MW00639618

Australian Adventure

Other Books by Constance Helmericks
We Live in Alaska
We Live in the Arctic
Our Summer with the Eskimos
Our Alaskan Winter
The Flight of the Arctic Tern
Hunting in North America
Down the Wild River North

Australian Adventure

Constance Helmericks

PRENTICE-HALL, INC., *Englewood Cliffs, N.J.*

Photographs by Ann Helmericks

ACKNOWLEDGMENTS

To my many friends and "mites" who have helped me in discussions, correspondence, in bibliography, in travel assistance, I would like to express my debt and my sincere gratitude.

These are almost too many to mention, in fact, but I should like to express gratitude especially to my literary agent, Clyde Vandeburg of Hollywood, one-time cowboy of the West, and a very unusual literary agent, indeed, a traveler, adventurer, and entrepreneur in Australia as well as in America;

To "Van's" friend and my friend Art Linkletter I would also like to say many thanks;

To Jack Whitehouse, President of International Public Relations;

To Columbus Line of Hamburg-Sud group, we extend thanks particularly, to Pat Hewson, Vice President;

To Ansett Airlines in Australia, represented especially by John Tyrell, for much assistance in flights about Australia;

To the Knutsen Line we want to extend our gratitude for making Jean's voyage possible for two months out of Perth and around Southeast Asia;

To Comlaco Aluminium Ltd., especially in the person of Dean

Bunney of Melbourne who did more than anyone to help us coordinate a year of Australia wanderings;

To the Kaiser Aluminum Company, and especially to their Vice President, Robert Sandberg, we give special thanks;

To the Alcoa Company, and to the Kwinnana Works at Fremantle we give thanks;

To MacRobertson-Miller Airways, Ltd. of Australia we say many thanks for taking Ann from Darwin to Perth;

To Captain Svend Simonsen of Santa Barbara for teaching us navigation—even for a dry desert run, as it turned out;

To Bill A. Beattie, pastoral consultant of Melbourne—the author's views on ecology are strictly her own, however;

To Thiess, Ltd. Toyota Dealers, especially to Mr. J.J. Tiernan, Sydney, we wish to give thanks for the loan of a Landcruiser which, unfortunately, got a bit mashed up, before it was turned back in to the Company;

To Hayman Island and the Royal Hayman Hotel, and to the proprietors of Dunk Island resort, on the Great Barrier Reef, our deep gratitude for guesting us at these resorts;

To Mrs. Peg Robinson of the Cairns District and Travel League, who made us feel that Cairns, Queensland, is perhaps our most special "home" in Australia, it would not be possible to express too deeply our thanks.

Then, thanks finally to Gilbert Barrett, assistant in the many technical and mechanical problems of putting this manuscript together (as once before, with a book on arctic Canada) for dinners out meanwhile, and endless errands attended to, and multitudes of friendships and conservation committees shared, the author would like to express her grateful "thanks."

Contents

Australian
Adventure

Chapter 1

HOW AUSTRALIA HAPPENED TO ME

It was the year Jean had turned eighteen years old, Ann had just turned sixteen, and Grandmother at 84 had passed away; and for me it was a time to think young. Because young is now, and now is the time.

It was a time of high-level noise in the city; the students from the high school across the street threw their leftover lunches into the arroyo, while at night strange men were running contraband through the storm drain underneath the school.

It was a time when sweet fresh air and blue sky were vanishing, and people's behavior often became violent and erratic what with the sheer, animal crowding of their endless numbers, trapped in a complicated technology. Yes, even out in Arizona where we lived.

Even here, the varient tones of light were becoming flat. All over the United States much of the natural, clear, wonderful color was actually being destroyed. In fact, I recognized to my horror that color was being taken away from the whole world, leaving a flat ugliness under the pall of pollution, in which a new generation moved in a dim, man-made wasteland.

As the sun began to hide her face and the stars their fires, there was surely not a moment to waste—I wanted Jean and Ann to at

1

least be able to remember COLOR. After all, SOMEBODY must remember—it is essential to truth.

It was now that writers of northern hemisphere civilizations wrote books reflecting the morbidity of the times. Such books looked inward—what was there to look outward to now, certainly not the view? Playwrights wrote plays born of a mood of pessimism and corruption.

That was when Jean and Ann and I decided that we must go away to Australia and take a look around.

Our eyes ached to look across open space. Our spirits needed to find a place yet populated with wild animals, with strange and wonderful monsters.

So we searched for a land where the sky so blue comes right down to the ground, and the land is surrounded by the blue sea.

A kind of sky country. A kind of sea country. Fantastic, wonderful. And our lives and our book would not be morbid. My heart leaped then. It was to be Australia, and we would be immigrants there.

We were to travel that marvelous continent for a year—camping out and sleeping on the ground—with our 4-wheel-drive vehicle parked beside one anthill or another. During this year Jean, Ann, and I were seldom under a roof. We were vagabonds in the great Outback, which probably will never know the plow.

But, of course, in the end we returned to the U.S.A. Beloved America, there will never be on earth again a continent, a nation, so blessed. America, a dynamic force, free. A power of initiative and creativity without precedent in history. Certainly the quality of those free minds which got America into this advanced technological age, acting as men of goodwill, under God and working together, can find the answers to relieve her of the woes which technology itself, spawning pollution with mindless overpopulation, have created.

Our great dismay was only to learn that Australia, too, is going down that same road, following the American, English, and Japanese lead. Urban Australians are a greedy, materialistic lot: They worship "progress," just as we, and they "conquer the frontier."

They have a philosophy in Australia which is a counterpart of the old American frontier philosophy, which goes: "If it grows, chop it down. If it moves [hops], shoot it." But there is hope. They are beginning to change now.

2

Will that last, great, free giant, the sky country, the sea country, be able to profit from America's tragedy, or will she too overpopulate and destroy her beauty? Will she learn in time?

Beloved Australia, beautiful desert, brothers to Americans, we thank you for your goodness to our wandering family.

Chapter 2

TO SYDNEY, PORT OF ENTRY

People think of Australia as a "young" country. Why is that? It is really two hundred years old, dating from the official discovery in 1770 by Captain James Cook. (There is evidence that many other people saw Australia long before Captain Cook came. In medieval Rome there was even a word for "kangaroo.") Has it stayed young because of its enormous size? Because of the ferocity of its deserts? Its isolation? What do we really mean when we say, "Australia is a young country yet, you know?"

It was young for me, anyway, if my two daughters and I could go on safari through the "great unfenced" and just be simple, carefree vagabonds—for an entire year.

What about the kids being out of school? Let's dispose of this silly question once and for all. It would rarely be asked in Australia of kids sixteen and eighteen. Sure, the girls would return to school later, but this was to be a rest period along life's way. Australians would find it curious that there are people in America who reject the idea of such a rest period.

After lots of dreaming and months of preparation, we were at last underway.

I could almost feel the influence of the strange continent pull-

4

ing us as we drew near. It cast a spell, which even our ship seemed to feel, perhaps because of subtle changes in the water currents. The final approach, after days at sea, dismissed the northern half of the world almost as though it never was.

When you slide into Sydney Harbor at six in the morning, the beautiful bay opening up to you with the city, still half asleep, hidden inside, you think little of offices and shops, of old hand-bricked streets with their Victorian bluestones and new sky-scrapers, for the Aboriginal past is not far away. It is right here and now.

The eternal sea washes the beach. The ancient continent pokes through her thin veneer of modern industry and through the artificial green of a million trees imported from England. Here is a city of 2,800,000, but still part of the same worn, stone-age, eroded continent; far fresher and cleaner than the despoiled shores back home, because only a few of our predacious race have come here.

Australia is old in time, a living link with the earth's past, and there is nothing quite like her anyplace else on earth.

In another geological age, Australia was connected to Antartica, to New Zealand and to New Guinea, and was probably separated from the body of Southeast Asia by only a few long water crossings. It is believed that the dark tribes of the desert came here as the last Ice Age forced them to flee its advance, perhaps from the region we now call India. The stories they told the first Europeans to arrive in Australia were of a time when the earth was cold. The word *myitting*, in the Bibulmum language, means "in cold times." Again, they remembered when Australia was completely covered by forests of tree ferns and other giant trees, and real dragons roamed.

Here live the oldest race memories of man on earth. When white men found these people they still used phrases and snatches of phrases from the times when, they said, God was dreaming of the things he would still create. Before God made things he dreamed them for ages, and so Homo Australis remembered, and called this the Dreamtime.

The means by which the race memories of the Dreamtime were conserved (by various tribes speaking as many as five hundred different languages and dialects) and by which the stories of magic were handed down through the generations was rather remarkable. A special group of dancers and singers put on shows continuously,

5

traveling from tribe to tribe and from area to area; it required two generations of singing and dancing to circle the Australian continent. The ones carrying this holy trust—by means of body movements, ritual ceremony, sign language, and mental telepathy—brought the story of God and Man and the wonders of creation, replete with many wondrous animals, to every remote corner. These religious dancers and singers were revered and hosted with foods wherever they went, unmolested in an age when other men did not dare to venture from their own tribal territory.

Like men the world around, the aborigines had habits which were barbaric by any standards, in contrast to their strange spiritual insights into nature. The Dreamtime continent lay alone and isolated in Stone Age savagery while the rest of the world passed into other ages.

The climate grew drier and drier. Temperatures grew ever hotter. The forests vanished, or changed in character to dry-area types of vegetation, except for a few surviving pockets which can be seen today. The physical environment became so harsh that only the barest subsistence by hunting and scavenging could be maintained. The people were cut off from outside ideas, and they never learned to fish or to put to sea in ships. Nature provided no big animals which they could herd or native plants they could domesticate.

How did they survive at all? The whole continent, totaling over three million square miles, supported only around three hundred thousand of these human beings, living in perfect balance with nature's meager supplies. Today there are about one hundred thousand left, half of whom have white blood; and from a low point of near-extermination in the 1930s, they are now on the increase. They are still in the transition stage of learning to live with encroaching "civilization."

Most civilizations are found in the Northern Hemisphere. You can turn the globe of the earth and from one view it is possible to see nothing on the world except water in this hemisphere.

Eroded and weatherworn, driest of all the continents, inhabited by one race, one culture, and one nation, Australia remains the most sparsely populated of the modern nations. A trickle of white men who came from England and Europe to inhabit it during the last two hundred years have remained essentially alone.

Today there are twelve million white Australians and they live mostly on the rim of the continent.

What should we expect the Australian personality and temperament to be like, given this background? Will he be friendly like the stereotype of our old Western ranchers? (Some of our old Western ranchers were *not* friendly, and are still not.) Will Australia be an exciting place to be, with a lot going on? Will it be stagnant in ideas? Perhaps it will be many contrasting things. We must wait and see.

"Are you ready to meet the press?" our captain asked me.

After quarantine and docking, what looked like the entire news force of Australia came on board, about twenty-seven of them, boys and girls, carrying notebooks, cameras, and tape recorders. The whole mob of us went into the ship's sedate German lounge, where coffee and whipped-cream cakes were served.

The press conference had been called by the Columbus Line after their public relations firm in Sydney learned that they were responsible for bringing to these shores, as guests of the line, an all-female expedition of explorers. Also, we were the only passengers to disembark from this particular freighter on this particular day at the only eastern port of entry. Consequently we received a welcome generally reserved for royalty.

The customs officer, also on board to greet us, politely waited. Later he confiscated two books which were on the best seller list in America and some leather boots (which could possibly bring contamination to cattle lands into which no hoof-and-mouth disease has ever been introduced). Two things which Australia worries about are human morals and hoof-and-mouth, you see.

"What do you think of Australia?" was the first question from the press. We hadn't left the ship yet. The bearded young reporter who led off the interview smiled mischievously, while his mates knowingly cocked their ears with pencils poised. This question must be routine.

"We already love Australia," we replied in truth. Dutifully, everybody took this down. "That's beaut. What are they saying about Australia in America right now? What do the Americans think about us?"

Here was a mind-stretcher. Nobody I knew had ever mentioned it, so I just said I believed the Americans thought it to be a swell place and the Aussies real swell people, that they were almost like

7

our neighbors, ha, ha, and well, they certainly were very much like us Americans, in fact. And I tried to think off the top of my tired head. I mentioned that I was really looking forward to seeing the geology and geography which would be reminiscent in a friendly way of my very own North American Arctic.

"Australia is *like the Arctic*?" questioned the sophisticated young of the press, shocked awake and suddenly interested. "How is Australia like the Arctic?"

"Because of the Precambrian rock. The Arctic has too cold a climate to grow crops. Australia has too hot a climate in the center. They both lack soil. Perhaps more than 75 percent of Australia has only Precambrian rock or rock-sand—like Canada, you know."

The scribbling went on furiously. Some of the reporters admitted that they had a soil problem as well as a drought problem which was intrinsic in their country's makeup. Scholars in the Australian universities studying soils and ecology already knew this and a great deal more, of course. We told the group that we would try to see the whole continent by car, camping out, and we told them in generalized terms how we proposed to exist.

These reporters probably had never been outside the half dozen cities of their country, or the small suburban villages in which some were born. They had never been into that vague 90 percent of Australia known as the Outback, where we were heading. It was inexplicable to them why anyone would want to go there.

A peculiar characteristic of Australia is that you have extremely close-packed urban settlements along the shoreline juxtaposed against enormous continental emptiness right at their backs. There are innumerable tiny villages and signposts, to be sure, out there beyond, bearing Aboriginal names and English names, but they are of the Outback or Never-Never, far more remote psychologically from the urbanites than the countries overseas which Sydneysiders face.

"Well, hello there, Jean and Ann," said a blonde, mink-hatted English migrant into her tape recorder. "We are very happy to greet you here in beautiful Sydney Harbor in behalf of the National Wool Board. I noticed what wise travelers you girls are, for today Jean and Ann are wearing *wool*. Yes, there is nothing quite like *wool* for you also, our dear listening audience out there. These world-traveled, fashion-conscious young American girls here today

8

find that *wool* serves veritably every purpose, isn't that so, girls? And I note that you, Jean, have selected—oh, you clever girl!—for your ensemble. . . ." Jean looked about to faint.

Trapped, Jean stammered into the microphone, while the world listened. The fashion expert, a former English showgirl whose act broke up and stranded her in Sydney, had found a stage career strictly limited Downunder, so she just carried on with expertise about fabric and texture, pleatings and skirt length.

I came into the interview unannounced. "May I ask a question as a newcomer? Do women in Australia receive equal wages with men for work?"

The directness of the American mind, its pathetic eagerness to attack all basic issues at once and to solve all problems at once, is not necessarily shared by all cultures. Rather taken aback, the Englishwoman hesitated. There was dead silence on the air, and then she recaptured her blithe stage warble.

"Women receive about three quarters of the man's wage in some offices and banks, I think," she replied. "Which reminds me, do you know that for the career girl there is no material so completely serviceable and adaptable as *wool*? Of course we don't expect that all women will be working, do we? Just until they get married or something like that. And women are not constituted to do the same kinds of work which men do, are they? I'm sure most women don't want it. No more than a man would want to spend his life as say, a secretary? Therefore, women are not usually qualified to earn certain very high wages which men earn, ha, ha."

"But doesn't *wool* get too hot to wear during 115-degree weather in the summertime?" chimed in Ann. This wool-headed dialogue was getting to her. The charming showgirl did not drop her warble.

"Oh, you would just be surprised," she reassured everybody out there. "Winters here in the south can be long and cold. Sydney climate requires our long snuggies, doesn't it? Our witches britches? And Melbourne, ah, those in our audience who live in Melbourne understand what real cold is, ha, ha. Therefore, *wool* remains our great and only real all-around friend here in Australia, our most loved and durable friend for all living purposes. . . . And in closing, Jean, dear, tell us what *you* think, what your young friends in America are saying about Australia?"

There was a long, mute pause. (*Friend*. The crazy picture came into my mind of one of Jean's best friends in America. It was Stephen, her cat, and they were having their breakfast together out of the same plate.)

"Well," Jean said, finally. "I can't think of much to say. Except, most of my friends right now are Germans." A kick from Ann. A kick from me. Jean stopped, caught up in a blush.

"Come now, Jean, surely your friends in America sometimes say something about Australia when they are holding a conversation? What do they think about us?"

"Well, they know it's down there somewhere," Jean stumbled on in almost classical honesty, "but they don't care, I guess." (Glares, and kicks under the table.)

The interview terminated swiftly at that point, with good wishes from everyone for our happy exploration of the Outback.

I invited the English girl to lunch with me at the hotel later, and I got a chance to ask her more questions.

"What wage, specifically, does a shop girl make a week? The woman who stands behind the store counter, I mean." I felt less than nice, asking such questions, but I am an American, and Americans always ask such questions.

"Much more than back home in England," she told me. "Australia is prospering and going ahead fast. There is no real unemployment." Finally, she said that the pay was around $35 for the five-day week, or just over $6.00 a day for eight hours. Men in the building trades, truck driving, and manual fields, who made up a large percentage of the population, earned around $70 a week. In other words, Australia wage scales were like ours about forty years ago. You just turned back the clock.

We were talking in terms of Australian dollars. Their dollar at that time cost $1.12 in American money. Along with this, the national average Federal income tax (taking men only) was 40 percent. Pretty high taxes. There were no state income taxes in any of the states, and no sales taxes. If a man made over $10,000 the government took care of him fast: a 60 percent tax for him.

To be meaningful this information must be compared with prices. Here once again, the American was due for a shock. Prices at a glance appeared to be low. But they were no bargain for the people who lived here in their own little inflation, which was spiral-

10

ing now like one of their desert dust clouds, far into the stratosphere above wages.

Take housing. Rents amounted to three quarters of some workers' total wage! The most modest quarters took nearly all a worker could make. Young people, as in all cities, packed together in communes under one roof, in order to afford a roof. Half a dozen working girls would rent a two-bedroom house or flat for $150, and many were higher. There never were enough apartments for rent for the burgeoning young working population. Every young married couple's greatest dream was to be able to own a home, and, after a lifetime, most did. But the banks charged such high interest rates that the overall result was a pay-as-you-go way of life which limited most people to the small, modest, and often poorly insulated bungalow. The high cost of obtaining credit seriously hampered the building of large commercial structures such as hotels and discouraged other business expansion.

As for food, the downtown snack bars took a tremendous toll of the low Australian wage, where a cup of coffee cost up to twenty-five cents. It was not unusual for three people sitting down in one of Sydney's charming coffee houses to spend, say, $3.00 for a between-meal snack. How did these people afford their constantly-filled coffee houses? A modest steak dinner, though, could be obtained for anything from $1.25 to $2.50.

Many shops showed clothes at prices similar to U.S. costs. A secretary or shop girl, unless she sewed, would be obliged to spend twenty to fifty dollars for a good dress or suit. Despite these prices, young beauties were to be seen parading in the expensive leather boots and metal fashions of the day. Some of the most beautiful clothes in the world—from Paris, frequently—including twelve-hundred-dollar ballroom gowns, appeared in Sydney and Melbourne. How could the average wage-earner afford to live here?

The fact behind the fashion parade—these thin, willowy, twenty-one-inch waistlines, these busts fashionably petite and demure—was that the working girl's diet consisted often of only a biscuit or cracker all day long, washed down by the inevitable, life-sustaining, dribbling, English cup of tea, and possibly for weeks at a time. Perhaps the same holds true for any large city in the world and its working women, in our booming times; and lovely, leggy Australian girls do have a special style!

11

But a city feeds off the hinterlands which give up their wealth. How many kangaroo miles does it require to sustain one multi-million-dollar downtown block? Can this continent, comprised largely of tracts of sterile rock and sand—and one nearly continuous strip of alluvial soil running north from Geelong up the East Coast into Queensland—support a population beyond its present twelve million?

Through bustling streets our taxi whirled. Signboards screamed their wares: "Drink *this* lemonade. It's thundering good." "Join the Total Absolution Society." "Take Vincent's Tablets for Fast Relief of Headache." These were ineffectual rebuttals to the massive alcohol consumption in a thirsty man's land.

The cab radio voice was British classical. The cabbie's voice was cockney. We knew then that two languages were spoken.

The cars traveled on the left side of the street, and the traffic patterns combined with their speed seemed precarious to me, particularly since all was completely in reverse of my normal habit. But after all, this was an upside-down country, lying at the bottom of the world. I must continue to expect things to be upside-down, mustn't I? Here is where Jean and Ann had an advantage in their extreme adaptability—they took to it like ducks to water.

"You girls watch your step when you go walking across these streets. This crazy traffic could flatten you."

"You watch yourself, Mom. Better not go out unless Jeanie and I are with you. Just think how it might read: 'Elderly, absent-minded tourist gets clobbered. . . .' "

When we got into the hotel, they put all three of us in a great high-ceilinged room which echoed the retreating tread of British monarchs. We took a satisfying look at the vast antique pull-chain toilet and the nine-foot white tub standing on slew feet. "I'll ring room service," said Ann, decisively. Just then flowers arrived from Wolfgang. "Please, there, will you send up two crab sandwiches and an asparagus sandwich? And three milkshakes. American style, one banana and two chocolate. Thank you.

"That's marv," she said groovily, when their order came. "That's beaut."

We found ourselves very much alone with a peculiar problem which I hadn't been able to solve from the distance of America. I am not sure yet what all the factors were that solved it. The problem is,

12

after you land at Sydney, do you circumnavigate the continent by going clockwise, or do you go counter-clockwise?

Chapter 3

MELBOURNE AND THROUGH SOUTH AUSTRALIA

The girls and I were aboard a diesel-electric train headed south—and clockwise-down the coast from Sydney to Melbourne. As you travel south you are going to a cooler climate. The shores of Melbourne and beyond, where the continent ends to drop off westward, are washed by Antarctic seas.

Our train rolled through a landscape of gray-green eucalypts, called "gum trees," and neat, fenced green pastures called "paddocks." At times the scene was like a serene Gainsborough, with fat, sleek, velvet-eyed animals drinking at ponds and where flashing brooks were set with flowers. It was September and early spring. But the impression of the once-green countryside of England was exhilaratingly shattered the next moment by flocks of rose-breasted cockatoos, called *galahs* in the Aboriginal language, flying up in an exotic cloud.

We were going by train six hundred miles south to Melbourne because we had friends and advisors expecting us there, including several corporation representatives we were to meet, and there we expected to take delivery of the vehicle we needed, a Toyota Landcruiser.

But there's many a slip 'twixt the cup and the lip, as the saying

14

goes, and at that very time our car, a gift from the company, was disappearing somewhere en transit between Japan and Australia, never to be seen again by anyone as far as I know. Our gift camera met a similar fate.

Four months later we were to get the replacements, first our camera, then our vehicle. Meanwhile, I had to pick up out of pocket, somehow, some kind of a car—a sudden, horrible pain in the wallet which mere words fail to convey.

In Melbourne we were taken in hand by a firm character who had that distinguished British bearing and accent which reassure the visitor instantly that it is a safe and wholesome and really fine world. This man and his wife drove us to the motel they had selected for us, ("They must have *heating*, Mildred!") and sometime later dined and cocktailed us in their flower-bower of a home, and took us sightseeing, for which I was deeply grateful.

Jean and Ann did not participate in all my little tours with older people.

"But where are the girls today?"

"Oh, the *Cap Blanco* is in, and there are these fine ship's officers . . . American girls don't always go everyplace their parents go. . . ." I felt a searching gaze? kindly, charitable, but mildly curious.

These people liked the old tried and true ways. They did not—and this was really puzzling to me—approve of having a Bill of Rights drawn up for Australia, a subject that had recently been brought up for leisurely debate in the National Parliament.

When leading Australians visited America, the startling changes they saw over the years made them fear for the future of the world. All countries watched America and saw the increasing turbulence. America, the giant, was obviously a blunderer. Democracy carried *that* far won't work, the accusing eyes told me. Mobs in the street must *not* be allowed to take precedence over due process of law.

"Would you like to go with us to visit our new fourteen-million-dollar Cultural Centre?" And I went. It was built of magnificent stones hewn to simulate exactly a medieval castle, with a moat of water all around it, and it housed the country's most complete art gallery.

I hoped to see a Buckmaster, but none hung there at the time I visited. (Later I saw three wonderful ones hanging in the old Menzies

15

Hotel lobby—real Australian paintings, the Outback in the old days, done years ago by a romantic realist in the tradition of the classics.) I was shown a great vaulted skylight and was told that it was made of inset pieces of colored glass all individually hand-polished by one man, a work of years.

"Why couldn't the same effect be created by plastic?" I asked, and nearly offended a friend. And a little later, "Isn't the taxpayers' money needed even more for a modern highway between Melbourne and Sydney?"

"Well, for my part," my host responded with spirit, "I should not care in the least if Australia never acquired a modern highway system at all. Australia is getting along quite nicely without it."

The man had a point, too. Heavy freight could always be carried by rail, or air, or ship. Since all the important settlements lie on the shores perhaps the Australians won't have to see their land cut up by super-highways, and their air polluted by automobiles. There isn't enough interior commerce yet to justify much road expansion.

Mentally I compared this land to my home. Our federal government had just signed a bill permitting heavier, wider, and longer trucks and buses to operate on our interstate systems. The federal highway lobbies and the trucking lobbies always won the game— or you could say that the complications caused by an expanding population won the game—and there was no end to it.

That a modern nation could exist without modern highways for freight hauling was a revelation to me. Don't knock it, I told myself! Enjoy it while it lasts!

On another day I went to the Royal Auto Club of Victoria, which occupied nine floors of a downtown building. Neatly attired young ladies waited at desks to pass out literature and attend the motorist's every complaint. I joined the Club, taking out the common, fourteen-dollar membership plan which would be honored in all states as we drove. The only drawback was that there was no free towing service beyond ten miles for local facilities. (Quite a drawback!)

The Club's mechanical department would check over my vehicle (still nonexistent) for me, but a fee ranging from $2.50 to $9.00 or more was listed for checking each individual innard. How could I afford to have them all checked? Yet many

16

people felt the Club membership well worth it, especially as
it also ran a string of private hotels.

With women friends I lunched at the Club. As we passed
along the buffet we selected from dishes which had overhead
either a stuffed animal head, or the whole animal, to identify the
ingredients: pheasant, quail, John Dorey fish from New Zealand waters, barramundi from tropical Queensland, pigeon pie,
southern bluefin tuna, German trout, haunch of rare beef, domestic white giant rabbit en casserole, saddle of mutton,
and so on.

"Motoring is a big thing here now," my friends said. There
were some fourteen brands of automobiles produced or assembled.
People lunching would sit and talk about their automobiles and
where they would like to drive on their next holidays. Few but
the young, or the odd, left the East, and its pavement.

Melbourne's air was clear that spring, blowing fresh from the
Antarctic. (Some mean persons called it, "the pneumonia center
of the South Pacific.") Where we dwelled in the French End
everything sparkled. It was such a quiet city, for all its size, that
from the ninth floor of our motel I could call softly down to
the girls at midnight, strolling with their young men, and beckon
them from my window. Then the girls would call back, in gracious, tinkling tones, "Coming, mother," and they would come
along.

One-fourth of the city was devoted to parkland and flowers.
There were two universities, the U. of Melbourne and Monash, and
newspapers dating back over a hundred years. The newspaper
buildings were not open during the two-day weekends, however.
They just locked their doors to the world's troubles and tuned
out!

Our prolonged stay in Melbourne almost broke up the expedition. But at last came "Jeep Day," when to the Sheraton on
Spring Street there chugged a baby-blue Jeep with a two-wheel
trailer attached for luggage.

The two-year-old Willys Jeep, Australia Limited, was ordered October 7. It was delivered October 26—from across town.
I paid $1705 for the whole deal, with license plates and the com-
pulsory police safety inspection and insurance fee. Then I bought
$32 worth of spare parts. The dealer may have known what he

17

put me through by the three-week wait. I used every bit of leverage at my command. Telephoning him to *please* hurry it up were the top officials in the Alcoa Company, the top officials in the Comalco Company (in which Kaiser Aluminum is represented), and the top men in the National Tourist Association, National Travel, and the Royal Auto Club. I had cash waiting in hand, and was on bended knee. But the Aussie of the common folk did not hurry, and he was the only one from whom I could get a used vehicle in four-wheel-drive within my narrow means.

I was to curse that Aussie car dealer a million times. I was to froth at the mouth. I was to get down and eat the road gravel. I had no title to the car I purchased. The man who delivered it assured me that my receipt of payment was all I needed. There was a temporary registration paper glued onto the side window. (This kept coming unglued and flying away in the Outback wind.) No title ever reached my hands out West. The spare parts belonged mostly to other cars. The timing of the engine was off ten degrees. The whole car shimmied, making even the side mirrors flap. Within the first fifty miles a door handle fell off, and there were no other door handles to be obtained anywhere.

As a final gesture of his contempt for the modern business world, the rock-faced car dealer apparently had dug out from his desk drawers every mismatched key that had accumulated in a lifetime of annoyances—an opportunity to get back at these troublesome females!

Delivery came at day's end. So anxious were we to get out of there, after a month in a $18-a-day room, that we handed over the good hard Aussie cash, threw everything into the trailer then and there, wrapped the canvas around it with a long, dirty rope, and left at sundown with Jean at the wheel and Ann map-reading. I was squeezed into the middle on the high, hard seat. In a big city, to begin one's new driving on the left side was simply breath-taking. The danger was compounded by approaching night and the worker's homeward rush. And traffic laws allowed all drivers coming into the mainstream from every side street the right of way, if they happened to be on your right hand. There were no stop signs on side streets. Driving was a free-for-all, because nobody knew who was going to give way, or who was going to zip his car in between, or who just might miscalculate the timing of his dash. Whew!

Somehow we made it. Traffic thinned out and night lights flickered on as our four-wheel-drive, coughing vehicle waddled out to the edge of town, finding the road for Wallengong, heading south and then toward the open West.

"We better find a garage in a bit. We better buy a mob of spanners (wrenches) to use all the time," said the girl mechanics.

A rugged tin can not endowed with insulation, the metal Jeep conducted the night's bitter cold to the inside. The dealer had promised a heater, that simple device which can be run off any motor. "What do ye want a heater for?" joked the blithe messenger when he delivered the Jeep. He was just over from Scotland. "It's warm here in fine Australia, don't ye know thot?"

We had the Jeep anyway, too late for arguments, and suddenly we knew we were going to love her. Intense cold and intense heat were to be our personal experience. Maybe that was all right. We would really get to feel Australia.

"Where are we going, Mom?"

"Clockwise!" I yelled happily, through the rattling din.

A small cafe with gas station beckoned. At the cafe we aroused the admiration of the Italian lady who ran it.

"Aaaah! You are Yan-kee! Henri, Mabella—Americans!" Her whole family came to listen to the Yank accent, their faces intent, radiating kindness. The questions about America couldn't come out fast enough.

"But—if you are Americans, for *why* do you come to Australia?"

"We love it. We think it's a young country with a great future, just like America when my mother was young."

"You *like* Australia?" Many European immigrants were heartsick, we were to learn, because most of them didn't have the means to return to their homelands. The country was hard on everyone, but Europeans had additional problems. They were not accepted into Australian life. They were called "wogs."

To the Aussie a wog meant some infection or disease. Or, a wog might be a strange, queer little bug or frog that jumps or crawls about. Many Aussies looked upon the newcomers brought over by their government as strange, not like themselves.

19

But, just as in America, a list of great Australians—the leaders, scholars and scientists— now include European names, no longer pure English.

"Something's awful with the spaghetti," whispered Ann. I had noticed it, too. I hated to say anything to our newfound champion of America, but the stuff was impossible to eat. At last I mentioned that the cheese, or maybe the sauce, had gone sour.

"Oh, no, that not so," the woman said, smiling. "Perhaps you are not yet used to this food."

"No, it's soured badly."

This could hardly be so, argued the woman, inasmuch as it never had been sour before. Her smile became fixed. "But tell us some more about America!"

Since no substitute was available for the sour food, we washed down what we had eaten with scalding tea, and left the rest.

"Mother, I hated to be impolite to that lady, but that stuff was so putrid it could have killed us."

"Yes, dear. Just eat your peanuts and candy."

Restaurants and cafes throughout greater Australia do not offer a substitute food or make amends if a serving is skimpy or sour. You pays your money and takes your chances. You don't send your plate back. At this cafe the woman may not have had any other food to serve, but neither would she have dreamed of forgoing her money.

Fortunately, to make amends, the Italian woman had placed a telephone call for us to the local caravan park. (The federal government runs the telephone system as a part of the post office. In addition to a yearly bill, anyone having a telephone had to pay five cents for each call placed.) We headed for our first camp-out.

Australia has an excellent national system of caravan parks. A guidebook describes where each is to be found and details its facilities: showers, toilets, and a shade tree. There were often laundry facilities, sometimes a small food store, called a kiosk, and there could be a resident or nonresident caretaker. There could be electric outlets.

The greater part of the Australian public could not afford to cross the country without this economical system. Also, camping appeals to the average Aussie; he doesn't like motels, even where they exist.

Camping was what we came to this country for: to live outdoors with no roof but our tent. There was no heating or cooling, but the same was true of most roofed lodgings. It has been said that Australians are an outdoors people. They adjust their clothing and apparently their bloodstreams to nature's temperatures. The general mildness of the climate makes this possible throughout the continent, except in the extreme south or in the Eastern Alps.

That night we slept for $1.10 instead of $18.00. The caretaker stood watching as the all-female expedition rigged a canvas fly half-shelter from the Jeep roof, and, studying printed instructions by flashlight, put up the three spring "stretchers"—low, folding cots—which would keep us off the ground.

"Feel perfectly safe here," he reassured me. "I'll be walking around a bit, and the park lights are on all night. There's some wogs camping over there in that camper, but they're roight."

"Roight-oh," said Jean.

"Good-oh," Ann echoed. "We're doing the oot-bush trick, y' know." Then, sotto voce: "He thinks we're Canadians, and almost one of them. We'll be Aussies by tomorrow."

"Good-oh." I echoed.

Later I awoke and most of the park lights were *not* on; thrifty, I guessed. In the bright morning our brand new folding camp table, the one item which we had not carefully put back under the canvas, was gone. Well, what the heck?

I must add quickly that the missing table incident was a unique occurrence. Australians regard themselves as having higher moral standards in their personal behavior than most other people, and there is some justification for this point of view. In what other country could a mum with two lively, nubile mechanic daughters travel and camp out alone for a year? Australia has had her occasional larrikins and swagmen, but life is nearly if not perfectly safe. When we got out-bush we would just hide our camps.

Oddly, there was no spectacular reaction on the part of passing young Aussies to the blonde young girls, as there would be in most of the world. Faces were stoical. The Aussies were deemed to be "shy with women." I didn't understand them. Sometimes I thought I was dreaming, because Aussie men did not smile, certainly not at women of any age, and in business the attitude was that the customer was always wrong.

21

At garages it was interesting to see the reaction when a customer drove in. Several men and boys employed there all turned their backs and walked busily away. One unfortunate one got caught—or perhaps it was his turn to wait on the customer. When there were several employees, only one would do all the work.

Water or oil for the car was never suggested. The girls always wiped our windshield. No extras were offered. Nobody ever offered us free advice. Nobody tried to sell us anything, or even tell us any news (there wasn't any). It was a peculiar feeling until you got used to it, I can tell you. Very strange indeed. I wanted to look into this—but how?

I can only tell our story from our own particular view and our own experiences. I have since been told that the real trouble was that we were not the Yanks who fought like hell in World War II and the Battle of the Coral Sea, where they saved Australia. Then, we would have really been *roight*. But the Aussies had no hugs or kisses, or even smiles, for female Yanks, it seemed. Had we been males it is unlikely that we could have passed through Australia without many a punch on the nose, as a general way of life, and a kind of means of communication. Aussies are fighters, not lovers.

The Great Ocean Road down the southeast shoulder of Australia was a narrow, paved, winding ribbon, glittering with spring rain. When two cars met, one had to go off the pavement a little in order to pass. Creeping by the turns, you looked below and saw the green, seething waters of the cold Southern Ocean.

Where we turned the southeast corner and headed westward along the south coast, farmlands and orchards were hacked from a forest of giant eucalypts, called "mountain ash," towering in cathedral majesty. Streams were stocked with trout. The fairy penguins would soon be swimming in from Antarctica to lay their summer eggs.

When the Great Ocean Road dipped to clean, uncluttered beaches of inviting sand, we were tempted to camp on the beach. Just as we started our camp an old man with rheumy eyes and a long-nosed, pinched face out of Dickens, got out of a pickup truck and approached us with a smile and a bow. With great courtesy he handed me a printed card. It said:

SHIRES OF BARRABOOL AND WINCHELSEA

You are in an area where camps and caravans are not permitted to remain. Please move to a registered camping area or caravan park.

> D.F. Ireland
> Health Inspector

Thanking the representative of the health inspector, we folded the tent, jumped the Jeep and trailer out of the sand traps beside the sea, and moved on. This, then, was why the seashore of Victoria was so clean, so unspoiled, strewn with six-foot calla lilies growing wild, and brilliant little falls of water coming down to the sea in pristine cascades. We saw why the few houses melted into the black hills. It was not by accident. To try to evade the conservation laws would be to court a nice fine.

We stayed in a cabin that night with beds and a butane burner, because it rained. The charge: eighty cents.

"Some men along the beach encouraged us to camp there. Why, if they knew we would get fined?" Ann asked the caretaker's wife.

"Well, they saw you wanted to camp there, so they hoped you would get away with it, you know," she said. "They're getting fun out of giving you a fair go to beat the law."

To the playful Aussie the spectacle of anybody beating the law on little matters like this could be a sort of betting game. Only, we would be the ones to take the losses.

"Another game is rushing cars," said Ann. "Or passing on all sides and racing. Mom, you can do absolutely anything in this country that you can get away with. Fun, huh?"

"Have fun," I said. "I don't think I'll do any driving this year."

"But—this could run into work, Mom. Aren't you going to help at all?"

The girls soon realized that I was serious about not driving. All those gears weren't for me. Here was just the land for that young person who never gets enough time behind the wheel to suit him.

Here start the roads that never end. Here the signposts will soon be practically nonexistent, until you get where you're going.

23

After you get there, if you look behind you, sometimes you will find a sign on a post. Here it soon leads into the Never-Never. This was the part of Australia which we intended to drive into; but we might never know exactly when we got there.

Unfortunately the girls said yes when the groundskeeper asked if hot showers were desired. He took his axe to the woodpile forthwith and fired up some absymal tanks. To justify the axeman's efforts, showers had to be taken in icy stone stalls having neither roof nor door, which we labeled the catacombs. It produced tiny needle spickets of water, and over a period of time your feet became yellow. We got underway again and Ann took the wheel with splendid spirit. We tootled along.

Then Ann's eyes bulged. She pointed.

"Kangaroo. I think."

It stood there upright on its haunches with long-fingered tiny hands folded sedately over a large stomach. There it sat, right beside a house, maybe six feet tall. (Large individuals were rare, as the species declined in numbers. The old man kangaroo of the big red species and the big grey may stand seven feet tall [only the very rare giant kangaroo gets this large] and can make a twenty-six-foot horizontal jump.)

"Isn't that a wonderful sight," I said.

"Fair dinkum, Mum."

A woman in the tourist business later told me, "Overseas visitors don't seem much interested in our Sydney Harbor Bridge, or our $58-million opera house. I reckon where they come from they have their own, don't you think? What they always ask *me* is to show them a wild kangaroo!"

Thousands of Australian schoolchildren have actually never seen a wild kangaroo. They have never seen their own nearly extinct, flightless emu. Yet these two animals are emblazoned on their country's seal. It is a sad situation. Except for the small, urbanized East, the other states go right on with the rapid extermination of kangaroos and emus, even by professional hunters—called in by private property owners—because the all-powerful grazing industry still regards these species as pests. Australia is a country without a single paid game protection officer!

Natural history societies promulgated by private citizens have been wildlife's principal friend, sometimes its only friend through the

24

years, while befuddled and indifferent government sits entangled in its own red tape, or even acts as an outright enemy of the nation's precious wildlife heritage.

We slept nights in the tent under broad spreading European pines. There were lamb chops and buckets of fresh boiled field "veggies" on this run. The barren seacliffs were carved into arches by the surf and all night long the sea roar was heard. Big black-and-white magpies sheltered in trees above our heads, and, being familiar with campers, waited noisily for food. They covered the blue tent with patches of birdlime.

Gusts of hail sometimes pelted the tent.

"Well, summer should be here almost any day now. Then we'll get warmed up." This was the characteristic philosophy this year, and every year, not only of people camping out in a tent for fun, but of people in houses and shops everywhere.

It was at this time that we ran into our first "link with evolution."

"Stop the car, quick!" and of course we jumped out, and ran right up to the animal which was ambling along the roadside. A thorny little thing, slow-moving, it looked like a porcupine at first glance.

But this was no porcupine! This was an Australian animal—we had chanced upon the all-but-unbelievable echidna (or spiny anteater) in the wild.

By the time we could leap forward the little fellow had gone into the radiata, and there, instantly selecting an excellent digging site, he was already half underground and sinking fast.

"Hurry! Oh, I've simply got to hold him! Run to the car, get the heavy gloves." Jean ran.

The animal kept on going down, down. "Hurry, he's going fast!"

"Shall I get the shovel?"

"Can't risk it. Might hurt him."

We never did get to see the head and long thin proboscis. When first sighted, he was round and puffed up, like a basketball. Now he became flat, like a big plate, only two inches thick. When we tried with gloves on to pry under the plate and gently lift it from the earth, the changeable glob of muscle utterly

25

astounded us. We could not lift it! The traction of its flattened body seemed to amount to hundreds of pounds of resistance.

The scoop feet hidden entirely under the flat plate body, continued their rhythmic subterranean excavation beneath a sheltering root, throwing dirt out at each side. He was easily the winner of the contest. There was nothing to do but let him sink to China if he wished.

The echidna can squeeze through a rat hole when necessary, by changing shape again. And although he weighs no more than three pounds, he is strong enough to upend all the furniture in a house when brought indoors for a pet, and if he decides to wedge himself into a corner or anyplace else of his selection, no human strength can remove him.

The echidna is a missing link between mammals and reptiles: a monotreme, a species which has only two members in the world. The other member is the celebrated duckbill platypus. As every school child knows, the platypus is a furred little animal that swims and lays eggs. However, few people outside Australia know of this cousin, whose structure is biologically similar, except that thorny quills replace fur, and its food consists of the small white termites of the desert. It is classed as a warm-blooded animal, but its intestinal structure is reptilian, and its body temperature lacks the usual controls. Blood temperature, with a bit of a lag, rises or drops helplessly with outside temperatures of weather. This animal lays an egg, yet it suckles its young inside a pouch like a marsupial.

The echidna is beautifully designed. He is no monstrosity. (In cold Tasmania the quills become a hair coat.) His long snout is the perfect tool for probing into termite tunnels and anthills, and his long, sticky, ribbon-like tongue is perfect for licking up termites by millions. His jaws are toothless, but when he grinds termites it is said to sound like a coffee grinder.

Termites are designed to eat dead wood. Their job is to keep the desert clean. There are few fungi in a desert to do this job, and too much deadwood lying around obviously is an enormous fire hazard to a dry continent. Therefore, it is natural to find a number of animals in the chain whose task it is to keep the termites, ants, and other insects under control.

While many zoos of the world house the echidna, virtually nothing is known about its breeding habits, gestation period, or

26

the suckling of little ones born from eggs—because no echidna has ever been born in captivity. In zoos the animals seem to lose their fertility. The great Australian naturalist Dr. Serventy pointed out that unfortunately zoos are not able to furnish millions of termites for meals. He suggested that these desert termites might be the fertility determinant for the echidnas.

Australian wildlife includes no indigenous big game. With a sparse food supply, life evolved in small, economical size, and is almost altogether nocturnal. We were very lucky to meet this echidna in the daytime, on a dull day, at the edge of the forest—a day when the temperature was about fifty-two degrees, and the sky, at the moment, overcast. Almost all wildlife detests strong, bright sunlight.

We climbed into the Baby Blue. "Darling, I give you an echidna on this day of your seventeenth birthday," I said to Ann. She laughed and started up the engine, threw the gears into position, and off along that road yonder she took us, ever deeper into Australia.

Chapter 4

LIZARDS LIKE JEWELS

"Food! Let's shop for tucker." At the next village, far south, we could smell the butcher shop from down the street, a kind of meaty, lusty, fresh smell. The hunks of meat were usually wrapped in old newspapers.

In the State of South Australia that spring half a lamb sold at the butcher's for $2.50. I always wanted to get that full half lamb and sit down and eat the whole thing in the bush. The children wouldn't let me. "We're not as fond of sheep meat as you are, Mother."

I couldn't locate the familiar red sign, so I stopped a man on the street. "Pardon me, could you direct me to the butcher shop. . . ." He looked startled. His face looked like a sunbaked rock. Disregarding me, he turned his back and walked on!

"Well, gee whiz, kids, I just can't understand what's going on in this country. With the people. That man acted just like the echidna!"

"Next time, Mom, ask a woman," the kids suggested. I did that, and it worked better. "Or get a shovel," the kids said. We were traveling the great State of South Australia.

In my own age group, particularly as a woman alone, I was

28

somehow missing the code. Art Linkletter says in *Linkletter Down Under* that sooner or later, without knowing it, you will offend someone in Australia, even at the point in a deal when things seem to be going beautifully.

There seemed to be no way to change the male attitude toward women, particularly in the older generation. Later I talked with women who said they just gave up, and addressed all remarks to other women.

In a grocery store I reached for a package of Billy Tea. The box showed a picture of a tall, portly kangaroo sitting on his great hind feet and pogo-stick tail beside a campfire, courteously offering an Outback camper a cup of lovely tea. "Hullo, Mate!" the kangaroo said. I put that tea into my shopping basket. Kellogg's Cornflakes appeared in the familiar package except that here in this young land the subsidiary did not find it necessary to enumerate the international units of vitamins and milligrams of minerals for the buyer's health requirements. The blurb only remarked, in a slipshod, carefree manner: "It's good for you."

We were now well along the south coast of the big continent heading into the open West, traveling the only state not settled by convicts, and the most industrialized state judged on a per capita basis.

"Australia's desert area is second only to the Sahara in size," I said. "Did you know that? I didn't. We're going to leave the greenbelt."

We were passing through two hundred thousand acres of government plantings of radiata, or Monterey pines, first brought from the Monterey Peninsula in California over a century ago. Funny thing about radiata. When carried to Australia, to Asia, and to parts of Africa as an exotic it grows twice as fast as in its native California, reaching a height of 120 feet in forty years. Today it is transforming marginal wastelands of low fertility and little rainfall into fast-growing softwood forests and helping to fill a voracious world market for the wood. In the states of Victoria and South Australia today it replaces the long-gone hardwood rain forests exploited by previous generations.

Ahead stretched a south coastal desert, receiving only five to twelve inches of rainfall, and that uncertain. The south coast of Australia is exposed to all the ferocity of the Antarctic storms.

Cliffs ranging up to 260 feet rise sheer from the sea, extending along this coast for hundreds of miles, forming the Great Australian Bight, which has neither rivers nor sheltering harbors. At some places the cliffs are buried by windblown sands. Tertiary sediments, chiefly limestone, form the almost flat, featureless surface of the plain.

It is believed that skeleton ships are entombed in those cliff faces and under those sands. No one will ever know how many vessels in centuries past were driven by the storms into the cliffs, to disappear forever into mystery. Survivors, if they were able to climb the cliffs onto the mainland, never lived to tell their tale. They died of thirst or were eaten by the waiting cannibals. The tribes were Stone Age men, and they were well accustomed to eating whatever food or stranger chanced to come walking along.

We passed through the town of Mount Gambier along our way, and went to see its two deep clear lakes, especially the Blue Lake. Looking down from the rim into an extinct volcano crater, we saw the lake lying 160 feet below, sunken within a limestone bowl and hidden like some mysterious, gleaming jewel, unique in all this continent. Homes in the town were made of white coraline—shells from the sea—and of gray and pink dolomite. You could imagine the ancient Aborigines regarding the Blue Lake as a place of Dreamtime, of sorcery and magic. Every winter the color of the lake, dull gray, changes on the very calendar day of spring to brilliant, living turquoise, and remains blue until cool winter sets in again.

At the beautiful Queen Elizabeth Campgrounds on the jumpup overlooking the lake, we were unable to pitch our tent because the wet fabric had shrunk. I went and grabbed three young Aussies, ranging from age seventeen to perhaps twenty-four. I was a Mum and could do that. They came promptly to the rescue, and with their strong hands they stretched the tent and pitched it. We stayed three days, until the tent dried and we dared take it down again. Not a smile crossed the Aussies' faces nor a word passed their lips.

When at length the Baby Blue rolled into the environs of sweet Adelaide, one and half million people located right at the edge of beyond, we found a city at its most lovely in the springtime, surrounded by miles of the glorious greenbelt. A short drive up to Mount Lofty lying back of the city revealed an idyl of bucolic woodlands, with many long-ago imported flowering shrubs and trees.

30

At the top of the first ridge of the Mount Lofty Range, whose ridges run north-south for 150 miles inland, the people had set up a tower commemorating the explorer Matthew Flinders, the first man (with George Bass) to circumnavigate Tasmania (then called Van Dieman's Land) and the Australian continent. It was Flinders who named Australia, and in his ship the *Investigator*, surveyed the Great Australian Bight and the south coast round to Port Phillip (Melbourne), and named Cape Catastrophe, Spencer Gulf, and Kangaroo Island. He also filled in the earlier charts of Captain Cook northeast along the Great Barrier Reef, and spent months charting the Gulf of Carpentaria along the *top* of Australia. His circumnavigation took ten months, nineteen days, putting into Timor in Southeast Asia for repairs.

At the very zenith of the explorer's career he was taken by a French vessel on his way back to England with the twenty-nine-ton sailing schooner *Cumberland*—England and France were at war. Following six and a half years in the terrible prison on the island of Mauritius, exploration's great man died of broken health at the age of forty.

At the campgrounds on the beach beside old Fort Glanville, we pitched a civilized camp, with the new folding table and five folding chairs (two for company, which usually came in pairs) set beside the sea.

Adelaide, on the Gulf St. Vincent, rainfall 21.9 inches was named after Queen Adelaide, and it is a little environmental nitche in which man can live. Renowned for art, music, and those humanities so loved by the English, the city has existed since 1836, a place of cathedral spires and private schools. Burke and Wills set off inland from here with camels, never to return. The overland telegraph line north to Darwin was completed in 1872, and Adelaide was the first Australian city to be linked to London by telegraph.

Adelaide never had much employment to offer people nor a lot of room to expand. The state of South Australia is the poorest in income and natural resources. Beyond Adelaide, westward, lies the Nullarbor Plain, facing the Bight, shared by South Australia and Western Australia, that mightiest of dry states.

As for Fort Glanville, where we encamped, its four heavy cannons defended this coast from 1840 to 1880 against possible

Russian invaders. Neither the Russians nor anyone else came to challenge the holders of Adelaide, and not a shot was ever fired. The toilets there were the strangest looking of all the Catacombs we had yet encountered. Finally the ancient guard explained: the Fort's old powder magazines had thriftily been converted into ladies' and gents' toilets!

I got on the telephone with the Adelaide branch of Comalco Aluminium, Ltd. Although spring was still fresh here, it seemed to me that the season was probably well advanced westward across the Nullarbor, or inland toward the "Red Centre." I needed advice. Which way should we go now?

Our advisor was an agreeable bachelor in his thirties, over from England four years. He quickly found his way to the tent, but he didn't sit down on our camp chairs. He and his mate took us out to a supper club, where an enterprising Tyrolean band was playing "Waltzing Matilda" and "Tie Me Kangaroo Down." Our trailer had pulled our cocktail dresses till then, but that night we danced and whirled, and drank the wines and champagnes of the Barossa Valley of the Mt. Lofty Ranges, which had twenty-two thousand acres of vineyards and wineries.

"What do you want to see in Australia? We'll try to help you," our advisors said.

"Aborigines and snakes," Jean said. She added, "We've seen an echidna and a couple of death adders so far."

"Hhhhmmmmm," said our advisors. I saw quickly that, living in Adelaide, they were not acquainted with either. "You could go either across the Nullarbor or up into the Centre and look around."

I already knew that. Thanks to the delay in Melbourne we had already missed most of the good season in the desert areas. The lost month would throw us into the desert in beginning summer no matter which course we chose.

"We'll probably give the Centre a try, now," Ann opined.

"You'll be right," they reassured us, although they hadn't been there themselves.

Much of the Nullarbor had paved road now—the direct route to Perth in the West, which I didn't want to reach too soon.

The Nullarbor—meaning "no trees" in Latin—is the most discussed desert in Australia because it has the only road link between East and West. Generally held to be about one hundred and fifty

32

miles wide, it lies between the Great Victoria Desert in the Interior and the Bight. Its original length, for the explorers, had been about 1200 miles, in which there was no dependable water supply or any food. The first man who tried to cross the Nullarbor Plain going west was Captain Charles Sturt. Having succeeded only as far as its fringes, he cautioned other explorers to heed the warnings of the Aborigines who told of lack of water.

Later, in 1841, the young bushman Edward John Eyre struck out on foot and horseback to find a cattle route around the Bight— for Perth had already been founded on the west coast (much as settlement was founded on the coast of California) and the historic problem, as we Americans can understand so well, was to communicate with Western Australia, which lay barricaded from the civilized East by this plain of death.

Eyre made it. But his white companion Baxter was murdered and eaten by the two Aboriginal guides, who in turn disappeared to furnish tucker for the strange tribes whose territory the party passed through. Eyre went from Fowlers Bay in the East to Albany, W.A., on foot and alone, for the most part, and he was the first man to reach Albany other than by ship—an incredible human feat. "On incredible human feet," Jean said.

About thirty years later, in 1870, John Forrest, the renowned water engineer, departed Perth and went overland, reaching Adelaide by the coastal route. He made a track which at last linked Western Australia to the other colonies; and a telegraph line was built.

Between 1871 and 1880 some isolated cattle stations were started at Frazier Range, Balladonia, Mundrabilla, and Eucla, on the Plain. But most perished in the baked, stony land. Despite bores and windmills to pump water, the pioneers saw their crops and stock wither and their rude homes disappear under the enveloping sand. Conditions became worse after the railroad was put in to link East and West in 1917, when more settlers came, because the combination of many and deeper bores for water penetrated into the salt water table which lay not far below, causing seepage from the sea. So much for life on a coastal desert. It did not take many years to destroy the exceedingly fragile biosphere of the Nullarbor.

As it turned out, the Nullarbor was the one part of Australia we were not to see. When we turned north into the Centre, we were not to get back there.

We filled our water cans a day later—thirty gallons—and filled up the tucker box with cans of food. We loaded the .22 rifle; for spring rabbits, we hoped. The unpaved road to Alice Springs was a thousand miles.

A gas pump man let us fill up the heavy iron jerry cans with thirty-five gallons of petrol, the large Imperial gallons.

"Hang on," and he helped the sweating gilrs hand up the last can into the Jeep. Jean checked the oil and decided on a couple of extra quarts.

"Just takin' a look around, are ye?" asked the man.

"Yep. How far does the pavement go?" asked Jean.

"You'll have bitchemen far as Port Augusta, 200 miles," the man offered laconically. It would be good to have the bitumen, we agreed.

"We certainly are stuffed," Ann told the man, indicating the ridiculous condition of the Jeep, with all its cans.

He suddenly went speechless.

"Whatever you do," the American consul representative had advised me over dinner in Melbourne, "don't ever use the word 'stuffed.' To them it means sexual intercourse."

Leaving the man in a state of suspended excitement after that blunder, we took right off and headed up into the interior along Spencer Gulf. We went into bush country with the Jeep and that night built our fire in the sunset, and, while the girl mechanics waded seaward for some relaxed play, I broiled steak over the coals.

The sea breeze dropped. As the sun set, the mosquitoes came out. Twilight found us pitching the bugproof tent as fast as we could. No "sleeping out under the stars" beside Spencer Gulf was possible—not at low tide. Zipped up inside the tent, we breathed deeply of DDT fumes—that dubious ambrosia of explorers in our times.

Now the wind rose, nearly carrying the tent away. We grabbed the camp table and folding chairs as they were being borne off. A big tent is a real monster in the wind. A person could get hurt from flying sharp metal tent stakes as they pull loose from the sand, or get rolled up inside the tent, unable to find the door zipper to get out again. But the gallant mechanics in swirling nighties soon set things right.

The rule goes: a small tent in the Arctic, a large tent in the desert. Lots of space is essential in this climate for air circulation. Our tent opened up on all sides with screens to keep out insects. We thought its blue color beautiful.

With such a tent and our "Portogas" burner, we had a real portable home and could stay anywhere as long as we wished, quite independently. Soon, in the dry interior, we wouldn't have to pitch the tent at all.

We had no lantern—only a big flashlight. We had no radio. "Early to bed and early to rise," was the motto which made my generation an intrepid one, I had always said.

Next morning nature gave us a break for a few minutes and we were able to dip our bods and wash dishes in the high tide running before our door. We saw that the sands here were made of billions of fragments of shells. We took the sign off the Jeep here, HELM-ERICKS EXPLORING EXPEDITION, and buried it. Suddenly it seemed too silly. Nobody cared or was here to see it except a solitary yellow centipede dislodged from a windrow of salt bush leaves.

The sun sailed high, and right there we made a change of plan. The famous little black flies of the Outback had risen with the sun. Millions of them crawled on us and into our eyes. They did not bite—they were just looking for water. The mosquitoes—called "mozzies" by the Aussies—belted us with red welts as we feverishly repacked the two-wheel trailer and struggled at rope-tying.

"We can't go on with all this camp work," I decided right there. "We're mad. We're going to store this trailer and all this junk the next stop up the Gulf."

It was the smartest thing I ever said. Already we had a cracked tire. We were bug-bitten and burned. Our collective hair was a solid mass through which no comb could run.

A friend of mine once expressed admiration for a Hollywood blonde whose hair was kept so coiffeured that he said "it was just like all one hair." Ours was like that, but not for the same reason. Ours was lacquered from sweat, wind, and grime.

"Oh, my lovely golden hair!" screamed the girls in anguish.

"Here, tie these scarves around your stupid heads," I growled. "You'll like them. They're covered with printed kangaroos."

We were soon to learn that this hot desert wind could dry out hair to the extent that in a bit, due to the strands breaking off, there could literally be no hair left!

35

We must jettison the trailer, the girls agreed, for reasons that made our cosmetic and comfort problems minor by comparison. The Aussies had put a Ford Falcon engine in their Willys vehicle, not the engine we had supposed. Jean wondered whether the engine could pull in the rough country, if we tried to haul a trailer, too!

Up the Gulf inland, at Port Pirie (South Australia's second largest port in export tonnage), our trailer with its load was placed in a storage shelter. We went on with only the Jeep.

Port Pirie's exports were generated from the Southern Hemisphere's largest silver-lead smelting works—Broken Hill Associated Smelters Pty. Ltd.—with byproducts of gold, copper-lead alloys, sulphuric acid, antimony, and cadmium railed from the state of New South Wales.

Just past Port Augusta, at the top of Spencer Gulf we really got into the Outback at last.

It was here at Port Augusta (railway workshops, wool, electricity station, salt works) that the truckers carrying goods in to Alice Springs, smack in the center of the continent where the rail ends, usually rolled their loaded trucks on board flatcars and rode the railroad track right on to Alice. The dirt road was too slow, too destructive to vehicle and driver alike, for commercial use.

With the tent pitched at the Port Augusta Park, we enjoyed to the fullest what the Australians call the "amenities," except that I had left our three sleeping bags in storage at Port Pirie, under the impression that a desert is a hot place. Also, our vehicle was so stuffed that it would hardly carry them.

In Port Augusta, Ann had picked up a starving little black-and-white male dog, a mongrel which we imagined had a sort of dingo personality.

The dingo, of course, is the wild dog of Australia. Some scholars believe that it may have come with later Aborigines to Australia only five thousand years ago. The Aborigines are held to be the only people who can tame the wild dingo. A woman would raise a wild pup until it was half grown, then break one of its legs, so that thereafter the dog would follow her, work for her, and depend upon her for scraps. Thus the generations of wild dingos became the followers and campmates of the Aborigines, from as far back as anyone could remember. At Port Augusta we saw our first Aboriginal people along the dusty streets, and noted that in these days their dogs were mongrels of all colors.

36

Ann's dog was in an abject state of starvation when she found him. The poor little mutt had been hanging around the fringes of Port Augusta, living only God knew how. With ribs standing out and sides shrunken in, the animal was barely alive when Ann came into the tent carrying him, and laid him out upon her cot on the tent floor.

She gave him only liquid nourishment at first, until his system could handle more.

He smelled, but Ann bathed him. She wormed him, too, in due time. Within a week his skinny body filled out and he came alive. Ann named him Lad.

We had heard that the Aborigines used their dogs for body warmth when they lay out upon the ground during cold nights. The degree of cold was judged as being either a one-dog night, a two-dog night, a three-dog night, and so forth. But I challenge the Aboriginal people to survive any night with just *one* dog to share among three people.

Chattering in the cold, the girls drove back to Port Pirie in the wee, dark hours to collect our sleeping bags, and never thereafter did we make the mistake of being separated from them. This was real desert—blazing by day, an Arctic hell of cold the moment the sun sank.

Into the stuffed Jeep the stray went, with a big bag of dried pellets for his provender. Thereafter he always slept with his head protruding from Ann's sleeping bag. Lad took to his sleeping duties as though *he* had "race memories" of being pulled over people and used for a blanket.

"Let's get one last ice cream cone for the road!"

The little store had no real door. It was open to the air, winter and summer. Its typical cuisine consisted simply of sweet bottled drinks and packaged candies, cookies, beer, and cigarettes. Narrow colored plastic streamers danced over the doorway in the breeze, to keep the flies out and let the fresh air in. Flies out, air in—that must have been the original purpose of oriental beaded curtains, I suddenly realized.

"What kind of ice cream do you have today?"

The girl behind the tiny, cramped counter looked at us sourly. She didn't know. Very slowly, shrugging, she opened up the small cooler which was heavily frosted.

"Strawberry and pline."

"Pline?" I asked, feeling foolish. "What's that?"

The girl looked at me in blank helplessness. We had reached an impasse in communications.

"Well, I've never tried pline," I said heartily. "Please give me that."

When I tasted it the flavor was, well—pline. It was white ice cream with no special taste. What the girl meant when she said *pline* was *plain*.

The strawberry tasted just the same, and was the same color. There wasn't enough syrup in it to be able to tell the two apart. You can pay extra for "double flavor" in your ice cream drinks, but you still won't get much flavor. If you always ask for *pline* you're better off—don't fight it.

Just think, there was gorgeous pure milk available in glass bottles at ten cents a pint throughout greenbelt Australia, and rich pure cream at just twenty cents a half pint, yet nobody on the whole continent made good ice cream.

We drove on into the desert, dripping ice cream. The few gnarled trees gave way to perennials about the size of our tumbleweeds. Each pulpy shrub may have weighed up to eighty pounds, was so solid you could have sat on it, and had hairy leaves. Widely spaced, some were green or startling silver-blue, some violet. They were members of the beet and spinach families which we did not see again. The loss to the world of desert growth by overgrazing cannot be estimated. Deserts once abounded with vegetation having curious medicinal and chemical properties, for one thing. From here on we would see mostly spinifex (Triodia), a bunch grass having the texture of barbed wire, and the low, typical gray acacia—a treeless desert.

All along the road were strips of tires, car parts, and sometimes the whole car itself, mute warnings to all travelers.

Driving through this Outback, with gasoline running from forty-five to fifty-five cents an Imperial gallon and needing four-wheel drive for a great deal of the thirty-eight thousand miles we had to cover, was going to be expensive; but it would be much more expensive to lose the car from breakdown in some remote place. The cars we met from here on looked as though they had driven through hell. They were the most beat-up wrecks in the world. Still, most of them made it. So, therefore, could we.

Give an Aussie a whole sackful of tools and by the next day they'll all be thrown on the ground somewhere, lost and broken. But give him just *one* tool, of any kind, and the Aussie will make that one tool serve all imaginable purposes. If his gas tank springs a leak he'll plug it with a bar of soap or a stick of chewing gum. If the fan belt breaks he'll use his wife's stockings or the baby's harness. If the sediment bowl gets a crack he'll remove it in the dark night, with his mate holding the light, and replace it with a desert gourd that he cut in half with his pocket knife. The Aussie always survives, he and his mate. Mateship has a special meaning among men in Australia. To survive in a penal colony or in hell you'd have to have a mate, wouldn't you?

The sight of any living thing in the desert is something to make the heart leap. We once saw an old tire strip on the road which seemed to be moving. And lo, it was alive!

We got out of the car for a closer look and our eyes bugged out in wonder and delight. The slow-moving "tire-strip" creature turned and opened its large mouth. It was sixteen inches long, covered with gorgeous yellow and blue beads, its tail so blunt that it looked as though it was chopped off with a shovel. Waddling on cumbersome, ridiculous, stubby legs, the creature looked up at the tall people, threw back its open mouth and attempted to hiss. But the poor thing couldn't hiss. It seemed to have no vocal cords or bubble box. Only a slight sound of protest emerged after enormous effort. He opened so wide that from our knees we could see down his gullet; the color inside his mouth was the most vivid coral rose, his tongue, drooping over the lower lip like a black stamen, like a rare orchid.

We assumed that this slow, pudgy lizard had those powerful jaws for nosing into burrows and pulverizing the bones of small desert rodents.

Ruffling the pages of our reptile book while he waited, we found he was *Trachysaurus rugosus* (the rugged one), or a shingle-back lizard. Australians call him Old Stubby, or Old Sleepy Lizard, because he seems sleepy and never runs away.

The girls discovered that they could pick Old Stubby up, if they used reasonable care, because these lizards lack the vertebrae to be able to turn their heads around, and thus could not bite if you held them properly.

In the springtime lizards appeared in great numbers along the roadside in their most brilliant colorings of all the year, and almost always in pairs.

But we saw many pairs lying dead and mangled, one little body beside the other, covered with blood and flies. "Operation Lizard Rescue" was put into effect in our own small effort to stop the senseless slaughter. We halted the Jeep at the sight of each pair, and Jean and Ann carried the jewelled honeymooners in their arms into the desert out beyond the road, where it was hoped they would be safe from man.

Naturalists contend that the greatest threat to these curious and harmless lizards of Australia is the "young man with the .22 rifle." Men traveling along the road to Alice carried guns, and they were shooting, very likely, at anything that moved—kangaroos, wild horses (called "brumbies"), wild camels, dingoes. This had been going on for a very long time before we reached Australia, but the recent increase of human traffic on the roads might yet, as in our own country, become the death knell of many species.

The next lizard we saw was a gorgeous all-scarlet fellow measuring about twelve inches—but he didn't stay around long. He was the Western Spiny-Tailed Skink, *Egernia stokesii*, and he also had a thick, pudgy shape.

"Reptiles are the main product in Australia," Ann wrote in her journal that evening at camp, and she was right in her way. "Australia has either 230 or 240 kinds of lizard, they *think*, because it is still unexplored, but hooligans are killing them, unfortunately, even before scientists can make a head count. I am beginning to realize how lucky Jeanie and Mother and I are to be here right now, to take a look around before they are all gone."

Campfire smoke curled up into the sunset and the stars came out. A covey of native desert quail scattered among the scrub. Doves called. It was almost like back home in so many ways, except that the Australian desert had no cacti, almost no succulents, and strangely, very few plants bearing thorns or spines. The sunsets were not as beautiful as those at home, because there were no clouds. The

40

yellow sunball set with a sudden straight plunge, nearer the Equator than we were used to. But the action was fast.

In her journal Jean was writing: "We had a very good day today. The deserts of Australia are: Great Victoria Desert (to our west), Great Sandy (north of us), Simpson (east of us), Tanami, Gibson, Sturts Stony Desert, and the Nullarbor. No roads into any but the Nullarbor. It is hard to define a desert's outline because real deserts lie in the middle of very arid lands. Desert boundaries are often based on vegetation growth and its density, but this can change. There are so many variables, such as the season, the landscape features like dips and potholes, the shade which may be provided by rocks, exposure to certain winds, and slopes having less exposure to strong sunlight.

"The desert," she wrote, "is a mosaic of microgeographic differences. It is characterized by *scarcity* of plant life, from absolutely nothing to an open stand of trees. Australia's deserts are among the least known in the world, being largely unmapped. So far scientists have concentrated on the desert fringes, for economic reasons. Little is known about the deserts' centers, not even measurements of precipitation or temperatures there. We are driving on the only road straight north through the heart of Australia. The unknown lies on either hand."

Chapter 5

DESERT AND ABORIGINES

Travelers here, seeing a snake, speed up the car and try to run over it—
putting on the brakes at the moment of impact for maximum skid
and crushing action.

I guess people feel righteous about using the car as a weapon
against all "wicked" creatures. But not us. The desert is snake
country, and we were only visitors. It seemed to us that all voice-
less, footless things of wastelands have a perfect right to be there.
They are part and parcel of the wild. They are doing no harm to
anybody. In fact, they are probably doing some very special job
which we, in our shortsightedness, are not aware of. A herpito-
logist's dream lies out there; it is an environment calling for study
and wonder.

Australia has about 230 to 240 different kinds of snakes,
including the little-known sea snakes, some of which nest on desert
shores. Of these some 66 are known to fall into the *elapid* category,
or deadly poison types. Not all snakes having very potent venoms
are dangerous to humans, because some of them are small-mouthed,
rear-fanged, or have imperfect venom-injecting equipment.

We saw tiger snakes, which have a venom similar to that of the
cobra and a semblance of the cobra's "hood"; the common death

42

adder; and Eastern and Western brown snakes—very deadly. Further north into the tropics we would be on the lookout for the Taipan, which may attain a length of up to eleven feet and has sometimes been called the world's deadliest snake.

There were others, too: the myall of the desert, the mulga snake, the whip snakes. The red-bellied black snake is not like its harmless relative, the racer of North America. Here in Australia, on some occasions (for reasons not clearly understood), it will actually seek out and hunt warm-blooded man.

But it is a curious fact that in this dangerous-sounding country death by snakebite is all but unknown. And not just because most of the population stays in the suburbs! It was so worked out in nature's subtle scheme that snakes and the large mammals live together in harmony, for the most part.

All of the deadly snakes are gifted with exceedingly keen perception, and seem to live in dread of being stepped upon. Moreover, instinct warns them that the large animal coming in their direction is not their natural food, and should be avoided at all costs.

There are exceptions, of course. But if these snakes were not so shy and quick to run away, the livestock industry all through Australia would have been in a sad state long before now. How many sheep, cattle, and horses die from snakebite is unknown, but, most graziers in Australia believe the number is very low.

The snakes we spotted a hundred yards or so ahead of the advancing Jeep were so fast that we seldom got a good look at them. Snakes use the tips of their ribs for walking or running. As soon as they feel unusual vibrations in the ground, those ribs really get into action, and they bound into the safety of the scrub. Unlike our own slow-moving rattler (three species of which are so rare now that they are on the protected list and a single specimen is worth many dollars), Australian snakes were almost never found dead along the road.

"The world's greatest collection of unique animals" was what we came here to see as we drove, but it wasn't going to be easy. Already, more than forty percent of all Australian wildlife were on the edge of extinction! Of these mammals over half were marsupials, a form of life which mostly vanished elsewhere in the world millions of years ago.

Australia had a marsupial lion in this region, prehistorically.

43

People still jokingly ask, "Did you see any bunyips?" These may have actually existed until quite recently in central Australia—diprotodons of the Dreamtime, to be found in mysterious rock paintings. Wombats, weighing up to sixty pounds, still exist in healthy numbers. The dunnarts—fat-tailed pouched mice (dasyrurids), including the numbat—are all but gone. If I could have seen a numbat-banded anteater—I would have been in heaven! Or a Lake Eyre dragon, which spends its life scampering about the glaring, white salt crust, with sunshades over its eyes.

Surely shooting was not the factor which was exterminating these animals scattered over such enormous tracts? No, the really critical factor was the rapidly changed environment caused by the introduction of vast numbers of livestock. Their hooves cut into the ground so badly that reseeding of native desert shrubs failed to take place. Along with this is the tragedy brought about when the English rabbit and the red fox were imported into this land (to hunt with hounds for sport, in the East). Before rabbits, there were warrens of Tungoos. Today they are gone. The poisons intended for rabbits, and the increasing range of the red fox, making his way out into the desert from the East, spelled doom for dozens of unique native species. The quokka, a short-tailed "pademelon" wallaby only ten inches high, is gone, as are eight species of the rat wallaby.

The Euro, a Wallero, was a grass-eater and the Dingo's natural food. Ninety thousand were said to be massacred in five years on one cattle station alone. Just as the American rancher wanted the jack rabbit, the bobcat, the coyote, and the mountain lion out of his way, so the Australian grazier swore death to all grass-eaters that would compete on the range with his livestock for food. He thus condemned the carnivorous dingo which, its natural food gone, was forced now to prey upon calves and lambs.

To help facilitate this eradication of "pests" the Americans shipped to Australia the fruits of their more advanced technology in the form of hundreds of tons of 1080 (sodium monofluoracetate) and other chain-reacting chemical poisons. So—just like us—the Australians, especially those in the grazing industry, are busily dropping poison bait by airplane, and setting out poison in various other ways over much of their land. In the clean-up a lot of other creatures, not intended for poison, get caught, including thousands

44

of desert birds and thousands of Australia's own eagle, the wedge-tail—another species despised by the graziers, and one on which there is a bounty in every state.

In South Australia there are fossil remains of *Thylacinus cynocephalus*, resembling a dog or wolf, and we saw a couple of taxidermy specimens of considerable value in museums. This wolf was living right here on the mainland until around fifty years ago, when the last one may have been killed off by settlers. Even today you hear stories of the "wolf" and its terrible depredations upon sheep herds.

Sometimes the wolf was called "tiger"—and from the town of Tantanoola, South Australia, came the legend of the famous "Tantanoola Tiger." It was an animal described as being either leopard or tiger which terrorized the area, killing many sheep. In 1893 a man named Tom Donovan shot the "tiger," which proved to be a Syrian wolf. Stuffed and mounted in the Tiger Hotel at Tantanoola, the presence of this animal in Australia remains unexplained to this day.

In time we were to scan tens of thousands of miles of abandoned lands which had been ruined by overgrazing. South Australia held some of the most abused of these lands. Driving onward we saw occasional shorthorn cattle and sheep scattered over "bare scalds" interspersed with what little remained of the natural desert shrubs. Through the seasons Australians had learned to expect an average loss of as high as 25 percent of their herds through starvation and drought, yet they continued to use the worn-out lands for grazing—the only means of livelihood they knew. Possibly they had to. Australia never was a soft land of milk and honey. It was a hard land which bred a hard people, who were forced to become oblivious to the sufferings of livestock. The emaciated, hollow-eyed cattle wander over unfenced wilds and when it is time for mustering (roundup) and marketing, all are grist for the mill.

Desert wild cattle are not tender or tasty. When an animal reaches the butcher shop of the small town out yonder, the shopper may find that the meat has been cut up in chunks and slabs with axe or pocket knife. Slime and guts and hair infest his tucker, but he's lucky to get it at all.

There are several enormous lakes shown in blue on maps of the interior. They are actually great, dry, moonscape, salt pans, or lakes of death. Lake Eyre, 52 feet below sea level, covers over 3,000 square miles. Underneath the earth lie salty seas collected in the continent's great internal drainage basins. The last "bunyip" was seen in water here in 1881. In this region all the rivers run inland, so that water may collect on the surface in floodtime, and undoubtedly there was a great central swamp here until very recent times. The only time in recorded history that Lake Eyre filled with water was in 1955.

From this point the land begins an imperceptible climb upwards through "desert steppes" to the Great Plateau, from one to two thousand feet in altitude, with a basement complex of Archean rocks—the Shield. Sand dunes north of this are "active," paralleling wind direction. A single dune can run uninterrupted for a hundred miles, rising a hundred feet high.

Fortunately, however, most sand areas in Australia are fixed by vegetation cover, and the sandy deserts are intercepted by stony tablelands. The sand plains have an ironstone gravel which helps to stabilize them, and there are also areas of coarse-textured deep brown soils, of red and brown hardpan soils, of deep red earths, and saline and sodium-affected soils. The organic content of all these soils of Australia is by and large very low. Siliceous hardpans and silicified surface stones occur extensively in the interior. A curious difference from Northern Hemisphere desert country is that there are virtually no *arroyos* or drainage ditches, and the soils are acid rather than alkaline.

Australian scientists know the soils of their infertile and arid continent as well or better than other countries' scientists know theirs—but they lack a long history of basic data collection. The Commonwealth Scientific and Industrial Research Organization (C.S.I.R.O.) was inaugurated only fifteen years ago. Our soil-survey program began back in 1899, and yet our non-irrigated arid regions have had only limited studies made.

It is not a certainty, but it is believed that the deserts of Australia are growing and on the move!

As the two girls and I drove onward into the Centre we thought about Aborigines. We had seen the dark men of the desert walking along the road and around Port Augusta. They wore dusty work jeans and broad-brimmed hats, and they had a restless look. Ann distrusted them, she said. They had a sooty blackness that was like nothing we had ever seen before. It seemed to us that a baleful hostility radiated from their glances at us, an impression enhanced by large red eyeballs (probably due to a lack of vitamin C but somehow rather frightening).

"They look like some of them just came from shoveling coal for the devil, don't they, Mom?" Jean remarked.

"Nonsense," I said. 'We mustn't have race prejudice."

Still, I too, felt uneasy— I didn't know why.

In any case," I said, "when we pitch our evening camp from now on we should make very certain that no Aborigines are in sight, or in the area. We certainly don't need them hanging around when we are camping out alone, that's for sure."

Back in Melbourne, I had met Mr. Dunstan, the incumbent Premier of South Australia, and heard him lecture on Aboriginal problems.

Mr. Dunstan noted that in his state many of the young tribesmen were restless. There was no real crime as such, but it seemed possible that gangs of malcontents might form and get into mischief. This, emphatically, Dunstan wanted to prevent. He said that assistance centers and hostels must be built and maintained at strategic places all across the continent to communicate with and guide and feed these landless wanderers. He felt that the federal government could best set up such a hostel system.

Antagonisms are always aroused by any imagined encroachment of the federal government upon the states' rights, but now at last, after generations of neglect by the states of their responsibilities toward the Aborigines, the federal government must, tactfully of course, try to persuade the states to modify some of their ancient concepts.

South Australia has taken the lead in one matter, passing equality laws so that black people would be admitted on an equal basis in all public places.

A growing number of young Aboriginal men have no prospect for marriage, and this is a grave factor in their discontent: the lack of women. The woman shortage is something new, resulting from a combination of circumstances. Because of the new federal minimum wage law of $35 a month, many stations will no longer take on the feeding of a hired man's kin. Thus his wife, sisters, and children are increasingly being relegated to distant missions for government-

47

supported care. In the old days, Aboriginal families found permanent homes with the station masters. It was mostly these station masters, carving an empire out of the wilderness, who domesticated the Aborigines' ancestors at the same time they tamed the country.

It was a reciprocal relationship: the blacks needed food, clothes, and money, and the whites desperately needed the blacks to do most of the hard work of station life. Only the blacks could endure the heat, thirst, dangers, and lonely, utter barbarism of Outback life over the long years' grind. Only blacks could furnish manpower; no other men could be obtained to work in the empty land. It was a marriage for survival of the two races. As one old fellow said to me, "Those were good days. We all ate out of the same pot."

But within three or four generations the old life began to change, even before federal government stepped in. The descendants of those early pioneers who fell heir to the properties (by lease, usually) were a different breed. They wanted to—had to—make money. Or more often the property was taken over by some outside, faraway corporation, which sent in professional management.

These new money-makers no longer wanted or needed large numbers of blacks. Black women weren't wanted around the house; they became surplus. When the government set a minimum wage in 1969 for hiring a man, many station people felt they could not afford to go on feeding the dozen or so relatives who had hitherto been an accepted part of the menage.

Hiring only the men and separating them from their families by hundreds of miles of distance, whereby they could visit only once or twice a year, played havoc with the once fairly balanced master-protector relationship, resulting in a state of social imbalance which apparently was going to have no easy solution.

It was not difficult to find Woomera, the weapon-testing range. We found the gate to the base, and the fenced, neat, modern town. Woomera means "spear thrower." In 1957 and again in 1959, England worked with Australia to test an atom bomb. It never was any secret. It was simply referred to rarely because it was rather less important among the more world-shaking bomb hierarchy about us.

England's first atom bomb was exploded on Montebello Island, Marlilinga in the south edge of the Simpson Desert.

48

The old guard, Bertie Dee, was unmarried and a bit lonesome after all his years out here, and he was quite delighted to see the mum and the two girls drive up. He offered to be our personal guide about the place. In his free afternoon hours we invited him into our tent for tea and cakes. Our tent was pitched beside the guard house, right outside the military fence.

I remember what terrifically wonderful weather it was the few days we camped there: the rainbow in the sky; the scudding clouds that blessed the countryside with a late, late spring, turning the desert about us instantly to green stuff and sprouting flowers. The tent was cozy inside while the tea billy boiled on the burner, and old Bertie, in between guiding us to Island Lagoon Tracking Station (there was an American there) and to the base movie picture house, and to laundry facilities and showers in men's barracks where he stood guard for us, was delighted with the exchange of conversation. For Woomera Prohibited Range covers 73,000 square miles. Lonely.

"I came over here and started with the government," Bertie said. "Here in Australia. My word, the swift years fly. You heard, of course, you youngsters, of the Battle of the Coral Sea?"

We had heard. "You ruddy Yanks came in and saved Australia, you know. Japs would have taken it, and Churchill himself gave it up. Well, they drew this line, see? The Brisbane Line. Ever heard of it? They figured here, the Aussies, to just let 'er go. Just try to hold the part south of the Brisbane Line. We won't forget you Yanks over here, indeed we won't.

"It was the Yanks built the road connecting the Alice to Darwin: did it with American money. Think you'll get to Alice? Think you'll go on beyond Alice and take a look around?"

It was probably going to be too hot, too late in the season, we thought. (How timid and cautious we were at first!) He nodded.

"They sent me on ahead of the bulldozers when they built that road," he said. "Because I knew the natives and could get along with them. I've lived my life with tribes. I know how they think. And I had no trouble picking up the Aboriginal dialects."

"A policeman on a frontier has to know a lot of different things. They had three different ways of talking, really—the spoken word, sign language, and mental telepathy."

49

"Why did you go out ahead of the bulldozers?"

"Official interpreter and liaison," he said. "My job was to speak to them as a Crown representative, and they understood that. We had to explain to them that we were building this good straight bitumen road from Darwin into Alice, and we told them that they, too, were welcome to walk upon it, and it would be helpful in their country."

"Well, I had a Land Rover and extra jerrycans of petrol, and water and the like, and often I would roll my swag out on the ground at night, and just live in the bush and wait for the natives to come up to me. They knew I was about. Word soon spread.

"Then, one time I had car trouble, and on this particular night I felt uncomfortable. I can't explain it. Things were perfectly still. Too still. The sun set and I was working on my car just a bit anxious, like, when I could feel the hair prickling on my neck, and I says to meself right then, 'Ho, ho, we have company, we do.'

"I just went right on working on the engine. I knew they were very shy. But also I knew the mob of them was a bigger mob than I liked. 'Oh, them bloody beggers,' I says to meself. 'Too many of 'em, and here I am on me own in the bush.'

"Well, out they came in a bit, the lot. Out of the bush like shadows. Lubras and Pickaninnies last. Naked as kookaburra birds. They can be deadly with those ten-foot spears.

"So, I put a few more sticks onto the fire and whistled a tune. Soon I was surrounded. I just went about my work, and now I always carried with me a good lot of sweets and lollies, you know. I made short time of getting out the lollies. They all had their hands out, knew what that was, all right.

"And I explained to them that they would be welcome to use the white man's straight, good road. Then, I shot off a few of me signal flares and made them some fireworks. Too far for the bulldozer camp to see me flares, but I shot them off anyway, made me feel better. Well, I got that car started. I drove until I could sleep far away, sleep well and sound, too, that night. Not a worry, really. But, everything's different nowadays, the bomb and all. Makes a man a bit sad, even a policeman like me."

"Tell us about shooting off the Bomb," we said. "Were you in on that, too?"

"Only as a policeman," he said. "Well I always kind of

50

liked the native people, felt sorry for them, wouldn't you though? They're not like white men, of course, but basically they mean no harm. It was all their country here for thousands of years. The government wanted to know how many there were back in the Simpson Desert, because we needed that desert there as a backdrop to explode the bomb."

He took a pencil point to draw it on my map.

"Weeks and weeks before we were ready for the blast, I had to find the natives and give the government's greetings, you see. We certainly didn't want to think that any people would be out there when it went off. The Australian government did everything in its power to get the natives out if there were some there. Who knew what or who was in the Simpson Desert? We kept flying over there for weeks and weeks, just looking for natives.

"They give me a helicopter with a pilot, and if I saw a native down there I was to tell the pilot to land. Then I had to jump out real quick and try to catch the native. But my word, say, do you think that's easy?

"They were afraid of the helicopter, and you wouldn't believe it, but there's a lot of places to hide in the desert. All I wanted to do was catch up with them so I could tell them in their language that there was soon going to be this great noise like thunder, with a big fire, and they must go away now, just go away, and stay away a long time. . . ."

"Why couldn't you go into the desert with a four-wheel drive thing, they way you did successfully before?" Jean asked the old man.

"Well, the terrain made that impossible," he said. "The sand dunes may go up eighty, a hundred foot high, with deep trenches in between them, so ground vehicles get stuck. And if you drive along a trench, all you can see is your own trench, anyway. . . .

"Well, we did our best," he said. "We worked like slaves, flying around in that heat, and making landings, and as A-Day drew near, I never worked harder in me life, I can tell you.

"I never did get to explain it to as many as I would have liked to. I did contact a few, and told them to tell the others. Often they ran away before I could make me speech. The bloody bastards. . . . Pardon me, ladies, I forgot meself for a moment. Please excuse the language not suitable for your ears.

51

"Well," he ended, "I don't think anybody believes that there was any natives living out in the middle of that desert, anyway. Ones I saw may have been just passing through. We think we got the message out, all the weeks we worked on it.

"You know, it's a handy thing we have deserts like thot in the world. Otherwise, where would we conduct our experiments?

"But—a man like me, thot has lived in another age, will never get used to this new age, I guess. A man thot remembers other things, I mean. I remember when the world was mostly bush. Now, to think how it's changing. The bush was a beautiful place. Beautiful. Wild, and free. A human being, if he didn't like civilization, could always go bush. If the laws seemed unjust, a human being could run away and just let himself be swallowed up by that great big beautiful land. The land provided him a living, too. Now the living has gone out of the bush. You can't make a living in it any more. What with the bush of the world being destroyed, where is any man to be free, to get away from other men?

"There is no place to hide," he said, and sighed softly. "I'm a policeman, and you see I've learned that you can't trust men."

Chapter 6

KANGAROOS TO COOBER PEDY

From the tent pitched at the Woomera guard gate we decided to go take a look at the famous Andamooka Opal Fields.

The fields lay seventy-two very rough miles away. Over the boulders with a Jeepful of clanging cans we went—but on the way there we began to feel a bit lost and uncertain.

At last a station homestead appeared beside the road. Against the girls' objections I insisted that we pull into the yard. The proud girls hated to ask anyone for help or information in this tough Outback, which thus far had not received us into its bosom.

A feeling of gratitude flowed over us, however, when we saw a woman coming to meet us. Picking her way through a shed filled with old truck parts, spilled oil, and kangaroo hides, she emerged before the big rambling wooden home. Never in our experience was any woman so glad to meet with another for communication.

We introduced ourselves and were invited inside. She was the grandmother of the managing family who lived there. We were seated in the large, homey kitchen, and our hostess explained that their property embraced fifteen hundred square miles—and it was good that we stopped, since this was the only house in the area. The property was called Andamooka Station. We were on the right road, thank goodness. When the black opals were discovered at One Tree Hill in 1930, the opal fields were opened on one corner of this station property, and there the town of Andamooka had grown up.

At the moment the large house seemed quite empty. The men—this probably meant just one or two white men—and the hired "black boys" were out mustering.

These people saw many cars go by, filled with adventurers and hooligans going to the mines, but few stopped here. After a while our hostess's married daughter came quietly and shyly in from another room, and we learned that there were small children napping. The young woman's husband came into the adjoining sitting room and at once fell asleep with his clothes on. He had been away mustering on the property for ten days. A halo of white dust enveloped the sleeping man. His Aussie hat brim lay on his belly, muddy with sweat.

"I'll make tea," said the grandmother, "and I'll whip up some scones." Hot from the old iron oven, they were delicious.

While the two women plied us with questions about America, especially "the Negro problem and race riots" we tried to learn what they knew of Aboriginal and desert lore.

"We've got pretty good boys here," they said of their Aboriginal stockmen and jackeroos. "They go walk-about two or three months in a year, but they come back. We have pretty steady work here." It was explained that when work was slack the natives just went walking into the desert, and this was their annual holiday. Later they came back to work—usually thinner and hungry, sometimes half sick. But go walk-about they must, at periods. They were wed to their land.

"What should we do if our car has a breakdown?"

"Never take a road off the main highway. Not unless someone radios ahead that you're coming," we were instructed by the two desert-wise women. "Some of these side roads go hundreds of miles to nowhere, or aren't used for months at a time. If you got stuck out there, nobody would know where you were, and *then* you'd be in real trouble. That's where strangers make their mistake."

We made a mental note: we would never take a side road by whim.

"On the main highway, you just put your car bonnet up if you have a breakdown. Anybody can see it from the air. Anybody com-

ing along the road will know immediately that it's someone in
trouble, and will stop to help.

"Drink your water slowly, conserve water. You drink the radia-
tor water the last. But never, under any circumstances, start walking
that endless road. Sooner or later, someone is bound to come."

But what if it is terribly hot, and a day would kill you? Get out
your shovel and dig. Dig a hole, under the car if possible, for shade.
Get down in the hole. Lie still. Wait. Hope. People in a really bad
spot might lie there covered with earth for days; that's all they can do.

Some people have learned how to rig up a crude distillery, if
any kind of short rubber hose or a pipe length is available in the
car—which it should be. With this, and a plastic or foil catchment
pan, a few pints of water can be condensed out of crushed shrubbery
laid in a pit. Maybe a pint each twenty-four hours.

In any case, remember—never, never leave your car.

"Thanks for putting us wise," we said. "Thanks for the scones
and tea."

"It was our pleasure."

Only a mile beyond, two lizards chasing each other dashed
across the road. We ground to a halt and grabbed the two terrified
things right from under our wheels—unharmed. Our catch this time
was a minor miracle, a valuable and rare prize pair. I don't know any
other people who have ever held such lizards—for this type moves
like greased lightening. A little over two feet long each, they had
mantles or big capes of skin supported by spines (colored bright
green when in an erect position) which could be thrown forward
six inches around the head like a halo.

These rainbow-hued big frilled lizards would be a coveted
collector's item. But we were no collectors, either by profession or
temperament. It made our hearts bound in joy to release the pair
and see them go skittering into the scrub.

Lizards of Australia include about fifty species of geckos, many
skinks—which are legless and may be incorrectly identified as
snakes—the dragons, and the big monitors called *goannas* (a corruption of the word iguana from the Americas) which may attain a
length of eight feet and are carnivorous.

This pair, members of the *Agamidae*, were special indeed, for
they were members of the Dragon group, the remnant survivors from
millions of years ago when real giant dragons roamed the earth.

55

The frilled lizards have all the characteristics to qualify for dragon: the spiny cape which can be erected to terrify enemies or rivals, the forked tongue (not breathing fire, however), and the habit of standing on hind legs to look about, while being supported upright by a long tail. On some occasions the frilled lizard can be teased into leaping up and down on its hind legs and snapping. It is an amusing sight. More amusing still, even unbelievable, is the sight of the frilled lizard in retreat from such a mock fray, when he will run off across the desert, going on his hind legs all the way!

With the passing of spring this encounter was to be our last with reptiles for a while. As the heat intensified, and because we drove by day, living things vanished from our scene. Animals here, (including man,) survived the desert by avoidance tactics. Their biological clocks brought them to the surface from their retreats at precisely the right time of day or night, according to the seasons. Only the plants, which could not run away, had developed into forms of life able to take desert exposure 24 hours a day, 365 days a year, and these marvelous mechanisms remained part of the landscape.

We took a look at the Andamooka Opal Fields but did not linger—we would give them a closer look at Coober Pedy. It was all surface mining. This field yielded about two million dollars worth of opals a year. A prospector paid a yearly license fee of fifty cents, and anyone could file a claim on a plot of ground extending 150 feet by 150 feet. The law for precious stones limited the claim size but it did permit the small person to have a go.

Prospecting in Australia was not very exciting, however. An individual could not "dig" the real wealth, as my girl Ann said. Everything below ground level in heavy metals, oil, gas, or uranium was owned outright by the federal government. No chance for a bonanza in the backyard existed here. The U.S. and Canada are the only two countries in the world that let men dig minerals.

Returning toward Woomera that night, the Jeep stopped. We then discovered that a water can had leaked—nothing but wet wraps. Soon we were freezing.

We could see the twinkling lights of Woomera. "I'll walk to town, and I'll be back with help in the morning," said Jean at 1 A.M.

Ann and I convinced her not to. We would worry too much.

Around 2 A.M. the welcome lights of a car came slicing up the horizon from Andamooka, behind us. The fellow stopped to help.

This was our first meeting with a professional kangaroo hunter. Driving a battered Land Rover station wagon with a big powerful searchlight mounted on it, he looked very fit and capable. As he leaned over our ailing carburetor I could see, by the light which the girls held, his keen blue eyes and ruddy cheeks, and realized with a fascinated horror that his hands and arms were red with dried blood to the elbows and his clothes were blood-spotted.

This young, happy-go-lucky merchant of death had seventeen kangaroos cut up inside his car from this night's hunting so far.

He was very good to us. While he worked upon our car with endless patience for several hours we were able to learn about his beastly profession.

Roo shooting is done at night, ranging over hundreds of miles of roads and dim tracks with a four-wheel drive vehicle having a suitable carrying capacity for meat. He sold the kangaroos to a firm in Melbourne which purchased wild meat—"mostly rabbits," supposedly. Every state including this one had laws against commercial roo shooting, but all a shooter needed was an invitation to eliminate roos at the request of a private owner. Meanwhile, the state of Victoria back East, while loudly proclaiming its conservation policy with regard to its own lands, conveniently had no laws to prevent dealers from acquiring wild meat from the other states, canning it, and shipping it abroad. Refrigerated trucks came regularly to Port Augusta for the meat.

I had various figures on the presumed yearly kangaroo kill in Australia, from naturalists, but nobody knew if the figures were accurate. One figure claimed that 100,000 kangaroos and wallabies reach the Eastern canneries each week. Another figure placed the wild meat racket at at least a million wild roos a year. These didn't include hooligan shooters and private extermination campaigns on properties.

Two of Australia's good customers for this meat were Germany and Japan. Big customers also were some of the finest names among American corporations, who invaded Australia after destroying America's wild horseherds for the pet food business. Now they turned to Australia for kangaroo meat to fill the endless procession of cans. Australia herself used this meat to feed domestic cats and dogs in cans whose contents went unlabeled. All this went on without the awareness or the consent of the Australian urban public, and on public lease-lands. And without the knowledge of the general public.

At the same time it is hard to believe, but true, that in 1970 the U.S. Department of the Interior was still supplying funds to states for government men to poison and trap America's so-called carnivorous "predators." For in the United States, as in Australia, the cattlemen and sheepmen lobbied strenuously to get rid of these animals, exterminate them.

This was the Division of Wildlife Services in America, under the Bureau of Sport Fisheries. At first they called themselves Predator Control Division. Then, in 1965, to enhance their somewhat tarnished public image, they changed their name to Wildlife Services and stepped up their program. Never was the word "services" so misused. The service they gave was death, or extermination, for wild animals.

With a Washington-based corps of up to nine hundred elite poisoners and a yearly budget of three million dollars, these men still laid their deadly bait injected with 1080 over the public lands of the U.S. West, eradicating coyotes, bobcats, kit foxes, skunks, racoons, hawks, eagles—every creature which might by chance be drawn to bait set primarily to get coyotes. One of every three animals exterminated was an accident of the program, a non-target animal.

They then strewed poison grain to combat resulting explosions in the rodent populations, thus perpetuating themselves in ever-growing bureaucratic busyness. They even talked the Indians into permitting government poison programs on the reservations.

Yes, merchants of death come in many forms. We have more kinds on a bigger and more sophisticated scale today than the world has ever known.

This kangaroo shooter here in a "young" country was only practicing a trade that was honored in the past, and being a shooter gave him a free life in the bush, you see.

He told us that he had "cleaned out about seven or eight thousand roos" in the area of central South Australia, he supposed, within three years.

"No wonder we never see any." True. The killer killed joy in the world.

We set off from Woomera after thirty-six dollars worth of car servicing, of a quality we hoped was superior, since people on this range handled rockets.

58

Puddles along the road turned the flat world into one big mirage. Campfires gleamed in this desert through which the lonely Sturt Highway pierced. And a certain white man's guilt needled us.

Not forty years ago the white man was poisoning the waterholes of the Aborigines—and he also shot them as wild animals are still shot.

Since this was such big, open country, it was quite a surprise when, traveling out of Woomera, we pulled up beside two hitch-hikers who were lolling beside the road with their neatly-rolled swags.

"But I'm not sure we should pick up hitchhikers," was my first reaction.

"You bet we should!" said Jean. "We won't have to be alone when we camp. Look, one of them's a *girl*! Look, they're both just kids, and Ann and I will have somebody to talk to for a change."

"A girl?" The figure certainly was. Wearing a blouse and skirt, too, and her head in a scarf. There was this tremendous smile, bright as the sun.

"I'm Jean, and this is Ann, and this is Mom. We'll make room for you somehow, if you don't mind a dog. Hey, where are you from?"

It took some managing, but the boy, about seventeen, and the young woman in her early thirties, squeezed in, all of us on top of each other, laughing and in an uproar.

I should have known where the girl was from by the laughing and uproar! America. She was from Phoenix. Her origin actually was a cattle ranch out of Wickenburg, carrying the postal address of Sandy Route, Arizona.

"What on *earth* are you doing out *here*?"

"We represent the Goody Health Food Stores," she said. "We're just starting up the chain in Australia, but here the name will be the Good-Oh Stores. You know, vegetarianism is quite popular in Australia, always has been. You can see why when you see some of the meat out here." We nodded. The little Aussie lad said nothing.

"Is he a vegetarian, too?"

"Sure. He's a good kid, too, aren't you, Wayne? I've been trying for three months to get him to talk. He's making progress. . . You have to get 'em young. Don't tell me you haven't heard of our health food stores yet?"

59

"It doesn't seem scientific to me that people can give up meat and not have their protein," said Jean.

Ann said quickly, "Anyway, we sure are glad to have you aboard. Tell us how you happened to leave your parents' cattle ranch, and end up eating vegetables in Australia, and where are the vegetables?"

Our effervescent female guest took out some small plastic sacks filled with oranges, apples, nuts, and raisins, and we saw that her entire hitchhiking rations for the dry continent did not exceed fifteen pounds. Good rations, too—not for prolonged camping in the desert, but just for getting from town to town, for a temporary period. She told us she always lived on this diet and the like.

"Did you ever see such rundown looking, mangy livestock in your life? Wait 'til my daddy hears about *this* . . ." She waved her hand.

The Arizona rancher's daughter loved animals so much that she rebelled against her father's way of life, and refused to eat any meat at all.

"Where's *he* from?"

"Sydney," replied the young Aussie in a low voice, all but drowned out by the Americans, and overwhelmed by age, sex, and years, as well as the greater worldly experience of his mob of companions.

"We haven't been able to get any Aussie boys to talk to us," said Ann. "Why is that, do you think?"

"I don't know," he said. "Maybe they didn't know you well enough."

"Stop blushing, Wayne," said Nell. "You're a big boy now, and besides, you're among friends. He works where I do. We were at Sydney, then the company transferred us over to Adelaide, and so Wayne and I decided we would just run up to Alice on a holiday and take a look around. Have to be back on the job in Adelaide next Monday."

"Speaking of food," said Jean. "We have this .22 rifle here, and we're hungry for meat. But every time we see rabbits, they've seen us first. They all scurry down their holes into the ground—hundreds of 'em—and we can't even get the rifle lined up on one of 'em, they're so quick."

"You have to get them at night, mostly," explained Wayne. "Before I became a vegetarian I used to be a pretty good hunter."

60

"Could you show us how to get some rabbits for dinner, Wayne?"

"Sure, why not?" said the Aussie. "I love to shoot."

"I love animals, too," Ann told the vegetarians, "But rabbits. Well, out here the rabbits are surplus, and it would be doing a good thing for the country, actually, if we ate some, don't you think?"

We all agreed that it would.

When the day waned we drove along slowly, on the lookout for rabbits. The boy rode outside now, hooking a long, skinny leg over the Jeep's fender, rifle ready. His rather retiring, sleepy personality came awake, with the result that a half dozen, plump, juicy rabbits were soon acquired for our campfire coals in the desert sunset.

These were English rabbits, different from any we knew. Their habits fooled us. Unlike our desert cottontails, these pesky things dug their own tunnels under the ground and lived in large communities called warrens. You could see why they absolutely destroyed the land. A single warren covering an acre might harbor literally thousands, and in infested areas the warrens were continuous. The rabbits sometimes shared their abode with giant lizards and goannas which were larger than they.

The European rabbit, *Oryctolagus cuniculus*, having arrived in Australia with the First Fleet by accident, came very close to ruining the continent's economy at one point. Being burrowers they survived and thrived. Early attempts to stop them included erection of thousands of miles of rabbit-proof fences, often too late to be effective. A Northwest Victoria fence was built in 1880, but rabbits had reached New South Wales by 1879. A Victoria-South Australia fence was built in 1887, but rabbits were already established in South Australia by 1886. Government bonuses were paid on twenty-seven million rabbit scalps in New South Wales alone. The Queensland government erected 650 miles of fence on its border with New South Wales. By 1900 the rabbits had crossed the formidible Nullarbor and entered Western Australia. By 1901 Western Australia started a 1,100-mile fence. But before it could be completed the rabbits had arrived and another inner fence had to be built.

Because of the impossibility of fencing a continent and the

61

general ineffectiveness of fences as a control measure, many of Australia's rabbit fences were abandoned. Others were converted into dingo-proof fences to try to keep the dingos in the wilder northern third of the continent. (Strangely, rabbits never acclimated in that north third, even though the dingoes would be justified in petitioning for some.)

Rabbit control is largely the responsibility of the lessees of the land today.

Methods employed since 1936 included trapping, poisoning, fumigation of warrens, and ripping the burrows. Then they tried using the disease myxomatosis, introduced by releasing infected laboratory animals. South Australia was the first state to try this biological method of control, and it worked. I do not have information as to whether the disease also destroyed other desert species. We do know that 1080 and others of the two hundred new and deadly chemicals released by the Americans since 1945 did so.

Now there is an emergence of myxomatosis-resistant rabbits and increased breeding in some areas, but there should be no return to the former plague proportions. The rabbits we shot bore no signs of disease.

After a big rabbit cookout, in which all but Nell participated—she held steadfastly to her fruits and nuts—we decided to travel on by night.

The car was so crowded that somebody had to ride lying down on top of the load, with Laddie (Ann's dog) standing over him. Going slowly we pushed through long lakes of water, gleaming white as milk under the starry night sky, and through scattered Aboriginal men walking on the road, wild looking, and with large red eyes.

And when we got through this: "We ought to take turns lying down. Would you like to have your turn, Mother? You can go to sleep."

So, for two consecutive nights of driving these young rascals put Mother supine atop the load, and as the Jeep pounced through ruts and "washboard" shimmies, and over the bumps and into potholes, Mother was catapulted into the canvas roofing to come crashing down upon dancing pots and pans and rattling tent furniture. The noise was like a boiler room. Red dust came up from the road and lodged on the "sleeper" smotheringly, as Lad's hinderparts came bouncing down on her face. And the young people talked and sang and laughed and giggled the miles away!

It was a wonderful beginning of our experiences with a number of young travelers like ourselves in spirit. I can see them now, those parties of gay young adventurers. Flaming deserts do not stop them. They are taking a look around. Around and around they go. Summer does not stop them. Some go clockwise and some counter-clockwise, and some, like us, head for the Centre.

Some hold jobs as they go around the Australian continent, taking two or three years to make the trip. They have packs on their backs, working here a few months, there a few, living close to nature in the quiet of great distances on all sides, enjoying great gulps of freedom. Hitchhiking is safe and respectable. The freedom they enjoy comes from an empty land, a gift of nature.

What were they looking for? I am sure they didn't know and couldn't tell you. They dreamed of finding a better world, out in the "Never-Never," perhaps. They were exploring, They were just practicing being young, and this was a land that offered them the opportunity.

We reached the opal fields at Coober Pedy at midnight and set up the tent in an unfenced school yard, for we could use the outhouses and the water tap there. At dawn came the howling of the camp dogs with Dingo blood—the same sad, universal refrain which one hears in Arctic wilds.

This tiny settlement was nearly world-famous for having perhaps the most beautiful opals in the world, and for being "the hottest place in the world" in summer. Four million dollars worth of opals are mined each year here.

Men who were adventurers, who loved freedom, who dreamed of finding wealth, had learned to hang on here by going underground. The town, while it now has a number of modern buildings on the surface of the bare earth, is literally honeycombed by the burrows of the past, a few of which are still inhabited by men. There are an underground

63

nightclub and an underground church. Historically the
town has had no women.

What really changed Coober Pedy from the old days was
the airplane. Most prospectors today do all their digging
here during the winter season and by summer the village
is nearly evacuated. There are two motels with dining rooms,
and a cafe or two, while air conditioning is unknown in
this little town.

In the early days the problem of water in this desert
camp was all but insurmountable. Water barrels as well as
food supplies had to be brought in from hundreds of miles by
plodding mule trains and camels. Today modern pumping
equipment brings up salt water from three thousand feet
below the surface. A modern solar desalinization plant
supplies tap water, but you must buy your drinking water
by the gallon if you wish to fill your jugs.

"You wouldn't notice it maybe at first, but there are
quite a lot of things to see around here," said an alert
Yugoslav immigrant when I walked over to look at the little
general merchandise store. The silent and grizzled storekeeper
opened my can of cold orange juice with a punch attached to
the counter with a heavy string, and handed me a flimsy straw.
It was nice to be spoken to. I turned to the sound of the
friendly voice, as we stood there.

"Oh, do you live here?"

"I live in Adelaide," he said. "But fifteen hundred people
still live underground in this camp. The season is almost at the
end here now. I'm in the mining game. They call me Yugo the
Yugo." He was fortyish, tanned to leather, workworn, and
had keen blue eyes. I liked his gutteral European accent.

We walked out together into the earth-packed street.
"It's a lonely life here, that's the only trouble with it," he
offered. "I lost my wife by divorce four years ago. She wouldn't
put up with this life."

I introduced Yugo to my mob of young people. "I'll take
you all out to my mine and you can pick up a few opals," he
said. "Would you like that?"

"Fair enough," we said, beaming. "Gee, thanks very much
for taking all the trouble."

64

"Hang on," he said. "I'll see if I can get John the Mad Russian to get his truck. My claim is twelve miles out. I could probably even get you a claim to buy, one that's already developed, if you like mining. Or, if you like opals, I myself happen to have some rather rare gems . . . ."

I rode with Yugo the Yugo in the truck with John the Mad Russian at the wheel, and we laughed and had a good time driving out there, while the Jeep with our mob followed at our heels, and Laddie, feeling very happy and gay, enlivened the holiday with his barking.

"This is Greek Gully," he pointed out. "A mob of crazy Greeks filed for the claims there, all in a bunch. But they're an untrustworthy lot," he added, gripping the truck door with a powerful, corded arm as the truck leaped along the track. The door was tied rather insecurely with a wire. "Here we are now. That's Mike Dobbs waving. I pay him to live right at the cut with a trailer, to guard the property. It's quite a good one, I've taken a lot of treasure out of her. That fella raising dust with the bulldozer there, he's my man, works for me from Adelaide, costs thirty dollars a day to keep him moving. How you doing, Sandy? Hey?"

I believed we were probably looking at a good example of a successful one-man mining operation. Big piles of dump surrounded the fifteen-foot deep holes and cuts in the desert, through which the truck wound. Altogether Yugo the Yugo had four properties staked out. He just put the other three in friends' names. It was easy to get around the law; anyone who was smart did that. (Possibly the law cared little.)

You had to be wide awake all the time with opal. Any ground uncovered by the bulldozer that hadn't been worked over that day had to be covered and hidden at day's end. It wasn't safe to leave any gem rocks exposed at night. To discourage people from prowling around he hired old Mike Dobbs to sit down right on it, and he would move the trailer to each new cut.

"Who steals the gems?"

"Well, everybody. Human nature, you know. Yah. I suppose you would say the natives are the most clever of the lot."

"Why do you say that?"

"They've got eyes that can see in the dark," he informed me earnestly. "At night they'll slip around—so will other men—and pick you dry. The natives can work without a light.

"Take almost any Aborigine, he can pick up an amount of opal-bearing rock that would amaze you. Right after any experienced mining man has gone over the ground. The Aborigine will lurk around, waiting for his chance, after *you* have gone to all the work and expense with a bulldozer at thirty dollars a day to make the deep cuts to uncover it."

The valuable stones were not easy to see in the dump. In their native form they were dirty and might not gleam. Yugo had hired one good Aborigine in past years to hand pick the dump. That one had "quick eyes of which you never saw the like," he said, and was "trustworthy."

"The only good one I ever had," he lamented. "The rest of 'em are no good, cheat you blind. Someone ought to take 'em out and shoot the lot."

The remark seemed a little tough to me. Was he serious? Or just a remark? Yugo appeared to be big-thinking and kind, and uncommonly generous by Australian standards, for he said he had paid that favorite Aborigine the sum of fourteen dollars a day for some pick-and-shovel work he had done. Not bad pay.

After my mob of kids had picked a few rocks we had to get going. Nell and Wayne had limited time, and my girls wanted to push on tonight.

"I've got some good Scotch," the outgoing mining men offered. "I'm living at the town's only good motel. Have a drink and a shower anyway. Your mob is welcome to my shower, I'm paying for it, hell. By the way, take a few towels while you're at it. . . ."

Later he showed me his rifle. I sighted along the rifle, feeling wild and happy, like in the old days when I was a hunter and the world was still a little bit wild. Yugo the Yugo held in his hard palm a number of loaded military clips. I was sighting through the window of his hotel room. It was a .303 Army carbine.

"Why the silencer on it?" I asked suddenly. "I know

what that is. It's a silencer, and I've seen it in the movies for killing people, and it's illegal."

"There is no law against a silencer in South Australia," replied Yugo in his fascinating, deep European voice.

"Hurry up, Wayne, you're taking longer with your bath than all the girls did, urged Nell.

"Hurry it up, Mom," urged Jean, "because you know Nell and Wayne have to get going!"

When we reached the Jeep Yugo looked under the hood. He really hoped to find something wrong there. He didn't want to let me go.

Darn that Melbourne car dealer! The Jeep was running perfectly now!

"Hurry, Mom, for heaven's sake, stop stalling, won't you?" Ann whispered. "Mother, you should be careful around mining fields to find friends who are really trustworthy, and—we have to go! If you're not interested in getting some opals, what are you stalling for?"

That night I lay on top the load under the dog's private parts and bulldust as fine as flour boiled out behind the Jeep. The Jeep interior was becoming a kind of tumbling disposal unit in which the Jerrycans danced to the tune of the broken kindling of the tucker box, and cans of food clashed together in discordant din. I reviewed the day.

I liked that good old man Mike Dobbs. Mike had seen little birds "waxbills," he called them, drop dead to the ground from the heat.

In the old days he remembered seeing men with their noses burnt off, with the bones showing through.

Yugo the Yugo had told me that it was hardly possible to drive just that twelve miles of rough track out to see Mike when temperatures soared to 120-130 degrees in the shade—there being no shade bushes in the area. Inside the truck cab it might get to 155 degrees. Better stay under cover, play it safe those days. You might not make it over to see Mike and get back. If your truck stalled along the way, it could actually be death.

"How did men survive summers in this interior in the old days?" I had asked Mike. He told me that a tent just like ours could be made cool and liveable if you know how. You rig a heavy canvas fly over the tent, making a double layer of insulation against the outside heat. Then you cover the outside layer with a thick matting of desert pine boughs. Yes, right here in the Andamooka Ranges and in the Musgrave Ranges and on up the desert steppes toward the center there were areas where such little trees grew. Some we called beech oaks. They looked like little pine trees with needles and cones, but if you burned the dead wood, an aroma of oak was given off. These wonderful "pines" existed under conditions of eight inches or less of rainfall, and through seasons of no rainfall; but they were vanishing.

"People are not allowed to cut the pines of the interior any more—but that doesn't mean they wouldn't do so if there was a real need for it. The disintegration temperature for protein—that is, the cooking point of meat—begins at around 120 degrees. People are meat, so far as the desert sun is concerned.

Actually, I mused, the amount of moisture available for plant life was several times the official rainfall records. Nature was crafty when she arranged those blistering hot days to be followed by chilly nights: dew and subterranean moisture resulted, to nourish life.

I awoke in what the Aussies call "pickaninny daylight," when the coldest hour of the night heralds the dawn. The Jeep was bumping along through red dust on that endless road, its lights stabbing the night. A feral cat slithered away. It hardly seemed possible, but these domestic cats gone wild had survived to inherit a continent, even as in America; they did incalcuable harm to the small native species.

Again I wondered, what is the desert, really? It harbors animals from other environments, not just desert species.

The building of water tanks fed by windmill pumps should help all life in this country to abound—if man would let it abound, that is.

The sleeping load of people sagged in their seats atop each other. The exhausted driver sought to hold the middle of the road. It was soon going to be sunup. One side of the sky, reddening, swept over us, and our lights probed layers of dust, just hanging there in the air, never settling all night long on that road and all over the whole land. Everything red and choking in red dust.

Slowly we drive down the valley between the ranges and entered Alice Springs, the most remote town, in the very center of Australia. The last few miles into Alice in daylight were paved. The citizens had paved the road in hopes of keeping their town clean, but this big dust bowl we had entered was appalling. Where was the famous oasis of yore?

Chapter 7

THE ALICE

Alice Springs lies on the Todd River. Shaded by eucalyptus trees,
the Todd characteristically runs mostly underground.

In its original condition long pools called billabongs lay hidden
under the shade trees and among rock crevices, to present a small
vision of paradise to the thousand-mile traveler. The problem was to
actually locate these life-giving billabongs. There is a story of one
camel train which reached the Todd with waterbags dry, and in desperate condition, only to be unable to pinpoint the pools. The
lives of the men were saved, indirectly, by a flight of wild pigeons.
Pigeons cannot live more than a short distance from water, and by
following their flight, the explorers found one of the billabongs.

Later the little valley in the Macdonnell Ranges saw the arrival
of the overland telegraph, 1,028 miles from Adelaide, en route to
Darwin on the north coast, 954 miles farther. The post was named
after its discoverer, Sturt, but its name was changed in 1930 to
Alice, after the wife of the South Australia Postmaster General who
ran the communications at that time.

It is here in the Centre, more than any place else, that one real-
izes how much Australia depends upon the air age. Alice is isolated,
cut off by forbidding deserts on all sides. It is the airplane which

supports a lifeline for the outlying homestead population who have been struggling for a couple of generations to settle the more hospitable desert steppes of the Centre.

The Flying Doctor Service (established in the 1930s by the devoted Methodist missionary, John Flynn, for the purpose of bringing medical help by hospital airplane to this population and to the Aborigines) played an enormous part in the drama of a developing nation. The government came in eventually to subsidize this service, and it was put on a regular basis everywhere. But this is where it started, from the revolutionary idea of one man.

Today the Royal Flying Doctor Service is still the lifeline of Alice Springs and its scattered population. Other private entrepreneurs such as Eddie Connellan and his bush airline came in to bring mail service to remote stations, and the number of local bush airlines with other services has continued to swell.

In a typical year the planes of the R.F.D.S. may log ninety thousand or more miles within the Centre. Connellan Airways serves six hundred thousand square miles, bringing the weekly mail to 120 station properties. Such is life in the Northern Territory.

Rescue and communications are the keynotes of the Centre. The remote families consult over the airwaves with the doctor, medicating themselves when problems appear to be minor ones. Everybody has a government-issue medical chest with numbered drawers. The doctor tells the listener which drawer to pull out for the medication needed.

Children who live so far away that they can't attend school get their regular schooling each day over the airwaves. Other families may elect to send their children by plane into Alice to live at the hostel during the school year. The airplane will return the children to their families during holidays. The mission started the hostel as an Aboriginal orphanage and for Aboriginal education. Now it is government-subsidized for everybody, and the law has ruled that all children under the age of sixteen must have schooling, either at home or at a school. The Territory led the states in this trend, because the Territory is run by the federal government. Now this law has been accepted by all states.

All of the thinly scattered Centre population depends upon increasing the availability of water as the town of Alice grows. Alice is the end of the railroad line at present. The town produces dairy cattle, citrus fruits, grapes, and dates. A fiber-plaster works, sheet metal production factory, joinery, cabinet maker's, some sawmilling and brick-making assist to a degree in maintaining the town.

The town serves as an outlet for copper concentrates from Peko Mines at Tennant Creek. There is a soft drink factory, three hotels, some motels, small restaurants, pharmacies, and a tiny shopping arcade; there is a large regional hospital employing many nurses (three hundred, I heard); and ten thousand tourists pass through the town each year.

One product which Alice has to ship outside is beef. Again the word water is the key.

The Todd River billabongs have disappeared under the assault of 6,000 residents. The dairy herd, which is a pride of the region, is limited by ordinance: the herd may not be expanded nor any other herds be grazed. When milk is at all available in stores, it is comprised of half fresh and half "reconstituted" (powdered) here and through- out the rest of the territory. Exactly two tons of fresh vegetables are raised for the local market within the 500,000 square miles of the Northern Territory: that's all.

Extension of water storage and reticulation is the subject of the day. The amount of water which can be developed here is still sub- ject to chance.

But worst of all is the unpredictability of rainfall in the cattle business. There have been several years of drought, following over- stocking of lands and over-optimism. Even when windmill pumps can bring up water to fill tanks, cattle can starve to death if the grass doesn't come up.

Cattle can go only about five miles from a water tank to get their daily food. All around each tank, in every direction, the ground becomes pulverized by hooves as the cattle concentrate near them. After having eaten all the forage in an ever-widening circle around the tanks, the cattle can become so weak from lack of food that they fall in their tracks. It is actually starvation, then, which gets the stock when drought strikes.

The instability of the Alice economy and its extreme isolation, making it necessary to acquire its yield from vast reaches of land that are intrinsically hostile, has seemed to attract wonderful people; outgoing, happy, friendly adventurers used to living by taking risks. People who help other people. People who have found a degree of freedom.

72

Everyone loves the spirit of the Alice. There is an excitement there akin to yesterday's America.

The average person can quite easily and safely make the drive to Alice as we did. What the average tourist might not realize is that the country he is seeing presents a spectacular and frightening aspect of growing man-made devastation. This town's fuel needs for winter heating are still met by consuming nine thousand tons of mulga desert scrub annually, helping to hasten the denuding of the surrounding lands. Only thirty years ago the mulga was so dense that camel teams had difficulty passing through. Now the region has no permanent carrying capacity: the degenerative processes set up cannot now be controlled. The remaining mulga, which pioneers battled with all over Australia, which pioneers believed to be their indestructible foe, is now dying from causes not fully understood. "The end of a tree which forms the only cover to thousands and thousands of square miles of semi-desert country must be taken as a desperately serious matter," writes Australia Professor N.C.W. Beadle, an authority on arid lands vegetation. Since 1950 a hundred thousand square miles in the Centre have been "lost." Eucalypts are growing scarcer than in the days of the explorers; trees like the river red gum, the coolibah, ghost gum, snappy gum, and the acacia forms called the witchetty bush, gidgee, myall, ironwood (not the same as our ironwood), and all the arid grasslands and shrub-steppe communities have been disappearing under the trampling of many hooves.

In Alice we pitched the blue tent sweatily and wearily. We stayed at Wintersun Car Park beside a violet-flowering jacaranda tree, feasting our eyes on rustling leaves and green things. It was getting very hot—we were along the Tropic of Capricorn. We looked as though we had been shoveling coal for the devil.

Again we offered the hospitality of the big tent to our guests. "What will you do now that you're here?" we asked them.

"Have to go right back," they replied, in a great hurry.

"Well, take a shower and grab a bite first," I said.

Within the hour the American girl and the Australian boy were deposited at the edge of Alice Springs, along the south road, sitting under a green-leaved tree. They were lucky. They caught a ride at once with travelers going straight through, non-stop, to Adelaide, where they had to be back at the store.

I met another old desert rat during my wandering of the town of Alice, and talked with him. He was a particularly disreputable type, but information is where you find it.

"Are there any mysteries of the desert that are yet unexplored?" was at the heart of my several questions.

"Well," he said, thinking hard, "a few seasons back we had some explorer here from America. Had a big name, that one, too, I reckon. Well, he had this idea. He was determined to dig up the bones of old Wombat Bill."

"Well, what happened?" I asked.

"Did it, too," the whiskery, beery, old fellow told me. "Nobody could stop him, even though some people would rather he wouldn't."

"What was the point of the digging-up?" I asked, very keen, and delighted to get this small nugget of local gossip about a fellow American.

"Well, he was one of our early pioneers around here, I guess you would call Bill. Everybody knew old Wombat. He had always wanted to be buried out on the desert. That was his wish, his instructions.

"Nobody in Alice liked the idea of having his rest disturbed. But this explorer, he come over here, and he got some black trackers and they went out on the desert and first thing we knew here comes Wombat Bill's bones along into Alice in a sack, and Wombat was famous, just like that!

"Really wasn't a whole lot of mystery about the grave to begin with. And I guess that was the last mystery that we had around here, far as I know."

"Jean," I said, "they have these big community dances on certain nights in Alice. I'll iron your dress, honey, if you'll take me to the dance in the Jeep."

"Why don't you drive yourself?" she asked. "You're mature."

"I'm timid, if you have to know," I admitted. "Please go with your old mum for company, will you? It might be fun for you."

Nobody had been to any dances in Australia all this time, but somehow the girls, with their very keen intuition about things, were not eager. "Take Ann," she said. "It's *her* turn."

"I don't have any intention of going and sitting and being a wallflower in front of the whole town while nitwit *men* look me up and down," replied Ann, shortly. She added, "I'm not on the beef market, thanks."

Ann had been escorted by two boys to a dance at Woomera, and she said that no girl, but absolutely *no girl* over the age of sixteen in Australia would show herself to the rude stag lines—unless she was looking for an evening of humiliation, that is. After the age of sixteen the girls sat home (unless they had a date) and the young men spent their evenings with the stags at the bar or club, showing their mates that *they* were true men, not just hung onto some woman's apron strings. Despite the preponderance of male population, both girls were certain that an evening of "dancing" at Alice Springs would be dismal.

After some arguments Jean, with the greatest reluctance, consented to escort her dear old mum as an act of filial piety. Ann remained with Lad to guard our possessions.

In the typical Outback town each hotel will take a turn at holding the weekly (or "calverey") dance. That way the hotels share the profits among them, but more than that, the destruction to the hotels is carried as a joint community burden.

On this night the dance was being held at the Stewart Arms. A lively crowd in every sort of casual garb was already whooping it up when we arrived in the "ladies lounge." Under territory laws the bars had to close at eleven-thirty. These were very daring hours—the most liberal in Australia, where the thread of Puritanism runs deep and wide.

Rough language or off-color jokes are never aired in the presence of ladies, and a man would not presume to sit down at a table with a lady he did not know. He might, though, send a drink over to her table and eye her from a distance all evening long—a distance that might well leave the stranger to these customs considerably perplexed.

At the same time, there are spasmotic outbursts of disorderly conduct in the form of drunkenness and fighting, as a quite "normal" male rebellion against the code.

A sophisticated world traveler, speaking many languages and conversant with most of the world customs, once described his brush with Australian male behavior to me. "It was in Paris," he said. "We were dining in the old Blue Room of the Ritz, when twelve *naked*

75

Australians came snake-dancing through the grand dining room. Quite an impressive sight, fine looking men, one must say. Two Russian Grand Duchesses fainted."

Well, Jean and I slipped into the barren "lounge" with its typically cratered walls, shyly took a table, and sat down. I didn't know whether custom permitted me to step to the bar and order our drinks, and nobody came to serve us. It was a strange feeling to realize that a woman, unless she had a man along to give her an identity, might not even get served. We felt miserably ignored and out of place.

"I wish we had never come here, Mother. I won't have my ego destroyed in this way. Why do you get me into things like this?"

I was about to muscle my way to the bar when two men came over to us. Soon Jean was whirling around the floor with one of them and I with the other. Returning, the men settled themselves at our table. This was quite unlike Australian practice. I looked around unhappily. What a greasy, scruffy-looking pair.

The sweating bottles of beer from the cooler stacked up. Suds soon were dripping onto our knees in running rivers. Aussie taverns are wet, runny places. And glazed paper napkins seem as though made from their native eucalypti. All of the other tables were running beer exactly like ours. The concrete floor was forming into a lake. It would be hosed down tomorrow. Men grasped girls in muscular arms on the dance floor. Girls tried to look pretty and kept a hopeful expression.

It was quite a while before I clearly heard the accents of the two men with us—one of them was an American. That was why he asked to sit down with us and easily did so. To an American casual friendship was the natural thing, with no self-consciousness attached.

Our new acquaintance turned out to be an old bush pilot, maybe the first to fly the Arctic Ocean coast of Alaska back in 1937. It turned out that he knew my old stamping grounds better than I knew them myself, or at least earlier. He knew the same Eskimos, and he could even tell some of the same stories I told.

"I've heard Serge speak of you many times," I told him.

"Yes, I flew balloons for him in India. Well, I always fly Serge's balloons. I've been flying balloons for Serge for eighteen years, too."

We were talking about the president of the Explorers Club.

From that moment on the men looked far less disreputable in my eyes, because I had understanding.

76

The local photographer came by and took candid pictures that evening. I will always prize them: all of us greasy and full of beer, happy with new (and old) friends, smack in the center of Australia.

Both men were far beyond Jean's age interest, and she now had no chance of others coming up to dance with her, because we had acquired escorts—to challenge this could provoke a fight, according to the male code. These men had given us an identity, by lending their presence to our·"frailty." So be it. The daring, hawkish old bush pilot and I resumed our stories and Alaska memories while Jean fidgeted and the music played on. Aussie rules are rough, because the woman has virtually all avenues blocked off for practicing any social independence.

The Aussies had begun throwing and shattering their bottles against the hotel wall. Nobody minded. Jean scratched a piece of flying glass out of her leg, ruefully.

"Can I please go now, Mom?"

"But I wish you would stay and have fun," I argued.

"Can't he bring you home?"

"I'll take good care of your mother. I'll bring her home safely," the flyer promised.

Jean left. For a moment I considered crawling under the table to escape the flying shrapnel, but the table, supported by one center leg, was no larger than a little parasol.

Crash! Smash! went the bottles.

"I'll play their Aussie game," he said, and threw a glass which shattered magnificently.

"You must be kidding," I said. "You can't be serious."

"It's fun," he said. "You should try it, an explorer like you. Did you ever try it?"

"You call this fun?"

"You don't know it but you are at the right place at the right time," he said. "There's a story here. If I see you a few years from now, remember this night, and I'll tell you some stories."

All around us the playful Aussies gathered in a cluster, talking to him. Not to me. Only one fellow said to me, "Yer a lady Yank, aren't ye?"

We were asked to drive out to another place to attend another party. The desert night was by now getting very cold, and the Aussies began throwing the girls into the swimming pool. The girls seemed pliable and delighted to get the attention. When an Aussie grabbed a girl she might feel that she was being grabbed by a playful, rib-cracking bear.

I was shivering with cold and wanted to go home. "Like that damned Libyian Desert, remember Libya?" said another American whom I hadn't known was an American. He was the fun-loving but actually very careful driver of our carload of bottles and people.

At length I was politely driven home and climbed into my sleeping bag to join the girls inside the tent. Our big square plastic flashlight had fallen apart again, and I couldn't find it in the dark. Anyway, it had been quite a night. I had never seen Aussies at play before. It was such a masculine society. For a moment I felt like Kipling in India—or like Hemingway in Spain.

The rains had taken effect and how lucky we were: spring dallied this year, coaxing out the rarest desert blooms. Usually the worst heat had hit by this time and withered all the flowers.

We were heading out toward Ayers Rock now, and the domes of the Olgas. The last night before we left Alice the girls had met two boys at the caravan park whom they referred to as Helmut and Hans. The fellows were from Switzerland. The girls kept babbling about these fellows as the Baby Blue Jeep ground and bounded through the hot, white, dazzling light and through the sooty black shadows of acacia into the nothingness of the desert. I, of course, was looking for the rare flowers.

Driving to lonely Ayers Rock at this time of year was a bit chancy because it was a 288-mile run out there by a dirt road turnoff, one which was not well traveled in summer. There was no gasoline to be had at Ayers Rock, we had been warned. That didn't matter—we had some with us. There were no mechanical services out there, either. We were desert wise: we knew we were risking the possible loss of our whole outfit, so far out of towing range. But that was always inherent in the Australia game, wasn't it?

Red sandhills rolled before us carrying Sturts desert pea, a great scarlet blossom drooping low to the ground on a little dry stalk. Sturts desert rose, emblem of the Northern Territory, covered rugged shrubs of the "blue bush" variety with hundreds of full-size roses of the most tender blue. The heart of each rose shaded into a deep velvet violet, with yellow stamens. The kangaroo apple, also a blue

78

bush, sprouted pea green "apples" upon it the size of golfballs—but not edible. This desert carried no edibles.

One of the most remarkable sights was the sprouting of myriad poplar trees, up to ten feet tall, their shiny round leaves dancing in the sun. If this desert had a few seasons of rain these trees would become a forest. Lacking rain, the poplars died off each summer.

The sand was heavy. Ann was coaxing the Jeep through the dips and over the dunes with an experienced hand. We certainly didn't want to get bogged.

We camped a night along the way. Solemn calls of bell birds were heard in the evening glow. They sounded like belled cattle. There was no other sound, nothing. No more tent or stretchers. "There is nothing that will hurt you in Australia," the C.S.I.R.O. biologist in Alice Springs had said. We lay peacefully out on the ground and were showered with stars all night.

We rose early. The moment the sun popped over the horizon it became too hot to endure, except when moving along. One wondered how the oldtimers survived without swift vehicles built high off the ground. The millions of small black flies which infest the Outback always rise with the sun. The Aborigines, like Arabs, were so accustomed to the flies that they did not bother to raise a hand and brush them out of their eyes.

This was a mistake. These flies, and a tiny, swift-flying gnat which stings the eyeballs without the victim being aware of it, cause the infection called conjunctivitus, which in Australia goes by the regional term, "sandy blight."

Slowly the "world's largest pebble"—Ayers Rock—appeared with the sunrise, turning from purple to mauve to rose, and then red. It is located in a native reserve, one of the few accessible to the public without special permit. It rises to 1,100 feet above the rolling sand plain and measures five and a half miles around its base, detached and standing there through the centuries in vast empty space.

The rock can be climbed on one side only. There is a foot trail reinforced by steel handgrips on the steep parts. Several caves and rock overhangs surround the base of the rock in which ancient Aboriginal prayer paintings can be seen. This is a very sacred place.

From one cleft in the rock a trickle of sweet water comes down into a pool at the base of the silent monolith. This pool, surrounded by bushes and trees, is hidden from the sun, so that it always lies in shadow and is always a certain source of water.

During the winter tourist season hundreds of persons come out from Alice to see Ayers Rock. Many come the easy way, on daily flights. Their guides serve them refreshments at a cookout. But the blazing day we drove into the public campgrounds we had it virtually all to ourselves. Except—there was a vehicle which turned at the campgounds to meet us.

"It's the boys! Helmut and Hans!" yelled the girls.

"But I thought we left them back at Alice. . . ."

"Helmut and Hans! Mother, don't you *remember*, we spent nearly all our time with them when we were at Alice Springs!"

I hadn't remembered that. Anyway, here they were, and they had driven all the way out here, by some coincidence, because, it was explained to me quickly in my briefing, although they came from Sydney they were taking a look around Australia very much as we were doing.

The girls, bedraggled and down in the dumps moments ago, were transformed into gay and sparkling scamps.

The boys did look like good fellows, I had to admit.

"We're a little late, but we made it," Ann was saying. "Mother had to stop and look at every flower along the way."

I had thought the trip quite fast, actually. More bumps than usual. On one bump I had bitten my tongue.

Jean had out her English-German dictionary by the time we skidded to a stop under an acacia tree; Hans had his German-English dictionary in his hand as he waved.

"They were brought over by the Australian government," Jean explained to me, "to work on timing devices for the military. They've been here less than a year and already Hans has taught himself to speak and read and write English! Could you do that, I mean, that *fast*?"

"They speak Switzerdeutch, a Swiss mountain dialect of German, actually," added Ann for me. "So it's hard for Jeanie to translate, and therefore mostly we all speak English."

"Those guys must really be smart," I agreed.

"Jean has been teaching Hans about fifty new words a day so far. But Helmut doesn't try so hard, I guess. . .But he's their expert mechanic. Just look!"

80

The tall and tanned Helmut was already lifting a heavy tool box out of their bus onto the ground. That tool box had everything! Those smart Swiss operated a garage on wheels.

"It is good to see you again," Hans greeted me, as both young men stepped up to shake my hand. "Many welcomes to Ayers Rock, this magnificent view. May we be of help to you in something? Please tell us."

The first thing was to prepare a camp for night. The two young men, bearded and about twenty-two, were living in a Volkswagen Combi bus inside which they had built cupboards and beds. On the outside they had painted an enormous map of the Australian continent, and on the top as a final touch to their adventure, they had wired a large set of bleached white steer horns picked up from the desert. The magnificently ornamented bus was named The Witchetty Grub, after that special worm which the Aborigines dig out from the roots of some acacia and eat hungrily for its fat content, either raw or cooked.

In a flash the blue tent was up, our five-gallon water jug hung on the tree, and I was delving happily into my pots and pans and tucker box.

"I'll make a wonderful soup," I suggested aloud to one and all.

"You should taste my mom's soup," Ann was cavorting gleefully, driving tent stakes with the new pals.

"Ha, yes," said Jean. "Mighty Grease strikes again!"

"How about some of this delightful stuff tonight?" Picking out a can labeled "Delightful Bake-Pie," I held it up in feigned delight. The boys tried hard to smile away their distaste. They, too, had been living on the horrid concoction—an overcooked, squashy, putrid meat mash, like dogfood. The contents listed on the can read: 35% pork, 28% beef, 9% cereal.

These percentages, not totaled, came to just 72 percent. I was always left wondering what became of the missing 28 percent. It was better not to think about it.

"Dig the cans later, Mom," said Jean then. "There's only forty minutes of daylight left. We can make it up on top of the Rock and down again before night, if we spring with our Swiss."

"Marv," remarked Helmut, promptly, when this was explained.

"Yes, beauty," Hans said.

81

The happy young people sprang up Ayers Rock, hopping into the bonza distance.

The next morning we saw a large bleached set of steer horns coming along the horizon, and a dusty Holden sedan named the Ugly Duckling pulled in under our tree. Like the Witchetty Grub, it too had built-in beds.

"We know these friends, too," Hans told me, and I shook hands with Kiwi and Claude. Kiwi was one of the fifty thousand New Zealanders who live in Australia. Claude was a real Australian, the only one among us.

"The new mites are from Swinging Sydney, too," sang Ann, overjoyed.

The new mates had recently traveled along with the Swiss in caravan style, camping out together. It was a roadside friendship.

It was interesting to examine each other's means of camping out. The Holden had really fancy cupboard work, which would not have worked in our Jeep. Our travel was the roughest and the bumpiest. All the others really envied us our four-wheel drive, though, because we could go places the others would not dare to go. We only wished we had a winch. But a good winch was too much for the loud laments of my wallet.

Within minutes of the newcomers' arrival, the two girls and four boys went out to climb the Olgas, thirty miles away. The Olgas rose 1,500 feet above the plain, or 3,507 feet above sea level, and they had deep ravines through which fierce winds occasionally blew. The young people were gone all day. I didn't miss the climb. I was very content.

While the kids climbed I walked with the water drillers who were trying to develop water at Ayers Rock so that motels, a gas station, and all the facilities of a modern wayside stop could be put up. We were lucky to be here before it was all "developed."

I mentioned to a driller that I had seen the poor Aboriginal wanderers with babies on their backs picking over the campgrounds' garbage cans.

"The Bongs? It was better in the old days," he told me flatly. "They are like animals, you know. They are used to hardship and they won't work unless they have to. They need the lash and hobbles to work."

No use to argue. I walked back to camp. A former mission superintendent at Hermannsburg, near Alice, had given a more enlightened and professional opinion. He said: "You can't turn a food gatherer into a food producer overnight. The Aborigine is not a simple nomad searching for a way of life. He is an efficient collector of his needs, with a social system that suits him, disciplines him, and is workable.

"To survive and bring up a family here, to have a language of at least forty thousand words, a culture, a religion, and a philosophy suited to him—these are hardly the achievements of dull and stupid nomads. The more we get to know about them," he said, "the more we admire them. But—we have to train them in a new sort of responsibility."

I took a nap for a while inside the tent. As I slept I heard the clank of my empty cans of "Delightful Bake-Pie," and tried to rouse myself. I should give them some cans, full ones. I heard the patter of dog feet then. Laddie had quietly brought dog friends inside the tent and was showing the Aboriginal mutts his newfound affluence. There was wagging of tails, but no sound but panting. Then they all went out again, in perfect and silent communication of some kind.

Acacia leaves made lacy patterns on the tent roof, moving slightly in the breeze. Last night I thought I had heard sounds of distant chanting, of clack-clack sticks, and *didjeridoos* around Ayers Rock. It was easy to imagine it. One couldn't be sure. It was the time of year when older men seized young boys without warning and performed upon them the most horrendous circumcisions among primitives the world over. The circumcisions involved a complete splitting of the penis from the under side, known among anthropologists as "subincision of the euretha." Missions and government had not yet, after over fifty years, been able to stamp out this gruesome, unsanitary custom. If anything, conditions were worse today because of the availability of steel knives and razor blades which could cut deeper and do more damage than the old stone-age flints. A female would be beheaded if she should witness the sacred *corroboree*.

One had to wonder how, with this custom, females were impregnated and the race continued. Some of the most religious and fanatical of the older men voluntarily went back to undergo the savage ordeal again and again as steps in their initiation as mystics.

83

When I awoke I went to the square stone washtubs of the camp, and there found myself talking with a newcomer, called Hillary. She was a perfectly beautiful girl from England, and at thirty-nine had the figure of a nymph, absolutely stunning in shorts, and a complexion like a clear rose.

"I and my traveling companion," she said, "are just taking a look around. I'm older than I look, really. Steve is twenty-one. He's a Kiwi, and we were talking this morning about now that we're here at Ayers Rock in the Centre, well, where do we go next? We can't quite make up our minds. It's such a big country and getting terribly hot now. . . . "

"I guess we have that problem, too. . . ."

"Steve isn't well. He was involved in an accident a while ago."

"Where are you from, to start off with?"

"Sydney," she said. "Swinging Sydney."

The couple had left Sydney months ago on their trek, taking a "working holiday." They had only a canvas fly to rig from the car for partial shelter, and they slept on the ground. They had come most recently from Darwin, and Hillary supposed they would return there.

"Get Steve and bring your pannikins to my tent right now, and we'll have tea," I said.

It was outside of Darwin, when he was working as a truck driver, that Steve's terrible accident had occurred. He had been crushed between two enormous cattle-haulers on the highway one night when one of the drivers backed up, catching the tall New Zealander standing between the multiple-ton trucks.

When I met him he looked wan, but game. His chest had been squeezed to the most remarkable degree of thinness I had seen in my life. It seemed a miracle that his heart and lungs had escaped being crushed and that his ribs had bent like springs rather than cracking.

"Oh, but I was too-right when me absent-minded mite finally put his stupid big foot on the brake and stopped backing into me," Steve explained, as I shuddered. "That stupid mite. He couldn't even hear me yelling.

"He's roight," he said flatly, to make it clear that all was forgiven. He had no grudge against him. "He's still me mite. But I don't like hospitals," he went on, rather breathlessly. "They had me lyin' there, me ribs caved in, and next to me bed was an Aborigine

84

with a spear-head broke off in his back. Made me feel unhappy surrounded by all that misery. So I get me clothes when the nurse was out, and jump out of that place, I did. I'll be roight. Only, me ribs is bent, and I wonder if I'll ever have a real normal-like figure again."

"But is there time to get back to Darwin again?" I asked the couple. "How about the Wet?"

The rains come during the four or five months from November through March, and while they are sporadic and unpredictable, they are nonetheless sufficient to deluge roads, fill river beds, spread out over lowlands for fifty miles, and often effectively block off parts of the North from all ground communications over a long period. The Wet causes species of vegetation to flourish, such as you would find in a jungle habitat, yet due to the opposite season known as the Dry, in which there is absolutely *no rain*, no true jungle forms. Because many rivers run from bank to bank in the Wet, ground travelers know that they must make their plans one way or another. They either have to pull out of the far North and stay out during this time, or they have to hole up at Darwin or at their station homestead, and stay put.

I wasn't the only one who was thinking about the North End, at this most unseasonable time to think about it. When our gang returned from the Olgas that evening they asked, "Why don't we all go to Darwin together?"

"There would be nine of us together," Ann pointed out. "Did you take a look at that tool kit of Helmut's? Say, you guys," she added with inspiration, "we need help sometimes with our mechanical problems, and, if you should need it, you can use our snakebite kit any time you want to."

"But we wouldn't want to go with people who kill animals," Jean said frankly. "We're studying things and just want to look, and no shooting them. We're really a reptilian family," she told the others. "Elizabeth Taylor likes jewels. My mom likes lizards."

"Hillary always cries if I shoot something," said Steve.

"The main thing, I think," I said, "is that if we go to the North End, we might just be able to make it before the Wet, but it will have to be a real fast trip. Let's build a campfire now. We'll have to thrash out the details, and to do this properly it will be necessary to have a good, old-fashioned pow-wow."

So we had a pow-wow there in the so-called "dead heart." At

first Steve wasn't sure he wanted to join up with the others. He was pretty much of a loner, he said. He wanted it made clear that he and Hillary would be free to travel slower or faster as they liked, or leave us at any time.

We wanted to take a quick look at Darwin, and then, instead of coming back south to Adelaide on the same track, we would take an alternate track in the North around the far west coast of the continent and on south to Perth.

Our luggage was stored with the useless trailer at Port Pirie away south on Spencer Gulf in South Australia. But did it really matter if it stayed there a while longer? We would get it sometime— hard to tell when.

As you go north toward the Equator it gets hotter by the mile, and entering the land of the Wet and the Dry, you find animal and plant life adapted to two violently contrasting seasons, and well equipped to survive after millions of years of evolution—although this was somewhat more difficult for man and for domestic animals. From Darwin to Perth would be a lot of driving, mostly on unpaved road. That's why, the first time around anyway, people like us would do well to have Helmut and his tool kit along, and travel in caravan with other vehicles, especially with the Wet about to bust loose any time.

I knew we were going to love the North best. It was lusher and supported the greatest abundance of wild animal species. I hoped the poisoners hadn't got to most of it yet, because settlers were certainly on the way to this very last outpost—the richest, the most exciting of Australia's lands, having the greatest potential of all.

The result of our pow-wow is easy to guess. We succumbed to the lure of the North. With recap tires unraveling and the Wet gathering, it was going to be a far cow to Perth!

Chapter 8

CAMPFIRES NORTH OF ALICE

The little caravan of four vehicles, nine people and a dog, sped in
good time along the smoking hot bitumen of the blacktop Stuart
Highway, northward. We were north of rabbits, north of sheep,
and the anthills began. For nine hundred miles this highway cuts
through the Centre from Alice to Darwin, following the old drovers'
trail. Along the trail today: gas pumps and pubs at Three Way
Roadhouse, Tennant Creek, the Devil's Marbles; Renner Springs
(Which marks the end of the arid zone), Newcastle Waters (the
junction of two old stock routes), Daly Waters, Mataranka (a
natural hot springs), Katherine, Pine Creek, Adelaide River—
each with its history of men's bodies impaled by Aboriginal spears,
and revenge by the whites in which whole tribal groups were exterminated, very much as happened in the Indian resistance against
the whites pushing West. But the fantastic changes which have
taken place in this century in America are far less apparent in
Australia.

Through the Centre the stony tableland spread before us. It
s like the hamada soils of North Africa and southwest Asia, they
ay, except covered with a broken silcrete and silicified stones,
giving this hardpan an intense patina which is known to the

scientists as "desert varnish." The surface stones, called "gibbers" in Australia, seem to dance in the heatwaves. Among the stones grow the perennial, evergreen tussock grasses called spinifex, and the mulga scrub, and all of it washed with the white lights and eyeball searing pastels of that first great Aboriginal artist, Albert Namatijira.

Millions upon millions of anthills stretched away to infinity before us. At first they were only two to four feet tall, but they grew larger toward the tropics. Each earth mound had passed through the intestinal tracts of billions of termites who built them from the soil combined with their own bodily excretions, until these rugged structures could survive any tropical downpour or cyclone like concrete.

The heat of the sun penetrates three or four feet into the ground, and the wingless white ants escape this death-dealing heat by housing themselves deep inside these earth homes. The red earth anthills we noticed were always shapeless globs with a melted-down look to them. Apparently they were able to stand up to the elements only because of the sticky glue from the insects' bodies, for the red pindan soil was soft. But, in areas of gray soils containing clay and silcrete, the termites built large structures with splendid pointed spires and pinnacles, and when their material would hold a shape, they built each structure so that it would knife-edge into the slant of the hottest afternoon sun, facing the equator. For this reason, the gray anthills were called by the people "magnetic anthills," and these were as hard and impermeable as grey flint.

The red pindan soils of the Northern Territory and Western Australia will not hold water for the farmer—water just sinks out of sight. Red pindan soil takes up thousands of square miles. Art Linkletter spent $50,000 developing a sprinkler system, using the natural artesian wells on his property at Anna Plains, W.A., only to have all the water that was pumped sink into the earth and vanish, leaving his sorghum fields to wither and die. Art had another problem, too, which is common throughout tens of thousands of miles in Australia: the water was too saline. Art was lucky that he lost only $50,000 that time. Other men have lost far more.

A curious sight among the anthills and spinifex was that of the campers lining up in shorts each morning to weigh in on the old bathroom scale the girls had brought along. We were all getting pretty big from our weight-lifting courses with the jerry cans, plus high-calorie camping foods.

Weighing became a morning ritual for all with the rising sun. We never knew exactly why we bothered, especially when sand worked into the scale and after that everyone weighed 250 pounds.

When we camped we made a circle with our vehicles as the covered wagon pioneers used to do, with our campfire within the sociable circle. At the first evening's camp Hillary brought out an artistically arranged tray of orange slices, apple slices, nuts, and raisins while the rest of us were opening our hideous canned meats with can openers and getting out frying pans. Suddenly it all seemed familiar. "Well, you see I am a vegetarian," the lovely Hillary explained.

Desert nights were so brilliant that I shall always remember the nights as much as the days. One by one the campers left the campfire and crept into their bedrolls. Hans was seated across from me on the other camp chair, as we wordlessly watched the red castles of the coals build and crumble and fall. You could see the stars not only overhead but clear down the horizon in a 360-degree circle.

"Why did you and Helmut come to Australia, Hans?"

"My father die last year. My father was a very good man, always giving presents and money to everybody. He was too good. My mother say he give too much, he give everything away. After he die, my mother is wanting for me always to stay at home, take care the cows, take care everything; listen to her talk about my father. But, when a man is twenty-one," he said, "it is necessary for a man to leave his home and mother and go out into the world, and take a look around."

Hans had milked cows, rising at four, all his life. For the privilege of going to school he milked the cows early and late. In Australia he was glad to get away from milking cows, he said.

But there was something else. "In Switzerland," the youth reflected, "today the people think only of making money. Everywhere they are greedy, they do not love their country, they do not care to help other people; even our beautiful lakes are becoming spoil from filth, and people throw papers down, their trash. I would like to find something for which to live my life. Something,

89

somewhere." He sighed, long and deeply, his young brow furrowed with his idealism. "Something beside just to make money all my life."

"Have a blast, while you last," called Jean from her sleeping bag, but was for the moment, ignored.

"Aristotle called it 'the unnatural perversion of money-making.' Do you think you find a better life in Australia?"

"It is much the same," he replied, with philosophical sadness. "You have to make money, even here. I like that, really. I like to make money. But—well," he said suddenly, taking comfort, "you have fine girls. I enjoy knowing Jean and Ann. I always think American girls must be very rich and lazy. But they are hard workers and they are true friends, the best friends I ever had."

"I am so glad you feel that way. Does Helmut like Australia?"

"No," he said. "Helmut will not even care to speak English. He does not tell even me what he think about, and I have known him for my best friend since we were little babies together. I cannot understand Helmut here in Australia. He will not talk to me, not even in Switzerdeutch."

When any of us tried to get to know Helmut, we got nowhere. Helmut was shutting himself up inside himself, something which is not uncommon with many new immigrants. Helmut's father-son relationship had been a childhood disaster. His father had been known as the most sour man in the village, and had been a tyrant to his family. When Helmut was faced with the problem of adjusting to a strange and harsh land out here, and strange customs, he had an impossible handicap. None of us, seeing that tall, tanned, stalwart body and handsome, bearded face, could have surmised the strange, hurt child who lived inside. None of us knew it then, but Helmut was emotionally incapacitated.

Goodnights were said. Once again, standing at my bedroll, I swung the field glasses over the empty land. I was always doing that. Good glasses can let you see right through night and darkness, and through brush as well, picking out solid bodies from the illusory.

The mystery of the origin of the min-min lights has never been solved. It was said that balls of light could sometimes be seen floating along, six to ten feet above the ground. I hoped I would see a flying saucer, a snowman—well, anything strange.

90

My glasses telescoped the millions of anthills marching away in the distance. The shy night-singing parrot is said to make its nest in an anthill somewhere, a bird which may be seen but once in thirty years. I put up the glasses and crawled into the sack.

It was hard to believe that during World War II at least 100,000 men lived in camps along this lonely road. The American soldiers pumped water out of bores from an underground artesian table estimated to cover some 25,000 square miles, and they raised thousands of pounds of vegetables in gardens. Even earlier than the Americans, Chinese coolies raised sixty bushels of rice to the acre along the Darwin River up north, and shipped it home to China for a profit. Nothing like this has happened in Australia since.

Corn, tobacco, sugar, peanuts. Many people believe these could all be grown, and cotton, too, in the far north, where there are some thirty major rivers which drain into the several northern seas.

Distance to markets has been too far. Distance also has been the reason why minerals have not been developed. Vast distances, lack of communications and transport, and lack of people made development uneconomical. When you push outward to the farthest places on earth and try "developing," you reach the point of diminishing returns on your investment. And so far three generations of puny man were just lost and swallowed up in the 523,620 miles of the enormous territory whose boundary lines exist only in theory on the maps, since no man sees them. "The land without memory," Ernestine Hill called this land. The total territory population now is given as 60,222.

Generally Australia is called a man's country, but curiously, the four outstanding writers are women: Ernestine Hill; Mrs. Aeneas Gunn; Mary Durack, now living in Perth; and Daisy Bates with her classic *The Passing of the Aborigines*.

Of course there are men writers, too, and I met about a dozen contemporary Australian authors in due time, struggling with the enormous odds of a continent whose science and civilization have the most meager research materials of any modern-day society. The authors themselves are scattered far and wide over the continent. Their names are known on book lists throughout the Commonwealth, but few Americans have ever heard of them, with their cheery writing of a world apart, of tastes for plain, honest sunshine and sand and human grit, and very little skill in writing about the complexities within man, or for writing dark things.

When the new explorers camped we eagerly brought out our books and passed them around.

"I'll let you borrow my Daisy Bates for *One Wet Season.*"

"I'll be glad to let you get a look at *The Bushman's Hand Book* if I can borrow *In Crocodile Land.*"

I prized my Daisy Bates, a paperback which was fast coming apart, very highly. Daisy Bates was an English newspaper woman who came to Australia in her early years, married a grazier, and had one son. On one occasion she drove her cattle two thousand miles overland. But we know little of her personal or family life beyond that cattle trek.

She emerges in the public eye as a woman over forty, with a tent and camp outfit, going off into the desert alone to live with nature. For the next thirty years she lived among the Aborigines, and it is for these years, from age forty until over seventy, that she will live always for people who seek truth. She was called upon for help by the government of South Australia to deal with recalcitrant tribes because nobody before her time or since knew them so well. She was called by the government of Western Australia for it was only she who could make the natives lay down their spears.

The Aboriginal peoples accepted her into their secret religious ceremonies, which no outsider may witness. She herself then became a part of Aboriginal legend, and she recorded their beliefs for posterity. The natives did not regard her as a woman. They knew her as a supernatural being and a mystic—which she seemed to become in time.

Daisy Bates was the only modern, educated person in the 1920s and '30s who was really in a position to testify to the passing of a people who had no recognition from the governments of the sovereign states, who had no medical care but that which a few lone missions gave, and who at that time were rapidly dying off from disease, destitution, confusion of identity, and heartbreak. Year after year she lived in the desert, giving them service with her own hands, nursing them when they were sick, watching them die, honoring their last earthly requests, comforting her "children," and accepting them as they were in all their wonder and their frailties—a Stone Age people. In the end she collected the old men's totems of the clans,

92

the mysteries of mysteries, covering them with canvas and preserving them beside her tent—what would appear to the casual observer to be merely a pile of interestingly carved poles and sticks, except that these sticks carried the history of the ages on them. The sticks were brought to her from far places and given into her trust, that they might not be lost as the people died. Eventually, when Daisy herself became too old to guard the sacred totems longer, they were entrusted to a museum.

Although Daisy was a strict disciplinarian in her own personal habits, dressing each day in the long black skirt, the shirtwaist, and high collar, and high button shoes of the proper English gentlewoman of her time, she recognized quickly that the "civilized" life could not be imposed on people who had not the material means to support it, who had no need for it, and whose delicate skins, for instance, could not so much as withstand soap and water care without breaking into sores, inasmuch as they lived their lives in sand beneath a blazing sun.

Native people of the warm climates have devised their own ways of coping with body exposure. They keep their skins soft and glistening and resilient as a reptile's by anointing themselves frequently with oils taken from materials at hand. In Australia, for instance, the oil of the goannas has been thoughtfully furnished for desert living— little oil tanks on waddling legs to fulfill the nutritional and even the cosmetic needs of man.

The most interesting of Daisy's observations deal with cannibalism, which she reports as being rampant from one end of Australia to the other. The great woman humanitarian noted that the most ravenous cannibals of any tribe were the women. Many women ate their own newborn babies, sometimes sharing the fat little nugget, dropped in a secret place, with a young child. The men of the tribe found this secret practice of the women repugnant and never themselves ate baby meat. Daisy saw quite clearly the plight of the Stone Age women, who were so vilified by both white man and black. These women were on the edge of starvation practically all the time, because the hunters permitted women to eat meat only after they the hunters themselves had dined, consuming all the choice parts.

At the same time it was often a fact of life that a woman must get rid of her baby as the only means of population control. All primitive hunting peoples expose a certain number of their babies in order to keep the population within the carrying capacity of their hunting grounds. This was always "women's business." The men turned their heads away and gave it no attention.

In Australia, the hunting grounds of any group were strictly limited, even though vast in extent. The tribes rarely came into conflict with each other because nature provided barriers of deserts which separated the human groups. Beyond these barriers of his own historic grounds a hunter would not venture. A certain balance of nature was thus kept. But when tribes were pressed by white men for their land, they had no place to retreat to, since the invasion of rival tribal lands meant war and death.

Females in Aboriginal life had no "rights" because they were not regarded as being people, and they "had no souls." All religious mystery or sanctuary was reserved for the souls of the male sex, exclusively. Women were but the vessels to carry the seed of the great spirit which would produce other men spirits to live in flesh in the tribe.

Pregnancy was believed to occur by supernatural means, not as the result of intercourse. A man wanting a child had a visitation by a spirit in some silent place, and was told that his wife would give him a child. A woman, however, tried to walk carefully past a rock or a pool, for if she made a mistake in her footing or perhaps even in the glance of her eyes, the great rainbow serpent hidden there might give her a child she did not want.

Phyllis M. Kaberry, another Englishwoman, tells in *Aboriginal Women* how she lived as an anthropologist among some tribes in the wild Kimberlies of the northwest for some months in 1938-1939. Phyllis found that these people believed that the necessity of being born of woman profaned the sacred Dreamtime Spirit. Therefore, this sin of being born of unclean woman, or being born into flesh rather than pure spirit, must be cleansed by initiation for males of the tribe. Males lived separately from females and could not speak with women throughout a lifetime, other than upon prescribed occasions in specified ways. It was death, in fact, to any man or boy who violated the strict sexual taboos or even worse, revealed magic secrets to any woman.

Phyllis spent her days entirely with the women. She carried a woven dilly bag on her back and a digging stick as she went on women's walk-about. But one gets the impression that the author enjoyed primitive woman's life very much, inasmuch as she was a

woman explorer on her own, and certainly not a dependent subject
of that male-dominated civilized society from which she came in
1937, to find a larger world.

In primitive life, Miss Kaberry wrote, men and women accepted
their assigned positions in the tribe and women, all in all, were a
happy lot. It wasn't easy to be a man, she pointed out—a man, as
hunter, had to supply meat. Only men used weapons. This was a
vast responsibility. Men painted themselves with magic ochres which
were never permitted to women. The magic, in order to be strong,
had to be secret. (The ochres had a slightly astringent and cooling
effect on the skin, she reports, and so helped calm their unsteady
nerves.) To outwit big game animals—kangaroo and crocodile—men
were called upon to endure hardships unto the death on the long
hunt. Men had to develop special cunning by means of magic to
evade evil spirits lying in wait. All this was man's business. Women
were not called upon for such disciplines as every boy endured from
the time he left childhood behind.

On the other hand, women trudged through their days collecting edible roots, grubs, bugs, little reptiles, and "such small deer,"
often loaded like pack mules. Europeans seeing them felt pity; but
where Europeans see only labor, filth and squalor, they cannot see
the religion, the magic, the gossip, the corroborees (dances and sings),
and the wide freedom of life lived as a food-gatherer in nature. Nor
can the European know the security—despite dreadfully stern male
kinfolk—which most women had in the Stone Age, where each person's role was fixed and sure, set by divine law.

Around the billabongs you can sometimes see the depressions
in the earth made by those Stone Age people. Each one was some
family hearth, where for untold generations the families lived, married to their land. Thrown down were their "billies" or water-
fetching shells, and the people loved and worshipped their beautiful
earth, blooming with gum trees, beefwood, oak, kurrajong, baobab,
bauhinea, pandamus palm, and the forty-foot-high bamboo
thickets along the waterways, whose blue, smoke-like flowering is
said to occur but twice in a century. Hidden canyons, caves and
clefts carry the picture drawings of these people today, where
strange butterflies flit through eternal summer and strange birds call.

So beloved is all this land, and so sacred, that each clan and
sub-clan and moity still holds certain animals in trust that may not

be eaten, and there are forests, hills, or river valleys that may not be touched by the hunter. Violation of the conservation taboos is punishable by death.

These were Stone Age men. Yet, "a feeling of grateful and affectionate respect for the land is a characteristic of civilized man," warns the Australian conservationist Leonard Webb.

The ritual of Kunapipi—six months of chanting in the night—is still practiced all across north central Australia. In this religious ritual, prayers are concentrated upon the earth. It takes place in secret retreats far from white man.

When ceremonial executions take place the white policeman and the court seldom have enough evidence to judge the true reasons or even the true perpetrator of the killing.

A blackfellow jackeroo working on a cattle station tells the boss that he must go walk-about for some contrived reason which will satisfy the white man. It happens that he has been selected by the dreaded Elders to be the *Mulunguwa*, the One Alone, to carry out tribal law. He has been designated ceremonial executioner. He cannot say no.

The reason: a man's grandfather three generations ago speared the gray kangaroo which was not allowed by his particular totem. Now the Dreamtime Spirit has spoken to one of the Elders and demands that the violation be avenged at this time, upon the proper descendant. Or again, perhaps grandfather chopped down a forbidden tree.

The execution takes place by stealth in the night when the unsuspecting victim lie sleeping alone at his bush camp. (All this is "blackfellow business," which the white man will never know.) The sleeper is garroted or stabbed through with a spear. Later the white policeman may be told that the trouble was a quarrel over a woman. This is an explanation which the white man has been found to comprehend readily.

"Pointing the bone" by using the thigh bone of calf or kangaroo or perhaps of man was a means of death when used by a strong medicine man or Elder. Until recent time it was very effective as a means of execution—all the medicine man had to do was point the bone at his victim and the victim withered and died. Such medicine men seemed to have enormous mental power for good or evil over their fellow men. Today the oldtime medicine man has lost most of his power in the face of white man's new and stronger magic.

Another interesting aspect of Aboriginal beliefs was that these very lease-lands of cattlemen through which our cars passed were "owned" by certain Aboriginal groups. Despite modern man's presence here and his laws, and despite visible changes in the land itself, was this land not given to them by the eternal, immutable Dreamtime promise?

Meanwhile the old Aboriginal beliefs were being challenged by the increasing mechanization of a new way of life each day that passed. It was only a few years ago that the old drovers and trail herds gave way to modern trucking. In fact, a few small herds are still driven to markets or at least to road points.

Australia's North End is the scene of the biggest cattle-hauling trailers in the world, called road trains. Commonly they are comprised of five units, including the prime mover, and will be 135 feet long in all. Ann climbed into the cab of one once and was shown twenty-six gears.

Their drivers are experts. If a fellow used the wrong gear when climbing even a small rise he would never be able to get the road train going again. He'd have to back down and start all over.

Road trains are possible in Australia because the land is so level. They would not work any place else, and here they are legal only where the population is very sparse, in the territory and in north Queensland, and in northern Western Australia.

Another reason they are permitted on the roads is that there is no railroad north of Alice Springs, or in Queensland, beyond Mount Isa. Road trains are obviously the only answer to moving cattle herds—but they are dangerous on the highways, and drivers must always be on the lookout for them, and should never try to pass one on a narrow road. Their optimum speed is around forty miles per hour. The drivers do not stop on their long hauls because it may take several miles to get speed up again.

In the territory it was our prerogative, for the first time, to venture into the hitherto-forbidden public bars which dotted this empty land. There were no other general refreshment stands in the Outback to which travel-weary females *could* go. Therefore, the situation demanded concessions on either side—barkeeps and traveling females must bow to circumstance and manage, somehow, to get along together.

How often we had driven slowly past those open doorways of the pubs of Australia, at every tiny town and roadstop, each with its crumbling exterior and small dog sitting in the door, and been assailed by the sure knowledge that for us (as well as blacks) refreshment here was not available.

But with our escort of males, and with the glamorous Hillary in her tight shorts, and being a large mob of people actually needing to spend money, we could walk into a pub, climb upon those tall, spindley, backless perches called barstools, or if none were furnished, stand straight before the high, battered counter and tip the elbow with our fellow travelers of the open road.

The timidity we girls felt in walking into our first pub was not assuaged by the glowering barkeep or slattern behind the bar, and even the Swiss boys, those new Australians, needed courage to enter the Australian man's club. Even Laddie was hard pressed to enter the strange territory of other dog habitues who enjoyed the prestige of belonging to strong masters whose territorial rights were won, no doubt, through many a victory in a saloon brawl. Laddie put his tail between his legs and cowered.

"Get that mutt out of here!" the barkeep bawled in a neanderthal roar, his face florid.

Helmut and our city Kiwi friend dutifully carried the little fellow outside. But he kept creeping cravenly in, as soon as we turned our eyes away.

"Can't you read the sign?" the stout greasy barkeep in his filthy apron reiterated. "The sign says, 'No dorgs allowed.' Wal? What'll hit be?"

Ordering our cold cans of orange juice and our beers, we luxuriated for a moment in the dark, cool retreat, setting our bottles and cans in a row upon discolored bathtoweling which covered the length of the bar to absorb spilled drink. On the wall behind the bar a calendar picture showed an Aussie running after a gleaming, naked brown woman, (called a "gin") underneath a leaning tropical palm tree. "When you're after gin," advised the caption, "go for Bilge's."

From a lighted electric juke box, that box which has conquered the world, the intrepid Slim Dusty was singing a cowboy ballad about a world which was happily populated with bush and kangaroos, and was asking to be buried out there where the dingoes howl. Nostalgia overwhelmed the patrons in this tawdry bar with dreams of yesterday—even as in the tawdry bars of Outback America.

It never failed to amaze me that those very frontier people who loved the howl of the dingoes and coyotes were always the ones that shot and poisoned them at every chance. Each man killed the thing he loved, including the way of life he loved, and his freedom, day by day, as he could never resist meddling with a good thing.

There were two men sitting together, and I spoke to them.

"I am a tourist and writer," I said, summoning my most frank American smile which all my life had never failed to elicit frank American smiles in return.

"Me cobber's in the refrigeration business," said the one, quite pleasantly. "And I work fer 'im sometimes. Don't I, Bob?"

"Refrigeration. Say, that's a good idea in this country. Do you sell any to the mines and all?"

"Wal, we're tryin'," said the boss cautiously. "It's slow. Some of these up here in this country could afford it well enough. But you know how it is—set in their ways."

"I wouldn't dream of having a car without air conditioning in it," I said without thinking, but saw that they were perplexed as to whether to believe this statement and that they felt on strange ground in general, talking with a woman at a bar, just as if she were a man.

I was trying to think of another subject when the younger salesman, with a provocative leer, suddenly asked:

"What do you think about the whistlecocks. The black-fellers," he said, and repeated, "We call 'em whistlecocks."

Right away I saw that he was not talking to me in the way Australian men talk to "ladies."

"I suppose you Yanks think the blackfellers are roight, eh? Most outsiders do," my barroom friend went on. "I suppose you jist love 'em!"

"Well, we really don't know any very well," I demurred, trying to keep calm, but definitely heated. "I've been reading a few books by some of your fine Australian writers."

This was the wrong thing to say. "Books!" my fellow drinker scoffed, while his more affable boss looked on impassively. It became clear to me that the Aussie working bloke suffers from a strangely heavy burden of hostility at large, more than from mere boyishness of spirits, and that nobody yet has succeeded in even guessing at some of the reasons. Baiting all strangers is a recognized custom and a game. Baiting women to the point of anger is usual if the Aussie meets a woman in a social confrontation in which he has had no prior experience or in which the rules and groundwork are not carefully prescribed.

"Wal, let me tell you something . . ." a belligerent voice was bellowing at me now like an enraged bull.

"I read," I interrupted in a calm, sociable voice, "your splendid Australian writer Alan Moorehead—his book, *Cooper's Creek* —how the blackfellows knew how to make flour cakes from a plant called *nardoo*, and there is apparently some narcotic shrub growing on the desert which they could chew in times of injury or pain, and it was their own discovery of anesthesia . . . ."

"What they do," he interrupted hoarsely, "the whistlecocks. They steal a man's socks when he puts them out on the line to dry. They have clever, savage minds. The Aborigine won't steal a full pair of socks from you, oh no! He'll go right down that line and take just *one* sock from each pair. Come evening, you go to sort out your socks, or maybe you start to put on your socks the next day, and *one sock* is gone, always one. They know how to get to a man. All through this country they do it to git even with the white man. Ask any bloke, he'll tell you the sime."

"Uh . . . why do you suppose they do that?" I turned to Bob, the impassive boss.

"Well, you know how a man can easily lose one sock," he said patiently. "The Aborigine knows how easy it is to not get all them socks counted after a washup, see? He figures the white man won't miss 'em for a bit. Now, I ask you, what good is just *one sock* to anyone? No, fer sure that Aborigine doesn't even want it. He is jist bein' pesky. They are resistin' the white man that came here three generations ago to civilize the bloody country, and I'll tell you them blacks is the dirtiest, laziest, most no good human bein's on earth, if you could call 'em human, which you can't."

"Come on, Mom, you better come along," said Ann at that moment, coming over to lead me out. She beamed her most charming smile at the two men, who received the smile with a slight, invisible ripple, well concealed.

"Oh, pooor Laddie, he's ready to just die in this heat," Ann fluttered fetchingly. "I gave him some water to drink at the hose outside. The hose is for people who want water, Mom. Never ask the barkeep for water, it just isn't done."

The men's eyes rolled along Hillary's legs as we went on out. "Poor dog," I agreed, hastening out into the hot sunglare.

"The dog, he's roight," said Jean curtly. "Hurry up, Mom. I want the Baby Blue to lead the parade. I poured water over him to cool him off. He's roight and Ann's roight, too, because she gets to hold the dog in her lap. Mom's roight but she's wrong if she thinks she can change an Aussie's ways or whip 'im in an argument. So— let's go!"

"It is time we go," smiled Hans, as I climbed into the high Jeep, feeling suddenly rather old and tired. From above Hans' neatly trimmed beard two wide, very young blue eyes looked with a kindly and idealistic glance upon a world brand new to him. Hans was a thinking man, even if he couldn't talk much yet.

"We're going to have to take better care of Mom," Ann said to Jean, as she double-clutched expertly, slowing down along the road ahead to let the others catch up.

"Want me to show you how to double-clutch, Mom? It's fun."

"Not now," I said, moping.

"You might need to know how sometime, you never know when you might need it." Silence.

"Mother goes through the world so perpetually innocent that I've come to wonder how she made it this far."

"She needs someone to take care of her. Mother, for gosh sake *think* before you flap. For gosh sake, would you go marching into some tavern, for instance, in our Southern states, and start talking to strange roughnecks about Negroes and Negro rights, and all that? Think now, is that really the time and the place?"

"I'm trying," I replied with deflated dignity, "to be a sociologist."

"I really like Aussies," Jean said suddenly. She was the first of us to acknowledge our grudging admiration of their sheer cussedness and truculence. "Do you know what I like about them?" she asked. Then she answered, "It's that you can't buy an Aussie. You can't even rent one!"

"But Claude, now, from Sydney. He is of a new generation," I offered. "There's a lot of hippies there, and don't you think he is a bit of a hippie?"

"Mother, your generation doesn't know a real hippie from a phoney. Claude is not a hippie. He's got a mod bod, that's all." Mod bod, hmmm.

"You seem to think I know very little about anything," I said, sourly. "Perhaps you'd care to help write the book?" Suddenly, I meant it. "Really, perhaps you would try a chapter, some place?"

"Okay, if you don't mind waiting a while. I just would like to set people straight on a few points," said Jean, "so you don't get them too mixed up. Ann and I believe we really understand the people a little better than you do. Excuse me, Mom, for saying that—we don't want to hurt your feelings."

"Oh, that's all right," I said morosely. "But I don't think that just knowing these Sydney boys like Claude, or the English girl, or our two Kiwis, is any real understanding of Australia . . . ."

Our little caravan pulled off the road just then under some trees. Trees were getting more numerous. Time for liquid refreshments and a stretch.

The sky was pale yellow and a haze covered the scattered open forest of gray eucalypts stretching, with anthills, into infinity. It was deceptive. This was still a desert where a person could easily die of thirst.

"What is it?" I asked Claude, as we watched the sky haze up.

"Fires," he answered. "There's always fires in the Top End."

Australia is a land of fire ecology. Perhaps all continents are. Perhaps it's just a little more noticeable here. One supposes that to a lesser extent, America was, too—only when you are quite alone in such a great continent, particularly without a radio in your car, fires can create a stronger feeling of unease.

Like the American Indians, the Aborigines from time immemorial set fires to drive out game. They also understood that fires created new grass and the regeneration of trees. The white man arriv-

102

ing followed the same fire pattern to make pastures for his livestock—but most ecologists feel that in Australia fire has been greatly over-done.

Some fires may burn for months on end, but the country grows back. Most species of trees are fire-resistant hardwoods. Their woody fruits have adapted to the desert to preserve the precious seeds of life, and indeed are so tough that the species cannot regener-ate without a fire to burst their cones. In other cases the parent plant or tree must be destroyed by fire for regeneration to occur. Where fire protection is not practiced, "ground fires" are a natural occurrence, burning off the dead brush, but rarely destroying the trees. In heavily protected areas, like much of the United States, dead brush accumulates to such an extent, that when fires do occur, tremendous damage is done.

Ahead of us now as we drove a number of kite hawks sailed laz-ily, making me think of buzzards. These hawks are also called "fire hawks." Actually, they were not as lazy as they seemed. They were busy hunting.

As our car passed through smoldering patches of ground on either side of the road, we could often see these hawks. The Abori-gines claim that the hawks will pick up smoldering branches in their claws and fly away to a nearby area and deliberately drop the branch to start a fire in a new place. This is why people call them fire hawks. They use fire to drive out game, say the Aborigines, just as man does. At any rate, fire does provide good hunting for them. They pore over burning areas diligently, catching grasshoppers, locusts, beetles, snakes, lizards, and small mammals running from the fire.

Although many times in our travels we felt as though we were riding in a bomb on wheels as we passed between fire and fire, in all cases we made our journeys safely. The nature of the Australian bushfires is such that they rarely pose a threat to man, being based mostly in grass and low scrub, and flaring up sporadically and sweeping low across the ground.

Claude led the way into a shady grove, and there we saw the graves of some of the people of whom Mrs. Aeneas Gunn wrote in *We of the Never-Never*. The Never-Never was thus at last identified to me. But still, it eludes one today, even as it did those first pio-neers of Australia's interior back in 1905.

Among those graves was the man who carried the first mail,

using a string of horses on his six-weeks' trek from Darwin. (His predecessor had died of thirst on the Barkly Tablelands.) This was the grave of the man known forever in literature as The Fizzer. The Fizzer had carried baking soda in his saddlebags and he would often remark that there was nothing more relaxing or good for a man's health than to pour his cup of water and drink it down with a pinch of soda.

When The Fizzer sat down beneath a tree to have a "fizz" at his evening camp, and he tethered his horses beside a billabong and put his billy on to boil, he was a man who was living on a completely acid diet: meat, damper (flour), and tea. The baking soda fixed him up.

The Maluka, the first cattleman, also lay here. He had died suddenly when he was only a young man, at the height of his adventure. During the tropical Wet people used to die from fevers in north Australia, some of which included dengue and malaria borne by the anopheles mosquito. After World War II these fevers disappeared, and nobody was ever able to explain to me why. We in modern times were not in danger from anything of this sort.

The character of the billabongs and rivers of the North End has been undergoing considerable change from overgrazing and the depletion of available waters by livestock. Thousands of hogs gone wild add to this picture, wallowing, trampling, and rooting up water lilies and adding to the stresses of life even for muddy-rivered crocodiles. Formerly heavy populations of native jungle animals are disappearing. Even the migrations of fruit bats, cranes, and parrots, which explorers described as darkening the skies, are surely not what they were fifty years ago. They are still here, but greatly diminished.

We did not have to fear malaria, but a protozoan which causes intestinal diarrhea in mammals, *Giardia lambia*, could well be here. Perhaps life is never perfect. We should be thankful to have only little worries. On the whole it might be wise to depend upon imported water and not fill our cans at waterholes except in an emergency.

Chapter 9

THE TERRITORY—OLD AND NEW

It was ten o'clock on a hot, sultry night when we reached that heavenly oasis at the cascades where the Stuart Highway crosses the Katherine River. Nights were no longer cold. By flashlight we peeled off sweat-dried clothes, donned swim suits, and frolicked in the clean, bubbling, roaring waters. Perhaps a hundred people gathered there beside picnic tables under gracious, hundred-foot-tall paperbark gums and little pandanus palms. Australian fireflies flitted, carrying pale green running lights.

"What about crocodiles?"

It was safe here. The crocs were chased by the soapsuds and shouting of white man even if they got up this far from the sea.

There are probably few really giant crocs left. The graziers made relentless war against them. Recently the professional shooters for leather had been stopped, except in Queensland, in an attempt to build the supply back up.

The estuarine, which likes to lie about the estuaries of large, tropical rivers, has been known to grow twenty-six and a half feet long and weigh several tons. It may travel as far as four hundred miles up river from the sea. A relic of a bygone age, it is magnificent even if formidable, and should not be totally exterminated. It must be studied in relationship to the total environment in which it lives, it must be appraised as a resource, and control must be handled by intelligent decision, not just left to chance.

Biologists are pleading that the natural ecology of these northern rivers, which includes the crocs, be preserved. In some rivers in Africa, for example, a little-understood relationship has been discovered between healthy herds of crocodiles and some species of fish. When crocs were shot out, fish populations mysteriously declined.

We drove into the city of Darwin on the north coast the next day.

Charles Darwin never saw this port, which was named for him in 1839 following the five-year voyage of the H.M.S. *Beagle* when the same ship came bearing in here carrying Darwin's old friends, Lieutenant Stokes and Forsythe. (When a settlement was started, for a long while the people called it Palmerston, as they resented the "sacrilegious" attitudes of the scientist who had galvanized the world's long-held shibboleths.)

A tribe of magnificent Aborigines, the Larrakia, met the old *Beagle* wearing naught but a fourteen-inch bamboo split through their flat noses. They practiced no circumcision. Food was abundant here in the tropics, and little if any cannibalism was practiced. The Stone Age men who met the *Beagle* extended friendship and received it from the scientist.

Darwin's development awaited the passing of centuries, hampered by isolation of two thousand miles of desert or several thousand miles of uncharted navigation and the problems of adapting agricultural and ranching methods to an unfamiliar climate—i.e., learning to graze cattle with crocodiles. Here "mean annual rainfall, sixty inches" may mean complete drought alternating with complete flood, interspersed with both tropical and desert cyclones.

Our bar-tread tyres rolled into Darwin, thump-a-thump. Past Southern Cross Machinery, past Napier Mounted Disk Plows, past Heavy Duty Toolbar Cultivators, past English Electric Diesels Australia Limited, past Australia Blue Metal, past the bus stop ("On time with Buntine Roadways") and Cresco Fertilizers, past Constrictor

Elasticator Castrators, Pioneer Asphalts, McMinn Motors, all giving evidence of filling the basic needs of a raw frontier. "For service that's smarter, go Arnhem Air Charter."

Soon the tent was up at a caravan park and I was watching, fascinated, some remarkable ants which moved about in a mass by jerks and rhythms, as though animated by separate electrical impulses. When you stamped on the ground they jerked faster. The single trailer sink in the ladies' room of the camp court was clogged with half-drowned beetles.

We of the open road could see why, I thought while taking a steamy, beetle-clogged shower, the Aborigines developed a philosophy, in fact a religion, which has no place for material possessions. All equipment here falls apart. Each day something else gives way. The handle was off the frying pan. The plywood medical kit was rotting out on the bottom from contact with the metal Jeep, which itself was all squeaks and rattles.

I asked Annie if she would like to help me gather some information during the few brief days that we were in Darwin making our repairs. She said that she would. We went to the government Aboriginal Welfare Department, introduced ourselves, and Annie was given every assistance in drawing up her report. Ann then became, in her own words, perhaps "the world's only seventeen-year-old with her very own locked attache case." The following is Ann's report on the Aboriginal Reserve of Bagot, today a part of the City of Darwin.

In Bagot as many as forty different tribal groups are represented, and all of these people are on different levels of familiarity with modern Australian society.

It took modern man approximately five thousand years to develop from his own Stone Age days to the space age, yet the Aboriginal people are trying to achieve that transformation in three or four generations.

When one thinks of social progress one has the tendency to think along terms of material gain. But the real problem lies in acquiring the patterns of thought that go along with them.

Travelers from all over the territory come to Bagot, for various reasons: medical help, vacation, walk-abouts, visits from bush and station properties, runaways, and so on. For the ones who stay the transition steps are applied by the government in a practical and very workable manner.

Let's assume an entire bush family walks into Bagot and remains. Chances are their previous contact with Europeans is limited to distant missions. Most likely, they have never lived under any kind of roof other than a "wurley," and their existence has been one of hunting, food gathering, and day-by-day existence. They are moved into a small, concrete building with no furniture or cooking facilities.

At first they are provided with literally just a roof overhead. Every day a sanitation squad completely hoses down the buildings. Communal showers and toilets are available, but for many, the corner is the toilet. Their meals are provided, and the family takes daily instruction in hygiene, child care, cooking, and various community tasks.

The next step, if the family desires it and proves capable, is to apply to move to another home. These homes have private showers, toilets, simple furniture, wood stoves, cooking utensils, and gardens.

The family education continues. The last step is into two-story homes with all electrical appliances including stove and ceiling fan. The very final step is homes built in the regular community, and "integration," only the Aussies call this "assimilation."

Under this plan each individual is allowed to move forward at his own pace. Some never leave the concrete huts. Progress for these people covers a very long period of time. The men must be trained for outside jobs and become family providers and breadwinners. A wife must be able to keep up in standards with her husband.

It is all very painful and a bit sad. Many times deep emotional depression sets in. Progress is made in mad spurts and relapses, in a zig-zag pattern. Women are usually more easily domesticated than their men, but being subject to the latter's abuses and excesses, are caught in between. Children grow away from their more conservative parents.

All this stretches out over a lifetime. What terrible problems these people and their "educators" face!

Originally, many different things were punishable by death. Even being late to religious events could result in execution, in one tribe.

108

Obviously, white law objected. So, to get around white men's laws and still fulfill the old tribal law, this tribe had all the relatives of the condemned man bleed themselves into a hole in the ground until it equaled the amount of blood in the condemned man's body. Then the hole was covered up, and that man was considered killed by the letter of tribal law, though his life was actually spared.

Suicide is unknown in this culture. So is competition.

Mr. Wilson, the Superintendent of Bagot, mentioned that there are "funny things which can happen to Blackfellas." He meant death and disaster due to black magic.

After Bagot I drove out and visited a special residential Aboriginal high school called Kormilda College, set up two years ago. Kormilda is a word from an extinct tribe, and means "tomorrow." The word incorporates also a concept about future orientation of people. By choosing to use a name taken from an extinct people, no jealousy or discrimination among living tribes was invoked, and the very fact that the tribe is extinct is symbolic of how life evolves and goes on.

Of the total of 4,500 kids at Kormilda, only 27 so far have reached the Grade Seven level. But they hope a teachers' college will grow from this, and eventually a school of art too, where Aboriginal art, dancing, languages, legend, drama, and music will attract students from all over Australia and the Southeast Asian area, as well.

"They have the ability to learn," the director said of the Aboriginal kids my age. "If they can comprehend English they can comprehend the subject. But they do not always accept our values, unless the value can be proven to them."

Northern Territory education, I learned, while supported by the federal government, is organized and run by South Australia by tradition.

While Ann was assembling her information about the Aborigines, I was receiving an education on another subject, pastoral production (beef), which at that time represented about $17½ million a year in returns to Territory producers, with a 37-percent increase in revenues over the year before. About 1½ million beef cattle are grazed, each animal being generally worth about $118 on the hoof.

A lot of these cattle were the old Australian shorthorns, but

109

quite recently Brahmin cattle have begun to play a part in northern beef, and so do Zebus, which are ideal to endure the heat. The big property owners bring in bulls valued as high as $2500 to increase the quality of their herds. Getting quality breeding stock is slow because of the enormous expense of these deluxe bulls, and the distance. Another factor in slowness is that this stock, most of which was bred and developed originally in Texas, can not nowadays be sent direct from America due to restrictive quarantine laws; so the graziers of Australia have to wait many years to obtain them from the small, slowly-growing Australian reservoirs. The strict Australian laws forbid importing even test tube semen.

The eradication of infectious diseases in cattle had been started eight years before by the C.S.I.R.O. working in the territory. Among their 1½ million cattle, 30,000 blood tests had been made during the past year at a cost of $1 per test. Pleuropneumonia is always present, ever since it first crept in back in 1880; active cases are found every year. Brucellosis, or contagious abortion, and tuberculosis were also present. The former is incurable in cattle. The latter is not practical to cure. Such animals should be destroyed when found.

The causative organisms of common diseases in cattle cannot survive away from cattle. Many vaccines are cheap and easy to use, and blood tests for diagnosis simple and reliable; but in a land mass so vast that no one can afford to fence it, a major problem is finding all the cattle out there. About the best that could be done was vaccination of cattle while branding on the stations, as well as all cattle being trucked south from the territory on their way to market for slaughter (a little late for efficacy of treatment). "It may be many years before TB is reduced to a satisfactory level in cattle," said the government man who took me to dinner. (I mentioned steak—he countered by offering Chinese food.)

A later friendship, in another part of Australia, with a farmer turned forester, revealed clearly why so often we did not like the quality of beef and mutton we bought at country butcher shops. A lot of mutton is marketed that is full of cancer, a malady with which sheep particularly are affected due to the clear, rare atmosphere and high radiation combined with deep sunburning after shearing. To eat meat which has cancer of this sort has never been proven to have harmful effects upon the diner—although proposals to use "clean" parts of infested animals are turned down by the U.S. Department of

110

Agriculture. I can say personally, however, that some meat can be quite unesthetic at a country butcher's!

Tuberculosis in beef is more dangerous. We ate our Outback steaks well done. The feral hogs are subject to TB as well, as are some of the several hundred thousand wild Asiatic buffalo.

The buffalo have a 150-year-old history in a special region which they inhabit in the North End. Brought from the island of Timor in 1824 to supply the Fort Dundas settlement on Melville Island, they were spread by man to the Australian mainland settlements, and ultimately went wild. Shooting began in 1925, in a galloping, Buffalo Bill era which wrote a short page in Australian history. The government stepped in, slowed down the modernday Buffalo Bills, and regulated the professional shooters. Now the government abbatoirs handle an annual kill of around 6,000 head in season, on a sustained yield basis, plus another 6,500 that are rejected for human food and are processed for pet food.

Some control of the herds to keep them from starving to death and totally destroying the habitat of the North End is necessary, for the buffalo's wanderings are limited by arid desert to the south and the Timor Sea to the north. They have to stay where swamps exist. It is good to have the buffalo as an added big game resource for Aborigines.

Strange as it may seem, the greatest problem in the tropics is that of producing meat! Tropical lands have much of the world's "hidden starvation" from lack of protein.

Only in the upper few feet of the earth's surface can there be storage of the remains of former animals and plants (good soil nutrients), but in the tropics these nutrients are rapidly destroyed by the intense heat, leaving no organic matter in the soil. In no place are phosphates more needed than in the lands near the Equator, where minerals must be continually replaced due to the leeching action of tropical sun and monsoon rains. North Australia, lying twelve degrees below the Equator, falls into the category of lands which always will have special soil problems because they lie within the "geography of hunger."

We know that subtropical deserts at twenty to thirty degrees yield to savanna as we approach the Equator. From scrub forest they rise slowly to rain forest, which looks green and enticing. But *all native growth near the Equator is useless to man*

111

at present. The poverty of the human inhabitants of such lands is the greatest on earth. The Kwashiorkor latitudes, we might call them—renowned for protein deficiency disease.

The livestock grazed on native vegetation grown on these soils may have but little nutritional value. A beef cow in northern Brazil or in arid India or in north Australia does not contain the nutrients in its flesh that we normally expect, where it grazes such vast deserts of sand and rock and scrub bushland that may be totally sterile.

On each side of the Equator the tropical scrub, dry grasses, and dusty soil occupy the largest areas of land on earth: in Africa, in South America, in Asia—and in Australia.

Of the estimated four billion acres that are available for food growth in the whole world, four fifths are already tilled, and two thirds of the human race is underfed, say the United Nations figures. However, the most critical soil nutrient which is in short supply—nitrogen fertilizers—can now be synthesized by passing nitrogen gas with oxygen through intense radiation, thus producing nitrogen compounds; and herein lies the hope.

Of course there is also the crucial lack of water, for a quarter of the world's population lives in land that has to be irrigated: India, China, Egypt. A recent survey concludes that a great portion of earth's ten million square miles of the Dry—less than ten inches rainfall—is beyond the conceivable range, economically, for artificial watering systems to be set up. Most of these lands also have uncontrol led human health hazards, such as the tsetse fly, typhus, yellow fever, dysentery, malaria, yaws, and leprosy. These areas also have very complex communications and transportation difficulties, involving the spanning of jungles, swamps, and mountains. Therefore, Australia's North End holds great hope for production for the world, along with some other similar equatorial grasslands.

Beef is one of the answers to the ever-more-crucial protein shortage of the world. Some experts think it might be possible to feed two billion people from the U.S. soils alone, but not on beef. Our best soils are giving way to concrete cities, with more land being put out of production every day. In producing food it is not difficult to add carbohydrates to food supplies. It is more difficult to produce fats and oils, and still harder to produce high quality protein, which is the most needed of all.

112

"The rapid respiration of life" in the hot lands makes every moment a contest between man, the animals, and the microorganisms, as to which will consume the nutrients first. In such heat even sterile foods are subject to chemical reactions which cause losses in flavor, texture, color, and nutritive value.

It is this rapid respiration of life which has made soil building or herd building nearly impossible. Every higher order of life is consumed rapidly by those parasites which feed on it, which in turn are rapidly consumed by others, and on down the scale.

Most people are not aware of it but this principle applies also to the fish in the seas. The commercial fisheries of the world, always near land, along ocean currents, and in cooler waters, are not found in the tropics. It is believed that bacterial invasion in warmer waters limits the building up of large fish herds of a common species. Absence of a good continental shelf may also limit coastal fisheries, as illustrated by Australia. At any rate, tropical waters contain fewer commercial fish. Coastal villages of natives may live on fish daily, but commercial packing plants have not been tempted to settle on tropical coasts or South Sea islands.

To increase the world's supply of protein food the overseas capitalists are taking up land rapidly in Australia, a friendly and stable country. And in this rush the North End today holds the most promise.

Development must come from outside; the Aussies do not have the means. Their State Agriculture Departments are understaffed, there are only a token number of agricultural colleges, nor is there much extension work. The lack of education among working farmers and graziers, and their lack of capital, make most research meaningless, anyway. Unfortunately, the Australian Government has set up no National Reclamation Act, such as was put into effect in the U.S. in 1902, to help its own people get hold of their country. The latest advances require enormous outputs of capital, for, to repeat, it is nearly impossible to regenerate many soils along the Equator. At best, it is going to be a big gamble.

The territory's local cattlemen are now trying to improve a few pastures since the C.S.I.R.O. at Katherine had proved that nine-month-old shorthorns, when fed Townsville Lucerne treated with phosphate, gained a pound daily even through the perilous Dry, and were ready for slaughter by age 2½ years with a live weight of 964 pounds. (But normal weight is around 1600 pounds at the same age in any Western state today!) The C.S.I.R.O. found that a similar "mob of weaners," on *natural* pasture, always lost weight during the Dry, and at age 2½ weighed only five hundred sixty pounds—if they survived at all. It was proved, therefore, that application of phosphates to fenced paddock lands enabled the grazing of one steer to three or four acres. Darwin people could get phosphate at the Townsville price (east coast), thanks to the territory freight subsidy (the subsidy also assisted them in airspread service to distribute the phosphates). If only more people could afford it!

The aerial spreading of Townsville Lucerne, a high protein clover vine, with six pounds of seed to the acre, is done during December and January to ensure good germination during the Wet. Government analysis to test the Townsville and other legumes was provided here at Darwin: it was found that protein was increased 50 percent in this cattle feed by using phosphates.

Throughout the history of Australia nutritional and disease problems have always decreased animal weight by about 25 percent right into this time. Big capital hopes to do something about this, with the help of new feeds, new phosphates, and new imported breeding stock.

In the respect of land availability and challenge, Australia is indeed a young country and wide open—but only for corporations bringing big capital. This, basically, is why Australia is so much in the American newspapers today. The news media reflect the corporate excitement at home, and in turn the ideology and the challenge is caught up by the small American, or perhaps by all thinking people, because Australia offers a hope to solve overwhelming problems of approaching world food shortages.

The excitement in the air around Darwin consisted of a strange mixture of the old and the new. Water, for instance, was limited in the swelling city because the fruit bats (called flying foxes) kept landing on the power lines and cutting off electricity from the Manton Dam pumping station. Some twelve hours were needed for repairs, while pumping capacity was halved, each time a flying fox descended to take a nap. The three services and the Darwin City Water Council agreed to cut water consumption by appealing to Darwin residents to consume less. Reserve supplies always dwindled to a near crisis by the end of each Dry. A $10-million dam on the Darwin River thirty-five miles from Darwin was being designed, rather slowly,

114

by the Snowy Mountains Authority, twenty-five hundred miles away.

Meanwhile the flying foxes returned for a visit last July, and the reservoir on Bullocky Point went down to 600,000 gallons by Dry's end.

In the Territory more than 60 percent of the population were under thirty, and 55 percent were unmarried. Many "wogs" came here from Greece, Italy, Germany, the UK, Netherlands, Syria, and Thailand. Over half the population were a work force. Just 2 percent were self-employed, or capable of generating employment for other men. Only 4 percent of the territory people had an elementary education.

It was pretty much the typical frontier population anywhere: unstable, fluctuating up to about 117 percent throughout a year, but slowly stabilizing as people came in to stay. It will always be somewhat unstable, however, because these are earth's marginal lands. Only young people can thrive. When people grow old they retire from the tropics or the Arctic and return to the comforts of the temperate zone.

As for tourism, the Territory is viewed by the Australian Tourist Commission as their most important promotion after the Great Barrier Reef.

Tourists to Darwin are drawn from the U.S.A., Japan, Hong Kong, Malaysia, and Europe, usually coming up through Adelaide and the Centre; but 75 percent of them are Australian. Most use the coach service and most holidays last but a week or two, but those coming by private car are on the increase. They spend their time in the new motels and a few camp out. They spend $12½ million a year in the territory, and tourism rates as the fourth largest industry, following mining, cattle, and building.

About 43,000 tourists came to Darwin the year before we were there, and the year following our visit was the big centennial celebration.

The Territory also has great hope for minerals. The minerals are here, all right: everything except diamonds. The production was $28.2 million in 1968, doubling since 1966. Oil exploration is going on off the north coast with frantic excitement, each company trying to get there first before another worldwide company beats them to it. The general geological outlook is the most promising of any place in traditionally oilless Australia, with the exception of Bass Strait on the southeast coast. Australia had been thought for many years to possess no fossil fuels except limited amounts of coal.

One of the excitements in the Territory this season was generated by the presence of U.S. Steel. This company announced its entrance into the territory fun and games by acquiring leases of four areas covering 7,373 square miles of land and water on the shallow Gulf of Carpentaria near Borroloola on the Queensland border. The leases stipulated that the company could have a try for all minerals, except oil and coal, for twelve months.

At the same time the company had moved the $10-million oil exploration rig SEDCO 135G into the waters of Joseph Bonaparte Gulf by separate agreement with the federal government.

This remarkable oil exploration rig had on board all its exploration instruments, its scientists, its technicians, and thousands of dollars of meat and groceries intended to be the men's food. It was completely independent and outfitted for exploration in a wild part of the world.

Imagine the shock to U.S. Steel when the rig was met in these seas by that intrepid little band of men in tropical shorts and knee socks—from the Australian Department of Health—who insisted that every item of food on board must immediately be *destroyed*. The reason was that the food came from outside Australia and conceivably could bring contamination.

Tons and tons of food were thrown overboard twenty-five miles west of Darwin, and the remainder was brought into Darwin and burned (with no thought given to air pollution).

The rig was completely re-outfitted with Australian food supplies, including the delicacy of territory beef, and U.S. Steel carried on. It moved to its drilling position with only a few precious weeks of delay, sixty miles west of Port Keats in Bonaparte Gulf. The rig carried its "brains" within it in an air-conditioned, spacious cabin. It made its own fresh water, used three tons of fuel oil a day, and cost $20,000 a day to operate; could drill in as much as six hundred feet of water, using thirty-foot lengths of pipe some thirty inches in diameter at the top to sixteen inches at the bottom; it had its own cement-making factory, turning out sixty barrels a minute (cement is needed for lining the drill hole, and for plugging the hole if there should be a blow).

116

Yet while the Australians were busy focusing on the traditional bogey of contamination by imports, little thought had been given thus far to the dangers of contamination of the seas, or the possible upset of the ocean ecological balance. Contamination of the oceans is beginning to lead to the death of large numbers of plankton, which are responsible for manufacturing oxygen for most of planet earth's needs. The plankton's health safeguards our lives.

But perhaps the greatest project in all Australia was the Nabalco bauxite find on the edge of Arnhem Land. Nabalco is a consortium of Swiss Aluminium Ltd., Colonial Sugar Refineries, the Australian Mutual Provident Society, the Bank of New South Wales, the old Elder Smith Trading Company, and others. One of the super-giants of our age, this consortium will build a plant to take 500,000 tons of bauxite by the end of December, 1971.

After Nabalco, the second largest mining venture in the territory is the Groote Eylandt manganese operation. The third biggest is at Frances Creek, with three to six million tons of iron ore under contract to sell to the Sumitomo Company of Japan. This ore will be railed to Darwin on a government railroad of limited capacity and would be shipped from Darwin.

Schemes to make money out of the Territory are many and varied. Right now eight companies are conducting experiments on *forty-four thousand square miles*, by government permission, to see whether it would be commercially practicable to collect and merchandise the native mulga scrub for the wood chip industry.

The clean-sweep removal of the ground cover, no matter how despised a species, means exposing naked earth to the pitiless sun, the wind, and the forces of erosion. And it will raise the ground temperature by at least twenty degrees—certain death to all small ground life in the vast areas of removal.

If the mulga is removed, will the grasses come back? There might be a chance for ultimate improvement in the condition of the land. Only time will tell the answer to the daring experiments and testings going on in this gigantic laboratory, the Territory.

In 1969 it was announced that Federal Members of the Territory Legislature would have voting rights from now on in federal elections. That was a step forward, anyway. Harold (Tiger) Brennan huffed that to all intents the Northern Territory was regarded by Canberra as a mere suburb of the haughty capital—"one of its

117

paddocks," I think he called it. And, of course, he was right.

I knew what he meant, for I was a resident of the territory of Alaska for twelve years prior to its statehood. Territory citizens have virtually no rights. Their land is usually plundered by outside interests, if there is anything there to plunder, and they are universally sold down the drain.

Wallamen Falls, also known as Stony Creek Falls, are 70 road miles northwest of Ingham, Queensland, on Stony Creek, a tributary of the Herbert River. Sheer fall is 970 feet, the second highest sheer fall in Australia; total descent is 1,150 feet.

Three at Campfire: the author and daughters Ann (left) and Jean (right) take a lunch break along the trail in South Australia. Lunch usually consisted of meat broiled on the open fire and a billy of tea.

Queensland homestead in the Northern Alps, typical of the homesteads in this area—the Gorge Range of the Eastern Highlands of Great Dividing Range, Northern Queensland.

Camping with Toyota and canvas fly was our mode of camping during our early travels along the east coast of Australia, in the wet season. During the dry season a mosquito net replaced the canvas fly, as flying insects then became a problem.

The Big Goanna, Gould's Goanna (Varanus gouldii), also known as the Sand Goanna or Ground Goanna, is the most common and widely ranging of all Australian Goannas. It is found in both the deserts of the outback and the wetter coastal areas. The color and pattern will vary greatly, depending on its habitat, from light (yellow predominant) in the desert areas to very dark (black predominant) in the coastal areas. It is among the largest lizards in Australia. This specimen, a full-grown adult, is approximately five feet in length, and was found along the North West Developmental Road, north of Coen, on the Cape York Peninsula.

Winching the Toyota out of a ditch along the North West Developmental Road, on the Cape York Peninsula. The winch proved itself invaluable on more than one occasion.

Toyota helps missionaries stuck in Archer River. This, the first crossing of the season following the wet, proved too much for the missionaries' tractor. The faithful Toyota came to the rescue. The scene is the Archer River crossing of the North West Developmental Road, about 40 miles north of Coen, on the Cape York Peninsula. Ann, on the left, hollers directions as Jean drives.

A typical windmill and sheet-iron homestead of the outback area, near Wollogorang Homestead, Northern Territory. The sheet-iron walls and stilt construction are typical throughout the outback.

Aboriginal women at Weipa Mission, located a few miles east of the town of Weipa, on the Embly River arm of Albatross Bay, on the west coast of the Cape York Peninsula. The mission station was established around 1892. The township of Weipa was established about 1956 for the purpose of extracting and shipping the bauxite found here. The Weipa bauxite deposits are now believed to be one of the world's largest.

An Aboriginal stockman tends branding irons in the fire during the stock round-up and branding at the Silver Plains Station, 25 miles east of Coen, on the Cape York Peninsula.

The white station owner and an Aboriginal stockman brand a calf during the round-up at the Silver Plains Station, Cape York Peninsula.

Chapter 10

THE LAST OF THE BILLABONGS

"Gotta fill all these jerry cans full up with petrol," Jean was saying at the gas pumps, scanning the way we were packed with a practiced eye.

We had said goodbye to Hillary and Steve, with beer running down our knees, in the steamy lounge of the Victoria Hotel in Darwin beneath a slowly-revolving ceiling fan.

Jean and Ann still had two young men each for our party's guard—what kind of a time would we have had outrunning forest fires and trying to get served the basic survival needs at those Outback bars, were it not for these wonderful guys?

The Swiss had corrected some of the mechanical faults of the Baby Blue and one of the boys often relieved the girls at driving it, or sometimes one of the girls drove another car. I always had my own driver, with this shifting around.

We had to hurry along. When the Wet descended upon this remote northwest it would revert to crocodiles. Trucks and cars would be bogged, mired in mud, and the rivers would be impassable—those dry bottoms through which we today jolted with guileless ease.

This was the North in which the explorer Leichhardt disappeared forever a century ago, trudging forward with a party of three white men, two Aborigines, 13 mules, 12 horses, and 270 goats, to furnish bonza tucker in all likelihood, for unknown tribes. Only twenty-five years ago white men on lonely boats vanished along these shores when they plied some coves and rivers for crocodile hides. They were killed for reasons known only to the native mind and to acquire their kidney fat—which is a good enough reason.

It was a North West (Australian spelling) in which as recently as 1958 a group of "woolly primitives" were discovered in the Tanami Desert who had never before been seen by white man. Wailbris and Pintubi ragtags, they used wooden and stone-headed spears when a government patrol ran across them, just a decade ago, in that area bordering Western Australia which we would soon traverse all alone!

We were retracing our way to the turnoff at Katherine when the Baby Blue came to an unceremonious halt by the side of the road. A broken fanbelt. Spare parts, however, turned up a *refrigerator* fan belt for our supposed spare. This was too much! I started right there in my rage to get down and eat the road gravel but Claude from Sydney said in Yank slang: "Don't sweat the small stuff. She's roight. We'll get a roight fan belt at Katherine, then you can write a letter to the Royal Auto Club of Victoria about how thot bloke treats the public, and it will be published in the automobilists' journal for all to read.

"I'll just do thot," I said drily, taking a drink from my canteen, and I gave some thought to the wording of the letter right there: a scorching blast.

"What you have to do, Mother," said Ann, "is show that bloke that you're too tough to kill."

This problem quickly disappeared, and we found ourselves in the swim at cooling Katherine Gorge.

The Gorge lay twenty miles up the Katherine River by a little dirt road which was floating with small mobs of graceful kangaroos wafting alongside the car, and was regally surveyed by two tall gray cranes, called *Brolgas* or the "native's companion."

The place was not a national park, but was kept in all its original beauty by a bright young man named March, who with his mite was making a marvelous living by furnishing scenic boat tours.

At the Gorge site we found that camping space was free and available to all comers. Here began the famous pools created by the Katherine River flowing some thirty miles through 200-foot cliffs,

120

honeycombed by subterranean caves. We made our first real acquaintance with the old-time gorgeous setting of the true Australian billabong.

We had seen Mr. March's large curio store and restaurant along the highway. He also had the concession for Katherine Caves downriver in the opposite direction. When we talked with him at his little trailer house he told us other ideas still came to him. For instance, he had found a spot in which nature lovers could live and play just a short flight across the water in Southeast Asia. March probably made $40,000 gross yearly just from his boat rides on Katherine Gorge.

He was an example of the new Aussie, the far-seeing businessman in tourism. He had started with nothing but his own mind, and he still worked with his own hands.

It was now the off season and time to mend and overhaul the fleet of boats tethered in deep water under the overhanging trees of the billabong. Time to build new washrooms and install more public benches and garbage facilities at this money-making site, which the enterprising young man kept immaculate.

Were it not for such a young man one wonders what indeed would become of Katherine Gorge, which, for all practical purposes, we might call the "last billabong."

Only one-sixth of one percent of this great, over-grazed, empty continent (or five thousand square miles in aggregate) is preserved in what are called "national parks."

The term "national park," too, is misleading. They are parks operated by the state, to serve all the people of the nation, and so are called "national." These little nature reserves actually have no real, permanent legal protection, and they receive almost no care. There is no park system as such in Australia. At any moment a change of mood in a state parliament may destroy these reserves.

Australia's bureaucrats care little for the testimony of their country's scientists. The Australian Academy of Science, founded in 1954, has made surveys showing where real national parks are needed to preserve samplings of every kind of habitat, including their recommendations for anthropological reserves (the sacred places of the Aborigines) and including historical monuments. But there is not enough money. The day-by-day business of the nation goes on and the Academy's recommendations are lost in the shuffle.

A National Parks Authority should be created. But the main

121

trouble is that the jealous states won't give up lands to the federal government, even with the enticements of money, honors, and the prospects of vastly increased tourism. The cattlemen's and sheepmen's lobby cares little for that.

Politicians have little interest in preserving the last unclaimed billabongs, most of which were taken over long ago by the graziers for their livestock, unless, like this one, the billabong is inaccessible. So it remains that a private citizen, untrained in science, is the sole guardian of such a precious place.

This person's interest normally is that of pleasing the public, and making his business popular with them. Unmindful of the barking spider which comes out hooting at night after rain, unmindful of the water lily which blooms one night and dies with the rising sun, unaware of the flappy-footed Java sparrow which is so fragile that it walks over waterlily pads, uncaring of the shyness of the fish-eating Johnston crocodile, the businessman runs motorboats on the water for a mindless public.

No shooting is permitted here, however, and the rock wallabies demonstrated their ability to hop up and down the sheer, rocky hills. Fishing is allowed, probably making considerable inroads among the native populations. The little "freshie" crocodile, so shy, left his wandering tracks in the sand along pitched billabong banks through the miles where we galloped barefoot in the poinciana, kapok, black acacia, and charming pandamus, where thousands of honey-eating birds with red eyes and golden eyes and turquoise eyes chattered and screamed at dawn.

Dawn on the billabong . . . the essence of the Dreamtime. No words can convey the pleasures of such precious waters of paradise. Hidden among the great, green trees brilliant kingfishers zoom, gaudy "magpies" call their cool organ notes, diamond sparrows flutter, and correllas, lorikeets, and all the brilliant parrot divisions of Australia have found their way hundreds of miles across ferocious deserts to settle in this haven.

This is not to say that we did not see flocks of big black cockatoos and white (sulphur-crested) cockatoos everywhere, even in the most arid desert scalds. In the midst of the desert it was a sight to come upon the bands of huge, hearty, crested parrots sitting on the ground by the hundreds in a flock, or sometimes roosting on low acacia scrub.

122

The parrot families that migrated to Australia some thousands of years ago were gradually forced to make special feeding adaptations as the continent slowly dried up. Today these parrots make long distance migrations and make their living just from dry seeds and from grim boles of hardest wood. In dry, open forests you can see them sometimes sixty feet above ground hunting grubs by using their mighty beaks to slit tree trunks. The Princess Alexandra parrot, the Bourke parrot, and many other beauties live here.

What naturalist will ever know all the mysteries of nature now vanishing in Australia? The parakelia is a plant with watery stems which can keep livestock alive when all else fails. It can cover the sand with pink paper daisies. There is a ground creeper which has tiny, furry barbs with which it clutches small birds and animals to their eventual death, and then feeds upon them. There is the banyan spider which weaves a strand so strong that native women would wind it around a finger when they wished to have a finger drop off at a joint. (This was a common token of grief at the loss of a male relative in the Australian world, as it still is in the New Guinean world across the water.)

The wood dove and diamond dove; the flood-bird, a cuckoo which tells the coming of the Wet: they are here.

The jungle fowl is here, too, looking like a small, brown long-tailed pheasant. He is one of a number of Australian birds, including the Mallee fowl of the south, and including the twenty-pound, five-foot-tall plains turkey or turkey bustard, which the pioneers gladly ate for dinner. There is nothing like these "game birds" in the Northern Hemisphere. They belong to the group called megapods. These birds are close to their reptilian ancestry in that they bury their eggs in wet leaf mold and hatch them by chemical heat, just as the crocodile does.

The male turkey for instance, is a wonder. It is he who guards the earth mound where the eggs lie buried for three whole months. Each day he scratches off the top layer of earth, takes a reading of the temperature by means of his long, sensitive tongue, and satisfied that he is keeping the eggs at exactly 92 degrees Fahrenheit, carefully covers the mound up again, until the eggs hatch. As many as twenty-two baby birds may hatch out on the same day from these buried eggs. The babies make their way out of the ground like little reptiles.

Night on the billabong. No one will ever know how wonderful the billabong can be by night until he has camped there and gone to swim in the black velvet water under a pale sunset sky as the sleepy birds hush their last cackles in the trees and the evening stars pop out. There is a crescent moon. You may think about scorpions where your bare toes walk. You may think about a big hairy Australian spider like our tarantula (they call it a triantelope) which is shy and harmless and lives in a hole in the ground. You may think about that "harmless" type of fish-eating crocodile whose pool you are about to share. But the sweat and fatigue of the day throws off all nonsensical concerns. You cast yourself into those cool, velvet depths, only thinking, "Look out, fish and crocodiles! Here I come."

Out into the very middle of the billabong you crawl. The crocodiles have given way to you with no argument—you hope. Sometimes you experience a shudder or two, thinking that one might follow your toes. It is mighty dark down there in those black waters. The top layer of water is warm from the day's hot sun. Deeper currents caressing your toes are cool. Crocodiles? Oh, well, You turn on your back and float face up to the sky, lost in a blissful dream. Never again will you know water as sweet as billabong water.

Everything is still. Not even the sightless, barking gecko is out tonight. Motorboats should never be allowed to disturb wilderness like this. Lucky for us, no tourists were here in the off season, so we had the billabong to ourselves.

Next day we rented a small rowboat from March at a fee of one dollar an hour, divided between seven. We set off on the water to explore, with the understanding that most of us must swim it because obviously the little boat could not hold us all together. Only I knew how to row, but the others soon learned.

We swam a number of miles up and back through two lakes, with some of us tracking along the sandbanks, and you can believe us when we report *we got sunburned*. And we got exercise that day!

We got out the Shell map of Western Australia. This state takes up just under one million square miles and covers one third of the Australian continent.

Across one of its empty deserts the new Shell map has stamped in red letters a legal warning and humane instruction for motorists: "Shooting of Horses, Camels, Donkeys, Cattle, Sheep and Goats Strictly Prohibited."

A day later found us at Wyndham, three hundred miles away over mostly dirt road. When the little road crossed above the shallow, murkey billabong of the great Victoria River, which drains into Joseph Bonaparte Gulf in the Timor Sea, we came upon a collection of big semi-trucks parked there. Many times we were to be a part of such a scene—greasy, exhausted drivers lying under a tiny tree or panting in the shadow of their trucks waiting for the mid-afternoon sun to lose a part of its lethal sting. It was almost impossible to risk going on in such heat now.

I remember the Victoria River crossing well. Maddened with heat we saw water. We walked right in. When Helmut's Swiss toes were nibbled by something on the muddy bottom, we all screamed and scrambled out. Of course the Victoria River has the big crocodiles which trail back and forth from the sea.

"Probably gabbies (crabs)," Claude thought of the nibbling. Our clothes dripping mud, we fell into the cars again and went onward. When heat gets that intense out on the open road you don't care about much. Near Wyndham we dry-camped in a desert open forest as was our custom, using one of the infrequent road camps where road machinery had formerly been berthed. The road camps left hard, level ground cleared of bush which was, we hoped, snake-free.

Again the blazing heavens revolved around us all night, giving a direct view into those unimaginable distances of space out there above, which are available to ponder on this desert.

The folding cots, called "stretchers," were sagging now, and we slept upon the ground rolled up in light blankets, like true "blueys," those Australian vagabonds who carried blue blankets in days of yore. One by one the campers took their canteen baths at night out beyond the campfire's gleam, as each was inclined. I would wet my gown all over with clear water for cooler sleeping. The flashlight and bug spray at my side, my canteen for a pillow, I never had a care in the world as I slept soundly, all wetted down for the night.

"But," said Ann, "when we come back into the tropics the next time around, I think it would be a good idea to buy a family size bug net and hang it on the limb of a tree."

"Too roight," said Kiwi, whose native New Zealand held no bad bugs or snakes.

The old, hot, humid coastal town of Wyndham is the only

deepwater port in northwest Australia. It was attacked by Japanese aircraft back in 1942, and the real wonder is how they found it. It lies at the end of Cambridge Gulf, a forty-mile deep, narrow, treacherous tidal rip gulf, its waters restricted to daylight approach for large overseas vessels, which must obtain pilotage service from fifty miles out beyond the mouth of the gulf (and this service is available only during the April-December meat shipping season).

The abattoirs, whose records show 30,000 to 35,000 cattle slaughtered here a season, historically drained the blood down the head of the gulf from a small creek, where bloated estaurine crocodiles lay with open mouths swallowing the grapefruit-size clots, and growing fat and monstrous.

We walked out onto the jetty where the ships came to load meat, looking closely below our feet for crocodile mouths, but did not linger long. The meat works had closed down for the season at the time we were there. It was 112 degrees on the docks, and probably about 130 degrees inside our cars.

"Here, take your salt tablets," I said. There was a hose outside the slaughter house for workmen to get a drink of water, and we stood there and turned the hose on ourselves, all seven of us.

We let our clothes stick dry on us as we went on, our garb being filthy shorts and sandals. Nothing mattered but to avert heat exhaustion, dehydration, or collapse.

We now drove into the area of one of the most talked about and exciting experiments of the continent when we approached the Ord River. A new town has been built, called Kunumurra, upon which the mighty state of Western Australia places great hopes.

We reached Kunumurra about six o'clock on a Saturday morning, too early to buy petrol or to find an open cafe. At the adjacent Kimberly Research Station, however, I did catch an early rising scientist just coming out of his modest government bungalow to get into his car, sleepy-eyed. He said that there were only very light monsoon rains in this area, about thirty inches, but still it did offer to Western Australia virtually her sole chance to try to raise such crops as cotton, rice, sorghum, safflower, and other cash crops upon the vast plains here.

We gazed upon those new fields early in the day. Clouds of white cockatoos had gathered upon the newly turned soil and were picking both cottonseed and locusts indiscriminately.

126

The scientists and their supporting staff of fifty were kept busy with shotguns, I learned. The farmers shot them, too. Oh, well, chemical treatment would soon take care of a few million birds, and America would be glad to help in that.

The damming of the Ord River which flows into that Cambridge Gulf earlier described, on a coast as precipitous as fjord-dented Norway, was intended to provide controlled irrigation of these cultivated fields during the deadly Dry.

Some twenty-eight farmers at this time had taken parcels of government land. "Are they making a go of it? Are they making money?" I asked the early morning, friendly, French-Australian agronomist.

"Some of them. The best of them are," he replied.

The only crop right now was cotton. Rice was still a government dream. The Kimberly Research Station, founded in 1945, was funded jointly by Western Australia and the Commonwealth. If these flat, blacksoil tablelands yielded as was hoped, the damming of the Ord furnished a pilot project which could be applied to other Kimberly rivers.

When we drove over the modest Ord River Diversion Dam, we eyes its crocodiled depths (not very deep) with studied skepticism. But a second, much larger dam, the real Ord River Dam, was scheduled to be built between canyon walls thirty miles up the river within three years, which might create a large man-made lake and power project. Now in the late Dry, just before the Wet, it was hard to believe that the Ord as we saw it was a river which, from December to March, emptied into the gulf at over one million cubic feet per second: a fairly big river, it drained 18,000 square miles. It has been a great economic misfortune for Australia that her only big rivers flow into the most remote and sparsely-populated tropical seas on earth, two thousand miles by air from the Australian centers of civilization where water and power are needed.

Now not only did Western Australia intend to produce new crops and open up new world markets from this barely cockatoo-scratched frontier in her arable extreme North West, but it was here only that she might develop the electric power which could be transmitted hundreds of miles across the desert southward to supply growing communities, and to attract worldwide industries to the Perth area. Such was—and is—the dream.

The Kimberleys of Australia is a legend of legends in itself. An area of mountains (and rainfall during the Wet) which is three times the size of England, the land has no railroads, few roads, and few bridge crossings over major rivers as yet.

Under the Beef Roads scheme about a thousand miles of road have been built or upgraded since 1960, costing eighteen million dollars. Before 1960 the only way to market cattle was to drive the animals overland to the Wyndham Meatworks, an ordeal which only the fittest man or beast survived.

Shorthorn beef still forms the basic Kimberley economy. Since 1880, when the area was opened for settlement in million-acre blocks, terrible deterioration of stock and pastures has occurred. Like our Arizona ranchers who fought Apache Indians only three generations ago for the land, the Kimberley pioneers lived in stockade houses with narrow windows through which a rifle could be thrust, and many fell to the spear. Even today, many a steer is lost to the natives and to white cattle rustlers whom the Australian grazier calls "paddy dodgers."

The wild Kimberleys still has a vastness and emptiness that staggers the imagination. Only a few white men preside over the Kimberley Range at homesteads which their grand-daddies settled nearly a hundred years ago—enjoying their privacy, no doubt, in this most isolated corner of the continent, and enjoying the north-ward-flowing wild streams and rivers which furnish water in the world's driest continent.

As we drove slowly across the Ord River Diversion Dam our eyes lifted to the mysterious Kimberley Ranges which hung upon our inland horizon, from which this Ord River came.

The Diversion Dam, opened in July 1963 by Sir Robert Menzies, then Prime Minister of Australia, had been extensively researched beforehand for its engineering feasibility; yet no scheme had been the subject of so much bitter controversy. In the capital of Perth over two thousand miles away, the subject of the $48-million investment was on the lips of all, and was the pride of the state, although few of the Australian multitudes who would be paying for it would probably ever see it.

An American consultant agronomist later told me that at the Kimberley Research Station the Aussies had set up work which would do credit to the Rothamstad, England; to the Rowett Insti-

128

tute in Scotland, and the University of Leeds—but not one single experiment was being done there that actually applied to the problems of north Australia. At the University of Western Australia (Perth) pioneering studies have been made on soil deficiency problems. But the professors know most about soils in England, Europe, and usually any place else except Australia, and perhaps not one has ever been further north of Perth than fifty miles!

As we drove southward, skirting around the Kimberley Ranges, I was so anesthetized by heat that I was grateful not to be called upon to do anything much but be carried along. I'm sure I don't know how any large population will be lured to the tropical north, other than the few of that special breed who live there today.

The wise traveler, like those truck drivers we saw, lies down right where he is and goes to sleep under his truck. Explorers, too, crawled into cover at times when their internal clock indicated it. But most city people, used to a schedule, accustomed to pushing on against all internal dictates, will run quickly into trouble. On a day of very intense heat he pushes too far. He blows his stack right then. In the scorching deserts of Australia, Death is always waiting for the uncautious man.

The Outback is serious business now and always, due to these temperatures soaring to the very threshold of man's endurance—not sometimes, but routinely, day after day. People can die from heat very suddenly—apparently normal people. What happens?

In Perth later we learned that a veteran Australian government man died along this road not long after we passed. The man's death, as nearly as could be ascertained, was somehow tied in with an emotional tantrum he had, perhaps similar to my road-gravel-eating acrobatics over the fan belt. This man had had some car trouble. He just died there beside his car.

Our three vehicles were slowing to a stop along the dusty track. There was a little group of trees and a big bull under the trees.

Swinging out of the high Jeep I just kicked that deluxe bull out from under the tree. He gave way with no argument. Then, cooked from heat, I lay down where he had been among dried piles of manure, only dimly feeling my sunburned back against thorns and little piss ants, and let the flies walk over me for minutes on end, nearly unaware. Oh, I was all right. I knew that. If I could sleep a few minutes I knew I would make it okay. The boys were rustling about,

129

making refreshments. "I can't get any real rest in this place," I mumbled.

Then Claude brought a cup of iced orange juice from his cooler in the Holden sedan, and I rallied to open a can of tuna chunks, which I ate with a stick.

We traveled early now, breaking camp fast. I gathered up and packed equipment each daybreak, but left the science of loading to the girls. I took Jean's advice and just left the worry to them, enjoying what Jean called my "oldstership" and its benefits. I had a capable pair of girls. Yes, really capable, even though when I dug for food I kept coming up with such things as hair-brushes and battered boomerangs instead.

The greatest hazard to Outback driving was dust. The suffocating dust clouds were so dense when one car met another that you might have a collision. For eight miles before you met the other fellow you'd see the plume of his dust. "Desert varnish" of a glittering moonscape vied with thousands of cast-off beer bottles lining the road on every hand. Worse, the pile of horrid bottles and filthy tin cans and trash proliferated suddenly every time the road brought you to a shade tree, while at water holes, sitting under a tree became virtually impossible because of the years of accumulated filth and trash.

We left the open forest of the north after Hall's Creek, but were to have the delightful experience of one more tropical gorge, one which was truly hidden and unexpected in the desert, creating its own greenhouse.

Keigie Gorge lies ten miles by dirt road off the Great Northern Highway, from Fitzroy Crossing.

Another big river flowing out of the Kimberleys, the 400-mile-long Fitzroy, like the Ord, could produce at peak a million cubic feet per second. But unlike the Ord, it flowed west into the Indian Ocean at King Sound.

Rarely navigated because of snags and sand bars, its habitat was tropical but surrounded by thousands of square miles of arid land, with brightly-colored parrots screaming amid fig trees, banyans, and water-storing baobabs (called "bottle trees"). The mere 850 cultivated acres of the Fitzroy bottom land so far were but the forerunner, it was hoped, of another agricultural area for Western Australia. Art

Linkletter had one of his properties here, if you could find it, known as "Art's Fitzroy."

We drove right across the bottom of the Fitzroy River at the Crossing in the late Dry. A rat couldn't have found a swimming hole. But this river couldn't have been crossed if we hadn't done it fast. A curiosity of the village was that the pub was located on one side of the river (the pub was here first) and the small post office and hospital on the other. These amenities would be cut off from each other during the five months of the Wet, so you had to take your choice, for you couldn't have it both ways if you stayed here.

"There's a crocodile living in Keigie Gorge up the river," I heard a grimy little man say to someone at the pub. "Several people have seen 'im."

Jean and Ann and I and the Swiss boys hastened to drive there at sundown, arriving just about dark. (Claude and his Kiwi mite elected to stay at the pub.) Mr. March had been here, and had thoughtfully provided trash barrels, fire places, and rest rooms. He was just starting to work this place, and the motorboats would be brought in right after the next Wet. Fortunately, there was no one here but us, as yet.

The little truck had brought us through a tunnel of tropical vines, where we breathed gratefully of wet things. Then our Jeep suddenly came to road's end, with no warning whatsoever, and our headlights shot into space. Below our front wheels was a slick mud dropoff, and deep water. Brakes, brakes!

We got out in the deepening twilight, sensing the moist jungle with every fiber, and its strange sounds and its pregnant silences, and we breathed deeply again, listening. The drop-off disclosed the deep, green, gloomy water, murky, and somehow hideously repugnant even to the uninitiated.

We cooked our supper almost in silence and laid our swags down there. The place held all the loneliness of the original Australia.

"I'll take the side near the fire. You take the crocodile side," I told the girls, when we arranged our beds. It was an old Australia joke. When a couple of mites traveling with their horses camped at a billabong they might take turns for the safer sleeping place on the ground, on alternate nights, because in those days the crocs might be out walk-about around the river banks.

131

The night was black as pitch. At length it came—just once, then silence. But I could always say I heard it. A gutteral bellow, right there only a few feet away in that green, murky waterhole. An erupting, hollow belch, so cold you shivered and snuggled down into your blanket.

"Bull crocodile," I whispered. We all listened, shivering delightfully.

"If sewers could only talk," said Ann, "they would sound just like that."

Next daylight, carrying my field glasses, I made my way up the cliff on our side of the river before the others might rouse and spoil the hunting. I must hurry.

Full daylight came swiftly. Why had I not wakened earlier? For a half hour nothing stirred the placid surface of the water below. Every moment counted now. Birds were shouting their staunch hearts out in the gum trees to the rising sun. I started my climb back down the black, iron-ribbed cliffs. Fairy mists of night smoked from the water. The scene was like the dawn of creation, the very beginning of time.

Once again, from long habit, my weatherbeaten glasses swung across the water, and nearby came to rest upon a form which was not there before.

The estuarine crocodile was floating high in the water. I could see his great shoulder, his girth as big around as two men. The length was nine to twelve feet, I guess. I could see his head, a perfect triangle. His long tail hung down into the water out of sight. Like a brown log he drifted, with the little wavelets of early morning lapping against his corrugated side, seeming to be carried by chance on a current until his position changed, and I knew that he saw me there perfectly well on my cliffside, and he knew that I knew that he knew. . .

At camp I handed the glasses to my mites. "There's nothing there," said one. "Only a rock in the middle."

"There isn't any rock in the middle," I said. The rock sunk.

This crocodile was protected by law and I was glad he was. There may have been more than one, of course. This is not to say that the big Fitzroy did not bring others up from the sea during floodtime to be trapped for a season or so during the Dry in the nine-mile-long billabong, along with some sharks, rays, and sailfish—

hundreds of miles from the sea! The interesting part was just how the crocodiles made their living.

The nature of this leviathan is to come hundreds of miles inland in the course of his hunt for food, for this animal lives largely upon land game.

His natural food in Australia is the kangaroo. To feed this great sea tank nature was faced with what would seem to be an insoluble problem—how do the two get together? This is a water animal, yet he must get food from land. How?

He will not venture more than six hundred yards from the water at most. He will not leave it at all during the Dry. His barrel body is so heavy that without water to support him, he founders, and his massive clawed legs seem puny by comparison to the enormous, bloated belly which drags the ground. Unlike the little "freshie," the slender-billed Johnston which was named for a sub-inspector of Australian police, he cannot run from billabong to billabong on nimble legs as the waters dry up. A denizen of deep water, he must catch his evening tucker by the fine arts of concealment and patience.

Sooner or later, a kangaroo will have to come to drink water. Hesitant, timid, instinctively distrusting the water's edge, nonetheless the land animals have no choice. Drink they must, or perish.

So it is that the estuarine crocodile, one of earth's most ancient lizards, a monster in prehistoric armor, has made a good living inland in north Australia since the Dreamtime. This great swimmer ranges miles at sea around the top of the continent, catching the giant sea turtle and similar marine snacks, and is often seen ten miles out at sea covered with seaweed and barnacles as he swims. But the meat of the kangaroo and such land animals must be endowed with special sweetness to this monster, when you consider that he has been found as far as four hundred miles inland. Further, he must have luck with his hunting, or he would not linger as he does, to grow into a submarine up to twenty-six feet in length, weighing several tons, and perhaps 150 years old. The Australian variety is the largest by far of all the earth's crocodiles.

After the coming of the white man, with importation of horses, cattle, feral hogs, and the Asiatic buffalo long gone wild, the possibilities for evening tucker considerably increased; and Crocodylus accepted all these additions to his diet. Graziers for three generations in north Australia have battled crocodile losses from their herds.

133

The great swimmer, the old sea tank, ranges in Southeast Asia and far up the muddy rivers of New Guinea, as well, taking land mammals; and occasionally his evening "tea" may consist of that careless native woman or child who has gone to fetch water at dusk. Crocodiles lie in the deep holes of rivers, usually under an overhang bank, where it is tempting to dip a water bucket. They may lie concealed in water lilies of blue and white and red with fourteen-inch blooms, camouflaging their nightmare presence in the most exquisitely beautiful, quiet places.

The technique of killing is to make a lightening lunge up from the water and either hit the prey a back-breaking wallop with the tail and knock it into the water, or grasp it by the throat in massive teeth, drag it into the water, and drown it. Once in the water no land animal stands much chance—the Estuarine crocodile twists and rolls to disorient and confuse the animal while he drowns it, and the weight of the armored giant is enormous.

Certain groups of man in north Australia could combat the crocodile successfully in its own element. Aborigines who wanted to cross a wide body of water that was teeming with crocodiles plunged right in and swam it readily. They knew that in most cases a crocodile will not grab a moving object. Often the croc will follow the object indolently but will not attempt to take it, being cautious beasts who like to look over a situation. They have been known to study their chosen prey for weeks or months before making their strike.

The Aborigines prepared for their dangerous swimming marathons by prayers. Special incantations, they believed, gave them a virtual guarantee of the crocodile spirit's permission to pass through its waters. The prayers rid the men of their fears and enabled them to put their best wits and energies at work to do what they had to do. Following prayer meeting each man acquired a sizable forked branch, all the leaves intact. The man always swam right alongside his leafy branch, using it partly for camouflage to deceive the saurians. When monsters began to follow after the swimmers more incantations were recited. When they reached close range a man would then leap nimbly out of the water and up upon his forked branch. The branch was frail and would not hold a man's weight, except for a moment, but that moment gave the swimmer a chance to outwit or confront

134

his follower. As a last resort a warrior would pull his knife (at the same time offering apologies to the spirit) and stab the persistent crocodile swiftly in the snout or eyeball. This lightening stab was a strong deterrent to the animal for any more close combat.

In hunting large food, such as a horse, the crocodile keeps in mind a number of water caves, quite often among the cypress roots, where he will need to store food too big to handle immediately. Only after the large food has softened and ripened in some secret, secure food locker for a number of weeks will the crocodile return to eat. Life for him is lived at a leisurely pace. He has time on his side.

Mama crocs are devoted mothers. Digging a hold in the moist bottomland, the mama drops several hundred rubbery white eggs about the size of golf balls, then covers them up with her own recipe of wet vegetation and soil, to create heat by the chemical action of rapid decay. She remains close by, guarding the nest, during the weeks of incubation. A clumsy intruder bush-bashing along the river valley, should be aware of the possibility of a ferocious, sudden charge at close range during this "nesting season." The charge of an angry mama crocodile can be as overwhelming as a freight train, it is said.

When the babies hack their way out of the egg sacks and up to earth's surface, each one is ready for a fight immediately and each one runs unerringly in the direction of the river. The satisfied old female then wanders away, and from then on they are on their own.

Seagulls and sea eagles haunt the water edges feasting upon the excess numbers, as do myriad land animals from rats to dingoes, thus keeping the world's crocodile population within manageable limits of the environment.

Primitive man, too, dined on crocodiles, small and large. He was an expert in plunging his ten-foot spear into the earth for testing nests along the rich, tropical river valleys. (Primitive man tested everything with his spear, which became an extension of his hand in a world where few things were safe for the soft, human touch.)

It was Mr. Dunbavin Butcher of the Victoria Fish and Game Department, author of many scientific papers and erstwhile visitor to America, who pointed out to me how truly primitive in concept most of our American wildlife laws are, and how abhorrently commercial.

In the U.S. the game statutes of most states regard all wildlife as a viable commodity, in line with the ancient hunting instincts. We shoot some animals for "food." We shoot others for "varmints."

Those others not so categorized we shoot anyway, because they are there. How many states have laws to protect the golden eagle, the raven, the porcupine, or skunk? Most of our game laws in America regard creatures as either nuisances or products, with an accent on the mass raising of deer, which are in demand by the hunters.

Australia is not oriented toward hunting for sport or hunting for food, because it was not given many food species or sport species by nature to start with—but also, Australia does not seek to *import* them to set up the hunting sports.

The state of Victoria and the Northern Territory (led by the federal government) now have set up, theoretically at least, far more enlightened systems than in America. Nowadays the Australian policy starts with the proposition that *all wildlife is protected*, unless otherwise regulated. Such conservationists as Mr. Butcher hope to see the day come soon when this concept will be honored by everyone in the land, even with the magnificent and terrible estuarine crocodile.

In the territory all guns must be registered, and this must be renewed each year. Right now we were seeing the last of guns in this land.

Chapter 11

WESTERN AUSTRALIA

One evening in the pindan forest we stayed at an abandoned road camp clearing, and were sitting about the campfire. In the forest, a few yards away, we could hear the voice of Hans speaking Switzerdeutch.

"What's he doing?" I asked Jean, as the shadows leapt back from the flickering blaze.

"Making a tape recording to mail to his mother."

"How good of him."

"Where is Helmut, by the way?" Ann asked.

"Hey, you blokes, did anybody notice where Helmut is? He's been gone quite a while."

"How long?"

"More than an hour, I reckon."

"Maybe he went to take a wash?" Claude asked.

"Does he ever?" someone laughed, shortly. Silence fell, suddenly.

"Well, when did he disappear?" I spoke up. I felt a creeping reluctance to use the word "disappear."

I turned to Jean. "Jean, go out to Hans and ask if he knows where Helmut is."

137

When Hans rejoined us he was just as mystified as to where Helmut could possibly be and why he would go away for so long into the trackless forest. It was dark night when his absence was noticed.

"Has he ever done that before?" we asked Hans, anxiously.

"No, never," replied Hans, with furrowed brow.

I turned to Claude. "Take my big flashlight. Climb up that tree here and tie the light near the top, as high as you can get, and start the red light pulsating."

"Don't you get excited," he replied to me curtly, not liking me to seize command of a situation. "There's no need to get excited, just calm yourself down."

"Who's excited? Just please climb the tree. Get the light going, and if he can see it he can find his way back. It's his only chance."

I wished right then we had a big rifle to fire, but we didn't.

"Did he take a flashlight with him?" somebody asked. No one thought so.

Annie was running about, breaking dead sticks and building up the fire. Jean got onto the Jeep horn and tooted. We all shouted. No answer.

All but Claude. He just seemed resentful, an enigma, at this moment of emergency. From the day we met him Claude had been the unacknowledged expedition leader because, after all, he was the only one who had driven the Outback before, and I think we all wanted very much to have his friendship and good opinion. Besides, it was sort of apparent that he wouldn't "play" unless he was the leader.

But now, obviously, there wasn't a moment to lose. If Helmut walked out there into the Never-Never he could get himself lost every bit as permanently as Leichhardt and many others did.

If he could not see the lights or hear our noise, there was little chance that he could find us by daylight the next day, either. In fact, night might be his best chance. I looked at Jean and we both knew. She was the only one of the lot of us who had trained a full year as a professional in search and rescue.

I can't overestimate the seriousness of the situation. I think we all cursed that moment under our breaths for the stupidity of it all, at the same time that we felt a grievous concern for the survival of our taciturn comrade, who offered so little to anyone else at any time. Still, no one put the light up in the tree.

"He probably walked the road back to thot pub back there," Claude concluded in Australian logic. "I reckon he's there, he's roight."

Ann jumped into the Jeep, and she and Claude sped to the tavern about four miles back. Within minutes they returned, empty-handed.

Then Helmut walked into our camp, smiling broadly. We all nearly collapsed in the enormous relief his safe reappearance generated.

"I told you he'd be roight," said Claude, and he and Kiwi went off to bed.

"But where were you?" I had to ask our euphoric comrade returned from the dead. "Why didn't you answer our shouts?"

"I go to sleep in woods," Helmut explained in his thick accent. He was pleased to have caused such concern and to have been missed. But after that incident I think all of us realized that something was seriously wrong with Helmut.

"I have to help heem," Hans told Jean, "and I do not know how I can help heem."

"We'll be in Perth after a while," suggested Jean, "and he should get a job."

"Yes, thot is for sure. I must get a job and work, too," replied Hans, realistically. "This is just working holiday. We need money soon. How long do you think the Mrs. Helmericks family will stay in Perth?"

"We'll be staying in Perth over the Christmas holidays anyway," I told Hans next morning as we all ate breakfast. "We have two things we hope to arrange before we can leave Perth. One is that we may have a wonderful invitation, I think, to go visit the Linkletter place several hundred miles south of Perth. The other one is that we hope we may get an invitation to fly to Tasmania from Perth for some of the hot weeks."

"Oooh! Linkletter's place. I have heard about thot. Of course, Americans, and you are Americans. Ooooh! The romantic island of Tasmania!" cried Hans, very enthused. "Thot is beauty, Jeanie. I am glad for you, my good friends."

The town of Derby, where this conversation took place, was located near the mouth of the Fitzroy River right on the Indian Ocean.

Derby (named after Lord Derby) was founded during the Kimberley gold rush in 1883, and has been used ever since mostly for the shipment of live cattle. The changes which have occurred, say, in California, since 1883, have been a great deal more noticeable than changes here. The passage by sea into this lonely port is restricted to a daylight approach and the town still has a colorful mixed population of Chinese, Malays, Filipinos, and Aborigines. A leprosarium is here, founded in 1946 by the Sisters of St. John. The permanently-flowing Myalls Bore provides for the "longest cattle trough in the Southern Hemisphere," and a famous Prison Baobab Tree—fifty-three feet in circumference, inside the hollow of which Aboriginal work gangs with ankle chains were once locked up—can be seen. And here now the site for the first tidal power station in Australia is now being considered at Derby where tides range up to thirty-five feet.

From here the Great Northern Highway zips straight across the edge of Dampier Land into which no road runs other than the track to Beagle Bay Mission—for this big peninsula is another huge Aboriginal Reserve the size of half a dozen European nations put together. The name Dampier came from an English pirate who, sailing to this northwest coast in 1699, deserted his captain and was later given command of the *Roebuck* to return and explore what was then called New Holland. Bad luck dogged his expedition, his vessel was damaged, and he returned to England to face court martial. His reports on the treacherous navigation conditions and abject misery of the west coast of Australia discouraged further exploration by others for many years. The whole region, from Darwin on down to Broome, that little town which lies on the south coast of Dampier Land, became historically one of the great pearl-fishing coasts of the world. It was pearls and pearl shell which built the Oriental and Malaysian population on this coast, they of the world-famous diving cult.

When we reached Broome, headquarters of the pearl industry in Australia, it was to see baked mud streets lined with open-air, screened tropical bungalows. The town had a population of about 2,000 with 3,000 in the shire.

In 1889, when it was linked with the overseas telegraph by submarine cable from Java, Broome was fast developing the character of an Asian outpost. It was not long before it had a boisterous polyglot of pearl buyers, merchants of questionable ethics, coolies from China, divers from Japan, the Philippines, Koepang and Malaya, European master pearlers, and an assortment of barefooted adventurers from the ports of the world wearing one long gold earring, a red bandana wrapped around greasy hair, and a cutlass in the teeth. Australia got a lot of its impetus for the White Australia Policy from the hard facts of life in the north and northwest, where Anglo pioneers found themselves far outnumbered by Asiatics, and the ports took on the air of a completely Oriental world feared by most Australians.

The big ideological battle is the belief of most urban Australians that whites cannot live in tropical conditions, and some now say that selected Asians, or "others," should be allowed in to populate the "rich" Kimberley area. This is an afterthought—after they threw the Asians out.

Certainly money and people are the key. The closer settlement of the North End can only be achieved at great cost and by the willingness of the population in the densely inhabited coastal belts down south to spread out and up to the frontier—and so far, they haven't really been willing.

To the Australian urban mind the development of the North is a venture of enormous significance. A battle against heat, isolation, high freights, the Wet, the Dry, and "wogs" is something one reads about in the newspapers. It suits the urban temperament little more than a trip by covered wagon to Los Angeles would suit most New Yorkers, assuming that L.A. was still unsettled today and would never innately possess the charms which L.A. at one time possessed.

Somewhere in the empty North, marked on the map as Kelly's Knob, a signpost holds its far-flung limbs stretched outward. The signs attached to such a post read:

ADELAIDE	1435	BRISBANE	1830
MELBOURNE	1815	SINGAPORE	1990
CANBERRA	1865	TOKYO	3820
SYDNEY	1900	DARWIN	320

Now the campers, their brains baked by blinding sun each day and splashed by stars each night, steered by the line of brown bottles glittering on each side of the track, and by the dead kangaroos alongside. (Many kangaroos were hit by cars at night. We never hit one in nearly a year of steady driving, because we took care not to, and because we were lucky. Many more had obviously been shot, because they lay in small groups or pairs.)

The wide-open land pierced by this one and only highway connecting South with North, although nearly uninhabited, was not always entirely private. It had a way of erupting people when least expected, at the most unfortunate moments, as in the case of Ann when she was suddenly caught in the headlights of a surprised truck driver at dawn. We can imagine him rubbing his weary hand across sleep-glued eyes, and sitting up straight with an awful start. He has driven this route for years and has bever seen anything like it. Hello, a kangaroo with a nightgown on! It squats and then it runs, now what do you make o'thot? Over there in the bush, too, it looks like min-min lights. (Our campfire.) Well, a man is liable to see almost anything out in the Never-Never if he drives that track long enough. Ann scurried for her life. The lonely truck passed with a cloud of dust that did not settle for the next half a day.

Only once, in all our driving, did we see a pair of wild emus, and this was a great thrill for us. These giants could be seen right outside Sydney at one time. Their original habitat was continent-wide.

Next to the African ostrich, the emu is the heaviest of living birds. It belongs to the ratites, forms which have lost the power of flight, possess no wishbone in the barrel breast, and grow so large as to be formidible enemies to anything that would attack them. With wings small and useless and flight feathers soft and flimsy, the bird depends upon its muscular legs which carry it on a 35-mile-an-hour run, and which can place a powerful kick.

A "sport" of hooligans is to run these birds to death with a car on the plains. One of the saddest commentaries on man was the Emu War in which, a few years ago, military forces were actually called out by the farmers to exterminate these birds in Western Australia.

But the Emu War turned out to be rather ludicrous. The herds of grazing emus, when driven across fields, broke ranks, and each bird cut out for himself at a marvelous sprint. Very few were shot in that drive, and the emus won the war. They have enormous, languorous eyes with flappy lids and long lashes in a tiny, ridiculous face set upon a long, rubbery neck protruding straight upwards from a bulbous body, and they react just like big rubber balls when pressed by pursuers. They can bounce off fences or other obstacles with amazing springiness. When grazing peacefully they make a bubbling sound like, "Boom!"

Their food consists of things like sour plums and emu apples, several kinds of wild, woody, bitter berries, and a great quantity of grass and seeds. The fruit of the prickly pear is eaten, and by voiding seeds in uninfested areas, the emu was a big influence in the spread of this pest earlier, the plant often being seen sprouting from emu droppings. This cactus was controlled by introducing Cactoblastis, whose caterpillar moth, from America, took care of the matter. Presently C.S.I.R.O. research proved that the caterpillars and insects which emus eat generally outweigh their damage to farms and wheatfields.

From 1945 to 1960 bounty was paid on 284,724 emus which were shot in cattle areas, rather than on farms, for the most part. Certainly many more were exterminated for which no bounty was claimed. The bounty still remains in all states. The cattlemen don't like the idea that, especially in drought years, when there is not enough food for livestock (and there never will be, so long as over-grazing continues) emus are forced to move into settled areas, foraging from streams or waterholes.

The breeding season of the emus, commencing in May or June, may last until September. Their nest is a bed of grass trampled on the ground with little or no attempt at concealment. As many as twenty greenish-black eggs are laid, measuring a little over five inches by three inches. The five-weeks incubation period is the responsibility of the male bird, as is the rearing of the young. Full size takes between one to two years to achieve, at which time a bird may grow to one hundred pounds.

Rather anxiously we sat by the side of the road in our vehicles, waiting for our two emus to make their long strides across the plain into the distance. Behind us three miles away a cloud of dust showed that a car was coming. Chances were that that car held men who would be glad at any opportunity to continue the Emu War.

"We're lucky to have some of the old maps, not the new ones," said Claude, consulting his Golden Fleece map.

"Why is that?"

143

"Well, you see, they are not putting out the positions of the bores on the new maps any more."

"Oh, how dreadful!"

Claude was choosing camps for us now according to where the bores were. The bores, or wells, were scattered about the huge, unfenced properties through which the highway plunged. In fact, the highway owed its existence to being a beef road, and ever more bores were being drilled adjacent to the highway for cattle-watering and cattle-loading purposes. Cal-Tex had put the bores on the maps for motorists, too, up until this very time, as a humanitarian gesture which could save a life in the desert. We might find two or three bores with windmills within a couple of hundred miles.

But—like us, the public in general had soon learned to use this resource for their camping out. I am sorry to say that the public made itself so repugnant to the ranchers who owned these bores and windmills and tanks, that vandalism caused hard feelings, so now the new road maps would no longer carry the locations of this water.

We were careful to leave no trash, and at the bores we took our baths standing under the tank spout in some instances, or the kids would climb up the high metal tank by chinning them-selves—the ranchers left no ladders—and go swimming.

South along the Eighty-Mile Beach, across the De Grey River, we went. Typically, the dry riverbed showed "pademelons" as we passed, looking almost good enough to eat. These wild melons, large, round, and striped, extend on vines along the sand where water runs. But they are inedible and bitter.

We passed right through Art Linkletter's Anna Plains and camped out on the property someplace, but did not pause to search for the house of the manager, or we might be searching yet. The vast property, bounded by the Indian Ocean in front and the trackless desert behind, was in the process of being sold at the time of our visit.

There was a plan afoot to build "the world's first nuclear harbor" in this area, at Cape Keraudren, north of Port Hedland. This would be a highly prestigious gesture for Western Australia and for the country generally, it was conceded—though not all physicists nor hydrologists recommended the gesture without qualification.

Although the Australian press was enthusiastic, the worldwide

144

agreement that no atomic blasts shall be vented on the earth's surface seemed to have been disregarded by some writers. Only Red
China and France did not sign this agreement in the early 1960s.

At Port Hedland, Claude and Kiwi decided to leave us and go on
their way independently. But the Swiss boys chose to continue
with us.

Hans by now had become very disenchanted with Helmut. It
was Hans who had pushed Helmut to Australia. It was he who was
behind their desert expedition. It was Hans who got their first jobs
in Sydney. It was Hans who got the vehicle, who made all the new
friends. It was Hans who worked diligently at learning English—a
few new words each day. Helmut had become a dead weight on
his friend, and this was one reason why Hans wanted to travel
with us from the first. He felt trapped, and he longed secretly
to find a way of getting free of his mite. The time would come
when he would be Helmut's caretaker no more.

At Port Hedland, named in 1857 and with a population at
this time of about a thousand, we were still a thousand miles from
Perth, but were soon to enter the Perth sphere of influence. Port
Hedland lay in the eleven inch rainfall belt. When we crossed the
Gascoyne and a few more like Quart Pot Creek and Pint Pot Creek
and such things, we would be "home safe," out of the flood area,
and south of the Wet.

This was just before the completion of the new, modern Walk-
about Motel at Port Hedland, and we visited the classical old-style
roadside inn, where the curious method of dining was to sit at a
narrow plank shelf just eighteen inches wide, with each diner facing
a blank wall.

Inland from Port Hedland lie some of the world's largest iron
ore reserves, including the Mt. Goldsworthy contracts, Hamersley
Iron, Mount Newman, Mount Tom Price—the biggest contracts,
written with the state government, which have ever been ordered in
the world history of the steel industry.

Only ten years ago iron reserves in Australia were guessed to be
minor. Now, suddenly, exploration has changed the guess: twenty
billion tons are estimated, enough to supply the whole world for
centuries to come. Contracts for three billion dollars are presently
let to Japan. Today the most enormous minerals rush the world has
ever known is on, making all former "gold rushes" look puny by
comparison.

Some fast changes will have to take place if Australia brings in the big companies to the Outback. At Port Hedland a new $1,500,000 steel and concrete wharf was under construction. A $1,800,000 dam on the Turner River to increase the town's water supply was being built. In fact, the companies decided they must build a new town. The town will be five miles inland beyond the tidal flats hemming the existing town site, in which all possible residential acreage is already taken up.

The twin towns would be linked by an industrial belt. The population is expected to reach 4,000 by the end of 1971, and 12,000 by 1980. The mines are building their own railroads through unexplored desert.

One problem was the control of dust associated with the handling of iron ore. World experience indicated that dust could be minimized, but not eliminated. Dust would be the price that must be paid for the development of one of the great iron ore ports of the world. "North of 26 degrees" was the cry to extract the wealth of the Pilbara, the Kimberleys, Arnhem Land, Cape York—to invade sedimentary basins, the great rivers, the broad plains of the emu, which together, said the leaders of man, "present a challenge and a potential as great as any in the world."

"The North can double Australia's wealth," said the leaders, "double this nation's population, its strength, influence, and standing in the world at large, particularly in the Western Pacific and Indian Ocean areas."

It was a bit like the excitement generated by a young Texas or a California shortly before the twentieth century. The momentum of humanity could be compared with that which characterized the development of the American West, except that pioneers could not come here without a job and pay check, and the excitement was corporate. There was a similarity of a dry climate and the vast distances separating the frontier from the financial centers of the East, and there was the same challenge to overcome alien geography—but the means were modern, mechanical ones.

Possibly the results would be much the same as in the American West in that later generations, like us today, might have some qualms about where all this "progress" would ultimately lead man, as he beheld his land.

Yet, where else could man march but "forward"? He had to do

something about the vacuum here. Population pressures on the planet urged him on. The Pilbara, now engulfed in a wave of mineral activity like a tide, lies closer to Singapore than Sydney. The Indonesian capital of Djakarta is the same distance from Port Hedland as Perth. Indonesian radio stations are heard by north Australians more clearly than those emanating from their own state capital! The great, gouged coastline of the northwest boldly faces the Commonwealth's Asian neighbors. Therefore, this geographical reality, and the political problems of the modern age, quickly reduce any real similarity between this region and the West Coast of America, and the covered wagon pioneers.

It was at Hedland that Ann and I made the horrid mistake of washing our sleeping bags. Their interior stench—the interior of our vehicle—was becoming hard to bear, particularly as we progressed southward each day into more temperate climes and more civilized society, and we must climb into the bags for warmth again during the night.

Jean was wise. "You and Ann wash your bags if you like," she said, "but don't wash mine. I don't advise taking the chance."

Well, here at Port Hedland's oasis we found the first completely automatic washers which we had seen in our wandering, and most of the machines were actually working. Big tumbler dryers also were available at this fine laundromat.

After a journey down to the bank for coins—(no business in this land is actually prepared for customers)—I started right in on all our musty, moldy, sweaty regalia. There was no air conditioning inside the laundromat, of course: a free sweat bath came with the washes. I worked like mad. At length the astute businesswoman brought a key and adjusted the dryers in some mysterious way, so that each dime inserted by me, her only customer, bought only three minutes of drying.

Now as everyone knows, sleeping bags require lots of drying time to fluff out all those gobs of wet feathers packed inside. Result: I ran out of time, money, and patience, as daylight ended. One bag—it just happened to be mine—had to be carried away still half wet.

I figured that the intense desert heat would dry it, ignoring the fact that we camped only at night when there was no sun. Well, why shouldn't the thing dry while traveling, if I spread it out under

147

our dancing dog's dirty feet? After all, wasn't our Jeep itself just one big red-hot revolving tumbler on these washboard roads?

Three days later the wet feathers were plainly rotting. Now also the nights grew colder, and the dew was so heavy it permeated even the dry bags of the others. We carried on with my pathetic dream of someday finding another town with a laundromat and another tumbler dryer. Someday I would just start all over again and wash and dry my hundred dollar bag. If not, it might be spoiled entirely, and I'd be cold and shelterless for all time to come. In that temperate (but intemperate) South we came almost to fear its striking cold, after our blood had been thinned out in the tropics.

The bag and I must have survived, because both of us are here. I only remember going on and on, like Burke and Wills or the ever-disappearing Leichhardt, forevermore.

We met a man along the road who would drop in at our camp-fire at midnight, or any time, for tea, and I see him, too, just going on and on in memory.

He was a fellow about thirty-three, and I first saw him leaning an elbow on our Jeep and talking to Jean way back at the Fitzroy. Mysteriously he would come out of nowhere with his truck, over that great horizon. We sat with him again at a Port Hedland restaurant, and he was always delightful and full of jokes, and he knew how to toss the compliments to mum.

Born in Australia, he was not typically Aussie, for this "loose hypothesis," as I came to think of him, combined a shrewd cosmopolitanism with a dark and swarthy skin, flashing hazel eyes, and a European flair of personality. In a land where month after month such roadside people do not speak with women he was a treat, for all his "woggishness," and were we not all "wogs" together, anyway?

I can see us now, the little campers, sitting late around the campfire out there, and along came that truck with the friendly wog. (We never did know what it was that he carried inside that truck, or why.)

"Are you roight, there?" came the friendly voice out of a big dust cloud.

"Yes, we're roight. How are you? Will you 'ave a cup of tea?"

A little shoreline town, population 250, called Onslow was really the last Outback town: low coast, marshes, reefs, severe tropical storms, lying on the edge of the Great Sandy Desert. On

148

the east mouth of the Ashburton River, it was a wool-shipping center, served by the State Shipping Company.

This Western Australia coastal desert extended 1,100 miles from Northwest Cape just short of Broome to Shark Bay. Other towns going southward from here are Exmouth, and Carnarvon. The Carnarvon district, 612 miles northwest of Perth, raises sheep and, in the irrigated land along the Gascoyne River, tropical fruits and beans. A NASA Tracking Station on Northwest Cape was being built by the U.S. Navy with a very low frequency radio station which would have a new permanent town around it, and this was Exmouth.

At Onslow we camped at a caravan park right on the beach under some trees and within half a block of "downtown." The town had blue ocean running on each side of it, being on a peninsula of land stretching right out into the Indian Ocean. The breeze sighing through American southwest tamarisk trees was delightfully cool to our parched desert senses. We swam in the ocean that evening, later, carefully asking first about sharks.

The tamarisk trees are today one of the species condemned in the so-called science of "phreatrophyte control," and in many places are being "treated" by chemical defoliants. These trees, along with cottonwoods, pinons, cedars, mesquite, chaparral, and greasewood— for which Australia has its own counterparts in every case—hold back and consume a great deal of runoff water in their root systems. In so doing they hold back floods and soil erosion in an otherwise bare land, but it is theorized that if they were gone, grass would grow, which is more nutritious for cattle.

At Onslow you needed only to pause a moment to give thanks to nature for the wonderful services given by desert scrub, which modern man is apt to underestimate. They are nature's own cooling and air-conditioning services throughout vast areas of the world, moderating otherwise intolerable temperatures, and it is due to this vegetation that life exists at all.

I wandered over to the town hotel which had all its battered doors hanging open. It was unbelievable. It had the usual three bars of the old roadside inn of Australia: one pub or public bar, where the public is regarded as being comprised of white men, only; one saloon used only by the blacks (many roadside inns in Western Australia serve the blacks through a window on the side opening to the

149

outdoors); and one ladies lounge, whose design was to isolate the female sex in that same queer attitude of propriety as that in which blacks are isolated.

All the rooms of the inn were in an equal condition of ancient decrepitude, yet this careful segregation of race and sex existed, something out of another age, carried on in the one tiny spot of habitation which was separated from all other oases by over three hundred miles in each direction. In practical application, however, the class segregation of people was mitigated by the paucity of space and arrangements. In practice everybody more or less fraternized, and all were most amiable there among the termites and cobwebs, the pitted concrete walls, and perhaps some dried vomit on the floor dating from the 1880s, who knows?

Entering the little cubicle called the ladies lounge, which is frequented by both men and women, I brought a short beer from the window adjoining the pub, and sank down in filthy clothes among the filthy, weathered wanderers settled there, while a flirtatious black man with large red eyes waved at me gaily from the adjoining open doorway to "his" room only a few feet away.

A glance about told me to my satisfaction that I was properly turned out for the occasion. My companions on the hard benches were two white men who looked the picture of dirt, poverty, and even illness. "He's quite an individuality around here," the innkeeper told me. The rugged old man was encrusted with red dust into the pores of his skin and the rings of his neck. His summer shorts revealed shins discolored from old wounds and scabby sores, some of which had knotted bumps. His arms and hands and face had sores and scars.

It wasn't leprosy. This was just the old Barcoo Rot. That's what they call it in north Australia—the ulcers developing from bumps, bruises, scratches and rope burns in the course of a working life out here. It is common to all the deserts of the world. In our southwest the last of it seems to have vanished, due to better housing and better hygiene, perhaps. In the U.S. southwest it was called Desert Sore. It never was so severe as here because our southwest lies as much as 32 degrees from the Equator.

The old man (he was eighty) had put in a full day's work in the broiling sun today, work which would probably have killed a college athlete. He was just a tough old death adder, as they call them in Australia.

His red-rimmed pale watery eyes looked out like those of some whipped animal from the battering he had received all his life from the elements, but he was still game and ready to go.

Another man I talked with briefly was a 67-year-old prospector. He looked like a starvation victim from some concentration camp, and I didn't believe him when he described to me his affluence, his vacation flights to Perth, and his mineral strikes. I believed him to be a welfare case, but proud. Imagine my surprise the following day when a woman in the park laundry told me that the old prospector really had found gold earlier, and was quite well off.

We were now paralleling the coast of the Indian Ocean north of Perth, and the wildflowers which grow along this coast, in a Mediterranean-like climate, are unique. We were lucky. As we drove south out of the tropics we were in time to catch many species which flower late in summer here, and the formations we saw now were fantastic.

In spring motorists drive up this road in droves coming from Perth. With the great love of flowers possessed by the English races, they journey forth with their friends, and tourists come on treks hundreds of miles to try to see some of the *seven thousand* species.

Plant life is actually less than 10 percent indigenous, but it is marvelous in its adaptations. Most species can be seen elsewhere, many invaders coming from the Malayan region, even extending to Tasmania—but it was a world of exotics to American eyes.

There was always a large group of cosmopolitan plants even before white man. How did they get here? The "high spine of the Andes" is suggested by some botanists as a possible migration route between the Northern and Southern Hemispheres.

The great majority of the endemic species are evergreen trees or shrubs which produce flowers during a short, hot spring. These are highly adapted to drought and to poverty-stricken soils. Many are fantastically fire-resistant.

But the thousand miles of coast north of Perth along the Indian Ocean has the truly unique flora of great sand plains, comparable on earth only to the South African Cape. The Western flora is thought to have had an exceptionally long, undisturbed development, shel-

151

tered between ocean and desert, springing from a land surface as ancient as any on earth. Here plants developed over ages unaffected by any major upheavals which elsewhere formed mountains or broke ancient lines of plant evolution by uplifting, submergence, or volcanic eruption. They evolved here in exceptional richness along the Indian Ocean strip, developing a copious nectar flow to enhance their chances of survival and self-perpetuation, glowing with gilded, bronze flowers of rigid, wire-like structure; or inventing blooms that are hard, waxen, and finely sculptured, or which have the touch of velvet gloves; or massing small blooms together densely clustered to form cylindrical, conical, or spherical heads, often very large, covered with wax to keep their moisture in.

In the better-watered coastal belts of the continent the original vegetation was a mosaic dominated by a particular species, such as white box, white ironbark, yellow box, and so on. Here the dominant plant form was the multi-variety banksia. Each belt had its own topography, soil, climate, fauna, and flora. But with "pasture improvements" these plant communities disappear and converge everywhere into one more or less uniform cow pasture, nothing else. Even where large native trees were retained the associated ground flora has been destroyed all over Australia for the benefit of livestock.

R.L. Sprecht, an Australian botanist, showed that weeds from farms have taken over most heathlands in Australia as the result of the use of superphosphates. Near Sydney weeds now form one fourth of the total flora. In Queensland 578 introduced weeds immediately moved into the native bush, spreading from roadside and railroad line. The same was becoming true of Perth's environment and the West Coast now, but the degenerating process was not as fast due to lack of people and slower "development" out West. Dozens of species of plants and flowers are probably becoming extinct along this highway now, with decline of healthy, whole plant communities upon which the individual plant depends.

We marveled to see the banksia along here. Their flowers grew in tall spikes on the bushes, a many-branched forest of elaborate candelabra. The huge, honey-oozing flowers grew strong to enable nocturnal-feeding honey possums to climb over them, their sensitive dark eyes probing the night and long, flickering tongues probing deep into each bloom for the nectars found therein. "Ever-lastings" or straw flowers, kangaroo paws, the famed blue leschenaultia, the

152

felted and woolly lamb's tail; gold, bronze, and coppery dyandra; dry-country or sun orchids; lilies; the four-foot-tall verticordia supporting great flower umbrellas of cream or gold—all are here. There are blooms fed upon at night by a little honey-eating muskrat; or by day, by the tawny-crowned honeyeater and such other glutinous and disreputable birds as you can hardly imagine. Eremophila maculata is a bird-pollinated shrub widely distributed in arid inland regions of Western Australia. It is visited slyly by the spiny-cheeked honeyeater and the yellow-throated miner. An excellent example of a flower adapted just for birds, its color is in the brightest spectrum of bird vision—scarlet!—and the flower tubes have been fabricated by the Great Flower Man in the Sky so as to guide the beak into a position that brings the protruding anthers hard against the bird's forehead, covering his plumage with gobs of pollen.

Here on the sandplains when heaths and mallees are flowering, an unceasing song fills the air, wafted lightly from far away, then near at hand, bell-like notes, melodies strong, then faint, gay, and saucy, or sometimes sad with that strange poignancy of a fragile beauty which trembles upon the arched earth. The flowers are shaped to make birds and mammals their messengers.

Even among the parrots there are some, lorikeets, which have taken to a diet of nectar. Their brush-tipped tongues enable them to exploit the wealth of the flowering eucalypt forests.

A rare species of carnivorous marsupial, rediscovered after being "lost" for eighty-three years, is the dibbler. It climbs nimbly over the wire-brush flower spikes, living, apparently, by eating some eleven species of banksia upon which it is totally dependent.

How do the highly-evolved mammals get the nutrition they need from feeding merely upon honey, which has no discernible vitamins or minerals? How is such nutrition accomplished in "wastelands" which we know have deficiencies in practically every trace mineral? The fur of the marsupials as well as the plumage of birds probing for nectar insures the propagation of this special plant world, while these creatures scurry busily about, collecting, carrying, and spreading the golden pollen dust from flower to flower and from plant to plant throughout the year. The proximity of the Indian Ocean enables these nectar activities and wild prolific blossomings to go on the year round, as the burgeoning of many species always overlaps with the decline of others, making the flower ecology possible.

153

Many of the large, spectacular western wildflowers could not be pollinated by insects. Some bar all but the most minute insects from their nectary, which will open only to the forceful thrust of a demanding bird beak. Or, they simply rebuff insects by omitting all of the facilities generally offered by flowers to insects. Those insects which do manage to enter the "birds only" flowers serve as an added lure for birds.

No particular wildflower family has a monopoly on bird-pollination, but the banksia family, the eucalypt family, and the pea family are outstanding in this. Any flower which is large or has a rigid, strong spike or head, has pollen dispensed and received an inch or more from the site of the nectary, and which is colored red to yellow may be suspected as bird pollinated, our experts tell us. Brilliant color, bizarre shape, large size: these are bird flowers! The flowers most often pollinated by butterflies are pink, and insect-pollinated flowers tend to be blue and violet and green.

The wanderer or monarch butterfly is found here. Indigenous to America, it was first seen in Queensland in 1871, and is believed to have entered Australia via various Pacific Islands and New Guinea by powers of natural dispersal, for in North America this species undertakes long migratory flights south in the fall of the year. The females lay eggs as they go, thus assuring the population of all areas. In spring in North America the monarchs return northward again, as birds do. It is believed that monarch migration of the same sort may now take place in Australia, as a withdrawal from the cold of the southern winter.

Of course, numbers of wasps and bees also contribute to the wildflower picture. These insects have been proven to prefer notched and scalloped petals, especially those with spots and special markings to guide them to the hidden nectar source. The deeper the nectar, the more elaborately developed these markings of flowers tend to be. At times the nectar-guide markings are present but invisible to human sight, being marked in ultraviolet, or in trails of scent. The preferred color of enticement here is violet-purple.

The fast-flying hawk moth hovers on slender wings while uncurling a long, thread-thin tongue which can reach deep into a trumpet-shaped flower. This moth feeds only at dusk. A soft dynamo-hum announces the moth's arrival. Quickly it pushes into the floral tube with head and back brushing under the anthers and

154

the tip of its long proboscis finding the hidden spot of nectar deep within the flower. Within a fraction of a second it is backing out, wings ablur, and with an audible hum it lifts away, flying straight and fast to the next flower. The plant is calystegia sepium. It is a creeper which climbs and covers the stunted mulga trees along claypan watercourses of the northwest. The flower is a deep rose. The moth, when he hovers and spreads his wings just at dusk, has two back wings which exactly simulate the rose petals of the flower he drinks from. Clearly, this insect and plant have evolved together.

By their shape the flowers ensure that pollen is distributed among plants only of their own species, and not wastefully scattered among other forms of flower. The flowers encourage "flower constancy" among their insect visitors by giving exclusive feeding rights to very few types of insects. In the case of the hawk moth few other insects could reach the hidden nectar. Therefore, the arrangement insures that there is an abundant supply for the chosen pollinator. Thus this flower fulfills its promise for the chosen insect, and for him only, and the insect in turn concentrates upon this flower where it has exclusive rights.

The beautiful rainbow plant has insect-trap hairs on its stem, and is nourished by insect bodies. Yet certain very tiny insects live as freeloaders on this plant, running along the stem without being caught, and dining upon less fortunate larger species trapped by the plant. This is one of two species of a family, the byblidaceae, found only in Western Australia.

In Western Australia we were to see the orange-tipped Christmas tree, so called because it blooms at Christmas time, and "throws wide its blazing incandescence."

The black boy tree ferns made me think of yucca. They seemed to be made of the same kind of pithy, reedy material, and were of a similar height, growing to four and sometimes seven feet or so. With their neat "grass skirts" hanging above a blackened, resinous tree trunk, each almost seems to start to life as some grass-skirted human being, especially as each carries a slender wooden vertical spike pointed straight aloft, like a spear. This is why the pioneers named this growth the black boy.

It was depressing to come again into a world of fences lining the highway on either hand. I had not expected them to stretch out hundreds of miles north of Perth. Less than eight thousand people live north of Perth, but these few have already turned the coast area completely to the pastoral business and to wheat growing. We found here, as always, that the places of grandeur or novelty were scattered out across vast distances in a land that was too often desolate, or offered nothing for the tourist but the private, fenced-in, often bare properties of the farmer and grazier—upon which we camped in quarries or stubble, between the fence rows.

The lovers of flowers, sand deserts, and heaths—the general public—while numerically far greater than the food growers, here as in America had little power against the commercial interests of great companies who lease the lands from an economically-oriented government to produce, produce, produce. Here the very arm of government itself in the name of science, the C.S.I.R.O., continues to be pressed to find ever more "economical" means to clear the land for conversion to crops, and biologists are hired under "Pest Control Division" to eradicate the dingoes.

Another type of plant community which naturalists are trying to save is the heath. So far only in South Australia had we seen a little of the heath as it used to be. In its pure, treeless form the heath is in coastal patches, such as between Geraldton and Perth, and from Albany to past Esperance (southwest corner of Western Australia), and in Tasmania. The related heath forest occupies enormous areas nearby. Regarded as "waste scrublands" which are useless for agriculture or grazing, the heaths fascinate the soil scientist because they offer a laboratory for the study of soil formation, of soil-moisture relationships, fire resistance, and mineral nutrition.

Heathland soils are utterly deficient in phosphorus and in most of the chemical elements deemed essential to plant and animal life. Yet, strangely, hundreds of native species flourish on the heaths and grow sturdier than pampered agricultural crops do on improved soils! Why? Work in these laboratories of nature might unlock the mystery. Therefore, the precious heaths should be preserved in every Australian state, a really serious matter because the new superphosphate treatment will change the whole face of the continent before we can fully understand these relationships. The danger is especially acute along the West Coast since the flora of the great sand plains here is unique.

An Australian patriot, Jeff Carter, in his book *Outback in Focus*, maintains that the Outback is slowly winning against modern man

156

with each succeeding drought, because it cannot stand up to the pounding of hooves, the burden of mass grazing asked of it. He describes it as "that huge tract of dry inland. . .covering three-fourths of our continent, which remains beyond the frontiers of agriculture." (This author excludes the Kimberleys and north Queensland because they are special regions having the Wet, and he did not go to Western Australia.)

Jeff Carter speaks of a sick Outback, of hundreds of abandoned ranches, and he advises that we all go talk with the geographers and botanists whose business this subject is, and get statistics on grazing rates since the 1890s. Each year, he says, it takes more acreage to graze one animal. The graziers may go down beneath the sands they tread, he says, and all of us with them, unless they are curbed.

He speaks of the population of the Outback, and I found that we had seen most of the traditional Outback "individualities": graziers and station blacks, tank sinkers, water borers, truck drivers, bush pilots, the shopkeepers, and publicans. "The frontier era hasn't ended yet," he tells us, "not by a long chalk. There are still hard-bitten men who live by the gun. They are the hunters . . . of kangaroo, rabbit, and wild goat. When times are good, a shooter can earn . . . for perhaps five months of the year, two hundred dollars a week, gross. But times are tough, usually. The hunters turn to shooting a variety of animals for their scalps: dingoes, brumbies, camels. . . ."

New people coming to the Outback are modern prospectors for uranium, manganese, bauxite, natural gas, and oil. You have to drive to special places, or fly, to see some of them. Modern machines are building roads and settlements. "But their form of settlement," predicts this thoughtful author, "dotted here and there. . . will bring little change to the Outback in general. Most products are taken away in crude form, and processed elsewhere." Just like the oldtimers, the newcomers were all profiteers and transients on walkabout, and their efforts were all extractive, putting nothing back but holes in the ground—the same old pattern.

The retreat of man from deserts is shown everywhere by the evidence of history. "Towns" or map names we visited, as this author points out, "exist for the benefit of local residents. The pub is a meeting place for locals, who see each other perhaps only a couple of times a year. There is little social or community life in the Outback, for there are not enough people for it. Some buildings are little more than humpies. One or two may be small homesteads with wide verandas, trellised and fly-wired, with low roof lines." That is Outback life: it just doesn't impress one as being permanent or real.

The Never-Never or Outback is rightly named, I concluded. The further you follow that track the further it fades away. You keep thinking you are really going to find something out there. Yet all the while even the distant mountain ranges recede, turning into low hills as you go on, and you have passed through them and out the other side, to find nothing there but a mirage of your dreams in the sky.

This is Australia. But Australia is much else. It is birds singing everywhere, the villages of people filled with the delightful presence of birds. Australia is clean-scrubbed, rosy babies, and gentle, patient, womanly women.

Australian voices are hushed, soft, gentle, cheery, melodious, a moderate society not given to extremism. You can camp closely-packed in a caravan park with a hundred people about you, and hear the crickets at night. May it always be this way! (But the young ones are beginning to carry their loud transistors now.)

Even big cities have that wonderful stillness. The fire and police and ambulance sirens in cities are musical, with their little ding-dong chimes tinkling. They don't seem to have many customers. Restaurants are hushed, even night clubs not raucous or shrill, their tribal drumbeat being carried out in far lower decibels than those with which we in the U.S. are accustomed to being assaulted, and the entertainment invariably in good taste. Water is delicious, having little or no chlorine added. Sleep in Australia is delightful beyond compare. The air is sweet.

Fruits and vegetables at roadside stands are absolutely the most plump, succulent, and delightful to see and to eat I ever had. Cauliflowers grow enormous and are as sweet as they look. The candies and pastries are of mouth-watering quality, made by European immigrants using pure Australian butter and cream. Some may have real alcoholic cordials inside—yum! Shops serve morning as well as afternoon teas, replete with yummies of whipped cream.

With plenty of good food, the Australians do not gorge to the extent that Americans do. There may well be other obscure reasons yet to be uncovered by science, but the fact is that cases of obesity

158

among the Australian city public are rare in spite of all the food available to them, because something unspoken in the culture taboos the "second helping."

The greenbelt countryside of Australia simply sparkles. It is fresh beyond anything Americans know. The eyes feast. The nerves relax. Such a greenbelt is the West Coast all around Perth.

I awoke in my sleeping bag under a big bush, which had successfully kept off the heavy dew. Each of the campers lay under such a bush that morning on a hillside overlooking Horricks Beach, almost to Perth.

We looked around cautiously as we pulled out gray, gnarled sticks for our breakfast fire, preparing for a swim in the cold, blue breakers of the Indian Ocean below. One of those roots turned out to be our old friend the sleepy lizard, or western shingleback. His color was gray here, like the roots. Others in the dunes could be death adders. We were bush wise. The spring was still fresh here, and snakes could be irritable, or stupid. We watched where we stepped, and what we grabbed.

Just three hundred miles to go now to the Perth metropolis. We all voted for a day of swimming, and say, that Indian Ocean in these latitudes was cold!

Under a big bush overlooking Horricks Beach I sat, musing and trying unsuccessfully to think about adjusting to city life.

Coming swiftly down along the "bitumen" you missed the dirt road you were used to, and you felt the expectant land undergoing a transformation from wide open desert to scrub forest and real forest, as you crossed the Murchison River (good-bye, dear crocodiles, is this forever?) on a real bridge into valuable sheeplands and wheatlands all *fenced* so that there was hardly any place to camp at all, except for sneaky sly old experts.

The Mobil Company had introduced their stations, with smiling and helpful attendants and little restaurants adjoining, where *free* glasses of water were served without complaint, and "pline" ice cream took the place of Outback beer. Showers at twenty cents were thoughtfully provided to travelers at each restaurant stop. But now our surroundings lacked Adventure. The saddest moment was when Ann said to the waitress: "Where does the Outback begin, or end? About here, do you think?"

"I don't know," the waitress said. "I never heard of it."

159

Chapter 12

PERTH

The Bibulmum tribes who roamed the fertile coastal plains upon which the city of Perth today stands and the delectable uplands of the Darling Ranges, were the largest homogeneous group in all Australia, says Daisy Bates in *The Passing of the Aborigines.*

They were gentle and religious, and they "sat down" in a rich country teeming with fauna, their very name signifying "many breasts" from the fecundity of their region. There were seventy groups linked by one basic language. Their homeland covered hundreds of square miles, extending from around Geraldton, three-hundred miles north of Perth to Esperance, nearly a thousand-mile swing around the southwest bottom of the continent, in the great Karri forest. They were the only natives in Australian history who were not cannibals—possibly because they didn't need the meat.

Their only god was *woggal,* the serpent-god of earth, sky, and sea, who punished evil-doers seldom. Their tools were paleolithic: the spear and the club. Women carried the digging stick, the scoop of bark or shell called a collamon, and a kangaroo skin bag. A campfire for winter warmth and a bough shade for sun shelter were their only homes. Fire was made by friction drill stick applied to the flower-stem of the resinous black boy tree fern. These people did not use the boomerang.

The first white men landed on the banks of the Swan River—named after the West's famous black swans—in 1829. Strangely, the natives here, like the Aztecs and Toltecs of Mexico, had rumors about white men coming long before white men ever came to their shores. In Western Australia the natives believed these visitors to be the returned spirits of their own dead.

"The pioneers of Western Australia were noble men and women," Daisy Bates says. "Nearly all of them were above reproach, and more than kindly in their treatment of the Aborigines. There is evidence that they did everything in their power for the preservation and betterment of the race. Schools were established as early as 1831, and reserve sanctuaries, with interpreters and ration-givers, and government inspectors. There were innumerable systematic schemes on the part of religious organizations, social organizations, and private persons. . . . Missions of all kinds were established throughout the Bibulmum area. The most outstanding of these was undoubtedly the great Benedictine Mission of New Norcia, eighty miles north of Perth [we drove right past this beautiful estate], founded by Don Salvado in 1846, among the dingo-totem tribes of the Victoria Plain.

"But, children of the woodland, dwelling in a squalor that could not be avoided in stone-walled houses, closed in from the air that was their breath of life faded away and died."

When we arrived at Perth it was to find a great garden city covering over two thousand square miles. Perth is the hub of an enormous 975,920-square-mile state, whose whole population numbers just one million souls.

Because people were pouring in here from the east in an ever-accelerating westward migration, accommodations were hard-pressed, and we scoured the city to find a place to stay. Only one caravan park in this city accommodated tents, and in this park there was only one good shade tree for pitching a tent under.

Concealing Laddie inside the Jeep, for the sign here said: "Dogs strictly prohibited," the two dusty vehicles entered the leafy glen of Perth Caravan Park, only to find that due to charitable feelings of the owners, practically all the dogs in Western Australia, of all sizes and shapes, were peaking out on their leashes on every hand.

In short order the two vehicles were pulled up, fees deposited at headquarters, food purchased at the kiosk, gents and ladies catacomb keys handed over, and the blue tent pitched beneath the one great sheltering tree. There was a small swimming pool. The season was into the hottest peak of summer. Destiny had it that we were to live here a number of weeks, as the girls and I awaited those tenuous arrangements which would enable us to embark upon the next, very radical, phase of our adventure.

Swimming in the ocean was available at many glorious beaches. Helicopter patrols and shark nets are widely used at Australian swimming resorts, and I cautioned my mob to be careful. "Australia is a continent, surrounded by hungry sharks," I reminded them.

"Mother, *all* continents are surrounded by hungry sharks!" Ann retorted. I had not thought about it that way before.

It was a time for catching up with oneself, at Perth. A time for learning about cities and culture, people and customs, even if due to the restrictions of life with Laddie, some of our best friends were dogs.

One of the things I tried to master was the telephone. My girls were much better at it than I. I had been in correspondence with a number of Perth people who were expecting us. It went rather like this, along the road:

"Please, where is a telephone booth?"

Passerby: "There are two kinds. Which one do you want?"

Me: "Well, ahem, ah—what are the kinds?"

Passerby: "Well, there is the red booth and then there is the white booth."

Me: "But which one should I have?"

Passerby: "Ye can take yer choice. The red booth is for public use on private property. The white is on public property and it is fer private use."

Me: "I see. Well—uh, thank you very much."

Passerby: "Don't mention it, Cheerio."

Our Jeep found a red booth. I hailed another passerby.

"Ye just puts in a two-cent piece in the one slot, and a five-cent in the other, which is really sixpence as the telephones,

162

ye know, haven't all been converted over to the decimal system
yet; and ye just don't pay no attention to these directions here,
they're obsolete, but you push this button here—see this button?—
and ye have yer call, soon as the operator answers. It takes both
coins to do it. Here, hang on. I'll do it for you. Yer a Yank,
aren't ye? Just takin' a look around?"

"Just takin' a look around," I explained.

Presently a perceptive Eastern executive of *Comalco
Aluminium* arrived at the tent. He took us right over to the plant.
Here we were introduced around to everyone. We at once solicited
their kind help in getting our trailer containing our proper clothes
shipped by rail to Perth from Port Pirie. They called *Comalco*
headquarters at Melbourne to send our mail out now.

"We were expecting you for a long time," the executive
said. "Guess you're good friends with Kaiser Aluminum in the
U.S.?" (I wasn't, but that would have been nice.) "Well, we're
here to do everything we can to make your stay a pleasant one,
you and your delightful daughters. This office will be yours"—
I followed my velvet-voiced host timidly into an unused office,
complete with carpeting polished desk, telephone—"and the secretary will be glad to help you with anything you need. You will
soon have a working knowledge of our aluminium fabrication plant
here. . . . Actually, we don't have anyone to fill this office right now,
so you might as well. . . ."

After that, I went almost every day to my office. This seemed
to be what you should do. If an office is given you, you go there.

After I got my office I made all my telephone calls from there,
but even this was not as easy as it looked because the Perth Telephone circuits were terribly overloaded.

Art Linkletter's man out at the ranch near Esperance said on
long distance that he would prefer that we defer coming down
there until after the New Year. I called my contact with the
Norwegian line of freighters that we contemplated a ride with sometime. The girls and I went to dinner then in a beautiful little
home having a formal garden high upon the hillside in the Darling
Ranges, overlooking the lights of Perth. The wife was a fifth generation Perth girl. The agent for the shipping lines, her husband,
was a former liaison officer in the British Royal Navy who had had
a lifetime of experience in carrying out delicate British missions in

163

India and Southeast Asia, and for some years now served the Knutson Line of freighters, on Australia's West Coast. Our hope: tickets to somewhere. Fun and travel, anywhere in the perimeter of that fascinating world known as Australasia.

"I know how Americans are," our English host, a man of great charm and dignity, declared. "I've studied them a great deal. I've read correspondence from America, and I think that we can, according to our directors of the Line, provide you with a ticket."

"There are three of us. One ticket only, you mean?"

"That's what the correspondence indicates," he told us with dignity. We thought that over.

On another day he and his fellow director took me alone to a beautiful lunch at the Palace Hotel.

"Well, where will the ticket be to?" the kids asked when I got home to the tent.

"I'm not sure. Some place. I had a cocktail. I think the ship takes you away from Australia for *two months*. Who wants to go?"

It was finally decided that Jean would be the one. It seemed appropriate for her nineteenth birthday a few months hence. Such trips must be booked months in advance. There would be two months of sailing those seas beyond north Australia along the coast of Malaya, to Port Swettenham, to Penang Island, Hong Kong, Manila, and four visits into the port of Singapore, shuttling cargo.

On another day I used my office telephone to call the Ansett Airlines in downtown Perth, and I also went there and met their people. Ansett is Australia's largest domestic airline. It is owned and operated by a man who might be called the Howard Hughes of Australia, a real Australian entrepreneur. He had had quite a battle, earlier, to get it away from government ownership, and had actually accomplished this miracle. It is, I can say now, along with Comalco and a few others, one of the best-run and greatest going concerns in Australia.

In Melbourne at the beginning I had gone to the Ansett central office. You can imagine how lucky I felt when their chief of public relations, who was authorized to issue complimentary tickets to special persons, turned out to be a reader of my Arctic books for twenty years. He had a wonderful personality, that man, and accepted me into miteship at first sight.

164

But many Aussies, even at top business levels, do not like to write letters, and it was the Perth office of Ansett that must actually book the Tasmania flights I hoped for out of Perth, where all-time human traffic jammed the facilities. I kept making calls East, thanks to my telephone, but time kept going by and nothing happened.

Meanwhile from my office I called our old Alcoa friends. It took two days to get through, because for one whole day their telephone lines were knocked out and they were incommunicado. They were just down the shore. Alcoa was expecting us to visit their great bauxite ore refineries where the raw alumina was made.

A full day was spent, including lunch, with Alcoa, which had leased 4,000 square miles of land for surface mining of bauxite south of the city. They dug 42,000 tons off the surface each week to supply their Kwinana plant, working two shifts of nine hours for a five-and-a-half-day week, with seventy men in the working crew. They had hired the first security officer in a country where the word "security" was still unknown. A former British Royal Navy officer again, he took us about. We attended a social hour given for an American minerals consultant who was to return to America. There was to be a company Christmas dance.

"Say, how about that?" I asked our security friend. "Could the girls and I attend the dance?" He seemed surprised that we might want to. I hoped I hadn't shocked him. He had little awareness of the American democratic tradition.

I always had this mother's inner vision of my girls suddenly bursting forth like butterflies and discovering the joys of the waltz and the two-step.

"I'll see what I can do." Presently, tickets were arranged.

Jean refused to go. Ann went with me, escorted by a Monash University boy from Melbourne who was taking the summer holidays at our park, living in a tent "next door."

As the three of us entered the private club which had been let to the Alcoa labor for the occasion, a man near my own age hailed me from the bar.

"Come. Set down. Have a beer with me," he said.

The evening was early yet. Ann was obliged to pass on through the open doorway to the inner hall. "It's a private club," I hissed. It's all right."

"Mother, my date is shocked. Women don't speak to strange men. . . ."

"But in a private club. . . ."

Ann was gone, floating, serene, secure with her escort. She looked gorgeous because I had just spent a small fortune on clothes for her fast-growing Perth social life, and it looked as if she might become a butterfly, and really enjoy her youth at last as I thought it should be enjoyed.

I felt shy here, but I had, after all, been guested by companies and industrial plants for years in lecture touring, so to my mind a friendly response to the hello seemed as right as "Swan Lager Refreshes." No one told me the name of the game in Australia. I'm not sure I know the name of the game yet, but I was to learn that Australian rules are rough.

Within one Swan Lager and ten minutes this friendly encounter within a private sports and social club became a total disaster. Even as I slipped onto the miniature stool on its spidery legs, a seat built for crickets, certainly not people, and faced the bar with its terrycloth bath towels to absorb the drippings, I felt uncomfortable. But I introduced myself, with my card, to the man and to his pugilistic and pugnacious-looking mite of neanderthal hairline and brick-red face, out of which stared suspicious little pig eyes.

"Are you sure I'm not interrupting?"

"This is a private club," the man reassured me. "Women set at this bar all the time."

He informed me that he was assistant to the club secretary, and especially considering his position in the club he was sure that no one could possibly object if I sat here. Unimpressed with a glance at my card, he threw it down in the wet towels.

I started asking him questions about the difference between pubs, bars, and lounges in Western Australia. It came down to: only men will be served in pubs. Only men and bad women. The only place "decent women" are served is in the lounges, and these admit only women with escorts as a rule. There is no law about it. But custom is stronger than law. (Ask any sociologist.)

But again, he elaborated pontifically, it may all depend upon the situation and each town itself. A woman has to "feel out the atmosphere," he advised. He recognized uneasily that custom was changing and the times were becoming more lenient to women.

166

We weren't doing well in our conversation, yet I felt fascinated by the trap of argument. There were raw nerves here, lying just below the surface, which hinted at information about people far more important than the mere barroom freedom of men. It is something "different" in this society which all overseas visitors sense very soon after their arrival, and which most are nonplused to understand.

"Well you could go to the dance hall," the man was saying. "But you would have to sit there and wait for some man to ask you to dance. Probably nobody would ask you and you would be a wall-flower."

My hackles were rising. "I should think you'd feel ashamed of yourself to talk to a visitor to your country, a stranger to the customs, in this way."

"We like our customs, and don't think you can come here and change them," he said.

"Nobody would ask you to dance and you would be a *Wallflower*," he repeated coarsely. (He must have got results with this line with other women.) "*Wallflower*. That's what we call it. That's a woman that sits by the wall and nobody wants at all. . . . do you know what a wallflower is?"

"We were not even discussing the subject of dancing," I retorted. "I have a bum neck, so dancing doesn't affect my life one way or another."

"Bum!" he seized on that, gleefully. "What do you call that, eh? Bum?"

"Bum neck. That's what we call a lame neck."

"What you mean to say is a crook neck," the pugilist corrected me, not unkindly. "Yore 'bum' is what you set on. We don't use that word here in proper society. It's not a decent word that decent people use."

Then, to my utter astonishment, he reached over suddenly and ran his hand right through my hair, ruffling it up on end, and I knew he wanted to pull it. His eyes glinted.

I fled, with as much dignity as I could muster, leaving him laughing with his friend, having put the woman on the run.

It was difficult, as I walked away from that encounter and re-joined my own group, where we sat and watched the Irish-jig-like pounding and thumping feet of the lusty dancers to a shaking floor,

167

to keep in mind that my good friends in Australia would far out-number in memory the unpleasant jolts I received.

I did not know if such rudenesses were an anachronism of the isolated continent they lived in or were more the result of modern times. Chivalry may have bloomed there in its time and in its way, but now, as everywhere, great social changes were on the brink. The intellectuals and the anti-intellectuals are always a part of every society. In normal, stable times they move in their own circles and tend to ignore each other. But in times of great social change their awareness of each other becomes heightened, and the name of the game is Uproar, or Hate.

The overthrow of Victorianism, with its English gentleman's code, its restraints on women, its sharp division of classes, its hypo-cricies, was even yet violently occurring in my own country, and in Australia the overthrow of Victorianism is just beginning.

In the East I had already seen a bit of the old-school-tie non-sense at private dinner parties. The masters of the Victorian way of life were capable of being pompous and effete despots. This type of Australian who apes the upperclass British is dubbed a "pom" or "pommie"—a slang term used by the working classes for the hated English. (The word may come from "pomegranate" and depicts the red, sunburned face that has not yet become accustomed to the Australian sun.)

A female child is born into a culture that does not expect or permit her to have any real determination about the course of her own life. A strong and wise male is expected to come along and decide all things for her.

What happens to those females for whom no one comes along is not mentioned. Not mentioned either in this Victorian code, much as in the U.S. of forty years ago and less, is what would happen when a female links her life with some all-powerful, god-like man who turns out to be neither wise nor kind, but a cad.

There is scant recourse in law for women in Australia. No state has divorce laws. It is a federal matter, one of the few things, in fact, with which the federal government is concerned.

Divorce takes five years, and can be obtained only on grounds of adultery. Should a wife flee her husband's roof for whatever reason, be it dangerous insanity, drunkenness or beatings, or whatnot, the law will not grant her any means of support until after six months. Consequently, most women have long thoughts about fleeing the most untenable marriage. The upper classes, however, may handle these matters with a degree of chivalry becoming to a gentleman, a prominent lawyer informed me. Here, custom may all but supercede the law. The great middle classes for whom the laws were set up to control their "morality," lack the chivalrous tradition. The middle and lower classes suffer much hardship from these laws.

In the blue tent at Perth I contentedly cooked on the little burner and sat at our camp table, while once again the rustling leaves made patterns in blue in the passing breeze—for Perth has the benefit of cooling ocean breezes every afternoon in summer—and the kookaburras cackled in the tall trees.

The kookaburra is one of Australia's most loved birds. Largest of the kingfisher family, he came originally from the East, and, like us, was a relative newcomer to Western Australia.

Hans had gone to work for the government railways. Having come from Switzerland to make tiny timing devices for the military, he now turned his considerable talents to engines with larger wheels.

"Hans, what do you do that for?" It was the boss, coming along through the vast railroad shops, taking a look at the new bloke at work in the grease pit.

Hans summoned his English quickly. "Well, you see, Mr. Ross, It is necessary. You do not do that before? Well, you see it is best to use plenty oil like this, here in all these places on the engine, for to stop the rust."

"Ah, well," replied the boss, gruffly. No one had done that bit of extra oiling before. "Ah, well, fair enough," said the boss, and walked self-importantly on.

"Good-oh!" said Jean to Hans, back at the tent at day's end, when Hans expressed his discouragement with union loafers, the bungling, the lack of oil in the machinery, and the don't care attitudes about train wheels. "Australia needs men like you."

"But it is really so easy," he replied, with his usual modesty. "It is too easy life. I get lazy." He who had taught himself English within a year now discovered that he understood far more words than the Australian workingman. Just as important, he was trained in the European precision methods, without waste of man-hours. On his job all day he listened impatiently to the quarreling and gossiping, like cackling hens, of many who only hoped to get

169

out of doing any task beyond each individual gesture with wrench or screwdriver which was closely controlled by union contract terms. Hans was temporary labor here, for the time being.

It was difficult for the new Australian to take pride in his work while feeling the union monolith slowly closing in on him. He waited impatiently to get enough money to enable him to move on. There was no hope of promotion under the Aussie union system except by seniority. This advancement was automatic, not based on achievement. It offered just $1.00 per year wage increase each year for a man's lifetime!

"I am thinking," said Hans at the tent. "When I go back to Sydney pretty soon, there must be some big change. I have Swiss friends. Very smart friends, too. I make a quid in this country, maybe I go into technical business for myself."

Meanwhile the golden days sped by. I went to see high government officials and learned that they could arrange with the big mining companies for me to get company flights into the state's Outback areas. But, the Christmas season seemed the wrong time. The Swiss were away—Hans to work, and Helmut off to the beaches to lie in the sand and dream.

Helmut did not try to get work. We could sympathize fully with Hans, who, though he said little, was plainly supporting him. When he was not at the beach Helmut mostly seemed to sleep away the days in the boy's Volkswagen "Kombi."

Jean and Ann thought a bit about getting jobs, also, in their impatience. But it seemed better to hold off and wait for either a positive or negative answer from the Ansett Airlines, about the island of Tasmania. The girls found State employment services for women were separate and work menial. It was probably good for the girls to do much of nothing for a while, and just live day-by-day tent life under the tree.

A young girl in our caravan park came to have tea a number of times in the blue tent. Her parents, migrant English, had reared her in Australia. She married at sixteen, the legal age of consent, as also did her three sisters, each as fast as she could. They all married Australian men. All were miserable in their marriages.

"After the baby was born things just kept getting worse. He drank. I knew I would have to run away again, taking the baby, just as I run away from Mum and Dad. I met a Hindu once. Well, I

170

thought maybe I could live with him. But he left town. Any man, I thought. Any except an Aussie, they're terrible. Well, I was very lucky. I met Willie. And here we are.

"Willie is Egyptian. He is very good to the baby and me. I filed for divorce back East. But that will take five years. Willie hasn't been able to get work in Perth yet. We are pretty discouraged. And if that Aussie husband ever finds me, he'll kill me. My lawyer told me to hide."

We had Willie over to tea. He was handsome. A graduate engineer, he was intellectual and educated in England. The big development companies coming to Western Australia's frontier were begging for engineers of all kinds, but all Willie was offered was a menial job, far beneath his qualifications. It had been the same with the desperate couple in Queensland three thousand miles across the continent. The young couple believed the problem was his race. They still hoped there would be less prejudice out in the open West.

Zonta, a young married neighbor, dropped in. She was very pregnant. There was no recourse for her and her husband but to live in their tent because he did not make enough money to rent a house. You had to pay a rental agent a fee of around $25, and nothing could be obtained in the city during the holiday "tourist season" for much less than $150 a month. Zonta told Ann that, unfortunately, her husband did not want children. So she had agreed with him, as the price of marriage, to give up the baby for adoption when it came.

Then there was our wonderful friend "Swedish Gene." The boy Swede fell quite in love with Ann, from the very first day he came whooshing into the court on his trusty motorcycle, having "crossed the Nullarbor" in summer heat, with his sleeping bag, folded tent, canteen, and small provision aboard. To Swedish Gene the intellectual atmosphere of Australia was definitely deficient, and he intended to return to Sweden ultimately, after his long working holiday, mainly because of intellectual loneliness. He had held many and various jobs during three years of roaming and practicing the art of being young.

It was at this time that Ann decided to develop her social life in that wonderful city of Perth, and I must say that she did quite well.

Emerging from the tent each evening like some gorgeous

butterfly in glistening eye makeup, she was met by a suitor of a prominent old-line Perth family, and almost nightly did the clubs and was, correspondingly, in the newspaper social columns day by day.

Off to teas and balls! Now, to the theatre! Now a wedding and champagne reception! Next, the American Ascot Races, where no American horse has ever run due to the strict quarantine restrictions, and where Americans remained a social myth with the sole exception of butterfly Ann, sitting with the boy's mother and her lady friends in the family "box," with fans and parasols.

I was making some moves to meet the Premier of Western Australia. Ann met him easily at an informal backyard party. "He doesn't talk affairs of state when he's relaxing," Ann told me. Photographers came to the caravan park and photographed the Americans living in a tent.

Ann had met Clive two years before, when he had lived for a few days right next door to our house in Arizona during his world tour. Clive took thirty pieces of luggage with him, and when he returned to Perth triumphantly, he was more than ever the man of the world that his parents expected him to be. He was twenty-six.

It is customary in Australia for all the people of means and social position to send their youngsters on a trip abroad, so that they may learn to take their proper place in their own country, intelligently. It is a social necessity to make that trip.

I had always thought that Australians were a very democratic people, much like Americans (this too, is a bit of a myth). So it brought me up short when something arose in a conversation and Clive distinctly said, "I don't go with working people."

What kind of Australian was this? Now, when we could see him in his natural setting, we understood a bit better what he meant and the reasons for his views. By "working people," he had in mind a far cruder level of people than we meant when we referred to American working people. Also, what Clive had in mind was the stigma of the kind of working persons I had sat with at those pubs. He and his friends, would not dream of lowering themselves to this public level. They just did not think about "integration." They had invented neither the word nor the concept for it, and neither had the lower classes.

"What are you doing now, Clive?" was one of my first openings when he appeared at our tent. "Do you work?"

"Oh, yes." He smiled charmingly. "Of course I always knew I would go to work for father. The old man made me start at the bottom of the ladder, too. Eight hour day and that sort of thing. It's quite fun, really."

So Clive really did work, and he believed in certain kinds of work and achievement—but he was definitely not democratic. He was the culture of the British upper classes and their way of life transported to Australia from long ago, and still very much alive.

"Mother," said Ann, "Clive is very charming, isn't he? Did you get an eyeful of that very pale green suit with the long French tails for the reception? Clive is always so pleased with me because everywhere we go our clothes perfectly match each other. And his mother, she is so very charming and dear, and you should see all their charming friends, all so wonderful to me"—She was beginning to talk just like them, in a charming British accent—"but of course, I realize all the time that he is, you see, Mom, a pommie."

"Yes, he's a pom. Well, nothing wrong about that, I suppose. You could marry him and become like Lady Astor. She was an American girl from Virginia who married a man in the House of Lords and she ended by doing a stint in the British Parliament."

"Sometimes, Mother," she sighed softly, "I wonder who it is that I really am, and whatever will my life be like?"

"It takes many of us a lifetime to find out, dear. But I think you are doing just right now at seventeen. This genteel social life you have entered is something precious, in a way, which has disappeared from the world we come from. No mother could ask for more, at the moment. I wish that that sister of yours would take up pretty clothes and Victorian social life as you do, for it seems to me that perhaps she is missing something along the way that she ought to try."

"I don't miss it!" yapped Jean, from the high limb of our tree. "I hate it!"

"Oh, dear, I didn't know you were listening, dear. Ann and I were just having a talk."

"Why does she stay up in the tree?"

"I don't really know, Ann. But I guess it's all right, if she likes it. She'll come down from the tree when she reaches that point in her development when she is ready to."

"Never!" bawled Jean.

173

It was all very confusing just who we all were, actually, having left our own country and all. But it was just as confusing back home, too. Jean and Hans settled into one of the long, quiet weekends of mending, reading, and car tinkering. I thought about going to a meeting of the American Women's Club.

There were wives of overseas executives living in Perth. It was interesting to realize that, instantaneously upon landing, they set about with great energy creating their own natural habitat which they had left so far away at home. The club was raising money for "worthwhile charitable institutions," was making tours to Parliament House, was giving teen parties, playing bridge, entering exhibits in the Festival of Perth, bringing in lecturers, visiting art galleries, giving demonstrations on hair-styling and wigs, and planning a July Fourth service for American Independence Day at St. George's Cathedral. The Very Reverend John Hazelwood, Dean of Perth, was to speak upon the types and causes of prejudice before the club.

It was Saturday afternoon and Hans and Jean had decorated the tent, and so had Ann and Swedish Gene, with colored paper chain links, and a small Christmas tree stood in one corner with a growing collection of wrapped gifts.

"Our camera has arrived, Mom. It's being held in Customs at Melbourne right now, but it's on the way to Perth. This will be our real Christmas. They told me at Comalco."

The camera would be Ann's exclusive property when we went exploring again. Jean was the Expedition artist, carrying her little kit of papers and inks and pens and fixatives throughout the land. It was difficult to get Jean into the mood to draw, but every few weeks she drew something, and when it was finished we were all transfixed with her beautiful work which helped us all capture more of the wonder of Australia.

"Hans and I are going fruit picking, Mom. You can pick your own fruit from the trees at a place up here in Kalamunda for a small fee. Plums and apricots, good-oh. Would you like to come along today?"

"I'll think about it."

"The man that owns the fruit orchard is about ten years younger than you, and he lived in the wild North and has a collection of boomerangs and artifacts. He's not married, and he's good-looking in a kind of Aussie way. . . ."

174

"Jeanie, I have courage with grizzly bears and crocodiles, but no social courage with strange men in Australia. . . ."

"I told him I was bringing my mother," she said, "and he seemed interested to meet you."

Beside the fruit trees was the man. There were citizens and children making merry, carrying their picking baskets. Some sat on the ground around. "This is my mother and we live in a tent near here," Jean made the introductions.

"So you live in a *tent*, you don't say?" said the man, immediately enthralled. "Now I've lived a bit in a tent, myself, and I have always liked to go camping. I would take it as a privilege to be able to see your tent."

When he came visiting that evening, he brought with him his small collection of artifacts including a ten foot native spear which was made of twisted desert roots, soaked first and then pounded straight, then hardened and blackened in a fire.

We struck up a conversation easily. "I've got a house, an orchard, and a car. And money in the bank," he said. "All I need now is a wife, ha, ha."

"Ha, ha," I said.

"My mother doesn't care about orchards, cars, or houses, money, or marriage," Jean told him. "All she cares about is wild adventures."

Digger was the most likeable Aussie I had yet met, in many ways. He had a regular job with the government utilities, he said, but besides that he employed five men regularly in small businesses of his own invention—qualities of industry most admirable to the American mind.

I looked at our guest closely. It was nice to have a guest come to the tent besides the juveniles with whom I regularly lived. The man had that desert brown, beat-up Aussie look, that makes most Americans look like poms by comparison. He was very fit, the lines in his face harsh, the shoulders powerful. The corners of the mouth, despite smiling eyes right now, were drawn down in a bitter line.

Marital life had not treated him well. "I'll never understand a woman," he reflected. "They're impossible to understand." His remark reminded me unpleasantly for a moment of dinner at Darwin with a far more educated C.S.I.R.O. man who said, smugly, "It isn't necessary to try to understand a woman. Here we treat them casually."

We decided over tea that we might be friends, but I was cautious. "I have something to ask you right now, " I said. "I have found that

175

sooner or later a Yank like me will do or say something that offends the Australian. . . .

"In Western Australia we just call ourselves swans. . ." he interposed.

"All right, do or say something that offends a swan. Only, you see, the Yank never knows that he is causing the offense. Have you known any Americans before?"

"No ladies," he said. "You're the first. I realize their customs are different in some ways, that's true. And women with red hair like yours usually love a fight."

"Ug, well, if I ever say or do anything that offends you, will you please tell me about it in a nice, gentle way? I want to learn Australian ways. And, of course, I'll do the same for you."

"Oh, I'll do that," he said. "I'll pull you up easy."

"Well, okay," I said. "So far so good. I'm here to learn about the customs and everything."

"Mom, can Hans and I have our cup of tea to take up in the tree? How are you two doing?"

"Just fine, so far, dear. . . ."

"Well," he said, setting down his teacup, "I brought you some colored stones in this bottle. Thought you might like 'em, makes pretty bracelets and rings. I set and polish stones, too, you didn't know that, did you?"

Although we had many stones back on the Arizona desert, and the hobby of lapidary never happened to be one of mine, I accepted the stones graciously from the calloused hand and set them proudly outside the tent corner when he had gone.

Within a short time Digger was visiting at the tent frequently. On my big map of Australia he showed me where he had crossed the Great Sandy Desert over a thousand miles as the crow flies, with a geophysical exploration crew, and it was then that I finally and reluctantly came to terms with the fact that invading the real central deserts of Australia would just not be possible for me with Jean and Ann alone, ever. The expedition Digger was a part of had six vehicles, including a bulldozer, portable welding equipment, and a water wagon holding thousands of gallons of water, besides drilling equipment for water.

Twice the mining company expedition got a bit lost, he said, when the surveyors were deterred from following a straight course

176

by the necessity of finding ways around and through natural geographical barriers. The leaders relied on celestial navigation. All desert expeditions simply had to be multiple-vehicle, completely self-sustaining, have sophisticated equipment, and be manned by very rugged men. They kept daily radio schedules and were assisted by airplane, the necessity of which spoiled that spontaneity of movement which was a large part of the charm of exploration for me.

"Say, would you happen to have some old newspapers lying around?" he suddenly asked, then.

"Sure. Here you are. Why?"

"Just thought this trick would amuse you. It generally makes people laugh."

Quickly making a tight tubular roll, and frazzling the roll on one end, he tore the newspaper with hard-palmed hands, pulled out the tube, and suddenly there blossomed a magic "tree" before my eyes.

"It's Christmas week, isn't it?" he asked. "I was always senti-mental about Christmas. It's lonely alone, especially at the Christmas season. Kids love these tricks with paper. When you see me, you'll always see kids around. . . ."

"Yes, I noticed that."

"Got some more paper? I'll show you another one. . . ." and quickly, he was off. Suddenly, I was laughing hilariously, and so was he, and we were really friends.

Next day he was back and took me driving for about seventy miles back and forth through the area along the Swan River and King's Park. I met him on my hands and knees, rising from my nap and peering through the lower half of the zipper from the female sleeping quarters. I had already found myself vehemently defending my glass jar of rocks from other family members. Isn't there some species of bird in which the male courts the female by laying colored pebbles at her feet?

"Oh, my! Just a minute. I didn't expect you so soon!"

Up I got, and went off with him in his carefully polished car.

"I want to tell you something you might want to know," he said as we drove. "I killed a man in a fight, once. I didn't mean to. It was an accident. But it's on the record. The law never forgets."

"Oh!"

"Well, I take you out some place, I just ask you don't think I'm

a coward if I don't fight. I don't drink, either. Just lemon squash.
Let's go into the lady's lounge here, and you have what you
like." We walked into a battered, unpainted lounge area, and took a
table, and while I listened, he told me that ladies don't clink glasses
when they drink a toast, but only delicately raise their elbows very
slightly. "I just wanted you to understand so as you won't think I'm
a coward if I walk away sometime if some bloke makes an insulting
remark, or something like that. . . ."

"Well, that's just the way it is in America," I replied sociably.
"Men don't fight. . . ."

"They don't?"

"Well, not the men I know, anyway," I said. "It's never happene
to me in my social life. So you can feel perfectly all right about not
fighting when you're with me, I'm used to it."

"Aye, then," he said happily, and we downed our terrible, sickly
sweet lemon squashes, and went on to drive around some more.

I learned the way he killed the man was that some really mean
Aussie taunted him about his wife's behavior, involving another man.
To the Aussie it takes far less provocation than this to fight, as we
all know. Only this time the mean Aussie had a bad heart, earlier
diagnosed by doctors, and as the result of taking a few lusty Aussie
wallops against doctor's orders, he inconveniently died.

The homicide left its lifelong shadow on Digger the workingman,
who became the only man in the country who dared not fight.
Divorce followed, and his wife took the children with her.

Charles' wife, of the steamship line, took the trouble to try to
find a house to rent for me in a fashionable area, hoping we would
make Perth our home. "You'll never meet anybody who is anybody
in a tent," she told me as a friend. "You really should take a house."
I appreciated all the wonderful help and the advice. But I waited
to hear from Ansett. Digger got films of Australian life, produced
and let out to the public by the mining company he had been with,
and projected movies on several evenings for the assembled
caravaneers.

Our tent became infested with small round bugs by the
thousands which came marching in through the door and then up
the walls of the sealed sleeping compartment, to drop down like
pattering rain on the bodies sleeping beneath. They didn't bite, but
they carried with them a horrid, bitter, all-pervading odor which in

178

turn drew more of their kind into the girls' boudoir. It was at that time that the kind hands of Hans kept replacing the family dishpan into which I vomited like crazy, and I was missing the Alcoa party.

The caravan park owner came around to visit. "Are you roight?"

"Roight!" I called gamely.

"Them little bugs always come down from that tree this time of year, I don't know why that is," he called in.

"*Now* he tells me!"

"They always go away soon," he promised, and left, busy with holiday vacationists from back East. "So many people would like to have their tent under this tree," he called.

"Yes, I know we're lucky to have this wonderful tree," I called back, wanly. Zonta came over and reported that her tent had bugs, too. All tents were taken down and there was a house-cleaning. The bugs marched away. My sickness may have been caused by other factors than bugs.

Digger was back, and he referred in conversation to "that episode in the park." He looked miserably guilty.

"What episode?"

"Well, you know. I put my arm around you on the back of the car seat. I don't mean to. It just happened. Will you please excuse me for that episode?"

"Sure."

"You and I are good friends. We haven't done anything to be ashamed of. . . ."

I perked up my ears and already felt better from my brief illness. Such conversation, I thought, from a man forty years old! Filled with Victorian guilt feelings, and over nothing!

He detested neckties but came to call nowadays carefully wearing one. Did he hope that the mere sight of a necktie would so inflame his partner that seduction in the dusty back seat of his old car would certainly take place? He brought a box of candy under his arm. It had an enticing picture in color of luscious, rich chocolates. But when I opened the box in an excitement which was not by any means simulated, the contents were dime-store hard candy in a land where "truth in packaging laws" hardly exist. Oh, well. I dug gladly into the hard candy.

Now he took me out in the evening to one of these open-air

179

drive-in facilities to which teenagers generally go, and he carefully closed the car windows as we talked.

I had already begun to catch on that frustrated lovers have no place to go in all Australia in which they can be alone to conduct a courtship of any type whatsoever. There is not a single hotel, in even the greatest city, where the morals of all people taking rooms, for instance, are not rigorously patrolled by an alert management. In this barbaric continent the population of any age, not just kids, take advantage of a fortunately-mild climate to sally forth to woods and fields, taking their cans of bug spray as they go, to sequestered spots that are guaranteed to be rough, thorny, ant-infested, and absolutely ruinous to nylons. In winter at Perth, night temperatures commonly drop to forty degrees, either inside or out, and women wear long underwear at this time.

At the drive-in refreshment stop there were other cars all about us, and I noted that Digger was very nervous about their presence. In my own country such symptoms are the sign of the married man. Here, I was just perplexed.

"For heaven's sake, what's the matter, Digger?"

"I know a lot of people in Perth," he said. "A couple of 'em might see me here with you, is all."

"Would that be so terrible?"

"Aye, the blokes would tell it all around the shop tomorrow. My mites, if they saw I was with a girl, would just give me a terrible time."

This incredible statement was to be verified again and again, actually, and was perfectly true! In Tasmania later, a college engineering student told me of a hazing custom which amounted to all-out war on love. Groups of young men persecuted any of their group who got engaged to marry, and dedicated themselves one and all to ingenious devices by which they often managed to sabotage any meaningful relationship between boys with girls, or between young men and young women.

Here in the car in a public place Digger watched his deportment and lowered his voice with exceeding ill ease, like a hunted man.

At length he drove me home, after another seventy miles or so of restlessly prowling the same roads, and deposited me half dead from his gassy old car, slightly less enchanted than I was the week before. Sprawling Perth, what with its factories and mills, and the summer burning of the tall grasses, was getting a bad air pollution

180

problem already, partly from frustrated lovers with roaming cars.

On Sunday afternoon Clive's mother arrived, bringing his businessman father firmly in tow.

She was a very pretty little woman, youthful, chic, dressed all in pink that afternoon: pink suit over trim figure, pink heels, pink gloves, and a romantic pink hat with a big brim and flowers. The couple took me for a long drive over much of the same run I had been making constantly with Digger, only less gassy, and we stopped at a more elegant place for Devonshire tea. Driving past the expensive private boys' school where Clive matriculated as a boy, she pointed out its impressive history, and the adjacent cathedral of many spires.

"Clive has always wanted to be married in that cathedral," she said.

She made it perfectly clear to me that while many girls in Perth wanted Clive, he had delayed for a long time. The family was perfectly wild about Ann. Ann was a beauty. Ann had such charm. Ann would be a perfect hostess. Ann and Clive liked the same things, the same people. They could have a beautiful life together, she thought, attending all the gay parties every season; in fact, gay things went on the year round in Perth, which was the perfect place to live. She felt toward Ann as toward her daughter, had she been blessed with one. Clive's mother felt that America was very much the coming thing now. She felt that the American girl had so much to offer to Australia.

"I am charmed," I said, thanking her sincerely for the great compliments.

"Oh, Ann is a most charming girl," said the mother in pink.

"She's a pretty good auto mechanic," I added.

"What? Oh, oh yes."

"Ann might want to go on to an advanced education in college," I added.

"Well, oh, do you really think college is necessary for a girl? Don't you think it gives them, well—strange ideas?"

"Well, no, my girls have already got a lot of strange ideas even before college," I said. "Hasn't Ann ever told you any of her strange ideas?"

"No, I'm sure I don't know what you mean, she's perfectly charming, and all our friends are simply charmed with her. I suppose

181

there are some strange ideas in America, it's almost in the air, isn't it? Ha, ha. But she's so young and sweet, she'll get over that in Perth, I'm sure. Clive agrees with me perfectly, when I said the other evening. 'Oh, Clive, you've waited long enough. You have broken enough hearts of the girls in Perth. Our Ann, she is the girl for you, Clive.' "

"You have a very nice boy," I said.

"Yes, Clive *is* a good boy, you know. He is so conscientious. He is a very sensitive boy, always has been so sensitive. He always has had a great interest in dressing right, you know, and always doing the right thing. One of the things he particularly loves about Ann is her marvelous feeling for fashions. She is just the kind of girl a man would be proud to take anywhere."

"Yes," I said. "I buy them." I had spent more than I should, I was thinking.

Back home again in the tent, I could hear the modulated voices of the women and children, our caravan neighbors, and they were among the sweetest sounds I had ever heard, like the birds. It was a most gratifying sight to see the little ones lined up with toothbrush and comb, helping each other in the bath compound. Imitating exactly the clucking, soft, cajoling tones of mother, the seven-year-old girl instructs the baby and lifts him up to the bowl, ever so carefully and capably.

The play groups of the children were active and bustling all day long in the open air and at the pool, with of course the occasional crying child or the childish quarrel. But the bawling does not compare with the incidence of crying in American children's groups. A child could do worse than live in Australia.

Play is subdued, less violent, less hysterical. Babies and infants cry far less. I lived around them in caravan parks and I observed this. Parents spend virtually their entire lives playing with, caring for, and enjoying their children as one enjoys pets, and it is a rare parent who becomes impatient with the little ones. Only one father in this camp of a hundred human beings (70 percent small children) shouted irritably at his child.

Yet the Australians are at a loss to cope with adolescents. The older generation, not understanding the changing world youth must inherit, does incalculable harm with its puritanical dogmatism. Australians are wonderful parents—when it comes to young children.

182

We got all our mail from home at last. We had been months without mail. The Jeep trailer came by rail with our clothes aboard just as we left. Comalco kept the stuff in their yard.

Poor little Laddie was killed. The dog was on an exercise run in the evening with Hans and Ann in the Jeep when an overtaking vehicle deliberately pursued and hit him.

Jean and kind Hans dug a deep hole over the gate and through the trees near our camp. It was the area reserved for the Boy Scouts. Wrapped in Ann's new pink nightgown the loving little body was laid to rest, with his water pan and his food pan buried with him. Thump of earth, and grinding sound of shovel.

No more would Laddie share Ann's blanket, crawling in beside her each night during the cold hours. The tent was lonely.

I visited the new grave bordered with neat bricks. A wooden cross was simply lettered, "Laddie." Gay wildflowers on the fresh grave drooped a little.

Ann did not go out on her date with Clive that night. Next day she telephoned him and told him many thanks for the abundance of wonderful times in Perth. We were leaving soon for Linkletter's place, and she would return to Perth only briefly.

She dated Clive again a time or two, but the magic in Victorian social life faded abruptly.

When the girls and I left with our Jeep we traveled light, leaving the blue tent behind in custody of Hans and Helmut. They needed the tent, and paid the rent to keep the place under the tree.

The temperature was 108 degress the Saturday we embarked for the Southwest, and our Kiwi friend Steve suddenly showed up!

Steve had come from Darwin by way of some of the Centre's most remote and lethal deserts. He had tired of Hillary and was alone. He looked terrible. Starved, ill, battered, he found us, and his appearance gave full testimony to what he had gone through. Crossing desert lands alone in his old car, with no one on earth to know where he was or to expect his arrival, he might well have ended a bleached skeleton on that desert had his car failed, or water or gasoline supplies given out—which they nearly did. He had been down to a few pints, it was that close.

Steve had gone wild in the desert. He had just gone bush, shooting his rifles all the way as he went. He had shot many brumbies—wild horses—just to see them fall. That cruel, crazy young man. Had he been in drug-oriented America of this generation, he probably would have been one to hit the drugs and "freak out!" Here he threw himself, destructively, upon wild nature.

"Well, come into the big blue tent!" we said, and we all hugged him and told him to make himself at home. Hans, who was the most stable of all of us, set to work at once to make tea and to give him food. After we left, all the men would get drunk and have a beer party for relief: Hans and Helmut, Steve and Swedish Gene, and others around the camp. That was okay as long as they didn't destroy the tent.

Chapter 13

LINKLETTER'S PLACE, WITH INSERT BY JEAN

As we drove south through the great *karri euclyptus multi-colours* the daytime heat was sizzling—but we were used to that. We gazed in rapture. Straight, limbless to the crown, the mighty pale gray trunks soared heavenward, their airy, feathery, gray-green canopy creating a magic forest, a forest of which legends are born.

In the cathedral hush the little birds sing all day in a chorus of prayer. Green parrakeets, sporting scarlet underwear, flash between the trees through dry fern glades.

When the sun drops and you sleep in the forest you go to sleep by watching just one visible star which moves slowly like a searchlight probing the forest aisles and on down the horizon; and there may be spatterings of red stains on dry leaves that cause you to wonder for an instant if this could be a sorcerer's blood trail.

We three had not camped alone for many a day. I at least was glad to settle into family aloneness again in the bush.

We were driving down Estuarine Inlet and to us, all was an unspoiled world. We stopped the car to watch the distant figures of people out wading in the inlet. They were crabbing.

When the girls waded out, two young Aussies allowed them to tag along. Soon four silhouettes could be seen a mile away. They pulled an old tire on a cord behind them, fitted underneath with screen mesh to make a floating basket to hold the crabs after scooping them up with a long-handled net.

That night between wheat farms and Granny Smith apple orchards—Australia's own hybrid apple—we camped in an abandoned placer mining operation. There were again rabbit tracks in the sand. We boiled and ate our delicious crabs under a full, yellow, rising moon, and an owl called, and small bats squeaked. Tracks showed that the red fox had managed within three generations of man to cross the Nullarbor Plain and, once a "pom" had now become an Australian.

One day we took a side road and swam at a place called Fonty's Pool. It was a swimming hole dammed up and beautified by three generations of an Italian family. We saw baskets and stone jars of flowers on every mortised wall. Art set in nature, it was an Italian garden of nobles on a wilderness shore. A line of benches set along an ivy-covered wall for two hundred feet permitted the dads and mums and aunties to sit and watch.

We swam in another great pool created out of the river near Pemberton. Framed by the tall, dreamy gray karri trees, the old swimming hole lured the public to picnic on green clipped grass, and there were free bath houses and facilities for all. From the opposite hill a sled track came down, where youngsters used a community sled on runners to plunge into the pool. Can you imagine an iron-shod sled used by a quarter of a million people—according to the signpost—without a single injury? There were no life guards, no visible law enforcement needed when this calm and simple population came out to enjoy wild nature.

We went to visit the State Trout Hatchery. From the first rainbow trout imported for breeding stock back in 1936, half a million fish are released each season into the sparse little streams of the southwest for the sportsman, and Western Australia requires no fishing license.

In the karri forest some of the tallest trees are used to house fire lookout stations. The girls climbed a 212-foot ladder to meet the agile ranger on duty.

The forest seemed to me to be a tinder box in summer. You could build a fire anyplace, however, at your own discretion, if you cleared an area of twenty feet with your camp shovel.

186

Each hot day gives way to cold, dampish nights at this season. The temperature contrast the moment the sun drops is hard to believe. Conversely, the moment the sun strikes your camp at breakfast, you have to move out fast or be struck dead by its gaze.

The mosquitoes were in the full frenzy of summer here. We used sprays over our faces and clothing when the car stopped. When we roasted our meat from the butcher's it was a fight to the finish to get the meat to mouth out of the swarms of ravenous flies settling on it the moment it came from the flames.

Our track: From Perth to Fremantle, Rockingham, Estuarine, Mandurah, Lake Clifton, Lake Preston, Bunbury, Picton Junction, Boyanup, Donnybrook, Kirup, Mullyalyup, Balingup, Bridgetown, Yornup, Wilgarup, Palgarup, Manjimup, Pemberton. (The preponderance of village names ending in "up" is from the Aboriginal language, in which "up" means water.)

South of the major industrial town of Bunbury there is no coastal drive as such, only zigzagging. Sight-seeing is difficult for the stranger because the sights to see are not marked or advertised, but mostly hidden.

Swiss and Danes came to settle the cool southwest corner. Our drive took us from the forest near Bridgeport to Walpole Inlet, to Denmark. The day was cool and overcast. Smoke filled the world from forest fires, and we hurried on, to camp on the side of Toolurup Mountain then, second highest peak in the Stirling Ranges at 2,800 feet, where Jean climbed the footpath to its top.

Storm was sweeping over the sky. We spread out our three cots on their legs tonight and put the sleeping bags on them in a closely-packed row, on the downwind side of the Jeep, which we trusted the forty-mile gusts would not blow over upon us. Over our beds we then spread the large canvas we carried, since we had no tent along. There on the high mountainside we lay, faces up to the sky and about to be washed, watching the storm, with thunder, pull its heavy blanket over heaven into sunset, cover the early evening stars, and finally zip them shut from our sight.

At moments the embers of our fire in the public stone fireplace blazed up and scattered fitfully in the gusts. Our tummies were full and comfortable from a hot supper. We worried not when the rain came down, simply tucking our heads under the big canvas.

There should be more national parks like Toolerup, its mountain so lush that it is not possible to see a hiker on its trail, or any other thing than those most airy and airborne of eucalpyts with tufts held aloft into cloud-like mist.

Jean found a small brown snake next morning as she climbed Mt. Toolerup who permitted her to lift him upon a stick with careful scrutiny. Most unusual behavior for the deadly western brown snake—if that's what it was. Its behavior may have been attributable to the cool weather or because it was a young and tender juvenile, like Jean. No conscientious tourist will kill anything in a national park, of course. A day later at Linkletter's Place a full size brown snake was fleeing my horse's hooves when one of the hands quickly killed it, lest it kill horses or sheep.

The neat grooming of all the land in this area today enables a truck to be driven over it anywhere. It was a newly-opened area, Esperance.

Esperance district has a nine-month growing season of winter, with fog and rain. A little snow may fall in the highlands. There would be a great deal more winter snow and rain than there is—rain ranges from nine to thirty-five inches—if the highlands were above the mere three thousand feet they attain. But of course, this is the problem with all of Australia. *Lack of mountains* has caused it to be named the "dry continent." Lack of mountains means that precipitation from on high is not caught in the way nature works in other lands, resulting in no flow of ground water down the slopes, and a dearth of rivers and lakes, and even, as one hydrologist put it, "no topography" over much of the continent. Even more serious in the long run, not only is there but very meagre surface water, but there is scant possibility of adequate underground water supplies in aquifers, and scant possibility of those aquifers being recharged once their supplies are used by man!.

Here we are 2,400 miles from the Antarctic with nothing in between but small islands. We face the loneliest ocean in the world on this corner where the Indian Ocean and the Antartic Ocean currents meet, where the strange and beautiful little rock fish look like jewels. The prairie winds blow around the year, keeping off the flies. Flies settle in thousands upon you if the wind drops for a moment.

The general climate of this south coast surprised me by its coolness in summer. When we drove back to Perth later by way of the

188

inland desert—Kalgoorlie and Coolgardie—we were to be roasted alive once more, by contrast.

In Esperance I found the Esperance Land and Development Company and talked with its manager, a former television announcer turned agronimist and big land salesman. This company signed a treaty with the government of Western Australia in 1950 which enabled it to acquire one and a half million acres of land to develop and then re-sell to the Australians—or others—in individual farm plots, making it possibly the largest private land developing company in the world. The money is American money. The selling agents are the Elder Smith Goldsbrough Mort Limited of Australia.

The company clears and develops water on one third of each farm plot to be sold. The extent of the underground water and the degree of its salinity, however, is unknown. Supplies from bores only thirty miles inland are quite saline at least for part of the year.

The farms offered run from 2,500 acres to 3,200 acres. Fencing—an essential item for running sheep—is left to the farmer. So is the building of his house and sheds. The company got the land for fifty cents an acre, and is selling it for nine dollars an acre.

But the plan to develop the Australians' own country and then sell it back to them in lots has boomeranged. Sales were not going well at the time I visited, because the Australian farmer could not afford to buy.

Art Linkletter had some money originally invested in this vast tract of land, but got out of it earlier. One of the first of the sheep pioneers in this section, he now grazes 22,000 sheep and about 1,800 black angus cattle on 16,000 acres.

But I shall let Jean take over at this point, and describe the experiences the girls had there, where only four men move the sheep mobs about, and the manager plots his strategy on a map each week as a general would move his armies.

LINKLETTER'S PLACE
by Jean

Aussies are more inclined to like you if you don't have much money. They may be a bit suspicious and resentful until you dispel your rich American image. They live in a big country where a man can work for years and still have little to show for it. But if you come to join 'em, not just look at 'em, you're right.

In short, this was how Ann and I found Aussies' attitudes by the time we were invited to stay at Linkletter's Place in the great southwest.

It was a cold, windy day when we pulled up and were greeted by the manager, John Hagon. We had lunch with him and then were shown to another house across the fields of sorghum. There were several buildings, including housing for temporary and permanent help, shearing shed, power house. Around us lay miles of fenced paddocks with developed water. It was a land that had had a lot of work and money put into it. John said to just make ourselves at home, and we'd see about things to do the next day. So we laid out our bed rolls on the floor of an empty house there, and I went out to sniff and prowl around.

The first thing I saw was a fenced back yard full of gum trees. The second thing I saw was Old Hefty. Peacefully cropping in the wind, without a care in the world, was a great big sheep with a long tail. Well, being a great grabber of animals, I set out to grab my first—though not my last—sheep. I was joined by Annie. The sheep was so woooooooooly that she couldn't see behind her.

The Kid and I have been in so many different situations together that we get along, and we think almost exactly alike, and that is why I knew she wanted to grab her first sheep and hug it, just as I did. We had a few *baaahs* which turned into barks and moos and we named our first sheep Old Heft, because of her mighty girth.

Mom and Ann and I then went up and cooked dinner for John as he was batching it, and there wasn't any wood the right size for the stove at our place.

After dark we drove through the cold, black night on the several lonely roads back to "our house."

The Helmericks are brave in facing anything but lonely, dark, empty, creaky houses. We hadn't slept inside a house for a long time. Also, we had been used to traveling with our adopted family of plenty of men! Anyway, after one exceptionally loud crash in the old house, the Helmericks grabbed the sleeping things, leapt into the Jeep, and raced to Hagon's house, fighting the billowing sleeping bags. John was awakened by three shivering creatures—the alleged brave explorers—covered with sleeping bags and assorted clothes, and he let us sleep on his livingroom floor.

Next day, however, we decided we must become accustomed to being indoors. Things always look different in the daytime. We found that if we bedded down before the power plant shut off—*that* soon became easy, after a day of work—we slept well. The beast responsible for the tremendous nighttime noises was a female cat, whom Ann and I named Mama Cat for obvious reasons.

John took us out to the yards to introduce us to the men and let us see how things are done on a sheep station.

Ann and I, having been temporarily farmed out on Arizona ranches before now, had learned to look a situation over carefully and then grab it. We may not know how to do a thing—everybody has to start somewhere—but we like to get right in there and learn it, "givin' it a fair go."

It didn't take long, knowing a big about Aussies, to figure out what the blokes had thought when they learned they were supposed to look after three Yank sheilas. They were understaffed when we came and had lots of work. Later I reconstructed the conversation that must have taken place soon after we got there.

"All roight. Now we're gonna' 'ave guests. Three Yank sheilas. Two kids and the Mum. Writin' book or somethin' like thot. We're to keep 'em 'appy. Put 'em on a 'orse or somethin', but keep 'em 'appy."

"Eh, look, mite. We're not runnin' a friggin' dude ranch. We ain't got nothin' but stock 'orses, an' bless me if I wanna be responsible fer no city sheila on one o' these 'orses."

"I know, I know. All I know is thot they're comin' an' we gotta bloody well look after 'em. How about Trigger, thot mean little Shetlin'?"

"Look, as if things aren't jolly bad enough wot with Mike gettin' married, and you gonna 'ave twins. Give a bloke a fair go, mite. We're flat t'the boards as it is. We gotta take care the stock. . . ."

But the fellows never showed a thing in their faces as to what they thought about the visitors. They were courteous, but their predicament was understandable.

George lifted his dusty old hat and scratched his head. Ann and I just waited until he thought. He looked as awkward as a bush Aussie handling a baby. Darb stood there self-consciously covering a rip in his "strides" with his hat. Brian was grinning.

"Well, wot 'bout the black mare? She's with foal an' thot oughta slow 'er down."

191

"With a mouth like 'ers, I doubt it."

"Holly's out. Wot about th' brown three-year-old mare?"

"She's not too bad if she's 'andled roight. But wot about thot little accident a few months back?"

"She does 'ave a bad habit or two at thot. But you got any better suggestions?"

"'ow's the gray gelding's foot?"

"Too bad, still, The gray mare might do, but she hasn't been rid fer a year."

"Well, give 'er a go and see 'ow she is."

George looked at us doubtfully. "Can either of you ride? I mean, a 'orse?"

"You bet!" we chorused eagerly. His doubtful expression remained.

"Well, one a' ya git up on this 'un and just ride 'er round the yard." I was elected, and after a couple of lunges and grabs, I was at last pushed onto the horse. Ann and I had always ridden bareback or with an American Western working saddle. We preferred bareback for it gives one a feeling of the horse's movements that the big Yank saddles don't. But the Aussie saddle was a real surprise. It's built smaller, lighter, and it lies closer to the horse. The stirrups are full length, but it resembles the English saddle more than the American. It has no pommel, but I never came anywhere near feeling like I had to grab leather the entire time I was on the place.

And that wasn't the only difference. I picked up the short reins, and held them loosely as I jounced across the yard. George shook his head.

" 'Owed ya ever expect to control a 'orse with thot TV type ridin'?"

It was then that I became acquainted with the Aussie style of riding. The reins are crossed just over the withers and held with both hands with the palms down and fingers curled over the reins where they cross. The thumbs are braced against the other side of the cross. The effect is of a rein curving under the outside of each hand and its opposite and protruding. The hands are held low and the reins are held tight. Frequently a set of neck rings is used to keep the horse's head low.

My stirrups were of metal rod, with a half circle dent in the inside of each, curving toward the horse's head. The purpose of these is a quick release for your foot in case you are thrown or fall off. The entire foot, to the heel, is put into the stirrup. This took a bit of getting used to.

I was assured that the best balance, and longest wear for your strides, not to mention your rear, is had by rising to the trot. The weight is back on a canter. A trot is considered the usual way to travel for miles at a time. Out of self defense, I tried this rising to the trot, and after many laughable miles of pounded rear, I suddenly discovered that it is possible and comfortable. It was a great delight to me the day I found myself really going up and down in rhythm with the horse, and the horse and I clipping off the miles easily.

The first day we brought in a mob of 4,000 weaners. These are young sheep. After they're weaned they're put with a mob in a paddock by themselves, to keep the older, stronger sheep from trampling them. I was amazed at how pitifully weak these little lambs are. I was amazed at the unbelievable numbers of ailments, diseases, medications, groomings, surgeries, shearings, dippings, and butcherings going on all the time. At no time in all the year is there a moment's lull in the compartmentalized paddock system. You see and hear and smell sheep in your sleep. In your dreams Australian horses prance and the sheep dogs run and snap at hurrying little heels.

While we on horseback drove the weaners through the pasture Brian followed with a utility truck picking up the ones that fell and couldn't get up.

We were moving the mob very slowly, their little heads low and swaying as 16,000 little rustling hooves kicked up the dust. Nine died on that walk. They succumbed on the truck bed. I saw their tongues loll out, gasping, their hearts racing, the flies crawling over them, and finally their open eyes burned out by the sun, and glazed.

Ann and I were horrified to see that some were literally falling apart from fungus. The fungus may have got into the range grass and soil, or it may have been communicated from the water tanks. Whatever it was, they were being brought to the home yards to be drenched—wormed—and given their trace mineral of cobalt by mouth.

Two or three were so sunburned after shearing, even in this mild climate, that the entire skin of their backs and necks flapped loose in one sheet, connected only at the neck and rump. As the stupid little creatures panicked to avoid our horses sometimes even

193

this came loose and dragged after them. Others dragged their hind legs unnaturally or had throats swollen with worms, or hides caked with dermatitus. When you get together such enormous numbers of sheep you are bound to see every disease in the book, finally, and it is quite an education.

The weaners were turned into the sheepyards, which are a maze of fences and gates constructed in such a way as to hold several thousand at a time. Gates can be moved to separate the mob into smaller and smaller lots as they near the races. This funnels the unwilling sheep easily into the races while keeping them closely packed. It also helps avoid deaths by trampling. There is a drafting gate which can be swung one way or the other to separate two thoroughly mixed mobs. As the sheep run through a race—a narrow chute—a center gate is swung back and forth putting them into separate pens. Most of this conglomerate was located under a large, open shed. The pens all funnel down to two races that hold sixty head or so, and over a hundred weaners each. A gate at each end of a race can be opened or closed to allow sheep to enter or leave. In the race they can be handled individually without being scattered.

We packed the weaners so they couldn't move much, but wouldn't be trampled. But the weaker always managed to fall, and you find many smashed little dusty bodies under the sharp, unsympathetic hooves of their comrades. Once freed and helped to their feet, they would usually run off stiff-legged after their little friends. There's nothing stupider than a sheep.

The drenching process consists of standing in a race with smashed toes and a special plastic bag full of medicine on your back, and the attached gun in your hand. You grab a sheep by the jaw, force its mouth open, push the cobalt-capped, rubber-tipped gun down its throat, and pull what seems like a ten pound trigger. The cobalt pellet and worm medicine are shot down the throat in the same operation.

It sounds simple. But the sheep rarely cooperate, and by the end of the day every muscle ached, our sinuses were clogged with dust, and we stank. We were sunburned and our hands could not have pulled that old trigger-pump one more time.

Near sundown we left the drenched sheep in the yards below the races, and left more waiting their turns in the yards above.

George found an English cross-breed in the mob that he said

194

looked pretty good, and he hauled it over to the killing shed. There he flipped the sheep on its back and was about to apply the knife to its taut throat. I thought to myself: "I can't watch!" But in two fast slashes George pulled the head back, broke the neck and cut through the spinal column. That sheep never knew what hit him. Blood spurted down the drain, bright foamy red. The kicking slowed as the blood changed to a maroon color and the veinule emptied. Quickly loosening the skin from the belly, George hung the carcass on hooks and punched the hide out in no time. Then he split the belly, dropped the intestines into a bag, and finished up dressing the carcass, which he bagged and hung up in the fly-proof room over-night to cool. Last he scrubbed down the floor with disinfectant again. It was time now to fire the cook stove, make supper, and wash your clothes or sew and those things you do in your spare time.

Tired as I was, I dragged myself over to the boys' place, which we used as a cook shack. Darb and Brian had made tea. They saw how tired Ann and I were, and they were sweet and considerate far beyond the call of duty when they asked us to share their tea with them. We had given it a fair go today. They accepted us.

Five-thirty came too early the next day. After we pushed the remaining weaners in the yards through the appropriate pens, we had breakfast.

I mixed up the biggest batch of pancakes I ever made, using my good old secret American recipe.

John Hagon and George arrived, and all waited expectantly. Well, this morning everything went wrong. The pancakes stuck in the pan. I couldn't understand how it was that I could control the heat and turn out beaut pancakes over a campfire, yet mess up so badly over this stove. I didn't eat mine until the last, when the men had fed. I took one bite, and almost choked. How could anyone get plain old pancakes to taste so awful? Then I saw. I had added to them and cooked them in mutton grease. Either everyone was too polite or they were used to mutton grease—anyway, no one said a word.

That day we finished the weaners, and Darb and I, without a dog, took 4,000 hungry, thirsty creatures through paddocks with feed and water, and out to another paddock. They were determined to go back and turn right, and we wanted them to go forward and

195

left. It took several hours, at a full canter most of the time, to get the big, sprawling mob moved. I honestly thought we'd never make it. My bum was so sore I would rather have walked, when we came trotting in at dusk. Where had the day gone? Darb said to me, "You're sure no piker." I asked what a piker was and he said it means someone who quits and lets his mites down. If he only knew how close I came to quitting so many times, but now I knew I never could quit.

The days that followed were spent much in the same way. We dipped and drenched and vaccinated and branded, and we moved sheep from dawn to dusk, two fellows and Ann and me together.

I soon discovered that the grown sheep weren't nearly as pathetic as the lambs. They still caught diseases and wogs but mostly they were big, strong, healthy, stubborn sheep, much alike in size and strength. The adults were separated into mobs of ewes only—to prevent out-of-season lambs—breeding rams, and wethers.

I learned that man has managed to breed, among his other monstrosities and inventions, sheep that don't ever lose their wool. This wool just grows and grows. A man told me of a sheep that had missed shearing for thirteen years. The wool, though ragged and torn, had some strands a yard long! From what he said, that was a really sorry-looking animal. Unshorn sheep usually die long before this, because the tremendous weight and bulk of the unshorn wool, when it gets wet, may make it impossible for them to get up from the ground, and they die of pneumonia.

The tails are cut off, or banded with an elasticator band, to prevent dags and fly-blowing. The manure clings to the wool and tail, causing painful and dangerous dags, or clots. Marino sheep are also mulsed around the anus to prevent fly-blowing. This is a surgical operation by which the hide is stripped off the whole area round the anus and over the tail stump. When this heals, the sheep have clean, bare pink bottoms where flies can't find a crevice to lay eggs in.

Wool is a problem when it grows too close around the eyes, so the sheep can hardly see out. Ram's horns may grow into an eye or get so curly that they get tangled in a fence if they are not trimmed. The fences are made of ring link, with barbed wire on top. This prevents sheep from getting tangled in barb wire, but keeps the cattle out of the sheep paddocks, too. Sheep and cattle in Australia also have a bad time from blow flies getting into the vagina and the penis sheath, but at Linkletter's controlled paddocks they were medicated.

196

Ann and I now better understood the plight of Old Hefty. She had been hand-raised, and one of her problems was that she had never been sheared or medicated. When the former employees moved away their forgotten pet was left behind enclosed in the paddock with our little house.

John Hagon heard us speak of her and laughed. "I wonder how that thing is still alive? She's been there for two years now without water."

It irritated me that he could know that an animal might be dying of thirst behind the fence and not do anything about it. But I guess when you have lots of important things to worry about you don't worry about one sheep. We carried water to her then in Mom's dishpan. But what Hefty needed was a plan for her future.

Ann and I suggested to the chaps that in their spare time we should shear her now. So they started up the entire machine to shear one sheep for Ann and me.

Well, the shearing shed can handle hundreds of sheep a day off of one engine. We went in there, dragging Hefty, and there was a bit of an odor, because sometime in the past some little lamb had got into the corner back of the machine somehow, where sheep are *not* supposed to be, and had died in there. Shearing is really a shocking business. Darb and Brian were as careful as possible with poor Old Hefty, yet the skinny pink thing that emerged was scraped with gashes.

Professional shearers who are working for speed and numbers frequently cut off ears and teats and all. The design of the shears is partly to blame for the amount of injuries sustained. I'm no expert but there must be some way to design a clipper so that it won't damage the sheep.

Sheep that are raised alone become smart, affectionate, wary, and individualistic. Once Old Hefty (no more) was changed into this skinny pink thing, she became nearly impossible to catch and grab. However, despite the fact that the hand-raised sheep in a mob may be more trouble to the handlers, one day this skinny, pink, long-tailed sheep appeared down a race with other ewes.

Everyone there pretended not to notice as she headed out to paddock and the water tanks with the others. She was later to cause trouble as a rebel leader when she tried to lead the whole mob into the back yard where she was raised by children. But everyone pretended not to notice.

197

One evening when the Kid and I were done in, as usual, Darb and Brian said the four of us could go rabbit hunting, driving the "ute."

They said they didn't shoot rabbits because there were too many sheep around, but they hunted without rifles. Well, this was a new one on me!

They were going to run the rabbits down afoot. Were they serious?

Ann and I had some misgivings about the humaneness involved for the rabbits, but it hardly seemed possible that men afoot and carrying a stick could get anywhere near wild rabbits.

We started driving cross-country with me at the wheel. The men rode the back of the flat-bed ute with sticks at ready, while I cruised. George was with us also, having seen his wife and twins for a couple of days.

Well, at first sight of a rabbit in our headlights, the blokes were off the ute and running like a pack of dogs. I never saw grown men have so much fun or display so much energy as I saw that evening. I could almost imagine them barking.

Those rabbits ran so fast, dodging this way and that, that we could hardly keep track of them and focus the spotlights on them and the men. Despite continual, untiring pursuit, the rabbits had at least an 80 percent chance of escape. And when they did make it down into their burrow they escaped clean, even if neurotic. All were killed clean or had their necks broken in a trice by the leaping men.

The mad pace kept up over the brush and between trees and snags at a ferocious frenzy until Brian badly turned his ankle in a burrow. This put him out of the running class, but as he could manage the clutch and brake, he was appointed new driver.

When I fell asleep about 2:00 A.M., the other two were still flat to the boards like a couple of happy dogs, barking after rabbits.

"Well, I'm knocked up," said Darb, "Let's go home."

Have you ever heard a full-grown, fourteen-stone Aussie man tell you he's knocked up? Some of the things they said we had to hear with a straight face. Darb meant that he was tired. And of course we made several goofs on the Linkletter Place that turned the sheepmen green and red around the gills, because of language differences.

198

Some of the things we loved the most were the sheep dogs at Linkletter's. George had a *kelpie*—an Australian breed—named Lass. (I've yet to see a female sheep dog called anything else.) Kelpies are small, thickly haired, intelligent, very fast, unassuming black-and-white dogs. Sheep people argue the merits of the border collie and the kelpie endlessly. Both are relatively small, wiry, alert dogs. Both have their fans. A man who owns a good dog is very proud of it, and well might he be, for a good sheep dog in action is fantastic. The good dog works only for one man, responding instantly to his signals, as well as acting on her own initiative as needed in droving. But I'm afraid that most candidates for sheep dog end up being shot. "A dog that takes drovin' as a game, does more harm than good," said Darb.

Darb and Brian were very good to us in quiet ways. When we asked them to, they would sometimes kill the hopelessly sick and injured sheep for us. I once asked why they weren't officially supposed to kill them, since the shearers won't touch sheep with cancer and such, and they certainly weren't good for breeding.

He said that Peter's Meat Pies took them away. I've always wondered if he was serious. They often kidded us and said that if we had it our way with all our humaneness we'd have to kill off half the mob.

When the blokes found out that we didn't have a mirror in our shack, a wall mirror suddenly appeared. At the same time their own shaving mirror mysteriously disappeared from their own wall. Chopped wood, the right size, appeared by our door so we could take hot showers. They looked after Ann and me like brothers. We worked hard, yet they saw our limitations and didn't run us down for them. We gave it a fair go there and they said they hadn't known girls like us for friends. They had never imagined it would be this way, that we were so interested in their lives here and in the whole complicated art and science of managing sheep. I knew we earned their deep and lasting friendship. Yet we must really have been more trouble than we were worth.

Even the strict John Hagon said that we were better workers than most jackeroos—beginning stock workers—that he was able to get. He called us "jilleroos"!

"Any time you want to come back, you're welcome," he said, and added, "and I don't tell many of them thot. And if you want jobs, I'll put you on the payroll as 'jilleroos.'"

It wasn't until we unpacked again back in Perth that we started discovering the little presents the blokes had hidden inside the Jeep load. There was a St. Christopher medal that Brian had worn all through his stint in Vietnam. There was a real, three-foot-long, carved ceremonial boomerang that wasn't made for tourists. I've never seen one like it before or since. And there was the dear old cracked shaving mirror all over again, which we had returned to them.

When they write the news isn't much, but we can see it all perfectly. "Killed a brown snake in the toilet," writes Brian. "Not much news. Miss you. The stupid sheep are stupid as ever. Wish you were here to help move a move a mob today."

Chapter 14

IN THE WILDS OF TASMANIA

We arrived back at Comalco in Perth just in time for tea. As we drove up to the familiar little plant an executive arm at that very moment could be seen reaching out the window with the teapot and dumping yesterday's tea grounds.

"I wonder," I asked the perceptive executive who had given me my office, "if you could perhaps telephone Sydney for me, where the Toyota vehicles have their head office? Ask the man if he will let my girls and me use a Toyota on loan, please?"

It was right then that the miracle happened. The executive in Perth talked on the telephone across the country with an executive in another company quite unrelated to his own, and in some kind of mysterious, Australian old-school-tie language the two men quickly reached a clear understanding that, as soon as I needed it, a Toyota Landcruiser would be mine!

The Jeep I was never to see again. It was sold, and so was the trailer, in Perth later by the girls. What we needed soon was a vehicle we could take possession of on the East Coast upon our return from the island of Tasmania.

With this firm promise Jean and Ann and I now had a completely new lease on life. When we returned from Tasmania to Melbourne our Toyota would be ready and waiting there to explore the north-east tropics. How wonderful that we would at last be able to have the make of vehicle which had been in the expedition's original plan! How wonderful that it would be delivered at the opposite side of the continent exactly where and when it was needed!

Sorting gear all over again, we prepared to leave Perth, hastily. Things going to Tasmania were limited to flight allowances. We could not take the big blue tent, or any of our camp outfit, or vehicle. We would be afoot in Tasmania, presumably in cold rain. All that could go to Tasmania were the sleeping bags, rain apparel, waterproof match containers, and a light skillet—things that you can carry on your back.

Hans and company would use the blue tent under the tree in Perth until they, too, left. Comalco would send back East by rail the lot just now arrived in Perth, so that we would have the right things ready to pop into the Toyota at Melbourne when the time came for the "second time around."

On three consecutive nights we all drove to the Perth airport to catch the 1:00 a.m. flight. On the third run we made it. The girls and I had to wait for empty seats, as our flights were free.

Dressed in our best cool-weather clothing we embraced our friends in farewell, as fan-props roared in the night. Hans was kissing Jean, Swedish Gene was kissing Ann, and Digger was kissing me. It was a good moment for America and the new Australia.

We were not to see any of them again, except the indestructible Hans, the intrepid Sydneysider.

The prop-jet Electra lifted into the night. The lights of Perth from aloft were a great panorama of friendly, blazing color. Then— all was black without.

It is quite an experience to fly over a completely dark continent. Since there are no other cities there are no other lights. From the air small hamlets are hidden. Only from on high do you fully realize how lonely, how absolutely empty this continent is. And how beautiful.

"Are you right?" It was the hostess, bending over my seat.

"Yes, thank you." I didn't need a thing.

At Melbourne next morning we hopped another plane, which turned out over the blue ocean, and a few minutes later we were set down, the only passengers to disembark that day, at the town of

202

Launceston, in that little kingdom in the sea which is Tasmania, lying two hundred miles off the south Australian shore.

The month was February, the height of summer. February is the time for explorers. It is the only month in the year when the "horizontal bush" becomes visible by peeping out of its burden of snow, rain, and fog.

There was nothing in the world like Tasmania when it was in its original state. Its mountain valleys were submerged by a wickerworks of the most impenetrable vegetation on earth. A bit of this is yet left.

Each spring fresh suckers shoot up, resulting in a dense, living canopy some twenty feet or more in vertical depth. This growth is flimsy. It will not support a walker over its top. Some oldtime prospectors pruned tunnels through it by saw and secateurs. Some explorers disappeared into the island interior and were never found. Getting lost, they could not find their way out. Some possibly fell into the "horizontal bush" trap they could not climb out of.

The pioneers found they could not burn some of this vegetation. It is watery and won't burn. But hundreds of miles of foot paths have been cut slowly through the years and are used today by the hiker and nature enthusiast. In this environment is it surprising that there has evolved a small species of kangaroo which has taken to the trees?

In the broad river valleys and lush plains herds graze and agriculture thrives in much of Tasmania today. We weren't too interested in that aspect. We came to Tasmania for the reason that all other travelers come: to walk, and to see beauty, afoot.

We were greeted by one of the Ansett executives, and I shall never forget my first impression of Tasmania as I was driven to the Gorge Gardens of the Tamar River on a day of clear sunshine.

A dam had been created out of the river in the Gorge, and there we looked down from a hill upon an enormous, clear green pool where hundreds of people were out swimming in the hot sunshine.

There is nothing quite like the sound of children at the water. A kind of screaming, roaring, contented sound came to us from the beautiful gorge from where we stood in the cool, imported yew trees and California redwoods, set among moist spreading tree ferns and banks of giant pink and pale blue and violet hydrangas. And a

203

white summerhouse and bandstand, of course. And a high foot-
bridge across the chasm.

Then we stood upon Bald Hill and looked out. The town of
fifty thousand lay beneath us: winding river, red-topped roofs
packed together neatly in folds of the hills, and no sprawling ugliness. No modern suburban development project!

It took the last fifty years for the population of Tasmania to
gain but 100,000 people. The total is just over 300,000 now, and
their only problems are insufficient employment, interbreeding and
growing inward—problems which you might expect in an island
kingdom.

With our back packs, sleeping bags, and suitcases we took lodging at an old Victorian hotel once owned by the pardoned rebel
highwayman Dickie White, which had been charmingly redecorated
in gilt and carpets, and in frills and gingerbread.

In such a hotel the door to any room is constantly being opened
by a maid with a pass key, who needs to do something. In the Australian hotel a "Do Not Disturb" sign is unknown.

It would be shocking to suggest it. Day starts early with tea in
bed. Double beds don't exist—just bunks, a token of monastic virtue.
Deathly silence hangs over all. The guest has a feeling he is being
watched; and this feeling is not idle imagination.

But the Launceston became our favorite hotel in the Downunder
country.

In the Australian hotel usually you might say that the customer
exists as a sort of stupid beast for the management and staff to tor-
ment. No one on the staff behaves other than sullenly. The customer
is growled at, bullied, and neglected. His eccentricities—God forbid
there be any! He is not babied. He is not reassured by comforting
signs placed in lobbies and halls. Ladies' toilets are carefully hidden,
although the "Gents" sign is prominently on display. At dinner he
is never offered a second cup. Typically the waitress forgets a critical item to sustain life and goes off forever. But worst of all, the
customer has absolutely no rights of privacy in the room he buys.
He is told when to bed and when to rise, and when to turn over.

My year roaming Australia gave me two rationalizations for
this peculiar view of hotel proprietors toward hotel guests. First, all
hotels still operate under the country inn laws of centuries past, when
inns were so far apart along the highway that they had no competi-

tion. Most of them were built and are still being built for the real purpose of conducting a public bar—for the federal laws say that no liquor license can be granted other than as a part of wayside lodgings (three rooms, minimum, to be in business) attached to it. The result is that practically all inns tend to be places of loud noises and barroom brawlings below decks. This unwholesome and ridiculous situation was combatted by passing a ten o'clock bar curfew, which curbs evening entertainment altogether, but at the same time permits the loud noises and noxious fumes of beer to permeate most hotel establishments. It is in this realm of reasoning that most family men "do not like to take their families to hotels," and they travel by camping, instead. The hotel industry doesn't care about that. They make their money from the bar, and the rooms and eats are an annoyance to them.

The second reason the hotel people treat the public off-handedly is that in ages gone by the publicans were more monied and more sophisticated and worldly than the rude classes they served. In Australia the publicans have not yet got over this sense of their own innate superiority to the public whose money they take.

First class hotel life in Australia may go somewhat like this:

Customer: "I need some hangers in my closet."

Clerk: "Very good, Madame. Hangers. Let me see. Hmmmm. Have you tried the housekeeper?"

"No. . . ."

"One moment, please. I'm ringing the attic. Yes, the housekeeper says it's all right if you pop up there and get them if you go right now. . . ."

Customer: "Well, uh, I must mention also the room is bitterly cold."

Clerk: "Do you call this cold? Ha, ha. It's our spring season, you know. John—he's our maintenance man—just *might* have an electric unit. There *might* be contact points in your room. Have you looked?"

"Well, no I. . . ."

Clerk: "I would suggest that you might pop down and see John. He's on the very lower level. Doing something in the furnace room, I think. Just look for numbers of wash tubs and empty rubbish bins and you'll see him about. . . ."

Customer, weakly: "Another thing, since you don't serve any-

205

thing to eat on Sunday, well, I'm quite hungry and. . . ."

Clerk, brightly: "Six blocks down to your right. Seven to your left. Sometimes the little snack bar's open. It's one of those stand-up places, candy and canned drinks, and I'm told they have a heating oven for Chico rolls and those Peter's Lamb Pies that the factory puts out in wrappers. . . ."

Customer: "Do they have a telephone? Perhaps we could phone them first?"

Forty minutes pass while the clerk fumbles through the telephone book and waits on six house guests who are more important than you inasmuch as they are men and busy.

It is often suggested in hotels that the guest pop over here and pop over there, but it's a different matter altogether when it comes to the maid popping into your room like a cuckoo clock eighteen hours out of the twenty-four-hour day. "Rap, rap!" goes the door. Almost instantly a bustling, motherly, middle-aged matron in uniform is inside your room, using that pass key with unbelievable effectiveness. Sometimes she brings a cheerful gang with her. They measure the room for new drapes and the like, and discuss at length their plans for redecoration in the year 2002. There is always some business to be discussed in your room because there is never a time that every fixture is in proper working order.

But we were soon to be out roaming the 26,215-square-mile island, returning to the excellent and comfortable Launceston Hotel many times between our trips, to the point where it soon became our second home.

Although Tasmania is only 190 miles wide by about 210 miles long, the island state has 900 miles of coastline, and lying in the cold seas 200 miles off the southeast coast of the mainland as it does, with a climate totally different to the mainland in every respect, it is a world unto itself. Tasmanians are Australians but they don't call themselves that. They are Tasmanians, and apart. Originally, even the now-extinct Tasmanian Aborigines were distinct from mainlander Aborigines, and of origin mysterious.

The Tasmanians were racially unique. Like mainland Aborigines, their problem was that nature furnished no crops which could be cultivated or animals which could be herded, so that settled life was impossible. Every corner of Tasmania was used as hunting grounds, so that dispossession of a group of European settlers meant death by

206

starvation or death at the hands of other native groups competing for the land. Those who were despoiled accordingly remained where they were, doing their best to kill the invaders of their island.

The Tasmanian story has a sadness, whispered by romantic hydrangas and old summer houses. Into this far, green island on December 1, 1642, came a sailing ship bearing Tasman, the Dutch navigator, whose men set forth in Blackman's Bay in a small boat. Back in the forest woolly-haired, black, broad-nostriled primitives peered out at the newcomers; but these primitives did not allow themselves to be seen by white man for another hundred years. The first explorers only heard human songs and saw campfire smoke. High in the trees, sixty-five feet above the ground, they also saw notches cut five feet apart indicating that in his adaptability man here had also taken to the treetops—in his quest for birds' eggs for food.

Next came a French explorer, Marion du Fresne, to the west coast of the island just south of Tasman's landfall, in 1772—North Bay. Here the natives had first contact with white man and "threw stones and spears": the French fired, wounding several and killing one. The natives ran howling into the woods.

In 1773, Cook's second in command, Captain Tobias Furneaux— after whom the Furneaux Islands are named—entering Adventure Bay, had the surprise of eight black men and a boy visit him, with an exchange of presents. The redoubtable Captain Bligh stopped here, too, in 1788. At first the natives were friendly and fearless. But "woman trouble" started soon.

Flinders and Bass circumnavigated the island in 1799.

The natives were frightened by muskets and disdainful of intoxicating liquor, and the women were unwilling to prostitute themselves.

"Washed by cold seas," the island was described by navigators of Holland, England, and France as a place of rugged mountains and gloomy forests "not likely to attract settlement."

But what a good place for dumping convicts Tasmania might be! Through the period 1618 to 1671 England's convicts were shipped to America, to the West Indies and to Minorca. West Africa was tried but they died too quickly there. Then Terra Australis, the Great South Land, was set for a dumping ground. In May, 1787, some 756 prisoners came to New South Wales, and soon the extension of penal colonies spread to Tasmania to disperse the mounting thousands who became dangerous to their masters. Also, the English needed a political strategy to beat the French in planting a colony in Tasmania.

At the same time these were the days of the great seal industry. The Antarctic's cold waters had evolved large herds of fur seals in much the same way that Arctic waters did. The entrance to Bass Strait became the center of this industry, loading ships with seal hides and sea elephants. Three early colonies were formed strategically which were really military posts, and these were Port Phillip (near Melbourne), Port Dalrumple, and Hobart. Ruthless American sealing vessels also participated in this history.

Introduced diseases, the lust of convicts and sealers, and the savagery of the free settlers were to wipe out the Aborigines by the early part of the nineteenth century, just fifty years from first contact in 1772.

So terrible is the truth of white man's behavior in this part of the world that official papers describing the first six years of settlement in Van Diemen's Land (Tasmania) were destroyed by officialdom. Convicts practiced cannibalism on each other in a frenzy of brutality. Military officers were kings. Feudal pioneer landlords who were crown favorites given land could flog their servants with impunity. (The inheritors of the crown land grants in Tasmania today pay no taxes.) Escaped servants became bandits and bushrangers.

Meanwhile the free settlers met native resistance in the hills. No longer were the blacks the friendly, arcadian people who delighted the French explorers.

Finally, the white settlers, to protect their lonely farms and their families, hunted down and destroyed the native marauders, with military authority backing them up. George Augustus Robinson, the "pacifier of the Aborigines," was a name to go down in the annals of infamy. A bricklayer and free settler at Hobart Town, he was salaried at one hundred pounds a year to distribute government foods at Bruny Island to the very last Tasmanian Aborigines, numbered at about four hundred and feared by twenty thousand whites, and he profiteered upon them. The last surviving Aborigine, of worldwide concern perished on Flinders Island of malnutrition and pneumonia, a pawn of the island's petty politics.

At the small museum at Launceston I was privileged to hear a single recording of the only song and language we have of these extinct people. It was a record cut by a very old woman of part white blood. The exterminated people left no photographs or records of their existence. Ghouls even dug up the last bodies to sell them for profit to overseas museums, smuggled out in bales of wool.

Something else which interested me very much at the museum were two lifesize mounted extinct Tasmanian or marsupial wolves in glass cases. They are precious. Not many museums in the world have them. Six feet in length, with the long tail of a cat, the dun-colored animal is unforgettable because of conspicuous black and white stripes lying across the last half of the back. It was locally called "tiger" therefore, or sometimes "hyena" because of its massive jaws and teeth.

This was the earth's last large marsupial carnivore!

Its natural food may have been predominantly the possum, largest indigenous animal of Tasmania, before wallabies were imported.

Our guesswork is an exciting pastime, because the prehistoric marsupial wolf may not be truly extinct. There were numerous sightings in the 1950s and 1960s.

Originally it ranged the Australian mainland, but could not stand up in competition, possibly, against the imported dingo, which arrived with one of the later waves of man perhaps five thousand years ago. But in Tasmania there is no dingo, and there is food and cover a-plenty. More food than ever, when white man brought his sheep, which it ravaged.

I was very glad when the museum biologist told me that the government of Tasmania had turned down no less than three proposed expeditions from America during the past year which wanted to search for the wolf. If indeed it does exist today, the wolf is so rare that man must let it entirely alone, only hopeful that it will be able to build back its numbers.

Our exceedingly genial Ansett Airlines hosts in Tasmania now helped me set off at "wolf hunting," and other things. My hunting equipment was my six-power binoculars and my two legs. The place was Cradle Mountain-Lake St. Clair National Park, a fortunately un-improved wilderness area totaling 520 square miles which has one foot track going across it in a north-south direction, connecting with side trails to scenic lakes, falls, and assorted peaks of the highlands. The fifty-six mile walk was to take me a week.

There was no bus service to the park entrance. but the Ansett people arranged a car-shuttle which delivered me there via winding roads. When the ranger and his wife showed me to my cold-water log cabin it was coming on nightfall of a characteristically cold, rainy day, and I was glad to see that the girls had arrived ahead of me and had a fire going in the big fireplace. The girls hitchhiked, and their journey to the park had taken them three days! Their wet clothes adorned every chair and bunk. They had slept in wet fields and under trees, and had interesting encounters with a number of people.

"Hi, Mom. We didn't think you would catch up with us!"

"Oh, hi there! How did the hitchhiking go?"

"Oh, Okay. These roads are awful winding. Somehow we went in the wrong direction most of the time, and people took us all over the island. A few cultural misunderstandings. . . ."

"When we stood by the road we used the old Yank gesture of thumbs up. But a nice woman took us quietly aside and told us not to do this. It's an obscene gesture in Aussieland, it seems. . . .

"Then a very nice, correct older woman offered us a ride, and she drove quite a bit out of her way and insisted that it wasn't any trouble. Well, she also had a rather smelly little dog with her, and she kept the window rolled down. Finally, I thought it would be nice to compensate her somehow, so I turned to her and I said, 'M'am, can I give you something for your gas?' Well, she turned around and stared me in the eye, and she declared, 'It's the dog!' And right after that, she turned us out at the next village. And the name of the town, on the sign, was, 'No Where Else.' Really, that was the town's real name. . ."

"I don't think we charmed the Tasmanians very much," remarked Ann, then suddenly squealed.

Four nocturnal brush-tailed possums walked right into the cabin and sat up on our wooden table and chairs at that moment, begging food. Their kind had been a dependable source of rich, oily food for the extinct Aborigines, and they had furnished thick fur garments for wintertime. The foot-thick kinky pelage of the animals protected them from cold and rain and leeches perfectly.

Next day in the rain the two girls started up over the high, bare mountain pass. Three days later, after a couple of short walks to try my unused legs, I followed the track when the rain lifted.

I spent the rainy days reading *Gustav Weindorfer of Cradle*

210

Mountain, about the wonderful life of the immigrant Austrian who
saved this area for posterity much as poet-naturalist John Muir saved
the Sierras. And I talked with the park ranger and his wife.

On May 18, 1968, Mrs. Joan Saunders, alone at the post, was
awakened in her bed at 3:00 *a.m.* by a howl which she will never
forget. The sound came from the yard of the ranger's house, where
large numbers of wallabies and possum assemble at the feeding
stations. The howl was followed by two short, gutteral snorts. This
was continued for ten minutes. The howl was so near, so real, so
commanding, and so thrilling, that as soon as morning came Joan got
on the telephone with biologist Bob Green at Launceston at the
Queen Vic Museum. There is no doubt that *Thylacinus cynocephalus*,
the Tasmanian wolf, on this date announced his return to modern
times. It was a howl heard round the world. "Here I am! I am
returned! I am not extinct!"

I met Major Ronald Edgar Smith of Latrobe, who is seventy-
eight and often comes to the park in remembrance of his days here
with the naturalist Weindorfer at the old chalet home of Waldheim.
The major told me that he had seen the "tiger" a few times, "but
not for forty years." There was a pound bounty on the animal. He
told me how the local policeman might pay bounty over and over on
the same scalp, so that he himself could share in the government
money.

Major Smith's father explored the Levin River in the 1860s and
spent his life as an explorer and prospector, and he saw the animal
only three times.

In 1954 on the West Coast, on the side of Mt. Sedgewick behind
Queenstown, Ranger Gordon Saunders saw one, he believes, when his
dog confronted it at thirty yards. When the animal turned back into
the forest he saw the stripes. Probably Gordon and Joan's little
daughter Cozette stood the closest of any person to the living prehistoric animal, when the child came back from a short walk and
reported "an Alsatian dog with stripes."

Still, the "wilds of Tasmania" hold some of the most ferocious
scenery known to man. Even if you don't have the luck to see a
Tasmanian marsupial wolf, it is a naturalist's paradise.

Cradle Mountain—Lake St. Clair Park sits alone in the middle of
a lot of wild country, remote from roads and settlement. Over fifty
years ago Weindorfer and his friends fixed the names on the lakes

and mountains and streams, and they had their own little private kingdom. They were a bunch of happy kids, boys and girls in their twenties, married and in love. Today you can walk the trails and envy them the pure, first world they knew.

The rain lifted, revealing the row on row of Matterhorns soaring into a turquoise sky above the high moors of buttongrass, across which a line of far-spaced stakes marched into distance, depicting the footpath. Because it rains 156 inches here a year, and in the highlands winter blizzards blow, rude axe-hewn cabins have been built at intervals in which the hikers spend their nights. You want to gauge your walk so that you don't get caught out on the ground at night, especially because of the leeches.

The blood-sucking leeches hang by millions in the wet, too-opulent verdure and drop upon the hiker's clothes, or hitch rides upon his back pack.

Make no mistake that Tasmania *is* wild, no matter where you have been before now. Death from exposure can occur easily much of the year should a fierce storm catch you on the peaks. In the wet beech and myrtle forests of the valleys it is nearly impossible, at any month, to keep sleeping bags dry. Starting a fire takes more than a expert in these saturated forests; it takes a genius.

And these mountains contain the most amazingly hearty snakes you have ever known. They glide out from ahead of the hiker's stride—little whip snake, copperhead, black tiger snake—through a habitat of roaring streams and black highland tarns and catchments of ice water, impervious to cold! Ranger Saunders told me he has seen a snake on two occasions out traveling through winter snow.

"We cannot speak of the end of winter and in the same breath the entry of spring," wrote Weindorfer. "The vernal development here is so slow, and consequently extends over such a considerable amount of time that there is no real seasonal demarcation."

Indigenous flora produce seeds, but usually not germinal ones. The majority propagate by stolons at above three thousand feet on the edge of the King William pine forests. In ponds Weindorfer discovered that the Mayfly larvae perform a service to frog spawn by raising the water temperature, and that by tunneling through the jelly they eat, they also help the frog larvae of these cold waters to eventually escape. Reproductive processes are speeded up for survival of the species. From time of fertilization until dispersement of

212

the larvae takes sixteen days, in which time the water temperature
may rise as high as 62.7 degrees—briefly. But 45 degrees in the air
is the blow fly's low limit of performance. Weindorfer was a great
and gentle man. He speaks fondly even of the blow fly's brusque
movements in sunny nooks which proclaim to the world, "I am
happy."

And so was I! It was my second day of walking alone through
the tender beauty of mountain flowers, through high green moors
where the black tarns gleam silver to the sky, and the high country
was all smiles. Little glaciers held tinkling rivulets with overhanging
moss cushions sprinkled with tiny stars. The guide stakes, each
topped with a red-white inverted tin can, went marching onward over
mountain and marsh, and so did I—carrying forty pounds—hypnotised
by adventure.

Each step was chancy, sinking so far as the knee in a peat bog,
or skidding treacherously on the naked roots of a hillside which were
like sleigh runners. But I quickly learned which mosses and shrubs
support one, and which don't.

Only in a few places may fires be built, because of the peat moss
underneath. I cooked my tea on rock ledges with dead wood. I had
slept the first night at Waterfall Valley Hut. The bed was planking.
The huts were in bad condition because they needed re-building, for
there was only Gordon Saunders to do it all. Outside "no-account"
hikers coming through these wilds left the interiors filthy, and the
rats did the rest. There was no danger to speak of from snakes on
the trail but there was in the cabins, because snakes eat rats.

As soon as the sun dropped, a huge plump rat came down from
the cabin attic where he slept by day, and leapt "kerpunk" right
beside my head on the bunk. By dawn he returned to his attic the
same way. Marsupial, I supposed.

The next cabin was Windemere, and I stopped early because it
was there, gauging my sun. Tomorrow would be the longest stretch,
to Pelion Cabins, eleven miles away. On my third day out I met
three boys coming from the other end, passing with a hello. They
said my girls seemed to be doing fine. They had carefully detoured a
number of tiger snakes by wading out around, through water.

The golden weather held. There was no clue that, coming
down from the highest, windswept moors, I would find a mountainous, wooded region which I guessed must be my first hunk of genu-

213

ine rain forest. It was the height of the afternoon heat. I donned shorts, and swung along in great style over ancient log bridges spanning mossy cascades. Blazes on trees were the signs now.

When I entered the rain forest I did not dream of its immensity, but it simply went on and on. Here the sun never penetrates, even at brightest day. Giant grass trees and curious palms standing in pools of black water, and giant tropical ferns festooning the trailside made it a botanist's paradise. Stands of myrtle glistened with billions of tiny, round leaves, whose dead members also lined the forest floor. Several types of evergreens such as celery pine and pencil pine were covered with tiny white flowers.

Proceeding wetly down around Frog Bog at length, I crossed the Forth River on a log so broad a team could have almost been driven over it. There the trail made its way upward again onto another mountain slope, the Pelion, and into more open country of a dryer type forest by evening. When the long-awaited Pelion Cabin hove into view I was relieved to make it by just nightfall, very weary.

From here on the cabins changed from the old handhewn type to modern lumber and sheet metal, and fell into the province of the ranger at the other end of the park. The night in Pelion cabin, the new prefab job capable of sleeping fifteen to twenty hikers, was colder than in the old log structures. It was a flimsy affair, set a foot above the ground on stilts to prevent rot, and was of that kind we may expect to get in modern days when sides of corrugated iron and plywood are air-dropped; these lack insulation against the outside weather, but they are dry. The cabins were always located in a dry belt.

Because the fireplace in the interior was choked with old socks, eggshells, tin cans, glass bottles, and unburnable foil wrappings, I made tucker outdoors, using the hut only to sleep in.

In every hut the axe was broken, and the lack of expertise of the youth meant that the only wood stored inside the shelter for the next arrival was green, unburnable trash, all brambles.

Because the weather still held I was able to scrounge dry "squaw wood" lying about on the ground. I had candle stubs and saved my bacon fat and the paper from my foods in my pack for fire-starting.

The night at Pelion was as active as usual. Before darkness fell I was inside abed, as the fearful uproar started out beside the door.

The author sadly views a dingo dead of poisoning near the Calvert Hills
Homestead, Northern Territory.

Aboriginal mother and children, with the baby suffering from conjunctivitis or the "Sandy Blight." This family lives near Burketown, Northern Territory.

Toyota crossing the Stewart River, 18 miles south of Coen on the North West Developmental Road, Cape York Peninsula.

Ann and government surveyors appraise our engine, while visiting with a mapping crew at the Nicholson River camp near Doomadgee Mission Station, Northern Queensland.

A view of the sheep pens at Linkletter's Place near Esperance, Western Australia.

Jean, stamping (branding) sheep at Linkletter's Place, wore goggles to keep the dust and dirt out of her eyes.

A typical old gingerbread hotel, now deserted, was once one of the most glamorous hotels in Perth.

A wallaby in the wilds of Tasmania was spotted near the hiking trail in the Cradle Mountain-Lake St. Clair National Park. This character just did not want his picture taken. Even the telephoto lens and an hour's belly crawl were of little avail. The click of the shutter sent him bouncing across the countryside.

Jean in the buttongrass, while hiking with her backpack during the wet season. The rain swollen stream in front of her gives evidence of recent rains. The grasses surounding her are alive with leeches, as were most of the hiking trails in Tasmania. This scene is in the Cradle Mountain-Lake St. Clair National Park in Tasmania.

The Old Water Diviner at Camooweal on the Barkly Highway in Queensland. An aged vegetarian, he lives alone except for his dog.

The road to Burketown, Queensland, is straight as an arrow for almost 150 miles. This is one of the few graded roads in Australia.

The cat and "Joey" wallaby are pets of the family living at the Moreton Telegraph Office, on the Wenlock River, in the northern part of the
Cape York Peninsula. This was our most northern contact on the
peninsula.

Rider chasing a calf at the Brunette Races, Brunette Downs Homestead,
in the Northern Territory. The rider was our host during the Brunette
Downs Races.

A water well driller gets his instructions from our host at the Eva Downs Homestead, Northern Territory.

Bread put there by previous campers was soon the center of a snapping feast. Possums. Or—was that the little Tasmanian Devil, marsupial of singular rapacity, looking somewhat like a small wolverine,
who was eating the shrieking, caterwauling possums?

Such screaming, like pigs being butchered, high and shrill! Then
the feral growls! The uproar, racing up and down the roof now, and
around the doorstep with bangs and thuds and keening, lasted inter-
mittently through the night, until the first whoops and chirps of the
cheery *kurrawong*, big black bird of the Downunder tall-tree country, with his golden eye and outsize beak like a pickaxe, heralded the
dawn. I looked for bloodspots or patches of fur, but saw none.
Were the night's doings a dream? Only the *kurrawong* knew, and
told everybody.

I was a bit stiff and sore this morning, and the long first mountain nearly broke my back, but let it not be said that any average middle-aged American woman can't walk with a pack on her
back all day when it is necessary to explore a little new country.
The lovely walk then took me in due time to the Kia-Ora Hut beside
a little falls of the Kia-Ora Creek in primeval wilderness, unspoiled;
and there silently I made my campfire in the fading light of the
westering sun. Then I washed my legs of mud in the icy stream and
laid out my sleeping bag inside the prefab hut, using some insulat-
ing mats available in the place, in the face of the encroaching chill
of high altitude night. Today I had passed along the face of Mt.
Ossa, 5,305 feet, highest in Tasmania, and breathed gratefully of
its chill snowbanks and glaciers in a month when temperatures in
the mainland's coldest city, Melbourne, might rise to 117 degrees.

In the dusk I took my binoculars and sat beside the Kia-Ora
silently focused into a wild pool. This is platypus country. It was
only twenty-five years ago that science "discovered" the famous little
marsupial swimming animal of cold water streams which Australians
occasionally caught by accident on their fishing lines. Platypuses furnished Downunder fur capes and stoles before the fur trade was
topped. Today water pollution may be an even greater threat to
the animal.

The platypus spends its life in remote mountain streams, and
only awakens by night. In the day it lies asleep inside its home up
underneath some mossy bank, the entrance out of view, underneath
the water.

To keep the home dry, furthermore, the platypus builds a very tiny doorway. The doorway is made so that when he passes inside, the water is wrung out of his coat, just as if he passed through a wringer.

Also, the platypus, which lives on small slugs, snails, fish, and larvae, has to allow for the fact that it freezes in the wintertime where he lives. The miracle, then, is not only that there exists a mammal which lays an egg from which young are hatched, but that it hatches the egg in such a wet, icy cave in the streambank. After hatching, the platypus suckles its young like other marsupials. The male animal has a small, poisonous barb on each hind heel. It has webbed feet, and a broad, flat "bill" for scooping food.

It was a downhill trek through dark forests of beech and green-mossed logs interspersed with areas of dry type trees such as the usual tall, straight, giant eucalpyti and a shiny, glistening tough mountain shrub adorned with clusters of bright pink buttons, and mountainsides covered with the famous warratah trees. I saw three specimens of the fast-moving, white-lipped whip snake. I learned that in the Southern Hemisphere the heaviest moss grows on the south side of the trees. The day passed as in a dream.

At 4:30 P.M. I was snoozing in the westering sun beside Windy Point Hut when two boy students surprised me, arriving down the trail from whence I had come. They were soon followed by two others, medical students, Australians all. I therefore shared the cabin this night with the four boys. Several possums and a tiny, dainty, spotted marsupial cat called "tiger cat" came into the cabin by candlelight to be fed.

The eleven miles next day to Narcissus Cabin were surprisingly easy for me. It was a gradual, downhill grade along a dry ridge, no bog, no slog. My pack was lighter now; but mainly, I was tougher.

It was my sixth day out and I was still sighting specimens I'd never before seen: a mob of a dozen enormous parrots all black with daffodil side jaws and daffodil underwings when they flew, and tails like yellow fans. This was the black cockatoo of Tasmania. A discordant ruckus high in the eucalpts. Out with the glasses. Some perched high on limbs listening to a "speaker" who was lecturing them. Others argued. Others were climbing about, parrot fashion, by means of their mighty bills, making the forest a gay place. Wood chips fell groundward.

216

From underfoot skittered a nine-inch, fat, heavy, umber-brown lizard, reptilian black with red undertones shining through.

Finally, I crossed the Narcissus River on a swinging bridge, and the end of the day's track was near. I was joined by the two Sydney students at Narcissus Cabin. One was a med student and the other a student ichthyologist.

The last day for me, my seventh out from civilization, consisted of a long fourteen miles out along the rain forest shore of Lake St. Clair, under and over giant fallen logs which were in heavy moss, and through tree ferns which climbed to the unbelievable height of fourteen to twenty feet. Tree ferns are a survival of the prehistoric days. I was exceptionally feted by the ranger's family at the final end of the trail where I was fed a steak dinner at their own table and sank gratefully into their own bathtub. The dedication of each solitary ranger, with his helper, at either end of this park was total. There is no telephone line across the primitive area and the rangers had only the most round-about communication with each other. The park was so remote that there were no roads or habitation for great distances.

When I arrived back at the Launceston Hotel, not having changed clothes for ten days, some members of the Launceston Walking Club descended at that very moment with a most pressing invitation.

Into the hotel flat sitting room they trooped, before I had more than greeted Ann and Jean. There is something about a hiker. He carries himself differently from ordinary people. He is blythe, buoyant, untroubled. He is like the cheery *kurrawong*. The atmosphere which these people brought with them as they came trooping into our rooms with an invitation for us to join them for another week in the bush, starting at 6:00 A.M. on the morrow, was crazily irresistible. All I really needed was a change of clothes, which I had ready, and a refurbishment of foods in my back pack. So away I went again, out-bush.

Jean and Ann, after I left, shouldered their packs and hit the high road for Dover, along the coast. They thought to work at fruit harvesting. They ended up diving with "hooker gear" and wet suits with a commercial fisherman who taught them how to pick abalones from the sea bottom in depths to thirty feet. But that is another story.

"How far? How difficult?" I asked briefly of my own trip.

I was told the walkers planned to split into two groups. There was the veteran "mountain party" who would push and cut their way through the bush across the mountains, bushwhacking it, and there was the South Coast Track party which had the benefit of a foot path. I was in the latter group. Easy.

I did not worry about the girls. Not only were they well supplied with cash, but hostels were available at fifty cents a day, and then they could always turn to Ansett or to Comalco offices if they needed a friend. (Of course none of our friends dreamed the girls were going to the sea bottom.)

And so—in cars the walkers headed for the wild southwest part of the island for a week's reconnoitering, as they were a crack rescue and exploration team. The little caravan of cars by mid-morning halted for campfire lunch—no people are faster in the world than the Australians at "boiling the billy" over an open fire, and consuming gallons of tea with sugar and milk—we did a little re-sorting, we split up our groups, and each group was on its way. We were to make radio contact with each other, optimistically, on about the third day out.

My smaller group drove on through the empty village of Catamaran on a single track and brought up at road's end at the shacks at Cockle Creek on a sea cove. Here the foot path began. The path wound over sixty miles serpentinely along a totally uninhabited shore southward from here around the flank of the island to connect Point Davey. The purpose of the Southwest Track is to provide a means by which shipwrecked sailors off the southwest coast could get to civilization in emergency. Totally remote, here lie vast wilds undreamed of. Unexplored.

Within the first mile I saw, sadly, that I could not keep up with my fleet young friends—Betty, Chris, Kevin, Lester—all thirty years or so younger than myself, and I already a bit tired to begin with.

We camped early in two tents the fellows carried rolled on their backs, and had a sweltering, mosquito-infested night of it in our sleeping bags.

The next day was just about the toughest day of my life. Immediately now, the Port Davey Track—built by one man hired for three years by the Scenery Preservation Board—became much tougher. It climbed straight up ridges, only to plunge straight downward to each beach that a shipwrecked sailor might possibly get off at.

218

Each beach was small, some only a few hundred yards in extent. Each was bounded by cliffs fronting the cold, windy Southern Ocean. With Antarctica directly two thousand miles away, the coast here is very heavy bush and rain forest, with hundreds of square miles of the same stretching inland from the single foot path.

We spent hours climbing hand over hand about the wild sea cliffs as the wind tore at us and I, at least, had to hand my packsack on ahead to helping hands. The one other female with us, while a little thing, proved to be surprisingly resilient and stubborn. The rule of the track proved to be rain forest ridges hung with moss, alternating with occasional sand beaches to which the trail plummeted like the sea eagle. The beaches coming at intervals permitted normal walking, then a sign on a stake would direct us to attack the soaring forest, hand over hand again.

It was a course of the most grueling gymnastics, and when the dull day turned to steady rain the sharply inclining track became a river of stinking mud out of which leeches came. Until now I had been in the bush only on sunny days.

Tears of utter exhaustion coursed down my face, but my companions may have thought it was rain. In any case, they had their own problems. I prayed for the day to end, or even for quick death to end this cruel forced labor. Alone a mile to the rear I dragged along, inch by inch. I was glad to be alone so that I could curse and groan. At intervals one of the tall boys carried my pack, "double tripping" his pack and my own at the last, as day waned alarmingly and there was no place to camp until the expected campsite could be won.

Our leader, Chris, was an expert at guiding us. Wet forest meant nothing to him, with his axe. In 1963 he had been a member of Cambridge University climbing team in Greenland.

When our young leader finally led me, in roaring, windy darkness around the last scary bluff above the sea, and I crawled on hands and knees clinging to sea grass and shrubs for dear life to the one cleared, hospitable niche in miles of Tasmanian wilds, and I saw the others around the cheerful fire, the cheery *kurrawong* hikers, I could only sit on a box and drink their hot soup, with wordless admiration of their great and noble spirits.

The leeches did not bother these hikers, and I found soon that they did not bother me. While we huddled sociably around our campfire on this cold, rainy night these inch-long, slimy, black, tar-like globs were gathering from far and wide, vast numbers of them.

"The fire draws them," Chris was saying to Betty. "They always love a fire. We can't sit here long."

When we swung out lights, sure enough, leeches were humping over the ground towards the fire as fast as they could hump, coming from every direction. My light picked up a leech on a moist stone four feet from me, waving its head this way and that, upreared. He was ravenous for a good meal of warm blood, and was coming after me. He was zeroing in.

I started checking my legs. They were covered with leeches! Suddenly everyone was in a panic, burning off leeches as fast as we could, and hopping up and down. We gave up our social evening at the good fire Chris had built with his axe work, and hurried off to our sleeping bags inside the tents.

I had already learned that in walking a rain forest track you cannot stop for long without these pests hunting you down. Any warm blooded animal is sensed with beautiful precision.

The leech will increase ten times its size with blood intake. Your blood is being drained out of you before you know it's happening. But don't try to pull a leech out. If the thing breaks off with the head in you, it causes trouble. Take salt, or light a match, and it will back out in haste.

When I got my leather boots next morning six leeches still hung from them, frustrated, where they had sawed hopefully all night.

We hiked up and down, through rain forest and sand beaches, all next day. At last we reached our goal, New River and the New River Lagoon. Distance from the start: thirty incredible miles.

Chris, an English migrant who had not hiked here before, dir-ected the girls to use putty, canvas, and tacks, and Betty and I then repaired the DPW—Department of Public Works—boats berthed on that beach, while he led the men over the hill for three hours re-connaisance, and returned with a big airdrop can of food. The contents were hard candy, package soups, pudding mixes, dried fruits bars of chocolate, oatmeal. No meat, however. I missed protein, the hardest of all foods to provide.

With two boats we rowed inland on the lagoon now, winding back into forested hills primordial. Fresh water was found near the base of Precipitous Bluff (four thousand feet) and Chris made radio contact with the mountain party.

The lagoon was covered with about five hundred very suspicious black swans. They sailed on ahead of us like tall, graceful ships. They flew in V-formation that evening on a practice flight, for when winter came they would migrate back north to a warmer climate.

The rowing put us five miles further from civilization, where we pitched camp beside the fresh water to await the mountain party. This meant that altogether I had about seventy miles to make this week, plus the fifty-six miles of last week.

The flies and mosquitoes bit like mad along the salt lagoon, so bathing was a brief affair. The whole world roared with insects to a degree that you couldn't hear the sound of an airplane if there was one—and this is my definition of wild country. I love that sound of wildness, the real thing. Not tamed, not sprayed, not improved. Beautiful, wild.

The mountain party arrived by night, halooing along the shore. Nothing stopped them, happy men and girls in their twenties carrying packs nearly as big as themselves. They were led by an English doctor, and some of the girls were nurses.

It was time for me to start the return walk. I would need three full days to make it. It was decided that Lester, the weakest and the only man inexperienced in bushmanship should start back, too.

I rowed five of us down the lagoon to the proper beach, then I set off at once through sand and then through the shallows, wading where the stubborn bush projected out into the water. Lester, age 27, soon overtook and passed me with his long moose legs. By unspoken mutual agreement I and the Tasmanian "city boy" knew we wanted to see little of each other, yet we had these wild miles to get over safely.

At North River, at the foot of the first bluff, I started hoisting myself and my pack, hand over hand up the killing track. Four hours hard work later the track plunged down another mountain to Surprise Beach in the same sheer manner, from upper rain forest. There Lester lay resting on the beach. He wanted to stay here. But something, some feeling, nagged at me. That beach would be pretty small in a sea storm. Also, I wanted to put the next big mountain,

221

1,000-2,000 feet, behind me, and we still had hours left before nightfall, which I could take advantage of.

Lester complied grudgingly, and we went off again, with him soon passing me. We had to pass clear on through each rain forest section where the leeches were waiting. Lester had been delegated to carry our tent.

Even at midday the rain forest was dark with only an occasional shaft of sunlight to gild the spreading umbrellas of the exquisite tree ferns, the horizontal scrub, the clumps of six-foot "cutting grass," the ti trees, and the slopes of dead standing brown ferns which the Scots call "bracken." Only an occasional dry log along the trail offered a rest, with a rock prop for your pack if you were lucky. Birds called at intervals but you could rarely see them. Roots, coiled and gnarled, awaited the careless foot.

The tiger snake, hooded and cobra-like, was revealed in sunny spots in the path. Always he awoke at a footfall and moved off. I saw the last half of such a snake, thick, black, sinuous, ending in the tapering tail when the coils glided away smoothly as the bracken parted at my stride. Quite close, that one. Fortunately a gentleman, in the way that wild things are.

In this month, February, the snakes were mating. Once in a while a big male may be looking for a fight, ready to take on all comers in true Aussie fashion. It is from this that the species gets its name, tiger snake.

Brian, at Linkletter's Place, told us of seeing a tiger snake chase a woman across a field to her car, and a very old man on Flinders Island, near Tasmania, reported having been chased himself by such a snake on that island, where he was clearing fields. I talked with one man who actually was bitten by a big tiger snake. This was the scholarly old historian Dick Fowler. He was bitten on Flinders Island by accident one hot summer's day in the course of farming. He said the reptile grabbed him suddenly by the thumb of one hand as he bent down to do something. It all happened so suddenly that there was little time to think about it. It was death, he knew. To his surprise the reptile hung on like a bulldog with its teeth and wouldn't let go. He couldn't pull it off his thumb.

Fowler resolved the problem by getting his shotgun out of the truck, and he shot off the thumb, snake, and all. Then,

222

wrapping up the stump, he drove three miles by dirt road to the little hospital in Whitemark.

By the time he got there he felt a numbness and a coldness creeping over his body even on that hot day, he said. Anti-venom was administered, and after a day in the hospital he made a nice recovery, except for being minus the end of one digit.

A girl hiker was bitten in a very private area of the body when outdoors behind a bush along the Cradle Mountain track one summer. She died. Hikers learned to be alert in the matter of untimely defecation.

When I reached Shoemaker Beach, Lester already had the little tent set up. He had a fire going beside a brook which ran under stones but left just enough water exposed to dip the billy. The tent sheltered under a fringe of conifers on the embankment, the crash of the sea before us being very loud tonight. The tent was actually pitched in a driftwood yard, showing that a storm tide might occasionally sweep the ground where the tent clung.

Lester had pitched a good tent, sagging just a bit. Then he had amused himself by laying down some stray drift planks over the uneven stones from the tent door to the waterhole, making himself a little paved street, and it was quite pretty. But he hadn't chopped more than about six little sticks for firewood. The hot day had vanished. A change in the weather was due.

Asked if he wanted to share my can of warmed tuna with me he growled, no, he always ate tuna cold, and not a thank you, either. He had not offered to share his sausages with any of the other campers during the week out, and typically, he offered none now. Silently we ate our separate meals, cooking in our own pots.

My morose companion, a natural introvert, picked a meagre handful of dry hay for tinder and put it thoughtfully inside the tent before retiring. The sky offered a few sprinkles now. *"That* won't start a fire!" I thought, but I said nothing and did nothing. I was just too tired to care. "That's his worry," That's what I thought.

Next morning nobody could start a fire. It had rained steadily all night and we awoke to that Tasmania which has been aptly described as "just one big, saturated sponge."

Now along with his stinginess and surliness of personality, the tall, pallid clerk revealed another trait not surprising in the extreme introvert temperament. He proved to be just as stubborn as the proverbial mule, and as set in his ways.

As the rain poured steadily downward it was his intention to start the A.M. fire—and he wouldn't give up. He had with him a miner's carbide lamp which insured that a steady flame could be applied. For an hour and a half he applied flame to his stingy pile of punky twigs. Each time the flame was withdrawn the fire went right out, of course. The fire just couldn't make it on what it had to feed on.

Of all things I didn't want, it was to stand around and lose body heat at the start of a very cold day. There was absolutely no way of getting body heat back once you lost it along this hostile coast. We still had two days travel ahead, two days to endure the elements on limited food. I tried my skills with the fire. Unfortunately, only an axeman who knew how to select certain wood and how to use an axe like an artist could have started a fire now, and neither Lester nor I were axemen.

"Well," he finally admitted, water dripping from his hat brim, "I'll eat my breakfast cold this time, and then I'll eat my lunch hot."

Soaking wet he backed inside the tent, carefully reorganizing his pack load. Mine was already rolled and loaded. Both of us were chilled. I couldn't even cover my hair because I had lost my handy head scarf. The world seemed raw and blustery indeed when your head was out in it, too.

Starting out ahead of him down the beach, I was soon puffing and clawing my way up the embankment at its end, and into the longest, toughest stretch of rain forest we had to overcome. Now the trail turned into a series of deep quagmires of black mud soup between the roots. Through it all I plodded doggedly under my pack, or in some cases, detoured the bogs by wrestling the bushes aside. I used bushes and trees to push myself upward with my arms when my legs almost wouldn't make the grades. I dug my toes in and the sides of my sneakers (rotting leather boots were carried in the pack) to gain every inch of toehold on the slippery, pouring mountains. Whoops! A flop here and there into the slimy mud!

Endlessly the forested mountain shoulder soared above into white fog. Rain spouts down the trees afforded an opportunity to drink, where in dry times an exhausted and depleted hiker could die of thirst. To drink I had to unbuckle my waist strap and wrest the pack off and get out my bowl. The way this back pack was

224

made, it set firmly on your hips, sparing your shoulder straps a good part of the load—and this was a good feature. But a feature not so good was that the load, attached to a rigid frame, rode so high up behind your head that you could not throw back your head to take a drink of spout water. In fact, in this steep country the high pack above your head was a menace. It gave your neck such rigidity that the position of upward climbing tended to unbalance you and push you off the mountain as you struggled. Similarly, if you missed your footing in the downhill swing, the high frame and load behind your head tended to push you face down to earth for a nasty tumble.

A loner's caution on this track was similarly alerted again by a fact that the brush-cleaner, in cutting the track, had cut the growth off about one to two feet above ground, with a slashing stroke of the axe. The result was a trail laced from start to finish with thousands of sharpened stakes onto which you might fall, especially when laboring under a load and in a state of physical fatigue.

Steadily I climbed upward and reached the top, which was a kind of tundra of buttongrass filled with bogs and tarns. The sea could not be heard. This must be higher than I knew, at least two thousand feet above the sea, and it had taken me hours to climb it. Now, onward through the clouds on top, and starting downward to the next valley over a series of endless lower ridges of rain forest, moss-shrouded, wierd, beautiful. The clean rain coming down, down, filled the moss banks till each puffed up ten times the size of yesterday. I crawled, covered with mud, on hands and knees, under and around time-taking windfalls. I was in shorts, so as to keep my long pants dry for sleeping, come night. I worked steadily at a speed calculated to keep body warmth, and the heavy pack on my back helped.

The dull light of the interminable day seemed to grow dimmer. I passed through somber glades which were like a dream. In these latitudes verging toward the Antarctic the days at this time of year lasted until nine o'clock. Still, would I make the next camp in time? Fog clouds drifted with me, dizzily.

At long last the trail opened out. There was the beach near Southwest Cape. I sighted a big, fresh arrow drawn in the sand there, indicating where Lester would be. There also were his long footprints leading right into Southwest Cape Rivulet. But the Rivulet was now a swollen torrent thirty yards across and becoming more dangerous by the moment. Just down below, the swift flood poured into the smashing breakers of the sea. Not a good place at all for getting floated away with a pack on your back.

I believed I could cross, with steady nerves. Taking a long pole to probe ahead, I waded gingerly across the fierce, muddy, foaming Rivulet. Following Lester's big footprints down the beach through sand I saw then his torn cotton shirt adorning a stake set up beside a tract of dense, sheltering forest of the dry area or eucalypt type. Plunging into this forest I found him there with the tent pitched, and he had a small fire really going! Lester had *finally* learned to use the axe to split dead timbers so as to obtain dry wood. I hadn't dared hope for a fire this night. I had to salute him.

He even had hot soup waiting for me. Pouring it for me into his own cup, he just croaked, "You better get out of those wet clothes and right into the sleeping bag."

I did that. There were about thirty leeches to be picked off, and I threw them unceremoniously into the cold from the sleeping bag. There was blood inside my sleeping bag now from my legs and lower part of my body as I detached the leeches, but the sleeping bag interior was dry and warm. I snuggled down, listening to the steady drumming of the rain on the tent and the wild ocean's roar.

The boy had selected a truly nice stand of trees. Crawling soddenly into his own bag right beside me, while I kept my eyes closed in modest manner, he rolled over as far as he could get in his half of the tent, and both exhausted, we were instantly fast asleep.

If shipwrecked sailors really needed to use this king's highway to walk to civilization on this coast, I wondered if a single one would survive.

It was the last day's march. Lester built a breakfast fire. He was still deliberating about whether he and I would drink both coffee and tea, hot or cold, with two buckets or one.

"When we're both soaked to the skin and about to get pneumonia who cares?" I said. When I went to the Rivulet to fill the billys and again when I washed up, the Rivulet was a terrifying sight and the wind near a gale. The people who followed us might be marooned.

Forward down the beach we quickly trotted on blue and shivery legs, and soon entered the area of great boulders, slag, and sea cliffs which we must pass. During this phase Lester stayed near me, and the trail, if you could call it that, was marked up and down and over and under the boulders, by little rock cairns.

Sliding my pack over an arch ahead and climbing through after it at certain junctures was an excruciating business. My knees were giving out in the joints. Any veteran mountaineer knows the signs. In Arizona we called it "canyon knee." Today I had precarious control, and I was afraid of falling onto the rocks. Today it was so cold, and the last day, that I gambled everything and put on all the clothes I owned, to keep warm, but also to keep from rock abrasions. Everything I had was now wet, and I knew that the sleeping bag, too, was about gone. One could really die of exposure here. It was only a matter of time and the individual's own condition, his endurance and grit, but most of all his emotional stability and common sense. How long could one carry on such inhuman labors without food and shelter?

As we retraced the way of the outgoing expedition a week ago, the tide was out. This meant the elimination of a slippery and hazardous piece of track, hanging above the cliffs, if we could but hurry across the rocks below before the tide came in again.

Momentarily I assessed it before the start. It could be a death trap. If the tide came in just when one of us slipped and broke his back, or even banged a kneecap. . . . Oh, well. We hurried on. Over the lower sea-slimy rocks we stretched and reached and chimneyed, and once on a big flat slab both feet whizzed out from under me, as though I hit grease. I fell smack flat upon my back, but was not hurt.

When the last of the boulder-strewn ocean front was overcome I released Lester and told him to go on ahead to the cars.

"I'll see you this evening, then, at Cockle Creek," he said.

The track headed inland for its final spurt across a neck of land, and even the hills leveled out to a degree, while the track was well marked and clear. Only when it entered the buttongrass plains and descended across a broad, green empty valley marked by stakes, was there a final obstacle course to run that I hadn't guessed.

During the three days that we were homeward bound the rain had been pouring down, in an area where precipitation is normally 150 inches and in some years may reach 185 inches.

The track I followed through the valley went deeper and deeper under water—something I did not see ahead, even with the aid of the binoculars. A small creek in the valley contributed to the general overflow, until I presently found myself wading continuously above the knees, and then it went to the hips, and then it went to the waist.

The water was not muddy here but lay over firm pasture bottom, yet was black in the fog which overlay the still world, and you could not see how deep the puddles were; nor was there any stick or pole available for miles around for soundings. The rain had stopped after saturating, yes obliterating the whole country. Each bush and tussack was loaded with jewels of water, while I, a saturated human water cart, plodded through, splashing.

I practically swam my way out at last. If I tried to detour the lakes I got into worse bogs still, and worried that at any moment I might step down into some really deep hole of a living, flowing stream. What with being buckled into the back pack, I might drown.

But there was once a wagon road here in the valley where I splashed; the track was right here somewhere underfoot. Remnants of old rotten bridge timbers floated around me. The pasture road at one time had been built up with little bridges in order to convey wagons or possibly some early motor vehicles near the coast. The long-ago road enabled man to gain access to the sea in the vicinity of Southwest Cape.

I tried then to walk upon parts of the old bridges or their supports across the swamp, but most pieces were adrift and would not bear my weight. In fact, they were an extra hazard. It was not long before night. I was very depleted now from many deep immersions, and dazed.

I proceeded along the submerged track with every possible caution, doing a job which had to be done, when suddenly, I stepped into a hole.

Down, down I went to the armpits. Both feet were wedged on the bottom between buttongrass clumps. When I struggled to extract a foot nothing happened. For leverage I grabbed a floating timber, but I only succeeded in pushing it underwater. I grabbed at some slender waving grasses. They were no use, either.

It would be twenty-four hours, optimistically, before the others would come along behind me on this track. Quite a spell to be anchored to the armpits in ice water. And—if the water rose a few inches?

By a miracle of ingenuity and strength, balancing on one foot, I drew the other foot loose by turning my ankle sideways in an

228

underwater contortion, floundered on across that worst puddle, and was on my way. Lucky for me I was wearing the slick little tennis shoes today so I could squirm loose.

At the last, to cross Cockle Creek, I tightrope-walked its two-log, high, wire-strung bridge above the river. It was almost too much in my condition. It had a booby-trap, rickety, wire-and-stick railing on one side that would have collapsed if you leaned on it for support.

I made it. Reaching ground, I turned my ear hopefully for the sound of a man chopping wood. Or the sight of an open fire.

No use. There was Lester, just sitting there in wet clothes, settling down for an indefinite wait in one of the cars.

But I found then a humble fisherman's widow. Inside a spare cabin, she built a fire in its fireplace for us, and I dined sumptuously on two fresh goose eggs and authentic "Australian lobster tail" direct from the crayfish pots. Lester never ate these items, he said, and thought I was a fool when I pressed two dollars into the poor widow's surprised hand. The widow had lost her husband at sea. She had some good things in life, if not a good pension: fresh cockles and mussels for the picking, lobsters and fish, a berry patch, beef cattle and hogs (which men stole from her), a kitchen garden, and a greensward out of a children's book of olden tales, upon which her stately ducks and geese waddled at the edge of the Tasman Sea. I slept that night in the farthest house south in wild Tasmania.

"You would be surprised how many marriages take place among the members of the Launceston Walking Club," someone told me when eventually the remaining walkers streamed, with back packs and bed-rolls, into the welcome warmth and hospitality of the cabin I had found.

On general principles I was glad to hear that. Certainly, if any justice prevails in this world, the girl who hikes deserves to get her man.

"Mother, you look wonderful!" cried Ann, when I walked into our hotel room. "You're so slim and firm! You've got a figure just like a girl's!"

Yes. Except that my feet were like clubs for some time, I looked and felt marvelous. Of course I couldn't get up and down the three flights at the hotel on the carpeted stair without hanging onto the bannister. But when Ann and I dined that evening, two traveling men from the mainland who were in their forties took it upon themselves to send us wine and dance with us. They were Australian millionaires and in the steel business: there would be plenty of dates to dinner for Mom when our travels the next time brought us to Melbourne and to Sydney. If only my "slimming course" lasted long enough!

"But where's Jean?" I knew instantly, with a mother's quick grasp of things, that I was missing one child.

"Jeanie and I couldn't get jobs picking strawberries," Ann said. "We met this bloke at Dover. He's got a fishing boat, and you'll never guess, he hired us for professional divers! He showed Jeanie and me how to dive. . . ."

"Where's Jean *now*?"

"Well, Mom, Jean turned out to be an especially good diver, much better than me. Diving's something not everybody can do, you have to have the temperament for it, and I caught a cold, so I came back to the hotel. . . ."

"*Where's Jean now*?"

"Diving. They went to sea for a few more days."

"*Who* went to sea?"

"Jean and Otto. She's his helper. He's from Germany, when he was a kid, and you know how Jean likes Germans."

"Ah, yes," I said. "So she does."

"The important thing," Ann hurried on, sensibly, "is you don't need to worry, Mom. Otto's a pro diver. He owns his own boat and he even owns an island, and he's very *sensible*. He keeps that boat polished, and the engine and compression pump and everything in just perfect working order. You know how efficient Germans are. . . .'

"Compression pump?"

"Yes, we use wet suits to keep warm in this cold water, and we use hooker gear. That means you have an air hose that feeds your air to you from the boat. Gee, we had a lot of fun with Otto already. He showed Jeanie and me an octopus in a cave, and he's been teaching us the names of all the fishes down there. It's a world of its own under the sea, Mom—once you learn to breathe, that is. Otto says Jean is a natural born diver. She learned it in no time. And I shot a big blue morray eel with my spear gun when it came after me. . ."

"Who mans the compression pump when you all take a dive?"

230

"One of us always watches it. You just set the dials. Two divers pick up abalones on the bottom, and just walk around with a basket. You keep one man in the boat to take up the baskets and lower them again. We work in about thirty to sixty feet usually."

Ann said that soon the Tasmanian season would be ending now. "And guess what? Otto says he always goes north along on up the coast. And we told him that we'll be driving north, too, pretty soon, with our new Toyota. He fishes along the coast of Queensland. Then, he goes on to Thursday Island and Divers Graveyard for a while. The water's very warm there. It's maybe three thousand miles from here. . . .

"You'll probably get to meet Otto one of these days, Mom," my youngest daughter told me. "He's anxious to meet you. We told him how you're not narrow-minded like most moms are [flattery will get you everywhere] and so he wants to meet you very, very much."

Even then I didn't believe a word of that. "Yes, I'm looking forward to meeting Otto, too," I said, feeling a little bit insecure.

Chapter 15

THE FURNEAU ISLANDS

Between the large island state of Tasmania and the mainland lie the forty-two islands of the Furneau Group. Ripped by the tides of Bass Strait, infested with a veritable treasury of deadly snakes, a nesting grounds of gannets, Cape Barrens geese, and muttonbirds, these islands, too, are very much worth seeing for those who revel in Australia's wonders.

On some of these islands cattle are grazed, and they have been the nexus of the strange "muttonbird industry" in which fat sea birds are plucked in season by hand from their burrows under the sand (burrows in which the deadly tiger snake also may greet the searching hand) to be dried and cured as an oldtime staple food of the Australian population.

The Furneau Islands can be reached only by small trading ship, and they have no public accommodations. The thing which makes them particularly interesting is that the population of their villages is made up of the descendants of white pirates, both Yank and British, of olden times, and the women whom they kidnapped and won in war from the Tasmanian Aboriginal tribes.

The largest of the group, Flinders Island, has the one airfield in this region. Ann and I accepted an invitation to fly with Ansett Airlines to Flinders for a few days, to be followed presently by Jean.

With its nearly constant Antarctic winds, legendary Flinders is not a hot island. On went every heavy sweater and all pairs of pants, shortly after we entered the old-time country hotel at Whitemark and were ushered into our bare little unheated cubicles.

It was carpeted, neat and clean. Paper flowers popped from vases in every cranny. Each evening we thawed out just before bed, with a hot bath drawn into the community tub—a thin pencil stream of brown, discolored water. Unlighted was the route to tub and toilet, as though to hide these facilities—for clearly the less used the better. Water is hard to come by on this island—only twenty inches of rainfall here. Drinking water was supplied each guest daily in a two-quart jug on his dresser, and the bath was a salt-fresh mixture.

At "tea time"—the evening meal—I descended from my frigid cubicle to a dark, frigid cubicle in the downstairs area, a standup place. Now, where was the dining room? The first door led into a broom closet. The second led into the men's bar: forbidden. The third was locked. The fourth led through a dark passage to a gleaming cash register, and I found myself unexpectedly *behind* the men's bar as a sort of impromptu barmaid. A sound of whistling blasted my ears as thirty faceless men in the bar saw a *woman*!

But it was time to eat. I could smell food somewhere! The proprietress, shocked by my wanderings, asked me: "What are you doing here? This is the men's bar." At length I got through another door and was permitted to sit down in the dining room, although, as the proprietress scolded, consulting her watch, the "bell hasn't rung, and you're two minutes early."

Typically the roadside inn guest will discover that his portion of meat, submerged under gluey gravy, is simply a little pile of sinew and bones which have been chopped and splintered by a careless cleaver. The game is camouflage. The theory apparently is that the customer won't know any different if you barely fulfill the letter of the laws of accommodation, and you give him as poor and stingy a portion as you can manage, for in this way, being shrewd, you save on food and get ahead.

If he doesn't come back—well, who cares about one bloke? Who does he think he is, a king or something?

There is always a lovable little chopped turnip in the soup. Lucky me, I like turnips. The ever-popular country vegetables served are coarse, gray-cooked beet tops, and sides of plain boiled pumpkin.

Three times a day you get your potatoes mashed and mixed

with mashed pumpkin as a regular dish: yummy. In a seaside room the seagulls fly over the tin roof, the cheap paper curtains stand out straight into your bedroom from the wind, a male hotel guest in dressing gown is crawling about on his hands and knees in the gloomy hallway upstairs, looking, he shamefacedly explains, "for contact points so he can shave"; and he finally does shave on his hands and knees, in the dark.

Time stands suspended in the nineteenth century. But it's all wonderful, really, because the nineteenth century isn't overpopulated · I really recommend it. Its discomforts are leisurely ones, not the utterly mad discomforts of our own.

"Could I ask your advice?" Dick Fowler's sweet wife asked me. She was an island girl, had lived on Flinders her whole life. "Next Christmas," she said, "that's a year away yet, I am asked to select some garden verse for our church publication. And I thought that perhaps you, being an author. . . ."

"What's garden verse?"

"Well, like Longfellow, and beautiful poets' works like that. The verses would be about flowers and the joys of the garden, and would bring a message of hope and cheer to people."

"Gee, Longfellow and flowers haven't crossed my mind in some time. Even my children don't have this in school any more. But, I'll try."

I would send her some "garden verse" from the outside world.

Her husband had been working on his vast historical work for fifteen years. It would really divide easily into three epochs, perhaps three books, the only works in existence about these islands.

He had charted a hundred shipwrecks of the old tall-masters lying under these seas. He was the only man to know where each one lies. In his head were the mutinies, the terrible deeds, the piracy, the murderous Captain Cook; Banks, whose valet for four years at sea is believed to have been a beautiful English woman who loved him and went along with explorers disguised as a man. In the historian's mind was Captain Blythe and Bougainville—he knew them well from their journals. He knew the great explorers, the convict ships, sealers and traders, each by name. The old historian of the island knew and loved them all as his family. He was growing very old now. Time, precious time, was running out. If he could only get them all down on paper as he knew them. . . .

234

This wonderful man, Dick Fowler, died a few months later, and his completed mighty efforts will be published in Australia presently.

Another fine work on this area is *Moonbird People* by Patsy Adam-Smith, whom I went to see in Hobart.

The beautiful girl Patsy first went to Flinders on assignment for a newspaper. But she ended up spending seven years as cook-helper on a small trading boat in the islands. She gets her title from a legend that the fat little birds were left behind when the moon fell from the earth long ago and went into its own orbit, and that the birds really belong to the moon. (Actually they are shearwaters, which spend the opposite season in the Bering Sea, off Alaska.)

As the fame of Patsy's several best-selling books began to spread around the Downunder countries, she told me people like to imagine somehow (she was divorced, and supporting children) that, because she adventured in remote places surrounded by men, her life was one fraught with endless romantic opportunities. Some would have liked to attach to her life, if they could, the spice of scandal.

Given any other land in all the world, and similar circumstances, love and romance might bloom, indeed. Never in Australia! When you are talking about Australia you are not talking about a normal land. It is probably the only country in the world that has never written love songs. This culture is so stern that the very inference of sex attraction frightens and outrages the men who are the most strict wardens of the unhappy Victorian code. It could happen only in Australia—that nothing ever happens!

In America our own critics tell us that for generations up until now we managed to educate the desire for sex out of a considerable percentage of all young women. But in Australia—can you believe it?—the actual male drive is blocked, is educated out of the boys as well. It is a culture which repeatedly drummed into young men: "Be *clean* in mind and body, son. Take cold showers, play constantly upon the field of sports. And should you ever have a lapse with some damned woman, the sooner forgotten the better."

The reader should read Australia's rebellious sophisticate, Sue Rhodes' *Now You'll Think I'm Awful*, for further verification.

I left muttonbird country and took a flight hop over to Hobart. Patsy and I were seated at cocktails in the late afternoon in a resort lounge, and Patsy, this elegant gal who looks somewhat like Shirley MacLaine, was explaining to me some of the difficulties of the exceptional woman who happens to be born in Australia. We were exchanging information in rapid-fire, low voices, somewhat as women who consider themselves attractive might possibly do in say, the chilly climate of Moscow.

Even at their age Jean and Ann said that Aussies just didn't know how to flirt or how to talk with a woman. (An exception to a degree was the very upper classes, but they were rare individuals.) They didn't respond to the proper signals. They didn't even *know* the signals. Some might regard modern woman, or emancipated woman, of the late twentieth century as some unknown, horrible, unleashed monster.

At any rate, as my monster friend and I sat in this fine, carpeted "lounge" we saw the area filling with a large party of gorgeous people, and we sat watching them. It was a private party. Gowns were full-length. Long gloves adorned bare young arms. Mums and dads were distinguished. In this society there was no large pool of divorced women. People here remained married forever.

Out of this group there came to our table now a girl of Portuguese descent. Patsy knew her well. The girl was in her late twenties and not married. She had no escort. She had been invited to this party, but was on the fringes, as it were.

The Portuguese girl, with her naturally merry disposition, her kindness, her industry and ingenuity, and a strong dose of quiet courage, all her life had had to make the best of it here in a world in which she and her family, no matter what they might achieve in scholarship or commerce or whatnot, were "frozen out." Her ancestor four generations ago had slipped his chains and swum ashore to a wild haven, to leave in this land a progeny of bubbling, friendly dark eyes among the blue ones.

The Portuguese girl kept smiling, and she loved and lived, somehow. She was the one who came to the airport at Hobart to see me off when I left, and the one to whom I would turn most especially if I were to say I have a real friend in Tasmania, although I left a number of good friends there.

By contrast was the day I spent with a petite woman of a rare arrogance of manner, whom it was possible to meet only by certain connections. She had me for tea at her home and then, slowly warming to the idea that I was a "visiting author," decided she would spend the remainder of her day driving me about and chatting.

236

Born in Perth to society life, this lovely woman had by pure spunkiness acquired a degree at law, against the staid advice of every lawyer and the sheer horror of friends and family.

It was her one rebellion. She could laugh about it now. In her culture girls of upper class, even there, are permitted only the one traditional career of marriage and motherhood. She explained that she never dreamed of using her law degree. That would be just too much.

A society wedding linked her to a general's son. He was an Australian born in Pakistan, of a father whose duties consigned him to the East Indian army. The father-in-law, a famous polo player in his youth, belonged to that age of colonialism in which officers had as many as twenty-eight servants for personal duties such as polishing boots.

The Australian general's son did not hanker for a military career. Attending a private school for sons of "better families," including British titled families, he became an empire-builder of lands, and today oversaw, along with vast properties in Tasmania and in south Western Australia, a recently-acquired 800,000 acres in the Nullarbor.

Perhaps the clever, sharp-toothed little women who marry wealth and position are inclined to be arrogant in any land. Yet, there was in her nature a quick, inquiring, intelligent mind, a deep love of beauty, a great flair for art and interior decoration, a love for the panorama of sea and nature, a tremendous zest for life in general, and strong bonds of class loyalty. Her culture did not engender in her any awareness that the age of colonialism is dead. She had no awareness that one has a duty to give as well as to receive from life— and so in keeping with that class which rules nations, she did what comes naturally and lived greedily for little self.

In Tasmania's little kingdom in the sea the couple lived their lives in a closed Victorian society of top hats and tails, of exquisite imported Parisian gowns, of formal garden teas laid by servants, and dinner by candlelight. It is a closed society, encapsulated, changing little, and only dimly aware of outsiders or tourists, who come and go like muttonbirds. In fifteen years in Tasmania this lady did not recall ever meeting a single tourist. Life in Australia for her group was a serene minuet of social events. Children were no problem. In keeping with colonialism you had a nanny to raise them, and they went away early to boarding school.

"Tazzy" is a tourist mecca for mainlander Australians only in the brief summer season. The Government Tourist Bureau, under an administration whose premier and staff have remained unchanged for thirty years, doesn't work unduly hard. Letters from outside are apt to lie about unanswered, even unopened. The Tourist Bureau has been given but a stingy, meagre little budget to operate on. Yet even Flinders Island business people want tourists.

On Flinders I heard the plaintive query: "Do you think our island will get tourists? We have some beautiful beaches here. . . ."

"Yes, indeed. But the Antarctic waters lapping against your beaches are chilly, even in summer."

"Yes, a bit chilly, I suppose. Yet, have you seen some of our beaches between the rocks? Beautiful symmetry. Such clean sand. . ."

"Charming. But you must admit yourself that the rock areas are a good deal more prevalent than the beaches. It would be an interesting challenge indeed in public relations if one could talk tourists into lying in their swim suits on those cold, sharp rocks."

And back in Tassy, proper: "But only last week a Norwegian vessel came into port, and it was just *loaded*. Every passenger on board was an American millionaire!"

"How do you know they were millionaires?"

"The Hobart paper said so. The tour was called 'Millionaires' Cruise.' "

"They're just people who saved their money by hard work, and are taking a vacation for three weeks," I said. "It's called 'Millionaires' Cruise' because Americans would like to think of themselves as millionaires for three weeks out of their lives."

"Oh!" sighed the businessman, disappointed. "Everybody around here is wondering how we in Tasmania can get hold of some of that American millionaire trade."

"But I do believe that tourism holds Tasmania's real future. Really," I said. "Tourism is far more important in the long run than agriculture and livestock raising. Even now it pays Tasmania as much as wool, I read. Yes, really. Tourism is more important than industry, too, I think. But not tourists lying on cold rocks. Tourists hiking. Tourists bush-bashing on walk-about into the wild country."

"Yes, I've always said we could improve on that," said the citi-

238

zen. "Put in some roads. Put a chair lift up the mountains. Then more people could see it."

"Oh, no!" I almost wept. "Please, please. Just let it alone. Please don't improve it. Then you'll have something really unique that tourists, certain tourists, will come here to see from all over the world."

"But Americans like improvements!" argued my perplexed friend.

"No, no," I wept. "You can't realize it, but where I come from the engineers have improved us almost out of the world, and there's no world left."

"If we had an American development scheme come in here with a vast amount of money, it would bring in more tourists." He seemed to have this fixation.

"Oh, but it's so lovely the way it is," I tried to impress upon him. "Just let it alone. Let alone the last habitat in the world for the marsupial wolf and the tiger snake, and it will soon be popular with the perceptive types of people. And at meals. At meals, serve larger servings of boiled pumpkin." (He looked perplexed.) "Don't ever feed tourists any fresh strawberry shortcake or your fresh raspberries from the bush. Just serve flan, like now, and half a canned peach. Keep on exporting the fresh fruits to Melbourne, don't eat them here, and you'll be right."

The trouble affecting conservation here is that the wilds of Tasmania offer the only source of natural water power available to all of the Australian nation. The Tasmanian Hydroelectric Commission might be compared to that dreaded juggernaut of nature lovers and sane people in America: The U.S. Corps of Army Engineers. For here in Tasmania also, they want to turn all into kilowatts, power lines, roads, towns, loud noises, factories, foul odors, and that sort of thing, in the quest for "progress."

Already three-quarters of the potential water power of the green island is harnessed. There actually is no water power of impressive potential, anyway. Rivers are not large here, nor the elevation great. Most of the rainfall is held back by the dense bush. But word of power has already attracted migrant industry, and even with the small population and three-quarters development an accomplished fact, and a shortage of power to the point of rationing the previous

239

winter, the government of Tasmania still wants to attract more industry, promising that it will find power.

To do this, a last dam project was even now in construction high in the hills on the Forth-Mersey, and in the wild southwest central area exquisite Lake Pedder, unique in all the world for its beaches of pink quartz sand and that pristine vegetation peculiar to Tasmania, was to be inundated, by building a dam on the Gordon River.

And even though power by nuclear plants was just around the corner, very near now, this whole land was to be invaded for the sole reason of short-term profit to be made by the government selling power to outsiders. The concept of "progress" is easily sold to people who need jobs and payrolls.

The Helmericks family had been in Tasmania about a month when Ann and I drove out from the Launceston Hotel with a young man representing Comalco one day, and visited the aluminum loading port at Bell Bay.

To fulfill its power commitments to Comalco the Hydroelectric Commission had been forced to purchase a New Zealand former tourist vessel, bring it eighteen hundred miles, and moor it at Bell Bay. There we saw this vessel at work producing ten thousand kilowatts by running imported oil-fired turbines. Comalco recently had jumped its production here from 58,000 tons to 75,000 tons of aluminum ore produced in one year.

"We'll take you around the plant if you like," said the young PR man, all eyes for Ann.

"Oh, could I just sit here? I'm a bit lame from bush-walking. I just hate going into places where there is crushing and grinding of ore, and boiling up of big hot kettles, and going through electromagnetic fields that could paralyze me. . . ."

"Well, that describes our plant perfectly, I guess," said the handsome young guide.

"I'll take over, Mummie," said Ann at that point. "Come along, Roger, I'll take the tour."

She hoisted her heavy photographic equipment, and I had to rub my eyes to realize how fast time was passing.

In her new light gray wool suit with red piping, and her gray hat with floppy brim, and her red blunt shoes and red shoulder-strap bag, she was now Ann the official girl photographer of great, worldwide industrial concerns. Around the edges of doors older executives peeped furtively at her passing. Her neat heels tapped. Her shoulder-length golden tresses laced with one false gold braid brought them out into halls on contrived errands.

For the remainder of our stay in Tasmania Jean remained under the sea and Ann remained nearly constantly at the side of the young PR man in his little red MG.

"I want to take you to some parties while you are here," Roger told her. "But when you go to a party in Tasmania, well, I'm sure it isn't what you are used to in the U.S. Pretty dull, really. The girls stay on one side of the room talking with each other and the men stay on their side with the beer keg, and that's about it. I must warn you."

"Sounds boring," said Ann.

"Well, I can assure you, confidentially, it is."

"I'm sure the segregation isn't the fault of the girls," Ann ruminated, trying as so many have tried to fathom it.

"Some of it's the girls' fault," Roger declared. "Most of them are empty-headed. They've never developed their minds, so they haven't anything to talk about, just chatter. But then, too, even if some fellow, well, like it might be myself, for instance, would really rather talk with the girl he's with, the other fellows make it tough for you. They rubbish you."

However, when he took Ann to Tasmanian parties, the fact was that Roger remained right there at her side the whole evening long, and so did several other fellows talk with her, asking her many questions about America and about the mechanical problems with the Jeep, and things like that, because they had been given to understand in advance that this is what an American girl would expect: to be talked to.

Well, we assembled all our back packs and suitcases and gear, and it was good to see Jean again among us.

Her social life down among the fishes with her friend Otto had made her into a capable diver and sea hunter, and to Jean, this was now the most important thing in life. It was something you just could not communicate to any land person, she said.

"Welcome home from the sea/And down from the tree."

"I don't think that's so smart," said Jean, as I hugged and patted her. "Who climbs trees?"

The girls were toting our baggage from hotel lobby to airport depot down the street in Launceston, when I paid our last hotel bill there.

Just as I was paying a group of the most flamboyant young women and young men I had ever seen came careening loudly into the lobby. Glamourous girls in leather boots and micro-mini skirts. Girls with glorious legs, striding and fearless. Girls laughing and bold And young men with sideburns, some with whiskers, polka-dotted vests, striped pants. Wherever this crowd went, they commanded attention, and they had money to spend.

I will not say I was sorry to see them arrive. I was glad. These were Australian swingers, and they knew perfectly well what they were doing. They were successful. They had it. They had no fear of Queen Victoria. They could come from but one stratum, I decided instantly, for they had all the earmarks. They came from the television or movie or stage industries in Australia, complete with Australian accents and all. They cared not for public opinion: they made it. They cared not for sacrosanct and sanctimonious halls of yore.

"What we would like," said one of the girls loudly, "is a couple of the biggest, nicest double beds you've got here. Not squeaky." Howls of laughter from the gang.

"We'll see what we can do, madam," said the cowed desk clerk, blushing. He led them upstairs as quickly as possible. But they would not stay out of sight. Oh, no, not those, aha!

They would make sure that Tasmania learned at last that there was an element in the public who preferred double beds. I laughed all the way to the airport.

Across the blue ocean the Ansett airliner swept to the mainland, and our family landed at Melbourne on March 10. It was Moomba Day. A day of fun and sports in the Aboriginal language, it meant among other things one million people lined up along Melbourne streets to watch one of the world's biggest parades. In fact, it had already been Moomba Festival for the two preceding weeks.

Patsy came to town and did a long television show about her newest book, and I dined out with another friend of friends met in Tasmania. When you can meet the Aussie traveling he is a great deal more friendly than if you meet him at his home, I learned. Anyway, this cute little millionaire lived with his mother, and he had made his money by answering an advertisement which took him to the United

242

States, where he trained in how to set up and manage a steel fabrication plant. Coming back to Australia, he then built his plant, and thereafter paid a royalty from profits to the American firm of twelve percent a year. The steel fabrication plant was so successful that he made his million within eight years, in a country where access to the millionaire road is strictly limited.

From our twelfth floor suite of the international hotel, the girls and I looked out from a vast, spacious room once again stuffed with luggage and crated expedition equipment, which had been delivered from Comalco headquarters, once again.

Sitting in his skyscraper quarters across the block, our Comalco friend Dean Bunney was very glad to be rid of that expedition equipment. For weeks it had been stored crammed behind his desk. Those Helmericks crates had nails sticking out from them. Dean was wondering if his thick executive carpet and the newly-decorated walls of his very own offices would ever again be quite the same.

"She'll be right," Jean told him, cheerily. He looked happier at once, hearing that brave philosophy of his rugged homeland.

Dean then set to work with another patient sigh to put out a nationwide search for the Jeep title which I had never received, so that their Comalco branch in Perth would be able to sell it in Perth. Dear Dean—whatever would we have done without you?

Now the girls and I saw a city that sparkled as at a ringside theatrical, our own city that we had come to know so well, an old friend. "Which do you like best, Sydney or Melbourne?" the visitor is always asked. These proud rival cities have a right to be proud!

These are real, living cities. Right downtown their hearts are throbbing and alive, where trams and busses, and throngs of vigorous walkers crowd one another in the broad thoroughfares, and every shop and theater and coffee house and bar and department store and pharmacy is bustling. Flowers brighten curbs and window-boxes. It is invigorating, even to the charge of the umbrellas; so long as you dodge them and don't get impaled, you're all right. For when the workers rush from the trams and along the streets from work, whole flanks of closed umbrellas pointing at you under windy Melbourne skies whipping up a gust, come galloping at headlong charge. Yes, I love Melbourne, and the dodge of the umbrella points.

Yes, I love Sydney, too. I love Australia, both the first and the second time around, I decided.

Chapter 16

MIGHTY QUEENSLAND AND THE GREAT BARRIER REEF

In Melbourne we were handed the keys to our newest vehicle, the
Toyota Landcruiser, on an extended loan to us.

"But when do you want it back? Where shall we turn it in when
we finish our exploring?" I still couldn't believe it.

"Any time. Any town. She's right," the manager said. There
were no papers to sign. He just waved us on our way. It was
insured.

The Toyota had just around four thousand miles on its speedometer and seemed in superior mechanical condition when handed
over. Instead of being canvas-covered, like the stripped-down tin
can on wheels our first time around, it had an insulated metal roof,
and this could be locked up at night. This meant we could go into
hotels once in a while, now.

It had all the gearshifts we wanted, and new tyres. Our great
pride was the "kangaroo bumper" which I had asked for, out in
front, so suggestive of safari, and its winch with a reel of steel
cable which could be run off the engine and which had a two
thousand pound pull.

So it was right on up Number 1, the Princess Highway toward
Sydney. Lyrebird country—what few of them are left. The most
beautiful bird in the world. Bellbird country.

244

It was koala bear country for the next thousand miles.

It was Australian public anger which stopped the commercial slaughter of the koalas for their gray, chinchilla-like fur, at a time when frontiersmen were eating roast koala and two million skins were being marketed for coats, back in 1924. We never got to see one in the wild, for this sloth-like animal is very hard to see sitting high up in the trees. He has sat in the forks through such long centuries of evolution that finally nature provided him with a thick, bare, calloused seat for him to sit upon. As the only animal equipped to dine exclusively upon the proliferating eucalypti forest, he fills a food niche of considerable responsibility. Endlessly, he eats his days and nights away, moving only to find fresh clumps of the bitter leaves. To add to his stability and contentment, the sleepy marsupial koala injests with the eucalyptus leaves a narcotic which causes his eyelids to hang in a perpetual droop: and thus he does his faithful continuous work of pruning the indigenous forest of Downunder.

This whole East Coast used to be covered with a rain forest of red cedar interspersed with the eucalypts. It flourished in innocence until the year 1842. The great red cedars, towering over 250 feet tall, extended from 160 miles south of Sydney northward for a thousand miles. Has anyone today ever heard of Australian red cedar? There isn't a stump left now within hundreds of miles of Sydney.

The cutting of this vast hardwood, Sequoia-like forest was done by convict labor, while charming ladies displayed ballroom gowns in Sydney and Melbourne and Brisbane, and opera singers and ballet dancers brought from overseas enhanced the evenings of the gentry, and gentlemen with lace collars bowed graciously in formal drawing rooms. Now it is rare to see a piece of red cedar furniture from that most precious of rain forests of an arid continent, because the gentlemen rulers shipped it all out of the country to England and Europe for their personal gain. Were they not brothers to the Americans here again? The thieves of the American forests we called lumber barons.

The forestry experts say now that if the federal government would allot seven million dollars a year to replant timber, Australia could be made independent of her timber needs by the year 2000. But if she does not greatly step up her planting, by the year 2000 timber may not be obtainable from any country at any price.

Northward along the coast lies the eroding land, poor in soil—it always was, for the forest was its great wealth. Forgotten by new generations is that time when climate was cooler and more moist than now, when such vast trees burgeoned that some hollowed-out ones served as church or schoolhouse, or kept pioneer families in residence.

Destruction of the cedar tip moth has been instrumental in keeping man from successfully regenerating the red cedar, despite its ready germination and rapid growth. The Forestry Departments of New South Wales and Queensland cannot do what they would like to do, for lack of funds. Originally these trees were scattered and dispersed within the conglomerate of the rain forest. To recreate that habitat seems a nearly insoluble problem now.

For nearly the first century after settlement the only effort put out in forestry was to collect a license fee from timber-cutters; and, incidentally, Australia and Tasmania produced in those days, and still produces, the most fantastic axe-men in the world, trained on giant hardwood. The crime was that the licensee could cut what he liked and waste what he liked. Often he cheated the Crown by cutting into Crown land. In a typical case a fine was just one shilling!

Only the best trees were cut, leaving the overmature and the deformed. Seed trees were destroyed for props in mines. An estimate of the ratio of wasted to used timber was eight to one. To get bark for miners' shanties a tree was just stripped standing, on one side only. This killed the tree. Wastelands were left.

By 1943 it was discovered that erosion of the earth was rampant along the East Coast. The stream flow was irregular in that precious East which has virtually the continent's only streams. State forests were microscopic in size. Rural desolation was general.

Regularly the primitive pastoral industry burned the land. We were soon to see how they were still doing it.

In 1939 an enormous fire swept 1,455,000 acres of Crown forest in reserve. Modern forest destruction today uses ball-and-chain, or chain-and-cable drawn by caterpillar tractors. The chains are thigh-thick. The tractors tow a two- to three-ton ball eight feet in diameter, which keeps the chains high enough to exert leverage on the trees. Gelignite is used to help bulldozers dislodge deeply-rooted, stubborn forest.

Still further north "Operation Blowdown" marked the
zenith in nature vandalism in Australia in 1963. Fifty tons of TNT
were exploded in the virgin rain forest at Iron Range on the remote
Cape York Peninsula. The purpose: to provide the army with
training in tropical jungle blasting! Result: a wide desolation of
gray ghost stalks. Of wildlife destiny in the surroundings no
statement is offered.

Within three days we were pulling into Sydney environs.

Many changes were going on in that exciting world port.
New nightclubs, dedicated to a newer generation, and all kinds
of bistros, discotheques, and fascinating shops found ways to stay
open now after 5:00 P.M., and even on weekends. In King's
Cross, where the hippies collected, small gang wars erupted. A
few larger gangsters moved in, where they found congenial environmental niches resultant from the country's prosperity. With ever-
growing professionalism, enterprising entrepreneurs arrived from overseas, appreciative of the market which tourists and American soldiers
(a thousand a week in Sydney) on their rest and recreation leave from
Vietnam, are quick to bring. We saw and talked with several of these
American soldiers in town. To me they looked very young, mannerly,
and academic compared to those of World War II. This new generation visiting Australia were a different breed. They caused no uproar
or disruption.

The new Australians, from Italy, Greece, Germany, and so on,
were quick to take advantage of the growing numbers of delegations
and conventions which business hoped to lure from overseas. The
city was urged to build more bathtubs. Some forty thousand Japanese
businessmen with their wives visit yearly nowadays, and the Japanese
do not prefer showers, but tubs.

Our new Toyota found its way into a suburb of Sydney, and came
to the hilly shoreside apartment of Swiss Hans.

As soon as we came walking in, we were met by the old cow skull
hanging upon one wall, exuding nostalgia. It had all our names on it,
the names of our mob, engraved for posterity. That sturdy, bleached
old skull had explored the length and breadth of the Australian continent, wired to the top of the boys' bus.

Quite a lot had changed about Hans. His beard was gone, though
he had mod, trimmed sideburns. His handsomeness, his grooming, his
new business suit told a story—what was it?—of sun and sea and cosmo-

247

politanism, all combined. The very aura of that metropolis, that city of over forty swimming beaches, twin city to San Francisco, lay upon him: the aura of swinging Sydney.

Jean and Ann hung one on each arm, as he told them about his new little red car. He would take the girls out that evening to lift steins with his Swiss friends at a cheery Swiss restaurant. (As for me, I had a dinner date at the luxurious new Wentworth.)

"Well, you see, I am in technical business now," he twinkled. I never did find out what kind of technical business, because I am sure it would be too technical for me.

Hans also had joined a volunteer commando group somewhat like our National Guard, and he was on call for the defense of Australia and rising fast in command. He played ball now. He went out for sports. We saw before us an Australian, but a new breed of Australian: energized, ambitious, going places, filled with a dream of a great and fair city he believed in.

Helmut had disappeared somewhere into that great city after the the boys returned. Perhaps he was saving money to get back home. Switzerland allows dual citizenship for her children, wherever they immigrate and however long they may stay. Besides, it takes five year of waiting to be permitted to become a citizen of Australia, or a citizen of the United States. This waiting period is a good idea. It is like the engagement period between a couple contemplating marriage During the time of the engagement the parties get the opportunity to know each other better and to decide if each really wants to take the final step which results in the marriage bonds.

A weekend passed with Hans. At its end, discovery. When Jean walked out on the sidewalk, there stood Otto of Tasmania!

We never discovered how he had found us.

"What he did, Ann, well, he rented a room in a house just a few yards up the hill! One that looks right into Hans' window! He leased out his boat in Tassy for the season, and now he thinks he could help us drive the Toyota north, and he would travel with us, if Mom would like to have him help the expedition."

"No!" I said. The reply came instinctively, without even needing thought.

Reluctantly, Jean went back outside to the sidewalk, then, and explained to Otto as best she could. "My mother gets upset, and

248

she needs me to drive the Toyota, and there isn't room for more than the three in our family inside it."

"It seems like your mother always needs you," Otto argued. "Why don't you come with me, Jeanie? I can show you some wild places that your mother never will see. How about going hitchhiking with me, then, to Queensland, and let Ann drive your mother?"

"Why don't you come inside and meet Mother now? She's right inside there, and she has wanted to meet you. You'll like each other."

"But Hans lives there."

"Well, Mother won't come outside to meet you. She says you are to come in."

"Tell her I'll meet her in Queensland up north. I'll see you in Cairns, Jeanie. That is, if you want to do any real, professional diving. Or, maybe you don't?"

And so, a bit upset, Jean took the wheel of the new vehicle out of Sydney on another day, and she and Ann and I set our sights for the wild, tropical north, and Otto was there day by day, some place just over the horizon.

It was goodbye to Sydney again, goodbye to shores where colorful bungalow colonies cluster, to Georgian balconies with wrought-iron curlicues, to the racing eighteen-footers with spinnakers filled by the northeast winds, and to the world's most beautiful bikini-clad girls, and that custom of "perving" or "bird watching" on beaches where men stare wantonly but never come over to sit with the girls and nothing ever happens. And it was farewell to that mecca where gather the nation's great yachtsmen, swimmers, runners, golfers, and tennis pros. The city where horse racing, lawn bowling, cricket, rugby, and surfing are king. Where all outdoors sports are king, and men commute to jobs and families that only interfere with play.

The Helmerickses drove north through New South Wales now whose initials, some say, should really stand for Newcastle, Sydney, and Wollongong, for the industrial might they have wielded for a century. One of the richest silver-lead-zinc lodes in the world, discovered at Broken Hill in 1883, gave this continent its charter to expand away from agriculture and grazing and hurl itself into the multiple fields of manufacturing and commerce. Today New South Wales is girding itself to keep its lead over the other states, for it is experiencing spritely competition from them, especially a competition based upon foreign trade. To man mines and factories was why each state now courted migrants from some thirty-five countries that made up half their labor force in some areas.

But the more educated professionals are not always courted; local people did not want competition in the professions. Or, if courted, the overseas intellectuals did not always stay.

It was a beautiful drive following the receding Wet as we went north. We were glad that we had not taken the inland "New England Highway." Our *Readers Digest* atlas showed that sixty-three days of rainfall is average all along this coastal green-belt, and flooding can occur at nearly any time of the year, but especially flooding of the rivers flowing inland down the western side of the coast ranges.

Queensland owns the eighty thousand square miles of the Great Barrier Reef. She even owns all the islands of Torres Strait within eight miles of New Guinea! Indeed she is a mighty state.

A state having great tropical rain forests, a state having Out-back to surpass the imagination, Queensland also has some five hundred waterfalls in her short streams, coming down to the Pacific from her Southern and Northern Alps. The highest water-fall, which we went to see, is Wallaman Falls, just under a thousand feet.

Then there is Brisbane, the state's capital, lying in its south, just over the border from New South Wales. Half the population of the state lives in that city of 700,000, and the city sprawls out to cover 385 square miles!

The small, modest homes of the people of the potentially richest state in Australia lend credence to the widely-held belief that here is a classless society. Because the giant state stretches far north into the tropics, human life is lived in a "tropical" way, and its customs, like those in our own South, have long been liesurely, procrastinating, and . . . well . . . tropical.

Queensland is the state of sugar, pineapple, and bananas. For the latter it is too bad that hill slopes are chosen for the express purpose of avoiding frosts. Banana growing, commencing as far south as Coff's Harbour, New South Wales, should move northward to avoid the frosts of winter. But this is too far from market. Growers like to use slopes close to the cannery at Brisbane for their plantations. Invasion of the native rain forest is the result. The life of a slope is ten years. Then the growers move on.

The vast arid interior of Queensland, including the "channel country" down which rivers flood the interior is, of course, a part of that limitless Never-Never all over again which we had seen before. But we shall never see all of this. It is too much. In Queensland's deserts the water brought up from underground may be boiling hot and so saline that often even livestock can't survive upon it. With some of this hot bore water small fish of ancient genera have been known to come spouting out upon the ground.

It was in south central Queensland that the prickly-pear cactus menace from America attained its nightmarish proportions by growing into inpenetrable forests attaining twenty feet in height.

Then there is the Brigalow Scrub. It grows in an area having twenty to thirty inches of rainfall stretching from New South Wales some seven hundred miles north into Queensland's interior, and estimated to cover anything from 11½ million to 23 million acres of acacia harpophylla—a pretty broad spectrum of guesswork. This valuable dry forest has so far resisted the complete destruction of the cattlemen hunting their wild cattle, because it comes back, no matter how cattlemen chop and burn, and no matter how rapidly the fifty million sheep which graze below the Tropic of Capricorn in Australia keep chewing away.

Some of the soils of Queensland are deep, heavy clays on flat land, where there is little erosion, but toxicity may be a factor. Following the Dry when heavy rains come you have the problem of nitrate poisoning of your livestock existing over thousands of square miles of soils which may be high in nitrogen content. The sudden forced growth of the Wet enables some plants to accumulate a lethal amount of nitrate.

The town of Surfers Paradise is what the Australian tourists immediately think of, though, when they dream of seeing Queensland. Of the several surfing towns along the coast, this one is the "swingingest." Of all places in Australia it is Las Vegas, Hollywood, and Waikiki all rolled into one, so far as Australian youth are concerned. Of course, we would give it a try along our way!

We took a little flat there for a week, washing clothes in the basement, drying out sleeping bags, eating curry rolls and dim sims at the beach snack bars, and gazing into shop windows. Some $70 million are spent a year along this Gold Coast.

The girls drove me to Lammington National Park, where I stayed some days at the guest lodge and followed the tracks through the forest with groups of walkers.

For here was an amazing Malaysian rain forest! The forest lies at about thirty-five hundred feet altitude, cold and dripping, not tropical in temperature but tropical in fecundity almost beyond belief. I walked into deep shadows where the strangler fig girdles the giants, where hoary nothofagus moorei, the Antarctic beech, takes his aged stand in representation with a hundred famous Queensland species.

The strangler fig is incubated in favorable mulch high up above the ground in a limb fork, then drops down to earth and spreads its roots there. Other airborne parasites are here, too, epiphytes locally called buckhorn and elkhorn, those great, heavy pulpy succulents weighing up to five hundred pounds, perching on limbs fifty feet above the ground or ten feet above the ground as the case may be. Some are so heavy that they have crashed to the ground and lie rotting about. Plush green logs are covered with pale violet toadstools.

Here is also the stinging tree, a little softwood with outsize leaves all out of proportion to the size of a small tree. The big flat leaves look like old lace from the minute perforations of insects which eat them. This leaf you musn't touch. If you do, the stinging and burning lasts a month.

As the tree grows larger the leaves grow less potent. When it is a tiny bush, it is deadly. But—right beside the tree in the same life group grows its antidote: a slick-leaved lovely thing, the wild lily. You just break off a leaf stem and squeeze its milk upon the stinging tree's bite. Also, the stinging tree, or gympie, has a trunk sap antidote for itself, it is said, if you know the tricks of the jungle.

The hardest wood in the world grows here: lignum vitae. Trees grow tall in a fantastic struggle to reach upwards to the sun. Antarctic beeches hoary with age are not replacing themselves as they reach the 3,000-year-old mark. Due to changing climatic factors, aided by the depredations of modern man, the beeches exist now only here in a few pockets, and along the West Coast of Tasmania,

252

on the South Island of New Zealand, in Patagonia, in a small pocket along the loftiest ridge of the McPherson Range (not protected) and on a cattle station leased by Texans much further north, called the McIllwraith Range.

Identified by signs along the nature trail were such rare woods as rose mahogany, brown malletwood, marrow-wood, saffron heart, tamarind. There were also the native Australian hoop pine and box pine.

Dozens of kinds of small orchids bloom in this mountaintop forest. Mosses and lichens etch rocks and trees in a green world. Since the leaves of the trees are far above, unseen, the giants do not easily give up their individual identities to that minute insect which is man as he crawls in the gloom about their enormous buttressed roots. The only clue we have to tell us that the season is fall are occasional strings of bright scarlet berries dangling. The only clue we have to tell us that this is truly Australia is that the dense bush is literally hopping with pademelon and the umber-brown lizard called mullet sleeps in a sunny spot on drier slopes, and the black tree kangaroos, which can jump twenty feet from limb to limb, inhabit such a forest to feed on ferns.

Birds of brilliant hue abound. They include a local mountain species of wild turkey, the wild pigeon, the rufus thrush, and the whip bird, whose vocalization is preceded by a whipcrack sound. Bower birds which exist only in Australia and New Guinea build a "bower" of dried grasses and sticks for the sole purpose of the courtship ritual in which the female is courted with pebbles and trinkets only on the basis that she approaches the special courting territory of the male.

Rain forest leeches are active and penetrating. After a day out walking the broad, manicured, and beautifully-graded park trails, hikers wash off the leeches along with streams of blood. But this matters little to nature lovers.

Two types of small fish inhabit the lower pools of mountain streams. We saw a brilliant blue-and-white, freshwater crayfish which looked as though some artist colored him with chalk colors.

Waterfalls and cascades festooned with the giant umbrellas of the tree ferns fall in spume forevermore over precipices in the park, catching shafts of glorious pure sunshine, to plunge into Stygian gloom.

The lodge at which I stayed at the edge of the ancient forest cost $6.80 a day, including three meals and three teas in between meals. I was seated in a place of honor at table with the owner, Bernard O'Reilly, whose book, *Green Mountain,* described how his family came here three generations ago, originally as timber-getters, to make a home in the wilderness. The knowledge of this forest they had accumulated and which they now shared with tourists was phenomenal.

No one ever got lost or hurt here. By chart the O'Reillys plotted each day where each tourist group would be at all times, and laid out the plan of action at breakfast time. About four thousand people came to stay at the guest house and go walking each year.

Nights were cold in the mountains and I was glad that I had brought my heavy sweaters and ski pants. Every evening a log fire burned in the recreation room, where bowls and scrabble were played, where women of no particular age carried their bird books for evening study, or plied their knitting needles. One or two elderly men made themselves companionable. I marveled at the sure instincts of my two daughters once again: the austere nature worshippers were not young people here.

Everyone in the lodge was tucked snugly into bed by ten each night. The management provided gigantic transoms over-hanging the doors of all the bedrooms and had them permanently welded open to the arctic night of the outdoors community passage. Sleeping was thus rendered a nearly public activity. In the dead silence after ten any person could be heard all over the premises each time he turned over in bed or gave a slight cough.

"Did anyone hear the dingo howl last night?" one of the keen O'Reillys asked one morning.

"I did," I said, and was immediately a heroine. Yes, only here in the park had I heard a dingo.

It was beautiful.

Ann arrived with the Toyota up the winding mountain road to get me. At the wheel she had a new young man.

A graduate of the National University Law School at Canberra, he was headed for New Guinea to become the new district attorney for the Crown there at Port Moresby.

"I suppose you have read a number of books about New Guinea and the natural wonders there," I said. "I admire your opportunity."

"Well, no," he replied, "I never had much interest in the outdoors, frankly."

"They named a vine after you over there, I think," I said. He raised a cultivated eyebrow.

"They call it lawyer vine. People get wound up in it in the jungle."

The remark brought a smile, at least. He was driving us slowly and capably along the narrow road of the forested mountain top. It seemed a shame that the bright young government man, so well trained in law, had no interest in people. He hated jungle and nature, and he had no knowledge of anthropology or sociology, only law. His mainstream of work would be the prosecution for the government of native killings and mayhem, without caring about the whys or wherefores of the primitive cultures. But perhaps too much anthropology would weaken a good prosecutor, anyway. He was interested in making money and a name in law.

All at once in the jungle beside us I spotted a great thick, mottled green tree root among the roots of trees, and it looked different. "Stop, stop the car!" I yelped. "It's real. I can't believe it. It's alive. It's not a root."

The young lawyer stopped, and then backed slowly.

"Careful, careful, don't run over him," shrieked Ann. Her friend from Surfers Paradise registered astonishment as he saw Ann leap from the Toyota and run for the snake, her mother close behind her.

The big green jungle python had been about to venture across this dangerous tourist-driven road when the thundering wheels of our car drove him back among the roots of the big tree. There he lay now, with blunt-nosed python head pulled back at an unusual sharp angle, like an elbow. Nine feet in length and as big around as a man's thigh in the middle, he was ready to strike a hammer-blow with his nose. The python, unlike the mild boa constrictor, does not make a good pet, because his nature is to strike with his nose and knock small animals off their feet, and

255

he may also have long fangs. After he has knocked a small rodent down, he then throws his coils over it, and in true constrictor fashion presses the breath out of it in about three minutes, then swallows his dinner quite quickly headfirst. Such snakes were designed to keep down the rapidly-proliferating rodents of a tropical jungle, which in turn were designed to chomp up the pro-liferating plant life.

It was one of the most startling and wonderful experiences we had in Australia to see a wild python in its natural setting in real jungle, and take our pictures of him at leisure. Every other guest in the park would have envied us now! Only this very morning early I had been taken for a drive in the O'Reilly station wagon in quest of just such sights as this. We had seen several lovely things, including the deadly red-bellied black snake at his ease. But this was the prize.

Ann's lawyer looked sick and shaken while we warbled on about the snake's charms. He shuddered from head to foot. We had an impossible task convincing him that this kind of snake is a "good guy," and all over Australia the python group is the farmer's best friend. The largest python in north, tropical Australia may reach twenty-five feet. It should be protected nationwide, but isn't.

I suppose that the majority of people over-react to snakes. We all have our phobias. I have mine concerning cars. When Ann drove those narrow, winding ribbons of half-roads through the Queensland hills at a merry clip, I kept eternally nagging at her to slow down.

It was Ann and I together, now. When we got back to Surfers Paradise Ann explained to me carefully just how it was. Jean had gone.

"You know, Mom, Jean hasn't been happy for a long time."

"For heaven's sake, why not?"

"She finds travel with you boring—she doesn't dig this tame stuff."

"Tame? Since when is traveling with me tame? And *where is she?*"

"I hate to tell you this, mother. *You* drove her away. She couldn't stand it any longer, your nagging about my driving fast.

So I put her out on the highway this morning. She's hitchhiking ahead."

At first I was very hurt and angered. Then I was worried. "She wants to go ahead and do some real diving, mother. Don't worry. She'll be right. Everybody hitchhikes here, you know that."

There was enough truth in this, and besides, I had to accept the fact that Jean was gone. A pack on her back, a little money, and her fins and snorkel. A thousand miles up that tropical Bruce Highway, she would meet us at Cairns. Otto the diver, the surley one, is there with his beach friends. I don't like him. He has never stepped up proper-like to meet the mother of the girl. My goodness, but raising kids takes some emotional stretching of all the bonds of reason and affection. But I'd better talk nice to Ann. After all, she's here. She didn't run off and leave me.

"They're cheeky beggars, I must say. And it's a bit dicey riding with you," I nagged in Australian.

"Well, do you think you could drive any better?"

"No, just resume." Birds were singing. A halcyon day. Ann drove.

A wise philosopher has said that happiness is a peculiar experience inasmuch as while it is happening often we do not realize it at the time. We can only remember. A halcyon day and Ann at seventeen, in Australia.

While Jean was hitchhiking to Cairns Ann and I picked up our own hitchhiker along the road, an American lad. As we drove and talked, it was apparent that he would eventually become a professor or a college dean. Already he seemed one. But he had been working at jobs in slaughtering and mining in Australia for some months past, in order to live and experience.

"We also have a family member who is hitchhiking this very road right now," Ann told him. "Maybe everyone needs to get away from the routine for a little while."

We carried the young man that day and the next. Driving into the lush hills on a side road marked Rise and Shine Road, we hastened to find a place to camp. Anxiously, as the precipitate sun made its

257

final dive to earth, Ann and the youth searched for a bare piece of ground that would make camping possible—and happily found it, in the guise of a deserted gravel pit on a ridge where a breeze blew some of the bugs away.

Here we grilled our chops and bread over the coals as the day birds ceased their warbling and were replaced by the night birds' cries, and occasional fireflies danced aloft, indistinguishable from campfire sparks.

The moon rose. All was loveliness. The sounds of peaceful nature combined with the very occasional rush of a late car on the road below. The distant hoot of the Interstate Train, a child's toy, evaporated.

At dawn's faintest light I heard dingoes howl. Their song ceased suddenly as a fresh breeze turned, and I slipped inside my down bag for the last two hours of night. When the sprawled bodies woke later broad daylight was upon us, the sun winking right in our eyes.

Ann finished making elastic-bound terrycloth pull-overs for the sticky vinyl car seats, which were taking the skin off our bare legs. Camp breakfast. Onward toward the town of Proserpine.

Someone lamented the lack of both soap and toilet paper in all public rest stops. You learned to carry your own and never forgot these.

"The public takes the whole roll away faster than any management can replace it," I remarked.

"But this is not to say the Aussies are dishonest, quite the contrary," philosophized Ann. "It only proves that this country lacks toilet paper."

"Americans find that no country has enough toilet paper for their needs," concluded the future college dean, with gentle irony.

At Prosperine we went to the Ansett offices for our contact, and the American youth departed with a large red pack upon his back.

Prosperine turned out well with Ann as our public relations representative. We were offered boat passage out from the coast here to stay some days at Hayman Island at the Royal Hayman Hotel, the swingingest of all Reef resorts.

Hayman is a natural park, containing palms, blood trees, hoop pine, Mackay cedar, sandpaper fig, Moreton Bay fig, black wattle. Jungle paths take you through flocks of cockatoos, seagulls, curlews, and currawongs.

258

It was a surprise to me to learn that there are only two true coral islands lying inside the Great Barrier Reef: Green Island, adjacent to Cairns, and Heron Island, used principally as a laboratory facility by the University of Queensland. This Hayman Island, like many others, was geologically a part of the continent.

The island consists of a horseshoe-shaped, forested mountain rising to eight hundred feet, containing at its base a natural tree-clad flat fronted by a sweeping shallow sand beach facing south to the Whitsunday Passage and a scattering of smaller islands. On this flat stands the Royal Hayman Hotel with its pool and gardens, capable of accommodating 350 guests in its beach bungalows.

Beyond the beach a half-mile-wide coral reef lies exposed at low tide but is covered by ten feet of water at high tide. When the hotel resort was built years ago this expanse contained exquisitely beautiful coral formations, strange shells, and *trepang*. But a massive storm had hit here before our time, sweeping away all that was interesting biologically—one of the countless catastrophes of nature.

What I was to see personally were swarms of tourists along the Great Barrier Reef gradually carrying it away, piece by piece.

An Australian Great Barrier Reef authority, Dr. Ian D. Hiscock, notes that "each year hoarders of shell collections comb the Reef and its cays and islands. Some do it to amass a hoard of pretty shells, which then collect dust on their mantlepieces, but many do it for money. The rarer the shell, the higher its market price. The higher the price, the more intensive the collecting and so for the desire for a quid, a species is lost."

I saw this, too. Everybody wanted some! Everybody got some, despite present Queensland laws designed to prevent it. What individuals did not realize was that the total monstrous onslaught of human beings upon the Great Barrier Reef environment was seriously degrading the whole ecology in a variety of ways.

Spear fishing, for instance, presently legal all over the Reef except for Green Island and Heron Island sanctuaries, is noticeably diminishing the native fish species. There is no doubt that spear fishing should be curbed and that much conventional angling from the continuous resort fishing boats should have some limits set.

There is no doubt either that the state of Queensland alone should not exercise jurisdiction over this great wonder of the world. The entire 1,250 miles of reefs lying in Queensland waters and beyond, said to be the longest ship pilotage in the world, should be made into a great total national park, in the strict meaning of the word, "national."

Our arrival at Hayman Island by launch landed us at the end of a jetty a quarter of a mile out from the island, and there we tourists boarded a tiny, narrow-gauge, Disneyland type of open air train whose cars were adorned adorably with festive red-and-white striped awnings, the train being pulled by a diesel donkey with an enormous false smokestack.

Clickity-clack the donkey engine pulled the cars slowly over warped and ancient rails. Gray old planking clattered, not nailed down, as our "train" moved toward shore high up above the water. Once ashore, the little train passed through a tunnel of artificially-planted bouganvilla.

Under the conditions of nature most Australian islands are not overly hospitable. When the island was leased twenty years ago from Queensland by private enterprise some 450 death adders were exterminated from its sparse acres to make it habitable for people. Other than the adders, many islands have no animal life to speak of. Kookaburras and gulls live on the snakes. There are parrots whose tough beaks tear the husks from jungle "fruit" of a woody nature, not edible by man. The palms from which coconuts dropped ominously close beside the bungalows had been imported. So had the hibiscus.

How do you go about choosing the best kind of island if you want to build a resort? Why was this particular island, five miles in circumference, selected? Well, in setting up an island resort you have to consider water. Distillation is too costly. You need an island which in normal years catches enough rain water to provide its needs, plus plenty of bars of salt water soap for guests in case.

Another factor is swimming. Only a few islands have good beaches. And what about shark danger?

In reply to my shark questions I found a generally accepted explanation that "sharks along the Queensland coast have plenty of natural food, and so they do not crave man on their menu." I never could accept this. Apparent to anyone with an eye to see is that the resort is built on such a long, flat, shallow shelf of beach that no shark in his right mind would risk swimming up here so far from deep water, and risk getting bogged and stranded.

What about other menacing types of sea life, of which the trop-

260

ics have an abundance? First, it is possible to catch and eat some types of poisonous fish. Some marvelous fish are caught on cruises out from the hotel, such as the red parrotfish, and little was known of the chemical nature of some of them. Since the Queensland government was too busy and too poorly financed to cope with anything but routine health problems, this resort had conducted some research at private cost.

More pertinent to swimmers are the Portuguese man-of-war or bluebottle, (physalia) the sometimes-lethal box jelly or sea wasp, and the speckled, gauzy, transparent butterfly fish whose fins look somewhat like graceful butterflies as it swims sedately along. These creatures are dripping with acid which burns like fire. The man-of-war is really a composite or specialized colony of many jellies, inflated by a gas gland in the center and trailing tentacles of fire up to twelve feet behind it. These tentacles can kill even large fish when touched.

Very few animals use them as a principal food source, partly because of their low caloric content and partly because of their unpleasant stinging powers. Except—there is one little fish which lives among the deadly tentacles.

Sea turtles eat the man-of-war greedily. If man kills off the turtles in the sea we can expect a most unpleasant increase of firy, gelatinous "navies"—they are actually able to sail at angles to the wind.

Another deadly little beast in the warm waters off Australia is an attractive four-inch octopus, smaller than the hand. It is the ringed octopus, Hapalochlaeno Maculosa. When it becomes angry the ochre bands on its body and tentacles and the dull blue rings change to a wild, irridescent peacock blue. One bite, unfelt, contains enough venom to kill seven men. The venom acts so fast that even if an antidote is ever developed it seems unlikely that it could be administered in time.

It is not always safe to run about barefooted on the beaches and shallows, for the ugly, six- to twelve-inch stone fish lies in the bottom of tidewater ponds looking exactly like some weathered, mossy stone, even to the irregularities of its spotted shape, awaiting the unsuspecting foot. The spines of its back are dripping with a poison so painful that little can be done but put the victim in the hospital under sedation.

There is even a horrid little beast which lives inside one of the innocent cone shells which lie upon the beach. Should you pick up a "live" one from the wrong end, a spear springs out and *boings* you in the palm of the hand.

Yet people in Australia, knowing these things, love to explore about their beaches and reefs; they simply use reasonable caution in what they touch. (Aborigines did their touching with spears.) This kind of exploring and prowling along shorelines and islands the Australians call "fossicking." Thick-soled rubber sneakers are advised.

But "fossicking" may be the greatest single hazard to the ecology of the Reef area, unless people can be educated not to disturb things, not be collectors.

The Queensland government puts out bulletins urging people to restrain their natural inclination to overturn boulders. A large proportion of living organisms on a coral reef lay eggs or browse under coral boulders, and disturbing their habitat when fossicking at low tide will seriously impede the growth of reef life. I myself found it hard to believe that an area covering 80,000 square miles of reefs, islands, and sea, and extending 1,250 miles from Rockhampton, Queensland, to New Guinea and the remote Solomons, could possibly be endangered by people—but this is so.

A coral reef is a living thing. The polyps which we call corals are tiny animals, eternally building their multitudinous castles of carbonate limestone; but they are also partly plants, whose fronds wave in the ocean currents and manufacture food by chlorophyll and sunlight. They also manufacture oxygen, for the animal part of the creature.

Coral polyps, therefore, can live only in depths which are penetrated by sunlight. This restricts their building area to fifty or seventy feet; below eighty feet all polyps perish.

Surprisingly, the majority of coral polyps emerge from their rock castles to feed at night. The experts tell us that the sea becomes a different place by night than by day. Unknown creatures rise from the depths by night to take oxygen and food (such as coral polyps and plankton) from near the surface; creatures which man, a day creature, in a powered vessel, does not usually see.

Eventually coral polyps die, as do all creatures, but their billions have left behind them permanent castles or reefs, which dead or living, dot the warm waters of the South Seas and which, in thousands

262

of instances, have caused coral atolls to form into permanent islands. Thus a part of their work has been to actually build lands and to attract land life: a most considerable work for nearly-microscopic creatures.

If corals live and build only in shallow depths, why do coral reefs come up to the surface from sheer, abysmal depths of the sea? The famous Great Outer Reef, which guards Australia's East Coast starting just north of Rockhampton, may extend in places thousands of feet below the surface. Charles Darwin in 1831 guessed that the gradual subsidence of the continental coastline during fifty million years must be the answer; and Darwin's explanation still is valid so far as we know.

By coincidence this continent sank at the same rate the corals built up. And so the Great Barrier Reef formed, and became the most famous and formidable continental barrier in the world, ranging from as far as 150 miles out to sea from near Rockhampton to within only ten miles at its closest. Even today ships use only a few of its known passes, for many treacherous corals rise near the surface on the inside of the Outer Reef as well.

Due to the protection of the Outer Reef, you have the most beautiful water visibility and the most beautiful coral colors here in the world, as well as the most exciting herds of fish from the deep. (There may be sharks, too, inside the Outer Reef, and herds of barracuda up to six feet long, the "wolves of the sea.") Divers know that while there are always some dangers in the sea, a man is rarely attacked so long as he is swimming free underwater. The swimmer paddling and fluttering on the surface is in much more danger of attack.

Today there is worldwide worry about the failing health of the Great Barrier Reef. "Already there have been almost irreversible damage to large faunal areas," say the marine biologists, "even far from large concentrations of man."

Currents carry oils, detergents, and factory metal chemicals, and affluents from sugar refineries pour from Queensland rivers. It is now recognized that even land clearing in river mouths, where most of Queensland's seventeen principal small towns huddle, has been slowly muddying the offshore waters during the past fifty years. Moreton Bay, at the mouth of the Brisbane River, for instance, is now mostly a soft, oozy mud bottom which overlies what was once a rich bay of living coral—now dead. Coral cannot live when it gets choked by mud.

Biologists believe that continued tampering with river levels by dam and weir construction will have harmful effects on aquatic fauna—and dams, inevitable with population growth, are just in the beginning stages on Queensland rivers.

Oceanographic seismographing is going on continuously throughout Australian and New Guinean waters. I talked with a young lad from Texas who was involved in this work and he told me that in a day's work about sixty explosions are detonated in taking soundings of the ocean bottom throughout the area. On some occasions it was necessary to detonate especially strong charges. On these occasions, he said, he had personally seen the sea filled with floating dead fish over as much as two miles from explosion site.

If this is so, only imagine, then, what the long-range meaning may be of numbers of oil companies continuously seismographing the South Seas. Even when the shocks do not visibly result in a stockpile of dead fish on the surface, is it not likely that the smaller creatures in the life chain are disabled?

At the time this is written worldwide concern is being given the population explosion of the crown of thorns starfish, which is killing the living coral reefs by its uncontrolled numbers. This has never happened before. It has been suspected that use of DDT in Queensland agriculture could be to blame, but no one as yet has isolated the specific cause of crown of thorns' horrendous eating spree. Whatever creature that normally keeps crown of thorns in check must be succumbing to some pollutant of man.

It is an emergency not to be shrugged off. Dead coral means coral that can be broken up and demolished by the sea. Not only does it spell the end of a coral ecosystem of incalcuable value and complexity, but if Australia's Outer Reef breaks down, this would leave a continent which has but very low altitude and almost no harbors at the mercy of the high seas.

264

Chapter 17

AT CAIRNS AND NORTHWARD

When Ann and I reached Cairns Jean was not there. A note at the
Ansett Airlines office directed us to a privately run guest home, where
we took rooms, and where Jean lived. But Jean was gone, with Otto,
on a walk along the tropical beach 150 miles to Cooktown! Her
note at the guest home said they would live on coconuts and wild
bananas and fish.

"But how will they cross those crocodile rivers along their
way?" I wailed.

Ann comforted me. "The new generation has most of the
Queensland crocodiles scared by taking their rivers for water skiing,
mom. Don't worry. Jean's roight. How would you like to be a
crocodile around here and have an outboard motor and water skis
going over your back almost every day?"

When Jean and Otto came back I must say she looked fit and
fine. Otto had disappeared off down the street.

"Have a good trip?" How thin and tanned she was! How
battered, tired, and contented with the world she was!

"Yep. Couple of police officers picked us up on the beach
and brought us in for questioning and finger-printing at Cooktown."

"Jean!" I was shocked. "Why? What were they after?"

265

"I don't know, really. Drug smuggling, I think. Of course we were just taking a walk, but it was hard to convince them of that."

"Well, I'm glad Australia is watching her shores and keeping a sharp eye out. Good on them," I said.

I met Otto—at last—next day, and we went on the launch out to Green Island near Cairns, and Jean and he taught me to use the snorkel and fins so that I, too, in a very small way, was finally to get a look at the sea world.

Most people will never undertake free-swimming long distances with an oxygen tank: it's a bit risky and many life insurance companies will not insure scuba divers. Anyone, however, even the most timid landlubber like me, can learn surface snorkling quickly, floating face downward over the gardens of lovely coral.

There are all the wonders of the sea at tiny Green Island, plus an absence of the more obnoxious and lethal creatures which dismay the timid, for instance, sea snakes. A few seasons ago sea snakes were legion, but they had been gradually and tactfully removed, one by one, by those who do not consider the sea snake compatible with tourist recreation.

The sea snake comes in many varieties along the Great Barrier Reef, and is little known because it lives in areas of the world which can rarely be closely examined by man. Being fish hunters, many have the unpleasant habit of attacking a swimmer and either hitting him with fangs or winding themselves around him when they see they made a mistake in chosen prey.

An experienced sea-world explorer went free-swimming at night using lights near Green Island, and he was able to see the oar fish, a remarkable creature which is known to but a few museums of the world and about which nearly nothing is known. Apparently the oar fish lives at great depths. It rises in the night, however, to feed. Growing up to twenty feet in length, its body is as flat as an oar, having a long, thin back fin, undulating like a serpent as it swims. So long and thin is the oar fish that for centuries it has been thought to be the sea serpent of many a legend. A completely harmless and gentle animal of the deep, a shy, plankton feeder, it has been seen in all parts of the world, but only rarely. One can only imagine the unbounded superstitious horror of sailors both ancient and modern upon sighting the "sea serpent" swimming on the surface with flow-

266

ing red "mane" erect, and lithe, inquiring head uplifted five feet above water!

Along the Great Barrier Reef I explored the sea cucumbers which were in shallow pools left by the receding tide, and I saw many when I snorkeled. They were black, nearly immovable except by the water currents, and they lay along the bottom, harmless to the touch. They have the curious habit of expelling their long, white, thread-like intestines if disturbed. Later, they grow new ones. In Australia they have an interesting history as an industry.

For many years a vast Malaysian, Asian, and Chinese market held *trenang* (the French call it *beche de mer*) in high esteem for food. Ships therefore put out to hunt the entire north end of Australia and the Great Barrier Reef for them.

Today practically every island having a few feet of permanent ground above tide will still show its rude boilers from those days; an old galvanized iron shed, a vat for boiling up *trepang* or *dugong* (sea cow) or turtle and then perhaps the old driftwood racks for sun-drying the meat. The cucumber-size *trepang* were reduced to the size of dried, salted lichee nuts, and slowly a cargo accumulated while the crew kept a keen eye on the weather.

Berthing a ship was never possible at a reef. Crews worked with small boats, or often were left upon the island with no boat at all for long periods of time until the ship came back for them.

Trepang fishermen lived a sun-blasted, lonely, dangerous life. Pirates roamed the seas. Bands of hostile natives were always capable of eating up the marooned workers. As for weather, they knew well the danger inherent in that sultry, still evening, when scum and plankton suddenly increase, and birds in flight are seen: this is cyclone country, in the summertime.

In a cyclone on the reefs there is virtually no protection. If you have a small skiff it may be shattered and sunk, or it may break loose and get away upon the sea. Your tent and provisions may be blown out of this world, your clothes and cooking gear lost. Many a person has crawled into the galvanized shed to survive the sand blast.

It is then that you should know how to distill sea water on a dry reef, in case all is gone and you should be stranded.

Just before 11:00 P.M. on June 12, 1770, the *Endeavour* got tangled in the terrible reefs off Cape Tribulation—reefs which are exposed to view at low tide in some cases and in the case of others, never. The place was twenty miles off shore, and it was a moonlit night.

Desperately the men heaved their cannons overboard (some of which a group of Americans were salvaging even at this time), their precious stores of food, their water casks. They cast off their iron and stone ballast also, to try to get the rising tide to lift the deep-hulled sailing vessel off the reef which impaled her. Much of the material they jettisoned still lies there on the ocean bottom, probably out of reach forever in deep sea chasms.

After several ghastly days hung up on the reef and battered by the seas, the ship began to fill with water from its injuries, and of course, sharks swam about, as they still swim. Dr. Monkhouse, the ship's surgeon (Monkhouse Point is just south of Cooktown) with that mind of a doctor which is so typically the dispassionate, analytical, thinking mind, suggested trying to "fother" the ship. The doctor had seen this done once. So holes were plugged with "some oakum and wool, chopping it small, and placing it in handfuls with sheep dung on an old studding sail, where it was stitched down firmly."

Free of the reef on the high tide, the slowly leaking *Endeavor* limped ashore to Endeavor River, where Cooktown now stands.

Here the explorers stayed their longest on Australian soil, from June 19 to August 5, and the ship's carpenters made repairs on a great new continent which was totally unpopulated by civilized man, under conditions which taxed the utmost in resourcefulness. The observations which caused England to choose Australia for colonizing were made during the weeks of the miraculous repairs of the *Endeavor*. Here the first kangaroos were seen, and the first Aborigines.

Much later, Cooktown became a gold rush town. Today it languishes in abandonment except for occasional tourists, of whom none arrive by a more ambitious route than did Jean with her "walk." The local individuals want a road built all the way along this coast to boost tourism dollars, and Jean knew that she was lucky to bush-bash it in her time with her nimble and bushwise companion.

There were a number of things to see around Cairns, and conducted tours abounded. Peg Robinson, representing private interests, not government, was the liveliest public relations person in tourism that I met in Australia, and Peg helped to "muster" tours and resorts for us there.

We went to the Bird Feeding Sanctuary, of course, where the wild birds of the parrot families came out of the forest and perch all over your shoulders and arms to be fed by people—real, wild birds.

Bartelfrere loomed nearby, highest mountain in Queensland, upon which as much as two hundred inches of rain falls each year, while Cairns below on the plain has but sixty-eight inches, an average temperature of 84.6 degrees, and an annual "festival in the sun." Mt. Bellendemker, the second highest peak in Queensland, is already doomed by the forthcoming road up to its peak for a TV station, even though technically called a "national park." There is continual and unrelenting pressure to invade the forests to mine, to grow maise, peanuts, tobacco, fruit, small crops, and beef. There is dairying and fishing here. People have to live. They have to make a living.

The public relations and tourist agency which Peg Robinson represented had done such good work that land prices had been boosted twice within the last four years among all the Bruce Highway communities. She agreed that if you are going to get tourism, you have got to conserve nature, or soon there will be nothing left for tourists to want. "The hardest job," she said in her soft, casual, likeable Queenslander dialect, "is to get the local blokes to see this point. If they'll have a listen to me, I would like to tell them."

Cultivation of sugar, begun back in 1863, still pushes steadily forward into the rain forests of the coastal side of all the Northern Alps. At the present moment the cane stops at Mossman—but where will it end?

Timber trafficking still exists. Half the timber sawed in Queensland is not supervised for girth limits, nor is the logger required to reseed. All a logger has to do is pay a few dollars rental, take out the timber from these mountains, and then let his lease lapse. Denudation would be far worse than it is, says Leonard Webb in *The Rape of the Forests*, except for the marvelous recuperative powers of the eucalypt species, and the self-limiting aspects of forest invasion: erosion, landslips, and take-over by weeds have historically driven settlers out.

269

There are 600,000 acres of alienated (not protected) native rain forest in north Queensland. This land is theoretically open for agricultural production and grazing. Most Australian farmers here actually "live on wood," as everybody knows. Investigations right now were up once again on the causes of decline in agriculture and dairying in the beautiful nearby Atherton Tablelands. They were never as rich as was thought. It is only marginal dairying and agricultural country, despite its greenness and despite money earned from its timber.

Only 18 percent of the great forest lying between Townsville (south of Cairns) and Cooktown is reserved as "parks." At least half the area is very rugged, including the lofty Bellenden Ker Range. The Crown recommended opening up just 27,000 acres of rain forest for logging, for the Crown felt that alienating virgin forest solely for beef cattle was not feasible economically for individuals of limited resources. Attention was drawn by the Crown to low fertility and to dangers of erosion of soils on de-forested slopes, some of which should never have been cleared.

But directly following this report the American King Ranch Company, long known in Australia, acquired 68,000 acres. Their land was mostly undulating alluvia with low hills, south of Cairns, at Tully. In parts it is swampy, including lower slopes of the main mountain range, rocky and steep, and covered by immature rain forest called "bastard scrub" consisting of trees four to five feet in girth, containing many commerical species such as silky oaks, ashes, maples, silkwood. Rain forest held by King is estimated at from 9,000 to 20,000 acres (lower estimate is King's). Rain forest soils are granitic, yellow earths, of precarious fertility when de-forested, yet this property now is called "cow heaven." At the time I was in Cairns a serious drought was on, and emergency roundups of cattle for immediate sale were taking place on the King Ranch property.

A member of the Queensland Parliment said reflectively: "Would it not have been better to have given this land to settlement to fifty families than to the employment of ten blackfellows at King Ranch?" This Parlimentarian was on the right track, though he missed the main point, of preserving the forest heritage.

Forest, soils, water: These are inseparable. Each keeps the other in good health. The Parlimentarian did not think far enough

270

to see that good permanent agriculture *depends* on good and permanent forestry policies. Clearing in many places has caused aridity and compaction of the soils, and that dreaded salting which is so common over much of Australia already.

The Parliamentarian and his mates did not stop to think that forests influence climate by acting as windscreens. Pyramid Mountain, a popular hike, offering a view of Cairns and the Atherton Tablelands, had its forest torn down by a cyclone just twelve months past. Forests reduce temperature extremes. Can anybody imagine the oppressive north Queensland heat, with a substantial part of the forests gone, and its effect on tourism? Forests maintain hydrological balance by promoting infiltration and deep seepage of rainfall, and regular stream flow. They increase the disposal of rain. The C.S.I.R.O. experiments to bring more rain produce few benefits for the country by comparison to the hydrological beneficence given naturally by forests at work.

No reforestation has yet been undertaken in north Queensland. Political pressure is felt from country towns and other interests which make a temporary profit out of government-subsidized settlers, whether or not these settlers succeed. There is still pressure continuously to invade even the state forests and parks to "provide more land for settlement."

My girls and I went driving on loggers' roads and saw ugliness and havoc. Only the barest fringe of red cedar forest had been allowed to remain around the site of Queensland's highest waterfalls, to give the illusion of some scenic attraction.

After limited salvage of larger trees by the sawmillers, the young rain forest will be bulldozed, thus sacrificing an enormous volume of commercial cabinet woods of thirty to fifty years harvest to come. It follows the horrid straight-line pattern by which, near Cairns now, the fires regularly enlarge eroding and weed-choked spurs which tower above the cane farms. Now the treeless "freehold" slopes are too steep to cultivate and too infertile to provide pasture. The life of these steep, seaside pastures is very limited. The leeching goes on for nearly a thousand miles of coastal slopes, presaging a future of flash floods, raising river beds by sediment, and predicting eventual expensive dredging for navigation into ports, and loss of crops, of buildings, and livestock by droughts.

The minerals of an undisturbed rain forest, curiously, lie on top of the ground. You can see this in the night by the phosphorescent glow, even of lower tree limbs. There is little underground.

Microbiological activities in the soil humus develop a soil structure which ensures permeability and aeration of the soil. Various species of microflora fix nitrogen, and assist in the solubilization and uptake of nutrients by the trees: gifts which many of our domestic plants lack, so explains an Australian soil scientist. Thus, the regeneration of native trees is able to restore soil fertility—an ability exploited by native tribes in all the world's tropics, when they rotate their villages about every few years and shift the site of cultivation. This works well as long as there is endless world in which to keep moving. But there isn't. When modern man settles in rain forests soil fertility immediately declines, the soil erodes, nitrogen is lost, weeds come, floods and drought result, and farmers go broke. Admittedly, it is a problem.

And so we saw that the lovely sloping forest land along Australia's East Coast has proven to be inherently unsuitable for agriculture and dairying and its fine appearance is deceptive. Once this native vegetation is removed the natural fertility is lost forever, unless you get the minerals out of a bag, which of course is what is being done here. Because people have to live and eat and make a living.

One of the nicest days we spent in the Cairns area was taking the Mulgrave and Russell River Day Cruise, a fourteen-mile launch trip along the jungle river.

As Ann pulled the Toyota into a little slot in the forest beside the river, a bus load of "golden agers" arrived. These Australian tourists are seen at the most unlikely places. Some tours take weeks at a time, and the tourists bring their sleeping bags and sleep on the ground in the desert. We all went off on a little open-air launch with a Mr. Sheppard, our tour entrepreneur, a captain to run the vessel, and a hostess to serve our charming morning tea. Every seat was packed. There were seats for thirty.

Later Ann and I stopped at the Sheppard's home for the mid-afternoon meal, and heard his story.

Sheppard had long ago seen the possibility for tourist cruises in such beautiful, natural rivers as the Russell, and recognized in his own love for nature that there were many others in the public who were likewise inclined. Far back in the 1930s (interrupted by his

272

service in the war) he had got his vessel and started these cruises. Over the years, the more that he studied his subject and the more he lectured to the public, the more he came to understand and love his part of the country.

He recalled a time when valuable food fish such as whiting, salmon, and barramundi were netted here. Even a nineteen foot sawfish once was taken, he said, in the Russell. It was a living river of unsurpassing beauty.

Now he had lived to see sugar mills upriver discharge their milling refuse into the river. The stench was terrible during sugar refining season. Chemical acids from the sugar plant turned the water to ugly filth periodically. This killed the fish and wildlife during milling season, October and November, until at last the river could not recover at all. Finally, no life came back. "The government has been looking into it for years," he sighed.

He described the joy of tourists being able to cruise a real jungle river, cameras bristling. But what was there to photograph now? We saw banks empty of Mr. Sheppard's friendly crocodiles. The crocs at one time had seemed to know his boat. Last year he had been able to show the tourists only one or two on favorite sandbars. The crocs were the high point, the fun of it. Now the excitement was gone. Poachers shot them, and the river water itself did not attract them any longer from the sea. The natural southernmost range of the crocodile is usually given as Rockhampton, where the waters become cool.

The pollution and killing of the river was as bad as the killing of its surrounding forest. The law states that a distance of "two chains" (one chain is equal to twenty-two yards) of natural forest must be left along all river shores, but this is disregarded. The law has no teeth because the state does not allot the funds to have any of the river shores surveyed.

I saw how farmers drained their lands for cane. The Eubenanjie Swamps were now being drained to divert the Russell River to Brampton Beach and there into the Pacific, so that twenty to thirty more cane farmers could be settled. I saw where cane fires, whose flames range forty feet high at times, scarred and mutilated trees right to the waterline, from "burning time." (Burning is necessary to harvest cane.) I saw where bulldozers pushed brush into the river, using it as a dumping grounds to get it out of the farmers' way.

Arguments to increase tourism invariably based their premise on getting the government to build more roads, but no move was made by that same government to protect forests into which roads already penetrate, with the result that lumber companies move right in and take "the lot" before the public even knows what goes on. In Queensland it almost seems as though the country is being opened for the cane companies and the lumber companies, for that is the result.

"I see the country go down and down. I'm sixty-three. Well, I won't be here," said Sheppard sadly.

For a long time forestry in this State was under the control of the Department of Lands, the minister of which was selected because of his ability to promote settlement. However poor the area, it was subdivided all along this coast from New South Wales into Queensland, and immigrant families were put there on blocks. The blocks could not, as in Western Australia south of Perth, support these disillusioned immigrants. The Australian public encouraged the government to continue in a long history of what might be called a big, wholesale land opening agency. The Australian states earlier had no conception of land conservation, no idea whatsoever of land economics, and no policy except to parcel the country out in blocks, regardless of consequences to topography or the qualifications of the settling "wogs."

It was a wonderful experience to live in the forests of Australia, not just for a day or a week, but for weeks and months on end, and feel the mood of the forests, after our many months in the desert.

Before leaving the Cairns area the girls and I were guests at one more resort island. Dunk Island, top of the Reef, lies thirty miles south of the coastal town of Innisfail, which has 140 inches rainfall. Dunk is a tiny island just three miles by two, with an elevation of eight hundred feet on its peak.

Its name comes from Captain Cook's patron, the Earl of Sandwich, whose family name was John Montagu Dunk. Its Aboriginal name was once Koonanglebah.

Backstopped by the two highest mountains (5,400 feet) upon which the monsoons hurl their water-filled balloons, this whole area, including large Hinchenbrook Island which is twenty-eight by twelve miles in extent and mountainous from end to end, "participates in

274

phenomenal rain." Here lies the rainiest area of Australia. But fortunately, this was the start of the Dry.

Brammo Bay, where our modern bungalow sat beneath palm trees, originally meant butterflies, for which Dunk, lying just an eight-mile launch trip from the mainland landing, is famous.

Groups of waterborne Aborigines used to use this island, so unusually hospitable, for camping. They were a people who did not mingle with the continental tribes. Originally the entire Reef area was their hunting grounds, a natural paradise of beauty and wonder, where they were no doubt very proficient at their way of life. Today we know almost nothing about the Reef and island peoples.

Fresh water on Dunk was thoughtfully provided by nature by a creek which never dries up. Only three quarters of a mile long, the creek plunges seven hundred feet through green and mossy passageways, sheltered beneath deep banks, upon which today's resort depends for water. While the tropical vegetation of fantastic richness and variety protects the creek and prevents its water from drying up during the Dry, it has also created its own special environment of part rain forest, part jungle. Should this growth ever be cleared away to any degree nature's paradise will instantly be lost forever. There is only room for a few bungalows on the tiny island, with a small dining and recreation area, and an airstrip and jetty nearby.

Dunk Island is associated with the memory of a sensitive and remarkable naturalist named Ed Banfield, who came here to live in 1898. Like Thoreau, Banfield worshipped nature and he was a poet by temperament. His writings remain as classical legend in Australia.

Banfield was a sick man when he came to this island, modestly well-to-do, educated. Arriving with his devoted wife, a white boatman, and two black helpers he was laid down sick and faint under a tree near the beach here. That was the start of his new life, which lasted another quarter century.

The shore party brought over by sections a cedar home which Banfield had designed, and he and his wife moved in. He lived thereafter on his paradise island making his observations of all nature and writing his deliciously phrased philosophies and his meticulous notes of the fauna and flora until his tragic and ugly death by burst appendix (unable to contact people on the mainland) at the age of seventy-one.

The species which Banfield found are diminished by 90 percent now, even though to the uncritical eyes of city tourists it would still seem to be enough of paradise.

Even in those days the keen naturalist observed that there was a growing accumulation of mud and a consequent dying of coral near his island. He recognized early that there was a gradual filling up of all the sea space between the mainland and the Outer Reef, with a lessening of the depth of the Coral Sea. This is documented by scientists today.

Banfield dreamed of Dunk as part of an Islands National Park, one which should never be improved, a wilderness area, including all its seas. The present owners of the island have set aside an acre for a nature sanctuary commemorating the venerated naturalist, who lies buried here, with his wife beside him. All of the island's hill country is called a "national park" and thus is eligible for state help with its nature trails. The goal now was to "make the island self-sufficient in food," as it developed tourism, I was a bit dismayed to learn. However, using just a few yards of the flat ground could satisfy much of this goal, perhaps.

As upon Hayman Island I set out and walked all the island tracks put in by the Forestry Department, and over the highest peak. In the A.M. I walked the high track. In the P.M. I walked the low track with the visiting Forestry man who had a small crew busy dynamiting track through rock.

Flying foxes hung head down high in the mountain, their faces snarling at one another with long jaws and ferocious teeth. They migrated seasonally all along this East Coast to southern Victoria. Their rain coats were their great, naked rubbery wings which they wrapped around themselves to sleep, and no rain bothered them or wet their thick black fur.

The girls and I returned after a few days to our tourist home at Cairns. Cairns, the end of northward railroad, lies at the top of a 530-mile sugar coast, making Australia second only to Cuba as an exporter of raw sugar. The coastal plain is narrow. A person flying this coast sees towns huddled at river mouths and jungle in between. Patches of smooth light green mean cane. It was like coming home as we rolled with the Toyota past The Pink Pussycat, past Mr. Leonard's Golden Scissors—International Salon of Beauty, and such

276

things, and found ourselves in a bustling, modern city of thirty thousand population, burgeoning with new restaurants and motels.

And oh! The glorious homes of Queensland! When we had motored through Marysville some days south, an area which was all under rain forest two generations ago, we fell in love with them. Who except Queenslanders have homes like these? Homes of steamboat Gothic. Great, high gingerbread structures of all colors, usually in soft pastels, they stand fifteen feet off the ground on their stilts. The stilts are man's way of outwitting the termites and also, in the tropics, to catch for himself each whimsical passing breath of sweet, humid air.

These are open-air homes for outdoor living the year around. A steep flight of front steps admits to a large verandah where the folks sit in their wickers in the evening dusk. Doors and windows by the dozens open up on all sides. All are open night and day. The windows are unscreened. Since most mosquitoes hang close to the ground (or are supposed to if they play fair), few filter in through these high altitude windows. However, bed nets may be seen hanging over many a bed.

The tall, narrow window panes of ruffled or partly colored glass are louvered. As the hours pass, they are adjusted to the sun's swing, so that rooms in Queensland always lie in the shade. The whole side of the house is comprised solely of these tall, vertical panes turned to admit equal amounts of fresh air with glass, making sure that the sun never strikes the glass. People inside may see out readily from the vertical slits of their castle on high, yet the nosy outside world can't see in—not even at night when the house is lighted.

These homes, made completely of wood, are very flimsily built for all their size. The whole house shakes when someone walks across the floor.

Underneath each house is an open-air carport, sitting room, or laundry facilities—usually all three. Green vines and flowers always adorn this area, freshly hosed down each day to produce coolness, surrounded by the lush, green lawn. Many homes have their own water storage tank which catches rain water, painted violet or rose or pale green to match the house.

When I drove past those first high, airy, delightfully rococo homes in Marysville I never dreamed that I, too, would soon be seated upon one of those big verandahs looking out upon the world in the refreshing evening breeze. But as I sat with the folks that evening and thought of the adventure and freedom which my girls had by comparison to the quiet way of life, the very limiting and restricting way of life, which Queensland girls seemed to live, it gave one something to think about.

While we reveled in parrots, the Alexandra palms, the lawyer vines, crocodiles, wild pigs, and cassowarys—those huge flightless birds of the jungle—while we learned everything we could about flame trees, native sasparilla and ginger, the Indian tulip trees with their large yellow blooms, the huge milkwood supported by flying buttresses, the native nutmeg, the native cashew, and the macadamia nut (native product of Queensland), and orchid terrestrial and epiphytal—while we were hiking and scuba diving and traveling with young men continuously at our side, this fun was not so easily available to the Queensland girl of Jean's and Ann's age.

There was a young girl of wan and apathetic figure who lived where we took rooms, the kindly landlady's daughter. Night after night she just sat there among the old folks watching television. She was quiet, mannerly, almost unseen and unheard—and by no means dynamically happy.

"Does Jennifer May have a young man she goes out with sometimes?" I asked the tired, patient mother.

"Sometimes," she replied. She was serving guests' breakfast on trays from her kitchen, which is the custom in Australia; breakfast goes automatically with the room, and a woman may prepare and serve up to eighteen breakfasts on fine china, and then wash up.

"But there isn't much entertainment for young people in Cairns," the mother said. "Most young men Jennifer's age are out at sports, you know. Then they all go to the pub in the evenings."

Young Australian girls often find their lives just wilting away. Wherever the action is, they aren't in it. And after they find someone to marry them, often to get out of the corner, they find themselves sitting in another corner.

The three of us were getting off now, from the familiar tourist home at Cairns where we had friends, bound for a remote bauxite dig of Comalco near the tip of remote Cape York on the west side;

278

we were to drive a single track not many people traveled, called the Queensland North West Development Road. Otto offered to help us drive there, but we declined his help to become the only females to accomplish this journey on our own.

"What's the use of taking any good clothes along there?" Jean protested as we packed the Toyota. "Where we're going nobody will be dressed up."

"Are you kidding?" Ann said, as she puffed, hoisting jerry cans.

"Yes, Jean," I echoed. "A good rule for women is always take along at least one good dress."

"You get to the very ends of the earth," warned Ann, "and if you don't have your good dresses along it never fails that everybody there is all dressed up, and then what are you? You're a freak."

We set off then, leaving our major baggage at the guest house, and sailed along in the Landcruiser, and the bitumen ended, bringing us once again onto dirt road, with no complete maps available beyond this—for we had not time to obtain surveyor's maps, nor could we have accommodated them without swamping the ship.

"Let's go bush." The sun was at ten degrees, taking its swift plummet to earth. Ann plunged the galloping Toyota recklessly through whacking branches, lopping off small anthills at a wallop. She brought us up expertly to camp along a river at a place drawn out for her with a pencil on a scrap of paper. Author-artist Captain Percy Tresise of Cairns, who had published a book with the Chicago Field Museum, had clued us in to this good camping spot.

Next morning was *hot*, following the early billabong washup under the figs and baobabs. Soon Ann took us climbing up a steep hill nearby, where she revealed to us a gallery of hidden rock pictographs along a large red rock face. Few people knew of these drawings. No state governments yet have the means to guard their precious treasures from the vandalism of the public, so these governments are well pleased if the public in general do not know where they are.

It was an experience to come upon this gallery of primitive art, and feel like the first to stand here. Thirty feet long, underneath layers of paintings of magic animals and men, lay a giant crocodile drawn under the cliff overhang. Sometimes many generations of man will use the same place for drawings, with each new generation making theirs over the ones of the old people—for such sites are sacred places and the drawings are prayers.

In searching for primitive pictographs you learn to look for the particular kinds of rock the Aboriginals liked to use. They liked overhangs which protected their drawings from the weather (though more likely from evil spirits), and they liked smooth, soft rock of a consistency which takes a good impression. It is valuable for the searcher for pictographs to crawl about underneath big overhangs or cave-like entrances, even on hands and knees, looking into corners, for some very secret drawings may be hidden upsidedown underneath.

Percy Tresise knew as much or more about Aboriginal art and its legends as any Australian. By trade he was an Ansett Airlines pilot. His interest in art exploration began when he saw many of his galleries from the air during his scheduled flights across north Australia's wilds. Following up the aerial mapping of his locations, he later made Landrover expeditions during his too-short vacations to the sites, taking with him a favorite Aboriginal friend as a guide. He wrote down stories partly from the interpreter and partly from his self-learned studies of many years. Colored films of the pictographs and his own artistic duplications illustrated his texts.

Some of the pictures showed white man drawn upsidedown, standing on his head. It seemed almost profane to view them here, and not very flattering to the viewer. Standing on the head is not a normal posture for anyone. These prayers wished us dead.

Consuming the last of our fresh fruit and milk, we drove on. The Dry was on as the track headed northward up the inland ridge of Cape York through open forest of gum trees. We hastened. The streams were still running. Their waters were clear, flowing over golden sand through which the vehicle waddled after a walker, who leaped out and walked ahead. At such crossings we paused to make tea under tall, lush trees and hear the birds, and lie down in the water to wet our clothes all over, refreshingly. It was the Dry coming on, fast. We slept on the ground under our big family mosquito net hung on a limb in the bush. The tent wasn't needed now.

I will always think of Cape York as the "real" Australia: the open forest, billabongs, lovely flowing streams, blue sky, vast distances of wilderness. River crossings were always a challenge. We were never quite sure if the rivers had dropped far enough to cross the vehicle over them. Jungle vines and cables of the match bean, with its beans four feet long. Wild pigs nimbly sprinting across the track just after the car has passed.

"Always look behind you and around you all the time when you are walking in the wilds," I told my girls. "Animals often cross behind you. They know the difference between your face and the back of your head, don't think they don't."

Jean: "Let's have fifteen minutes of silence, please."

"Okay, roight."

Silence. Drive, drive. Or, silently at camp, prepare food. Explorers by necessity must be too much together.

"Golly, what shall we talk about today?"

"How about World Events?"

"Can't. We don't know anything that's going on in the world."

"Then how about air pollution? How about overpopulation?"

"Too far away."

"Nix, mom, we've worn those subjects out."

"Gossip, then?"

"Haven't heard any recently. Haven't a clue."

"Then, let's have another fifteen minutes of silence," said Jean.

North of the trading post of Laura the single track, navigable only by four-wheel drive, and only during the Dry for half the year, goes on to connect tenuously the neighboring grazing properties with each other, and there are almost no signposts. The people, if you meet them, are so far apart that they almost never see their neighbors through the passing years. They are not vocal in expressing themselves. It is sometimes difficult for an outsider to talk with them. Some came in here to the Cape York Peninsula during the time of the potato famine in Ireland, and did not come out again.

Alone at camp, deep in the bush, you keep looking around and over your shoulder. You almost expect to see the "little people" so feared by the Aborigines. The little people are but four feet tall or so. They are very shy; even the Abos will tell you that they haven't been seen by anyone for a very long time. Yet you still feel them about, somehow. Their spirits are here yet, rustling the leaves in that great silence. The Aboriginal beliefs in the "little people," the *Burgingin*, are not wrong. Pigmy tribes still do exist just across Torres Strait in New Guinea.

Chapter 18

EXPLORING THE CAPE YORK PENINSULA TO WEIPA

One by one the government has set aside a number of Aboriginal reserves from the people's original hunting grounds, and following on the heels of early mission settlement, these reserves encompass altogether many thousands of square miles of wilderness. They take up practically all of the low, swampy, humid jungle lands of the coasts on all sides of the Cape York Peninsula.

Only the central highlands, drier and more adapted to grazing cattle, are the province of the white man. Natives get the coastline, white man the interior. White man gets the one government road. This is the general layout.

The parcels in which the government leases out land to cattle growers are all big ones. They run from five hundred to four thousand square miles each, and cannot be obtained in smaller blocks which I believe to be a realistic appraisal.

With a long winter drought followed by insufficient Wet, the "bushmasters" buried and lost in the tall kangaroo grass of Cape York may die in great numbers by starvation, when the dry grass holds no sustenance and billabongs disappear.

The stations of Cape York do not have fences around their enormous holdings. Their land lies mostly in an uncontrolled condition, virtually unexplored. The best the landholders can do is build some fences enclosing limited areas called paddocks, and under modern management very recently some are trying to find their wild cattle and get them inside the fence simply to count them. The people at a station called Merluna discovered their count five hundred head short in one paddock. It was believed the Blacks were still eating a good many; and some renegade white men may exist in some of this wilderness. No one really knows. The naturalist Dr. Serenti has stated that it is possible that the marsupial wolf could still exist in some of the wild parts of Queensland. Of course untended cattle, like wild animals, simply die from any number of causes, so that nobody knows exactly why they disappear.

Stations which can afford the investment are in the process of importing heat- and drought-resistant stock: Drought Master Studs, Brahmins, Santa Gertrudis, Poll Herefords. The greatest need, the Peninsula ranchers say, is for the Queensland Government to build them a beef road. The distance to market over present tracks is impassible, so that only a couple of remote ports are used for shipment now. We were lucky to see the country from the first track, before "improvements," and to see its wild, native vegetation and species, which alone in all Australia, are left in the original condition.

The roof of a typical old homestead will be covered with split wooden shingles in the southeast, and corrugated sheet iron here. The floor will be of thin planking, with the house sitting high up above the ground on stilts, and accessible by a steep flight of wooden stairs. Walls will be of sheet-iron, perhaps painted in white or pastel. The rooms (or room) will be very large and high-ceilinged. Some walls may be mud plastered and whitewashed, or lined with sailcloth (now sheet iron in the Outback). A verandah sometimes crowns square-adzed posts (metal today) stretched along the front of the house. Cedar joinery was the main glory of many old Australian homes.

Interesting to us from the modern world was that a similar service block containing servants' housing, a kitchen and pantry, a dairy and meat room, may be built twenty or more feet away from the main house, or may be linked to the rambling structure by a covered way. The kitchen is usually the largest room. It may be equipped with a large masonry fireplace and bread oven, with extensive work benches, and pot racks, and a large wooden central table.

Outbuildings may have come as much as thirty years after the first hut: barns, smoke house, brewery (in old historic homes), stables, forge, storage sheds, shearing sheds, and living quarters for workmen. Prosperous settlers in the southeast built two-story Regency style homes with stone or stuccoed brick walls, but never here.

Piecemeal growth, characteristic in type of the feudalism we find yet in some parts of Latin America, is still quite visible in Australia, but not in north Queensland or any of the Outback, for there were no servants as such and there was not sufficient manpower with which to do things, and there were no materials to work with. Raw, primitive frontier still exists, and will for a long while.

Today only large, heavily financed properties under the control of a salaried manager with his family in residence find it attractive to operate. A house a company builds for management typically may consist of a blend of impersonal fibro-cement cottage and separate office, with a cement-floored, sheet iron-walled garage stuffed with mechanical parts and fuel drums, instead of the old forge. A landing strip, whether or not a small plane is based there, is ready to receive the weekly mail plane. The old personality of the place has faded with yesterday, though the loneliness and most of the personal inconveniences remain.

Since the only road took us right through the stations, we dropped in at the homesteads grateful to find any human habitation.

The first station we drove through was Musgrave Station, and here we met its veteran owner, Mrs. Hales (pronounced Hiles), and her Scottish maid Betty. Encompassing a thousand square miles, Musgrave is a good example of the old Queensland homestead. It is one of few left still inhabited by the original pioneers, rather than managed by some city-based corporation.

Our hostess gave us our first wild "custard apples" from the Queensland bush, and, in addition to purchasing gasoline, we were given several pounds of beef, for which money was refused, like in the good old days.

Out beyond Musgrave the sandy track proceeded through dry forest until near sundown I called upon Jean to halt the Toyota, and

while each bar tyre straddled a washout, I walked to investigate a
white, gleaming structure back in the trees. The white gleam was a
large earthfill dam. Inland in the high country, surely it would be safe
for a real swim! No one who has not sweated over these endless
tracks until the Toyota is suffused inside with human sweat, no one
who is not beat half to death with endless gear shifting, can appre-
ciate what bliss the sight of water means, the thoughts of evening
camp under the trees, campfire smoke, fresh beef in a sack just waiting
for roasting.

I was walking in my sandals and short green cotton shift back
through the gum trees toward the gleaming dam when I saw a rare
species: A wild white man of the Cape York Peninsula.

There was his pickup truck. I hadn't seen that. In the truck lay
a couple of sweat-softened saddles, shabby and worn, and coils of
rope, and boots. The man was barefooted.

"Well, hello!" I walked up to the man, shook the calloused hand,
and introduced myself and explained our presence. The man was tall,
and like the American cowboy, had almost no hips nor waist, from a
life in the saddles. From the name he gave I realized that what made
him different from most Aussies I had seen was French or Spanish
ancestry. This made his brown eyes gleam as eyes do not usually
gleam in Aussieland. It was an inherited quality, in the genes. Then
too, he was a friendly man and most assuredly a happy man from his
independent, wild life in the bush, and he owned the dam and the
land I had been driving over much of the day, he owned it from early
times as had his father before him—and this in itself should be enough
to make any man happy.

We said but a few words, I don't remember what, each being
quite startled to find another human being here.

There was a gracefulness about him, and a graciousness which
stories attribute to the real Australian bushman, whether of Anglo
or Latin endowment, and there was modesty. Somewhere in the
area blackfellows, his only companions, were mustering with him.
He had just come for a swim. A person might remember the essence
of Australia in a moment. An encounter in the bush, the quick hand-
shake, a memory which stays. He gave us the dam for our night of
camping.

"You can't hurt anything," he reassured me, when I promised
to be very careful with our campfire. The forest was too wet, he

explained. We had seen a number of smokes that day traveling, and we wondered. It was mustering time now in the fall, and the black-fellow jackeroos were deliberately setting fire to the bush on every hand to drive out the "rogue" cattle which lay down to hide from them, and which they could not find in any other way, he said. Were it not for blackfellows, whites in the north would never find their cattle at all. If you lived with blacks for a lifetime or two you took to blackfellow ways and learned to track. The Outback being very resistant to change, you changed yourself to live with it, and after a while you may prefer sleeping on the ground to sleeping in a bed, and cook your meat outdoors beside the house, and adapt to the fact that there may be little else to eat when you are far out in north Queensland, cut off for half of all your years by raging rivers and monsoons. And if you stay on here, you may like this way of life. Those who don't, leave.

Again the girls and I bedded down under the net. It beat the tent life altogether. We had had our swim. Each night now we lay outdoors atune to the night glory, the sweet smells, the bird calls. Yet we were protected from all this glory of buzzing and creeping things, in perfect faith that the net would stop them at a tolerable distance, say, a few inches away. We did not worry about the cattle once we were abed, though we would not normally mingle among cattle if we were afoot. They were huge, horned, and dangerous.

Next day the girls and I moved on from Earthfill Dam, through occasional blackfellows on horseback, and cattle and smokes and spot fires, to reach the village of Coen, population thirty-five, called the Economic Centre of the Cape York Peninsula.

In earlier generations people who came to found Coen landed by vessel and forged inland by bullock teams pulling wagons—covered wagon pioneers, you might say. Now there was a mission hospital and hostel here for blacks, and a store and hotel. There had once been a mine.

It was Anzac Day, a national holiday, but we were able to fill up on gasoline, cold drinks, and fresh beef again. While Mrs. Taylor, who had been a pioneer baby in these parts, served tea to me in her home, my girls did the work with the Toyota as usual, and took care of every thing. We were given directions how to proceed. There were three different tracks going out of town, all of them being fourteen miles

286

out near the airdome. Two of the tracks led off to properties. Only one led on to Weipa.

We only found one of them on our first try, anyway, so we took that one. It was pretty dim. It crossed a nice jungle river and went off through gullies and thickly wooded hills, with many wild pigs.

Next thing we knew we were in a ditch, hung up there like a big square box, and we couldn't get out. The girls unreeled our cable and hooked it around a tree. The winch lifted us out, almost straight up. That was the first occasion we used our winch. Its reel snarled up on recoiling, like getting a snarl in your fishing reel, sort of.

"Just stand back, mother, leave it all to us, you are only in the way."

The girls figured out how to use engine power to unsnarl the cable and wind it neatly so that the coils would not bind upon each other. I worried—if a cable on tension should happen to snap under two thousand pounds strain in some of these maneuverings, it could be very dangerous.

"Seems to me this road to Weipa is awfully dim and rough," I said, when we had extricated ourselves by cable from another ditch.

"Mother, just stop nagging, will you? Leave everything to us, we know what we're doing. The sun's getting low. We'll soon be making you a nice evening tea."

"Oh, my, are you *sure?* I'm getting ready for tea, anytime."

"Tea will be served *soon,* mother," replied the poor dears, sucking on their bruised knuckles.

The girls could never get over the idea that the whole wilderness wherever we were was always teatime to me. During years before they were born I had lived in the wild on tea and wild meat.

We pressed on, to force pasture gates so thick and heavy that it took three of us to lift one hardwood timber aside, huffing and puffing. We pressed on, having returned the gate to its place, to stop again and drag burning brush out of the track, passing quickly with the Toyota over smoking ground to fresh ground beyond.

When we had tea and slept, I tied little strings on the trees to remind me which direction we were going. The girls laughed at mom for that one.

It was beautiful the next day. Real jungle. We could see lush forested mountains rising up beyond. Bushes parted and closed behind us. We were feeling our way with the wheels. If the driver couldn't get the feel, someone got out and led the way afoot. We had made only about thirty-five miles from Coen altogether, by the speedometer.

This darn road. We opened other gates through such complicated mixtures of wire and sticks that it took half an hour sometimes to get through—for we wanted to be polite and not chop them down, or anything.

"I wish I had our .22 rifle along," I said, suddenly. It was not the last time I wished for it, I can tell you. Alas, due to conflicting state laws, the trusty little camp gun lay inside a trunk on the opposite side of the continent, so that in Cape York wilds we found ourselves completely unarmed.

No more cattle or signs of recent man today. The Toyota pushed through ever thicker bushes, tunneling through them. The land was sloping downwards. The character of the vegetation itself had changed entirely, becoming pure jungle, containing types we had never seen before—and possibly had few botonists.

Jean pointed out that the road was heading persistently and stubbornly toward the east coast of Cape York, and we wanted to go west. Weipa Bay lay on the other side of the Peninsula, not over here.

"Mother," said Jean severely, and paused. Jean always took command in times like this. "We've got the wrong darn road. The streams, look, the streams are all flowing the wrong way, and look up there, the sun hangs wrong."

"Okay."

"Well, okay. Two whole days of following this darn track. Look, quick!" Something big and very black bush-bashed away from our very side at that moment into the overhanging cables of a rushing stream. Silence followed. Only the stream. Cassowary, we thought. Flightless giant.

"So, okay, okay. Let's go back to Coen. What's two days? Try again."

"It wasn't wasted time. Look at the wilds we've seen."

Surely very few human beings had seen this country where the dim track took us, down along the tropical rivers. Ancient track, made by one man. Good man, that. Not on any map, it took us over to the Peach River and Blue Mountain areas—so the locals later said—which drain through rain forest and jungle into the Pacific

288

rather than into the Gulf of Carpentaria. Due to the casualness with which the Coen pioneers gave directions and our own casualness in listening to the directions, we had worked into the wrong watershed. Ever-thickening jungle and wet-shadowed gloomy canyons, vine-laced, finally hung us up, and we retraced the trek back to Coen, gulley-jumping it, and gassed up again, got some beef, and started over.

Well, it was a sensible track this time, following the telephone poles, what the Aborigines used to call the "singing strings." When you follow the line, you're right. If you have some emergency you can always cut the line, and a party of linemen will come out in a bit and find you. No person would do this lightly, of course—but it has been done.

It was dry country again, inland, and the bush was cleared far back on all sides of the straight line road, except for a few rough ditch crossings, washouts. It was along here that Ann saw our most unbelievable and beautiful lizard—a prehistoric-looking goanna which was five feet long, and pea green (now fading to gray with the coming Dry) wearing yellow polka dots.

First we started taking pictures from the car. If you keep the engine running an animal which has allowed your approach in the first place may stay right there listening to the vibrations. After you take those first shots, you turn off your engine and take some more. Finally, if the animal will tolerate it, you slip out of the far door of the car and creep closer. If he is still there, you stand straight out in the open, putting one foot ahead of the other very slowly; if you walk in a straight line, especially if the sun is behind you and in his eyes, he may allow you to approach very close. This is partly be-cause the vision of animals in general is not good, and partly it is pure luck, and again there are certain days upon which wild animals may be approached, because they are looking for contacts with mates and friends. Or occasionally they may be looking for a fight, should they be pressed too closely.

We spent about an hour with our goanna, while he blew up his large throat bubble and let out air in lovely hisses, facing us, and stretched his dinosaur neck, and stood at intervals upon heavy hind haunches and flicked his six-inch-long, black, forked tongue in royal dragon pomposity.

All were aware that it was just possible for him to charge and

289

grab a bare leg if he so decided. Fortunately, he was a gentleman to the last, when we allowed him to move ponderously and regally away into the boondocks. His clumsy appearance was a deception.

Australian Reptiles, by Harold Cogger, says: "A large goanna (Monitor Lizard) at bay puts on an impressive display . . . the tail is curved and whiplike, and is readily used to flail an opponent. The head and body are raised high off the ground, the body is inflated with air and the loose skin of the throat is expanded to make a dewlap. The whole performance is accompanied by slow but violent hissing. . . .When moving at normal speed a goanna's gait can only be described as a rather comical waddle. The head and body are raised off the ground and slowly moved from side to side. . . .The same waddling motion is also used when running at speed. Only if really hard pressed and over relatively short distances, will a goanna fold its front legs flat against its body and run only on hind legs. To get an occasional view . . . when moving through long grass, a goanna will sometimes raise itself vertically by using its tail and hind legs as a tripod."

Near the end of that day we had made it beautifully all the way to the Archer River. Brawling through rocks and over clean golden sand, it was a glorious, clear-water river. As we had been forewarned, it was also in high flood, two hundred yards wide, much too far to hook a cable. We halted there and threw ourselves into the cool rushing shallows to "have a think about it," as Sir Reg Ansett would have said. I saw my green dress waft out behind me as I sat half afloat on the golden sand.

Just then we heard men's voices. With me leading the way afoot, the girls came cautiously along with the Toyota, pushing through the swift, shallow river. Approaching the two men, we knew them at once. Jean and Ann had talked with them back at Coen days ago. They had not been communicative with traveling women; when Ann asked them for travel information, they answered tersely and in grunts. They were missionaries. Now they were stuck.

They had a pickup truck with a winch on it and a heavy tractor being brought into Cape York for construction and cultivation, and of course the tractor got stuck right here in the Archer River. The tractor could not make the climb six feet up the steep stand embankment which floodtime in the Wet had carved on the opposite shore, nor could their truck pull it. The sand was too slippery.

Annie and Jeanie whooped with glee at the sight. The men in

290

typical conceit had treated the little explorers in cavalier fashion—
so the girls thought. They had gruffly told the girls not to come
far out here. "We haven't got time to rescue you," the good-looking
young one said.

"Whackadoo!" yelled Ann, zooming the Toyota all too recklessly past me and on across the rushing river, dodging boulders in
the same way she went through the ant hills.

It was plain to see that the missionaries were badly sunburned
and exhausted from their labors. "Can we give you a hand there?"
asked naughty Ann.

"No, thank you. I don't think you could. . . ."

"Maybe we can pull it out by using our two vehicles and
working together," put in Jean sensibly. "Our winch has a
2,000-pound pull. Mother, please get out of the river and go up
on shore. Go sit under a tree. You are only in the way."

Within fifteen minutes, with a bit of hooking of cables, the
tractor was slowly pulled out of the river, and the grateful
missionaries, much flabbergasted, were on their way. As for us,
we settled down to enjoy the beautiful Archer River tonight and
tomorrow. This crossing was the main highway for human traffic,
if any people came along.

On the north shore we hung our bed net. The stars came out,
and after much swimming and splashing, Ann stepped barefooted
upon a round stone like a plate, which turned out to be a surprised,
very-much-alive turtle.

When the girls went snorkling with masks and fins next day in
a clear pool of the Archer just below, and later decked themselves
out in leaves and ferns like mermaids and put flowers in their
hair, I never had a worry in the world. It was a friendly Cape York
River, where the rare palm cockatoo, with red wing feathers peeping
out of black, visits on occasion from New Guinea to wing its way
among the more familiar yellow-breasted sunbirds and among the
some 160 species of honeyeaters which are found in the Moluccas,
the Celebes, New Guinea, and Australia—but mostly in Australia—and
the green ant weaves its elaborate nests of stitched leaves in the trees.

Possibly there are lungfish *coelacanth*, (also called mud fish)
living in the Archer. I am not sure that anyone knows. This fish
lives in north Queensland rivers in some places. Growing to about
six feet this living link in evolution has lungs as well as gills. Found in

South America and Africa as well as in Australia, this living fossil can exist buried in mud during the Dry.

The well-armored, ugly fish, which weighs up to ninety pounds and lives much of its life in the ocean, can be most easily observed in some tropical rivers where it goes for a part of its life cycle. Some fishermen have called it "four legs," because the pectoral and pelvic fins of some types look like legs as the fish is pulled in. The color is said to be blue in the water, but it turns brown after it dies. It is not very good to eat.

Along the telephone line again, a barrel sat in the middle of the road. A station wife crossing the Archer had told us to "just watch for the barrel." On the barrel some wit had painted the words, "15 mi hour" and a large white X. This was the crossroads. Only the X showed that the road here went four ways, and we turned to the left or west. Nothing was to be seen of a track but bent grass for some distances. Characteristically, after half a day along the west fork we came upon a weathered board with an arrow on a tree: "To Weipa."

After that the road got better, with little bridges of boards and poles to take you over gullies and bogs. We found the missionaries again slowly tractoring along, and paused for tea with them in green forest. They would have to fly their tractor into the mission from the usual takeoff at Weipa Airport.

We continued on toward Weipa as darkness fell through enchanting, green, open forest glens, with the land sloping imperceptibly downward toward the gulf. Every eighth of a mile one big-eyed, grasshopper-eating little owl flew up from before our wheels, all white, lighted eyes.

I was satisfied that Jean was at the wheel. Jean took the car cautiously over those narrow bridges spanning little creeks of unknown depths.

It was well after dark when we got to Weipa, and everybody was at the movies. The wife of the boss came out and guided us to Unmarried Girls Quarters, and there we settled into a clean cabin that was to be our home and exploratory base made possible by Comalco. There was cafeteria food, a store, gasoline supplied for purchasing, communications, first aid if needed, and expert Toyota maintenance.

The chief Comalco mechanic said just nine cars had been brought up to Weipa by the men over the years he had worked here, all of them during the Dry, of course. We had already had a good

292

adventure. Usually the passenger car is assisted by a friend with a four-wheel drive and winch. For sixty dollars a car could be brought in by vessel from Brisbane, and that was more usual at the remote, self-sustained little bauxite camp, now fast growing into a city of sorts, a company town. All personnel were of course brought in solely by air. The bauxite ore is shipped out on great ocean vessels.

For a hundred years only the Bugi-men and Malays were in possession of three thousand miles of north coast Australia. Yes, the Bugi-men of Macassar, sailing in ships of straw under the yellow tiger of a rajah. Later they had little Dutch guns popping at their prows, the Asians blowing in and out with the trade winds in quest of the musty sea slugs, sailing *proas* under big square sails, and making contact with the north coast Aborigines. This led to wars and retributions, to kidnappings and murder, and their contacts are probably what brought the dread disease of leprosy to tropical Australia—where it remains today. While William Charles Wentworth and Sir Henry Parkes were debating before Parliament— the fathers of a nation—and Mark Twain came from America to delight the audiences in crowded theaters of the south, and railways were expanding, right here on the other side of this continent naked, betel-chewing Bugis with *kris* knives in their belts traded and raped and burned in Black Man's Land. All along the gulf you can find their traces today: groves of fine old tamarinds, fire places, Malay wells, iron boilers, graves with Arabic letters on their headstones.

Carpentaria tribes from Darwin to Borroloola today are half Malayan, with broad shoulders, high cheekbones, piercing eyes, a "cranky" temper, and the intelligence, energy, arts, customs, of Asiatic islands.

They were the first ship-builders, of the Celebes dugout canoe. They decorated their spears and shields, plaited and painted bamboo baskets, fashioned feather leis and necklaces of berries, and buried their dead in Muhammadan wrappings of paperbark eucalyptus. They left behind Malayan words in the Aboriginal languages. The *didjeridoo,* which is their bamboo oboe, is originally from Borneo. They brought arrack with them, blow pipes, and poison darts.

The blacks learned to hide in the bush when the next square-sailed *proa* came in, and when its crew ventured ashore for precious water, the bush attack was on, and there was human kidney fat for dinner.

It was always that way each year with the northwest monsoon: the fleets of thirty to sixty *proas*, each with a dozen outrigger hunting canoes, a queer little navy of a thousand Asiatic men: low prow on water, high square galleon stern, trident mast with two or three head sails, all coming in together with the high-piled clouds of the Wet. No charts—they sailed by dead reckoning across the sea, steered by two great wooden rudders, and using wooden anchors weighed down with stones. Their sails could be rolled up like mats.

Each *proa* carried some sixty fierce and lusty pirates with blackened teeth, oiled bodies with belt and *kris*, wild hair with headband or turban of red coolie cloth. Some were tatooed. Some wore caps of monkey skins. They lived on fish, rice, *dugong*, coconut meat and oil, domestic hogs, and Malayan fowls, cooked on a fire burning in a big iron pan set in sand aboard the ship.

To make a call on the *nakhoda*, the captain, you boarded at the prow and crawled on hands and knees to his cabin forward, which was a little kennel not four feet high that barely allowed room to squat and lie in. Each *nakhoda* had his run, luring the Australian Aborigines to hunt the *trepang*, and turtle shell, pearl shell, and pearls, which the blacks collected the year around and saved for barter in sarongs, sugar salt, fish, rice, arrack, beads, tobacco, and a live Asiatic chicken or two. The trade came to be worth millions; for the pearls and shells were sold in Samarinda, then finally to jewelers at Batavia and The Hague—and hence the cannon of the Dutch came to be on the *proas*.

By the time Australia woke up to the fact, the flotilla of *proas* in the eastward drift of the Dutch empire were sailing under the red-white-and-blue of the Netherlands while flying the red-and-yellow of piratical rajahs; and a stop to it all came finally by international agreement. Alfred Searcy, the first Customs agent, was sent to north Australia in the early 1880s, and he dealt with the matter deftly. His right hand brandishing a Colt revolver, wearing an Aussie hat and tropical shorts and knee socks, he boarded the murderous vessels one by one and typically, in the name of England, told them to "be off with you." And that was that.

In 1955 another lone white man, Australian geologist H. J. Evans came to prowl around Albatross Bay.

Evans used a little boat just nine feet long. He found he could explore this coast with it only early in the mornings when the weather was calm, for each afternoon the waves would rise dangerously. His progress was therefore slow.

This most unlikely way of voyaging disclosed to the trained geologist one of the world's greatest mineral discoveries—mile upon mile of red pebbles of pure bauxite lying upon the surface of the earth and gracing these far shores—which no other geologist had ever seen.

The remote dig discovered at Weipa today joins the Caribbean and West Africa as the world's great sources of bauxite, without which man's explorations of space would not be possible, not to mention his routine airlines. Weipa is strategically placed to serve long-term needs of the whole Pacific area, including Japan, and the developing countries of Southeast Asia, Australia's good customers.

Out of this fifteen years ago was born the Comalco Industries with a new alumina refinery at Gladstone down the East Coast, and the operation we had seen at Bell Bay, Tasmania. Weipa is a prime example of just how fast modern man can change the slow story of the world. In just fifteen amazing years the Royal Netherland Harbour Works, Ltd. had dredged the shipping access channel. The Royal Australian Navy came in to do the hydrographic survey, with the Queensland Department of Harbours and Marine. A meteorological station was set up by the Commonwealth Directorate of Meteorology, which did tidal stream observations in the rivers and bay channels, and took corings to show the nature of the bottom and the sedimentation and salinity of the water in the estuaries.

Every day you can see the scraper-loaders, assisted by bull-dozers, removing the few feet of soil covering the bauxite. Hough H400 Payloaders load the precious red pebbles into aluminum-bodied Haulpak trucks. Each giant Payloader can mine in excess of five hundred wet tons per hour. The bauxite is trucked a short way to an elevated dump station adjacent to the beneficiation plant, where ore grade is improved by sizing and washing. There, one thousand tons per hour go by belt conveyor to the crushing station, then through wet screening. The residue slurry is pumped back to the mine-out areas to be used as fill.

Probably the most thorough planning in Australia has gone into making the new tropical town. Weipa Township at Rocky

Point on the Mission River estuary accommodates the mining work force and their families, numbering 370. The population will expand eventually to around 1,250. There is a town center near the rocky point, having a wide vista over open water. It has a shop, snack bar, canteen, cinema, community hall, tennis courts, bowling green, and a swimming pool. A primary school is going. They await a high school and church. The town has its own water supply and sewage system. Cottages are all-electric with ceiling fans, fly screened, and made of bricks impregnated with insecticide. Louvered windows and house siding open each house to the natural temperature and breezes, reducing direct sunlight to a minimum. Green belts of grass separate groups of houses into courts, meant to give a sense of privacy and a sense of shelter. Shade and flowering trees were still small.

One of the girls drove me to visit the old Weipa Mission and the natives. Missionaries had convinced me before now that the value of their work is not to be denied.

Now I began to witness how the Government was taking up the old mission properties, often very large properties running beef cattle. I met a new government-trained supervisor and business manager for the property; and I met the slim liaison officer, a 21-year-old girl from Tasmania of no particular training, to whom a job was simply a job. There is a dreadful shortage of qualified personnel willing to live on remote native reserves or interested in the sociological or anthropological sciences, and the replacement of old-time missionaries by impersonal government people who are outsiders to the environment is not any notable improvement over missionaries. Still, the step seemed inevitable. Many missions had proven inept in management of the properties, and lost money for the natives rather than earning it.

Employment by Comalco was now of prime economic importance to the Weipa Mission Reserve natives. It was the first time in their experience that a man could actually earn a wage, for the missionaries never had money by which to pay people who worked for the mission—they only helped by food and services and prayers. One of the great complaints against missions was that the natives were getting tired of giving free labor for fringe benefits. All over Australia the natives had learned about money. Now the proximity of Comalco was making great changes in everything.

In order to reside at Weipa South Community, each family had to draw a wage—so this was a very special community, by Aboriginal standards. The houses were made of prefabricated aluminum, with concrete flooring, quite cool, and termite-proof in a way which old-time wooden houses were not. I went into houses with three bedrooms, shower, septic toilet, and electricity. The village had a preschool kindergarten and government-subsidized child feeding program, somewhat like Head Start in the U.S., besides regular elementary school. The Presbyterian Church, here for seventy years, still stood solidly. There was a branch of the Commonwealth Bank, a store, and post office, all operated by the Aboriginal people capably as their own.

I told Keith De Witt, the caterer in our village, of the girls cavorting in the Archer and viewing the sizable bream which lurked there, and screaming with fun as fish nipped at their twinkling legs.

"Well, a deep pool can be a favorite place for a crocodile to lie up, you know," he mentioned casually.

"What? But—not so far back in the hills from the sea?"

"Oh, yes. The estuarine may get as far as fifty miles overland. Remember, he comes during the Wet, in the flood. Little ditches may provide his walkway. And the Wet ended only just now."

"We saw a pet baby crocodile from the Archer here at Weipa," I said. "I assumed of course it was just a Johnston, the little fish-eater.

"What color was it?" he asked.

"Vivid green. Gray markings. Eyes glitter with an evil light, like yellow jewels. Beautiful little thing."

"The color is the giveaway," said the experienced Dutch Indonesian. "The Estuarines are bright, vivid green when young. Fish-eaters are always brown."

That pet was born there at the Archer crossing. What if his mama or daddy had been lying that very day on the bottom of that paradise pool where the girls snorkled? I made a vow to change my ways.

"Don't put a toe in the ocean here," the Weipa people warned. "We just go in the swimming pool. Sharks are everywhere. There are hammerheads chasing big sting rays all over the place and the sea wasps can cause death if you touch them."

Yet the native Aborigines had always swum and dived in these seas, these remarkable people. They believed sharks prefer white

297

man's flesh to themselves, and few whites questioned this. When diving, the natives for centuries took care not to show the white bottoms of their feet. They had knowledge of "magic" which, for the most part, protected them, and which most of us would not care to challenge.

Jean was to go sailing off on a cargo boat out of Perth soon, to be gone from Australia for two months, and Ann and I were going to explore with the Toyota some more out of Weipa, on up the line of "singing strings." But before Jean left there was just time to catch the Ansett flight out of Weipa Airport and go off to Thursday Island, which has many wonders to amaze the visitor. Besides, the girls had reason to believe that at least two old friends of ours were already at Thursday Island.

Chapter 19

CAPE YORK AND THURSDAY ISLAND

To get to Thursday Island the plane lands on a larger island, and a launch takes you over to Thursday Island.

When the girls and I walked the block or so up from the pier we found the entire first floor of our hotel, the Royal, occupied by the men's bar. Around to the side we went. The hotel registry was an outdoor cubicle window covered with cobwebs. It admitted into a tiny private "office." No one was there but we eventually routed out the manageress of aged, parchment cheek and dyed orange hair, a wraith from the memories of the youth of Somerset Maugham. There was a great deal of broken glass about.

"Where do we register?"

"Don't worry about it, dearie. The fare is eighteen dollars a day for the three of yez, meals included. Sorry, but you have to pay for all three meals whether you eat them or not, that's the rules here."

Enter the little row of six open-air bedrooms set up on a kind of terrace of concrete on a higher altitude behind the big bar, smeared by the drippings of tropical trees, and other strange smears and odors. Cantilevered windows on each side, doors open on each side, the air flows through from the tropical turquoise sea. A pitcher of tepid water is rationed each guest daily. There are no screens, no mosquito nets. Blast of the bar record player reverberates from stone walls. Somehow even the smells are different here. It is different from any of the Australia you thought you knew.

You know that just across Torres Strait is New Guinea, and just knowing that is wonderful. Torres Strait islanders are everywhere, a big-boned, tall, powerful negroid race of flashing white teeth. Many carry a combination of Poly-nesian and Melanesian blood, with a capacity for fun and laughter exceeding most races and far exceeding that of the main-land Aborigine. There are about eight thousand of them living in the Strait, whose inhabited islands number just eight, each with its radio communications, store and mission.

For untold thousands of years these hearty seafarers dwelled in this region, possibly never venturing into either the mainland of Australia or the great island mainland of New Guinea itself, because the residents of these larger lands were adept at defending their territories.

The magnificent health of the Torres Strait islanders is a historic testimony to the high protein diet of the sea and a disease-free environment; hence their laughter and good humor, and their great physical size.

Bright cotton clothing vies with red hibiscus shining against shiny black skins and black hair. With exuberant, beautiful bodies, an irrepressible love of life consumes them, while they are the scandal of staid Australia and their unhumorous Anglo guardians. On Thursday Island these islanders are to be seen drinking and sprawling everywhere.

This was the island to which our Aussie friend Claude had wanted to go back to stay. He loved the laughter and warmth of the islanders. He loved the mixtures of peoples, and their varying dialects and carefree philosophies. He admired their competence as divers and sailors supreme, the men who went down to 240 feet with "hooker gear," with only the old-fashioned helmet set on naked shoulders, to pick up the treasure lying in deep canyons among the dangerous and little-known currents of Divers Grave-yard, which lies between north Australia and New Guinea. (But this way of life had already passed.) And he loved to meet and

300

mingle with the diverse characters who come into Thursday Island when the fishing fleet is in.

Right away the girls went about making inquiries to find Claude. Claude was here some place. They found him living in a little shack in which he shared freely the favors of any number of native women.

I was not quite at ease when I learned that Claude had really gone native.

Many Torres Strait islanders were willing to share their women with the white men. Others got into violent fights. A part of the problem also—possibly the part which boosted the island's appeal for a young man like Claude—was that a large number of the most worthwhile and employable of the great black men were hired away to work, so that it was really a black woman's island.

The abundance of entertainment at Thursday Island, represented by the pool of willing women and by the hotels with their music and bars, was hailed lustily by the visitors from the sea, both black and white. You saw them with arms about each other: a mob of roaring convivial male miteship, and of course the liquor flowed.

An extremely high rate of venereal disease is a part of Thursday Island's problems, as might be expected. Ships carrying wild crews from seven seas converged at this happy port. Soon we came to see that many like ourselves were but visitors at the playtime island. They got off ships here at the docks at all hours, new parties each day. Were it not for the sanctuary of their own remote outer islands, where most islanders lived, these people might become completely corrupted—so many thoughtful Australians felt. But the Queensland government permitted white man to come only this far. Thursday Island was white man's limit. The other Torres Strait islands were banned to tourists, travelers, and all outsiders. Only the missionaries were there. And out there was one place that a fellow like Claude who wanted to go native could not get—if he wanted to.

Every night Thursday Island rocks and sings and roars. On Thursday nights the whole population dances and cavorts en mass at the Grand. On Friday night it goes in a body to the Torres Strait Hotel. Saturday is the night at the Royal. Although bars close at ten o'clock by law, the stalwart ebony figures and wild, red-flushed whites continue their parties along piers and shores and until late at many a private hangout, or aboard the vessels at anchor. At 7:30 A.M. the loud record player at the hotel starts its bawling for a new day. Those who run hotels cater to the public, and give the public what it wants.

The Director of Aboriginal and Island Affairs smiles enigmatically and makes no effort to explain away the untidy, brawling disorder of the "scandalous island," the island of accumulating refuse, of bottles and cans. The island of broken glass.

It seemed to me that people like poor Claude, carried away in their dreams of simple people and island paradise, had themselves regressed to infantilism.

The girls and I moved from the Royal over to the Grand, whose high porch looked out from a hill over the ships at port below.

Many people coming here detest the ugliness of the spoiled island, its unspeakable hotels and renegade white men. When we moved into the Grand it was, typically, having some troubles with escaping sewage along the path to the door. The fumes continued during our stay, from overworked facilities.

Up the flight of wooden stairs, the big open porch ran all the way around the open, corrugated, screened iron building. Our sleeping quarters were cool at night on the second storey, their doors thrown open. Ceiling fans whirred softly. No door keys existed on the island.

Here the colored customers of the bar and lounge did not come up the stairs. Over at the Royal they always kept trying to find a bed to lie down in.

Ann was being courted by a 41-year-old American skipper from Alaska, divorced and with seven children. Jean had found Otto. I didn't think we would stay long at Thursday Island.

Usually the blacks get their smaller craft towed out to the fishing grounds by the big ship. There they work four to five days or even ten days, until the ship is filled up and the catch iced aboard. Meals are taken on board. Sometimes the natives camp on wooded islands in the vicinity of good fishing.

One Saturday I met black-bearded, barefooted Bob Poorfish, the owner of a sixty-eight-foot, $30,000 trawler, and a party of us, including Ann, went out to his boat. He was a crayfish diver, buying from the blacks and working with them.

While Ann and I sat in the ship's little galley, every now and then a white man or two would unobtrusively slip away, only to be replaced by another who appeared from below.

The ships in port had almost the only private enclosed space in lots of ocean. The men were taking turns with some colored girls who came out from town with us. We had to maintain an attitude that was casual and impersonal. The colored girls liked Ann and Ann's mother all right as long as we were not in competition with them and their livelihood. It was a strange situation. Nobody spoke of what was really going on. The fishermen possibly regarded us as untouchable, and these were hungry, primitive men; and all of us were a bit outside civilization here, and out of our depth. The occasional white woman of higher educational aesthetic and romantic standards would have to make a firm decision as to which side of the fence she was on if she lived on this island.

It gave an insight as to why the British ruling classes had developed that chilly, repressive culture that they did. They had to remain aloof. They could not have ruled the raw lands and population they did if they had not practiced stern codes of self-discipline.

Thursday Island, so famous for its miscegenation, got along amicably for the most part, because historically there have been no white women. Trouble comes when white women come to a wild place, and bring civilized standards with them.

An Australian white girl, age eighteen, with her mother, had come over here to find work. Ann recognized her from the staff at Hayman Island. Days later on the street Lorraine told me the two women had been unable to find either jobs or satisfactory lodging. A sanitation law forbade camping out. They had been taken into a one-room hovel with dirt floor, belonging to a kindly black woman alone with her children, a temporary shelter until the husband's return from sea.

"Trouble started," Lorraine said, "when this lady and her relatives seemed to think they had the right to wear all of my clothes. They even put on my underwear, and used my lipstick."

"Heavens. What did you do?"

"Well, I just had to say no. I wasn't raised to share my personal things. But they were hurt and angry. They can't understand me for this feeling of privacy I have. They have no idea of private ownership of anything. Mum and I have simply got to find some place to live soon."

"Mom, guess what? We saw Claude, and he wants to shout you a shandy if you'll come to the lounge right now."

"Well, how is good old Claude? He just about spoiled part of my expedition for me in the Northern Territory when he assumed too much command for my liking."

The young Aussie greeted me with a swift kiss on the cheek, the most uninhibited Aussie I ever met, as he helped us all to chairs overlooking the ships at anchor.

"Oh, mum," he said, "it's like I told you before. The people here are the most beautiful people in the world. Here's Big John and Boogie Dan. Meet me mites." I shook the hands of two tall black men.

Claude had many women in his harem—and we all placidly accepted his arrangement of romance, on the surface.

Lorraine accepted a drink, but she sat there hungry for food and sick with uneasiness about her future survival. Inside she was deeply frightened. To top it off she now felt rejected and an object of no importance. I had hoped that Claude would have some survival ideas for the fair Lorraine, but he didn't at all.

Claude told her how wonderful the black girls were (but he only invited black men for beers with us). It was a man's world on this island yet again. Was it not also a man's cruel world in the mainland village life, which was all she knew?

Lorraine's mother, a timid woman who had fled a brutal husband, presently slipped away from our beery table, unwanted. Exit Lorraine soon after her mother; helpless and frightened women, wandering the face of Australia, up and down: alone eking out a miserable existence at kitchen work on $30 a week.

When we saw Claude again he could hardly walk or sit down. He was in constant pain. His face was gray. All he knew, he said, was that he was struck a violent blow from the rear, knocked flat, and then stomped by boots in the kidneys.

The assailant was clearly one of a crew of an Australian naval patrol boat in port. Three boats worked this port with crews of about six aboard—little gray hulls. I knew their captains by sight. The man with the boots was on one of those crews, But which?

During two days in the hospital Claude had brooded on revenge.

"I have friends here." He waved his hand toward the shiny, black, intelligent faces about us in the bar, innocent faces which had not long been in contact with what is known as the civilized world. "All my girls. They have male relatives. They have brothers, uncles, fathers, my mites. My brothers. We will find out who did this to me," said Claude.

"He shouldn't be out of the hospital," Ann murmured to me, as Claude turned with interest to the yelps of a dog fight which rolled through the men's bar, the ladies' lounge, and out the door, propelled by men's boots. "The way he happens to be out," Ann said, "is he wouldn't let the nurse wash him. The hospital matron found him up taking his own shower so she figured he was well, and the hospital threw him out."

The hospital undoubtedly had its fill of embattled adventurers. It gave them short shrift. A patient was discharged if he could stand up or if he became a nuisance.

Claude had never been x-rayed. There was no resident doctor here. Perhaps he had urological complications from injuries? His gray face dismayed me.

An enormous Torres Strait islander came up then. He kissed Claude on both cheeks, with deepest compassion and love registered in his face. Tears came to both men's eyes. The huge man enfolded the sick Aussie in his giant, muscular arms as one would enfold a young son, a baby.

It was this enfoldment, then, this love, which Claude came to Thursday Island for, and found, on the island of broken glass. Here was an expression of love which he could never express, for some reason, in his own culture. He found it here, that kind of love which accepts all, which does not question or doubt. Unlike stern parents or a demanding society, this love did not give itself on the basis of reward for accomplishment or for conformity to ex- pected patterns. Love just gave of itself when someone needed to be loved, when a white man needed love. That was what was so amazing to me to see. Renegades crave love, then.

305

The mixed-up young Aussie's cheeks were wet when he turned his gray face toward us. "They have found him. They know who the bloke is," he said in a low voice.

It was promised that the next time that bloke came into port with his patrol boat mites there would be a dozen native islanders waiting and watching. And they would take Claude's revenge for him, if he couldn't himself.

I certainly hoped I wouldn't be around on that day. Then, of course, we might expect that the loyal mites of the bloke on the patrol ship would take action in this native uprising, and the predictable outcome was a mass brawl for all.

So goes life on a paradise island, yesterday and today.

The Director of Aboriginal and Island Affairs was pleased that the law was growing up. It has permitted equal rights, including the right to drink liquor, only the last three years. You have to bear in mind, the Director said, that Thursday Island is a port where people are mostly visitors on holiday. He confirmed that progress was phenomenal. We saw black Navy seamen, we saw black faces in postal employment, truck driving, and in just about every island position. Women work at hotel employment or in the hospital. There was a thriving and bustling high school on this island!

There were some shady operations, of course. There were trawler operators who took cases of liquor out to sea and profiteered off native workers by tempting them to drink while on the job. Thirsty workers found the drink irresistible if available, at any price. But the workers were being given an opportunity to choose and to learn from experience.

The island's beauty might be of lesser importance than the fact of human growth. Integration was being practiced here, even though its practice easily led to degeneration. Black women, so Claude told us, want white babies: they gave their bodies away to all takers. The black men shared their women if the white man in the case was their friend. As for trash and broken glass, there was no easy answer. All those bottles of beer made a one-way trip to Thursday Island and never went back. Long ago resident pearl and shell buyers (these seas have the largest pearls in the world because they have the largest oysters) had removed the small beach by bringing its sand out for their own purposes, so that now only broken glass remained for a

306

shoreline. But man-made ugliness was limited to this one island, fortunately, as an experiment in freedom. Possibly a new beach could be created some day by building a jetty to bring in new sand from the sea.

Here at Thursday Island resentment hardly existed, nor was it stimulated by those little irritations people have to put up with from businessmen and government people of far-away Canberra—in this instance, Brisbane, Queensland—having no previous contact with Stone Age man. The wise Director turned a relaxed and smiling face to the complaints of missionaries and tourists who felt Thursday Island's atmosphere to be immoral. Immoral it might be, and shocking; but was the atmosphere not relaxed, contented, and free?

"That government which governs least governs best," was never more clear than here.

"Actually," ruminated the Director, sitting back at ease in his tropical shorts, "we are working ourselves out of a job, you know. They are taking things over quite nicely."

In the Grand Lounge where I did most of my research, I sat, at beers with a sometime crocodile hunter. He was telling me about Australia's great Arafura Swamp, of which I had not heard, for all my studies.

The big open porch listed like a ship under sail. The wooden floors shook. A bare yard of hard-packed earth sprouted frangipani and rubber trees, a breeze moving through the palm fronds, rattling them slightly. Through green leaves and the occasional splash of flaming hibiscus and rank yard weeds in flower among broken glass, stray dogs wandered begging handouts from the genial men of the sea; and from our hill we looked out to milky turquoise water. All shades of color moved in the clouds lying off New Guinea out there, and we saw two jetties, and bright ships riding before our door. Ships with the flags of Communist lands of Asia lay among other ships in our gaze, carrying perhaps but a dozen crew, encrusted with rust and odorous with fish.

The crocodile hunter was saying that the Arafurn Swamp along the Arafura Sea eastward across Carpentaria has about eight hundred primitives living there, visited only once a month by medical missionaries.

"How do I get there?" I asked speculatively.

307

"I'm going myself in a bit," he said. "Take the old ship for one last hunt. I know those shores well, but you can hardly find any really big crocodiles any more."

"I know you," I said. "I read about you in a book by a conservationist. You must be the same fellow. You're a poacher, aren't you?"

"Just one more hunt. Well, the way you could do is make arrangements in Darwin," he said. "You fly to Groote Island in the Gulf from Darwin. Then, on the return flight you land at Alco Island in the Russells. From Alco Island you go by small plane, or on the Mission steamer. The island lies just a half mile off shore in the mouth of the Goyder River. Then you go upriver into the swamp, that's the usual way. But of course I have my boat and that's best."

The poacher loved the wilds, actually, as such men do. As Ann once pointed out, those who make a living in the bush, have to figure out some kind of a product to bring out of the bush, or else they would not be able to make it there. Yet the wild yields so easily to the exploiters, it is so fragile, that with only a few it soon is ravished.

Even in the best days, men could make but a miserable living at crocodile hunting or from dingo scalps. It was the life itself which drew such men.

"Will you 'ave another beer?" asked the somber killer.

"Why do the Aussies drink such absolutely fantastic quantities of beer?" American tourists had wondered, as all travelers do. Drinking beer in a hot desert country, far from quenching thirst, creates an insatiable, raging thirst. And once having acquired a taste for this beer, the desert dweller proceeds from one year to the next with a constant yearning for ever greater amounts of this liquid.

Just combine this tormenting thirst with a civilization which provides few occasions for water being offered, and at the same time demand of all men that they be a mite with other mites in bars which are the only social centers of small towns, and you can understand why Aussie men become maniacal beer drinkers to the dwindling of their pay checks, and are the despair of wives.

Crayfish will never provide a real industry in tropical waters, despite all the vessels tied up here in hopes. Crayfish of the tropics are a country cousin for which meat-baited, conventional traps hold

308

no appeal, while their growth is very slow, with low reproduction rates. Crayfish are seasonal. They disappear into deep water during the off season.

Pearl shell harvesting is a small industry, too. Shrimps, called prawns in Australia, have yielded but small catches in the Gulf of Carpentaria recently, leading to screams by southern big city news media that "the Russians and the Japanese have fished the Gulf out." Nobody mentioned that as little as 0.6 parts oil to six parts water per billion will kill or immobilize a shrimp population within two days, and nobody mentioned that many trawlers had been dragging the Gulf bottom, and possibly destroyed that rich breeding habitat within a few seasons following its discovery, by stirring up its mud.

And so the restless men sit over beer, and when the tide changes all the adventurers jump up from the bar and bamboo lounge and run to their ships to make readjustments, as everyone lives by the tide.

Ann and I said good-bye to Jean at Weipa Airport at 8:30 A.M. and Jean took off for Cairns, Brisbane, Sydney, then Perth, where she caught her vessel out to Southeast Asia. She was to be gone for two months, and Ann and I were now on our own together.

After laundry, Toyota servicing and equipment overhaul, and food buying, we set out to explore northward up central Cape York whose shores we had recently traced in flight.

We were taking a nice, compact little outfit this time. I oiled my old arch-support leather boots with a drink of rich motor oil. Their soles were almost gone. The track cuts across from York Downs to the Telegraph Line. Once on the Line you go on to Morton Telegraph Station, whither our telegram already sped along, saying: TWO WOMEN PROCEEDING BY TOYOTA FOUR WHEEL DRIVE TO MORTON (Courtesy of Comalco).

We were not taking the track that brought us to Weipa, but another, over which we were the first vehicle since before the last Wet. The kangaroo grass was so high that it swallowed the vehicle. Birds and butterflies scattered before us as we went careening and bush-bashing along. Spider webs burst. Dismayed spiders found themselves suddenly plastered against the windscreen. Spiders came crawling into the windows, long-bodied, with two principle legs at each end. The barking spider in this area builds a web the size of a wagon wheel, which can catch small birds. We suddenly became female through and through. We stopped the Toyota and there was wild pandemonium to get the spiders out.

Often it was time to halt and pick the kangaroo grass out of the grill so that the car could breathe. Ann's progress slowed to a crawl. The wilderness was vast. We missed Jean's muscular and cheery presence.

Sightings of wild game here in probably the most remote bush left were the best of our journey: four gray wallabies and two small leaping bands of reddish kangaroos were our reward. Other animals we saw were one bush pheasant, a couple of strutting noble bustards or plains turkey, one frilled lizard three feet long and brown-speckled, a big sand goanna, and a fine, red, healthy dingo dog with sharp-perked ears standing in our road looking at us curiously, very much in appearance like a red, short-haired Chow dog, except for longer legs.

Once we got on the Telephone Line track we whizzed along, when suddenly there appeared sitting beside that untraveled line road a seriously sunburned, wrinkled, freckled, squinting, and tattered wraith of a human being. As we came to a halt in consternation we saw a filthy back pack lying in the grass, and a flat-tired bicycle!

Although the first impression was unfavorable, not to say shocking, there was nothing to do but stop and render assistance. A few minutes later our solitary idyll had ended and the crippled bike was lashed to the front kangaroo bumper, and we had with us an unsavory and unwanted guest.

The long-haired hippie was half in a daze from exhaustion. He was from Sydney and bound for Bamega and thence by ship for Thursday Island, of course, that mecca for such as he.

"Good heavens! Don't you have any shoes?"

"I lost them in Cairns," he said.

That seemed indeed a most strange remark to make in true wilderness. This was no hippie paradise, no dream for a city singer of bucolic delights. We shuddered for his sake. Swollen bare feet, filth accumulated on cuts and sores and scabs, long toenails. Was his age twenty-seven or forty-seven? There was no way to discern. He was ageless rags and filth.

Even people who profess to love the barefoot life close to

310

nature would hardly, if they had good sense, start on a journey one thousand miles into this area with no shoes. During his trip of three weeks from Cairns he had daily grown weaker, due to lack of proper food and exposure to the unrelenting elements.

"I'm sure glad to see you come along. I've had it," was all he could croak.

When we reached the flowing river before Morton, Ann and I were relieved, for night was coming on and this stranger was very strange to us. When the telegraph man and his wife and adopted Aborigine boy and their respectable dog came down the river bank to greet the first vehicle of the Dry, they seemed to get the same aversion to the stranger we had, a person that none here would be proud to claim as their own.

"We just picked him up," I immediately explained.

"Hey, you," said the telegraph man gruffly to him. "You can get out of that car now. Just get out and walk up the hill. The ladies will be camping here beside the river."

When the command was repeated the exhausted man, still weakly nibbling on the orange I had given him, departed for a tributary creek. He said nothing to anyone.

"Where did you find that bum? Where is he headed, anyway? He's the kind of person we don't need here." One glance at the unfortunate man seemed to unite the other people instantly in a common recognition of the type. I marvelled at their lack of charity, and my own.

Next day Ann and I wondered how the "bum" was, as everyone called him. We felt uneasy about his predicament, even though we disliked his presence. Ann slept poorly beside the tropical river's mysterious night splashes, she who was always so intuitive. Next morning she announced, "This means, mother, that we aren't going on any further, thanks to that bum showing up now. We can't camp out knowing he is in our country, we would be afraid. We can't take him with us, either; we'd be crazy to take the chance."

We noticed that a pioneer group sizes the bum up fast and accurately, and has even less tolerance for him than has civilization. Pioneers are practical people, above all. To them a person who throws himself onto others is both witless and selfish. There is no room in the wilds for someone who can't outfit himself properly and can't contribute something to the human struggle.

311

All day and next night as we ate and swam at the lovely cool Wenlock and enjoyed the Scammell's hospitality, our thoughts turned to the derelict.

The Jardin for which he intended to head was a hundred miles to the north. Too wide to use a winch, it was deep, very swift, and probably uncrossable for two months yet, the Scammells thought. Would he try to swim it? He could be swept away and drowned. If the river stopped him, what then? I urged the telegraph people to advise Bamaga. There were no police there, but if he did not show up there after some days of setting out on his hundred-mile-plus trudge, "somebody" would look into it.

So Ann and I at the Wenlock crossing lingered and listened to the night sounds of the wild river teeming with barramundi, a perch that goes up to eight pounds. Small swordfish and sting rays also traveled this river, and heaven knows what other things.

We were fortunate to know the Wenlock, for it is scheduled to have a dam built above Morton to pipe its sweet waters to Weipa. Thus one more wild river was to go. The creatures using it coming in from the Gulf would no longer be able to live. The run of barramundi, a fish which depends upon migratory access to both river and sea, would vanish. They came here for their spawning.

Because it was recognized that the valuable barramundi were threatened by man's inevitable expansion, the Nile perch, a sport fish which will live and reproduce in lakes created by dams, was to be introduced in Australia from Africa as soon as Parliament granted permission.

Returning back down the same track to Weipa after some days Ann and I met three men in a C.S.I.R.O. truck with full regalia neatly packed. We felt justifiable pride in having opened up the track for this season.

"We saw your signs," said one of the men, leaning from his panting truck. "We saw where you collided with a tree and took the bark off it back there."

I looked at Ann, and we laughed.

Toyota overhaul at Comalco, and a bath, and good food again. When we got back our brakes were all but out, the lights connections were out, and the kangaroo bumper was a bit "crook" from its life as a leaping kangaroo.

We were going to start south now. Before we left I talked with the aging Police Inspector. I was worried about the hippie.

"This exhausted man, he's pushing his bike for a hundred miles beyond the Wenlock River," I said. "He's going to try to get across the Jardin. I think someone ought to know his predicament."

"Did you see any of those anthills twenty-one feet high up in that country?" the enthusiastic Inspector responded cheerily. "I know that country like the palm of me hand. I'm responsible for all that country."

"But, Inspector, this vagabond, now . . . ."

The Inspector gave a disgruntled snort. "People like that got no business up here in this country, and we don't want them here," he said. It was all right for Ann and me, he allowed, we had connections with some very important companies and I was a journalist getting material, and we had a nice Toyota and equipment, and knew what we were about, he hoped.

"Now I have to go out myself and search for such people," he continued. "You have no idea what inconvenience they cause others when they get into trouble, and how much expense to the state. Last year the hospital at Cooktown released some lunatic, and he hit the track out of Cooktown. Lucky thing a snake bit him before he got far. We went out and found him lying beside the track, and carried him back. I said to meself, then, 'Thank you, Mr. Copperhead Snake, you done the state a favor that time.' And I still say it. Now I don't mind a man going bush if he can take care of himself and if he'll let us know whereabouts he plans to be, generally, within a few hundred miles. But if he gets into trouble we can't help him if we can't find him. Even my black trackers aren't miracle men. Fella like the one you're describing now, he could duck out from me, and he probably would, if I went after him. They can hear me coming. It's difficult to know how many and what kind of men may be in the bush. Because there's lots of bush."

The Police Inspector left before us along the same track toward civilization, firing his gun at dingoes all the way. "I'm a friend of the pastoralists, and I kill every dingo I can," he self-righteously proclaimed. (He, too, loved the wilds.)

Ann and I drove now toward Merluna and Wolverton Stations and on down. An eastern brown snake (or was it a Taipan?) was dreaming in the middle of the road. We stopped, reaching for the binoculars. He awoke and glided swiftly into the grass. This was Taipan country. The only way you could tell for sure was that the

Taipan possesses an extra scale near the anus. Lucky that the Inspector's sharp eye missed that one!

The country was turning from brilliant green to dry brown even as we gazed. Only the Wenlock and rivers north of it flow the year around. A traveler afoot in this could have a dry time soon, with no running creeks to swim and nothing to drink at teatime.

Ann and I reached the Archer to find the river dropped down ten feet from what it was when we were here before, and the area of the crossing was an unsanitary mess from travelers using it as a lavatory.

I called at the Mission and had tea with Mr. and Mrs. Lamb, missionaries who were some of the most friendly people we met in the Outback, and the nursing sister Beth Burden replenished our medicine chest. The big blue tent was disposed of at the general store. Again Ann and I camped in our old spot in the Coen River bottom. We thought it best not to drink the river water due to many cattle about.

We were offered no tea at the one dwelling in a 4,000-square-mile area where we called in Cape York. Owned by people in Florida, it was represented by commercial management. A modern young wife lived there, whose face was as hard toward traveling strangers as toward the dingo whom she described as a "nasty animal." The woman actually laughed when we told her about the stranger in rags pushing the bike. My hackles rose. Now I felt guilt about him.

Our experience was the same at another remote property we visited which had commercial management and which was owned by people in Texas; and they were expecting us. Here we were the ragged strangers. By means of very obscure, little-traveled tracks bearing no sign boards, we passed through many mysterious paddock fences to find this station home. Our way was adventuresome, because we were never quite sure that we actually would find it.

Finally, through a last gate, we came upon the far north Queensland home, and there was the slender young wife and the dashing blade of a Queensland husband, managers for their overseas mentors, garbed in smart riding apparel. They leaned against the gate and looked us over coolly. They did not ask us to come in.

After twenty minutes of awkward conversation, I said that if they would sell us a piece of beef we would be on our way, back

314

along their 47-miles guesswork track, of a property more than a thousand square miles in area. That is, if there was no objection to our camping on this property. At this point they asked us to stay the night. (In fact, our beds were made up. They had just been toying with us.)

I came close to declining, but having come so far across the seas and through the Outback I was determined to take a look at this cult of inhospitality and suspicion, and find out what it was all about. Later I caught on. These were upstart commercial people backed by American money, newcomers to Queensland, and they were trying to put on the act of cattle aristocracy the way they thought it should be acted.

First the couple led us out to weigh a number of prize calves in the corral, a dusty ceremony in which all the manual work was done by silent blacks. Ann and I stood by as time after time the young city manager slapped a gloved hand against the flank or face of the husky "weaners" in the chute. Each time he slapped the crazed animal would smash its sensitive nose against the steel bars. Ann caught my eye. We stayed on and looked. Smash, smash, went the noses, and bled.

At last we were ushered into the sprawling sheet-iron shack the Texans had provided their management, the kind of shack in which Queenslanders have always lived; open-raftered to the outdoors, providing a handy entrance for deadly snakes which frequently become unwanted house guests.

And, we saw, such a tropical, sweltering life necessitates a slave class to care for the needs of the white man and his wife, and, despite new laws, a slave class does still exist.

Three black women assisted our hostess in the kitchen with a wood-burning, cast-iron stove, to prepare a formal meal. The best cutlery and china were used, while we sat sipping tall rum drinks on the mosquito-ridden "terrace" outside, looking out across the wild. Ann and I had had delightful baths in a real tub, each given our own new bar of soap. We changed for dinner.

The black women waited patiently outside until we finished, near eleven, to clean up. This would take them hours. Conversation was not easy with these people whom we did not like and whose food we were enjoying, but we made it. Queensland has experienced strong national criticism for being the most archaic in its attitudes

315

toward blacks: the north of Australia is the south of the United States.

"They only understand routine. They don't respect kindness. You treat them like children." Where have we heard these phrases before?

"Madeleine has improved things around here in our four years. When I first came here, I was alone. I was a bachelor then. The white man who was here before me was sleeping with a black woman in this house." (A traditional north Queensland arrangement.)

"How have you improved their lives, Madeleine?"

"By the example she sets them of correct living ways," the station manager replied for his wife.

"Has she improved their diet, for instance?" This seemed to me more to the point.

"Yes, they have unlimited beef. All they want to eat. Man before us used to keep them half starved. You can't expect them to work if they're not fed," Madeleine said.

"Last week," Madeleine went on, with casualness, "the health officer took one of our house girls away. Well, I noticed when she was washing dishes that her hands were getting stiff in the joints, and numb and odd looking, like claws. It was the return of leprosy."

"Heavens! Don't you fear having leprosy around the household?"

"No," she said. "Many of the natives are arrested cases. We just keep an eye on them. The government controls it with sulpha now, you know, mostly. When they get symptoms the blacks know they must go away to the leprosarium near Darwin."

"Where's the leprosarium, exactly? You never hear about it."

"On East Arnhem," the manager said. "But many lepers hide out in the bush when they see the government team driving along. They don't want the white man's cure." (The Aborigines call the remote, hidden prison hospital the "Waiting Place For Death.")

Leprosy, or Hansen's Disease, was carried from person to person, and most people believed it to be associated with common filth of person and living quarters. Regarded as a "routine disease" here by the health manuals, and "under control," leprosy is actually on the increase.

316

It is generally thought that people of dark skin have a "weakness" for leprosy. There may be something to this theory, but I would like to challenge the theorists, myself, to go and take a look at the way white people live and then contrast this by the way the blacks live, sleeping on the ground in blankets and old rags in the filthy corners of "wurlies" of brush or in shacks like dog kennels, on some Queensland properties. When the blacks were wild hunters they moved about. Isn't it possible that by a few generations of crouching on the same earth with its accumulated filth, their life at the cattle properties has increased their proneness to leprosy and hookworm, at the same time that their nutrition may actually be in a worse state than when they lived upon wild game?

As for my favorite theme of conservation, these people of course had never heard the word. As soon as possible, they stated, they would destroy the rain forest on the lovely McIllwraith Range on the station property, and turn it into pasture. For eradication of dingoes they used strychnine, but next year they were getting sodium fluoroacetate, the 1080 chemical so widely extolled by those who use it in the American West, because the carnivore that has eaten it runs miles away from the bait to die.

The animal that ingests 1080 dies a horrible death. "Violent convulsions," so writes a physician who is a conservationist, "contort the whole body, with the most excruciating pain, affecting every muscle of the body. The nerves scream in agony. The back arches excessively *and the bones crack* [italics are mine] from the violently contracting muscles. And yet, many of these animals bear their abominable misery without a cry. Give a man these poisons and his screams would be heard for miles.

"These predatory animals are called varmints. It appears to me that the poisoners are more eligible for this name.

"Does any animal deserve such a fate? Can such a fate be representative of the desire of men?"

Early in the morning Ann and I departed these monstrous people as a fog lifted from the drying forest-savannah, and made for the main track and on southward. Our hostess did not offer a lunch nor did she radio the next station post—a truly unforgiveable breach of etiquette.

317

"What gives with these people?" I asked others down the line. Nobody was surprised at all.

"Oh, their manager said he was going to quit over there, the way we heard it, unless he got a wife. So one of the old-school-tie mob he's connected with, they got Madeleine for him. They say he never laid eyes on her until the day they were married."

"Oh, how interesting! Who was she? What did she do before marriage, I mean?"

"Some private school snip. Never out of the city before in her life, you know these girls in the best schools, they all want to marry a grazier. That's the way to get up in society. What they don't have any idea is, when they marry a grazier what they'll have to put up with out here—the complete isolation and loneliness. But *she's* not lonely! She thinks she's so much better than the rest of us she don't even come to the country rices once a year. Oh, they always treat travelers in an off-hand way over there. They're a mean bloody pair, and you should not get the wrong impression of Queensland from thot pair of rascals."

"Mother, I'm tired of shifting gears. Don't you think I ever get tired? You can drive for a while!"

"I don't want to."

"But my foot keeps bleeding every time I push on the clutch."

Ann had cut her foot seriously that very morning on one of the projecting sharp pieces of metal with which Australian Outback car models abound, and she was half crippled. (So was I.) We were in a bad mood from being guested at Monster Ranch.

"Come on, Mom. You'll enjoy it. I'll show you."

We went on, with me shifting gears merrily. Within a mile as we were going down a hill slope I pulled out of the road to allow the goods truck to pass. It was on its way to Coen on its fortnightly trip. The cheerily-waving trucker rounded the hill and disappeared over its crest. *Then* we learned that we were stuck. I had driven the front end of the Toyota up on top of a boulder at the side of the road, heading down grade. It was the only mile I ever drove on our Australia expedition, and it was disasterous.

Hours of thinking. Hours of struggle. The sun climbed and grew hotter. Water supplies were not too ample. No one

318

was expecting us. We had this crazy, teeny little car jack from Japan that you tried to crank sidewards in a half circle motion.

For miles around the country was dry; an empty land. The barest feeling of fear crossed my mind. Ann hooked the winch up on a tree and pulled out the tree. There weren't any good trees within range. She hooked up again and the cotter key broke when my resourceful little girl tried to pull the Toyota backward off the boulder and uphill. My slumbering foot infection burned.

Studying the map, Ann made her decision to walk to Bamboo Station. Maps were not adequate. The rule is: *never leave your car*. But Ann has an uncanny memory for details of a featureless country. She set off with our slim skinning knife on a strap for a makeshift belt, our Army one-quart reconnaissance canteen, matches, and wearing my flopping soft hat with a brim, and shorts.

I was very relieved indeed when three and a half hours later she returned with Fred Costello and another grizzled type. With a big truck jack about five feet tall and some heavy chains, they un-bouldered us. Lucky, that time, the ranch was so near.

Tea in another sheet metal station homestead, talking with the Mrs. and with visiting Bill Jackson of Wolverine Station there; the company was real, genuine old north Queensland stuff. When we left we were given a hunk of sirloin to choke a horse. The sun was already low. Ann and I went bush with the Toyota, dug a pot hole in the sand down in a creek bed under the trees, and crawled contentedly under our big net.

Another night we slept at the deep-gullied McLeod. That was sad, polluted with cans, bottles, papers, and human feces. Then, suddenly, we were back at Cairns.

The tragedy of Australia's Outback seemed similar to that of America where the individual families are being forced off the land, and a way of life which forged the character of nation-builders is disappearing. Here the old Queenslanders are forced out and properties are going into the hands of big corporations who can push "development." Old School Tie associations plainly influence selection of the Australian management of these properties, as we had seen.

Top Aboriginal stockmen make $42.35 a week. The black man's wife works in the kitchen for extra favors, such as medical attention, with no wages specified for her. Local customs decreed a small gift of money by which to attend the yearly races of the region. Housing and tucker are free.

Most Aborigines are not given the position of top stockmen in the wage structure. Most make just $16.55 a week, as ringers and jackeroos, as set by the government. They are not given all of this, either. The station manager or local police officer serving as social worker bank a certain amount for them. The Aborigines must, therefore, ask permission for each expenditure he makes out of his own wage, such as a pair of trousers. His guardian may then say "no."

Our last stay in the old tourist home in Cairns was a brief one. Winter was now advanced; the month of June was quite cold. Blankets were needed upon the bed at night. The night fogs were thick.

Jennifer May was still sitting with the old folks watching television from a dark corner. And the television news commentary was saying that a young man from Sydney had just completed pushing his bike all the way to the tip of Cape York, crossing wild rivers to do so. And had succeeded today in reaching Thursday Island, thus becoming the only visitor to ever arrive at Thursday Island by bike. How did I feel? As cheap and silly as all the other jealous gossip-mongers up there in the Cape York country should have felt.

Ann and I were going to take the Barkly Highway inland now to Mount Isa Mines, Queensland. Then we were going to go back to Darwin, but by a very roundabout way on back roads which would take us through the most remote cattle properties which exist, along the rim of the Gulf of Carpentaria. The season was well into the Dry—but this is the only season you could venture there.

We had enough experience now to explore country we would not have dared to earlier. We had earned it. We had spent most of a year at learning our bushmanship.

Little did Ann and I know when we left friendly Cairns that last time that we were to brush up against an experience which in retrospect I would now entitle, "Nightmare Alley."

Nor were we aware that fate was awaiting us with a light brush with death along the Gulf of Carpentaria in the Borroloola area, far out there on a lonely track.

320

Chapter 20

NIGHTMARE ALLEY TO MOUNT ISA MINES

Ann and I were driving through tall, green canefields in the Atherton
Tablelands, heading inland. You could have lost a whole train in
those fields—and sometimes did, in season. We were due at Mount
Isa Mines after the weekend, about a five-hundred-mile, easy drive.

The Atherton Tablelands are a clear example of the agricultural
failure of infertile soils which are ideal for forest growth. Species
include kauri pine, Queensland pine, she pine, maple, ashes and silkwood, silky oaks and other cabinet woods and hardwoods: klinki
pine and Honduras pine have been introduced. It was only marginal
dairying and agricultural country.

Only occasionally we met a lone car. At intervals the forested
hilltops fell back to bring us past scattered farmhouses and tiny
villages.

Ann and I were faced with a camping problem. The valleys were
all cultivated and had fences close on each side of the road. National
park areas did not permit overnighters, for they had no facilities, and
in any case, it was always our love to find a wild place that was
natural, and hidden. Some wild, lovely streams, including the Tully
River, offered momentary hope, but none provided a chance to get
the car off the road where it wouldn't be seen.

As the last shafts of the sun disappeared behind the night hills Ann spied a steep, leafy lane barely the width of the Toyota which tunneled upward sheer from the bottom of a hairpin curve at the base of a hill. Our Toyota climbed a couple of hundred feet up this in low gear quickly, with me leading the way into the gloomy forest on foot. This old track was dim. There was no sign that anyone had used it for years.

We topped out on a level spot, and quickly made camp. There wasn't a moment to wait before dark. My pile of sticks just would not burn, so with practiced ease I pulled out the primus burner and boiled our meat and tea. As the jungle night fell we saw why a fire was impossible. Phosphorescent spots and patterns began to stand out in ghostly lights on the leaf mold about us.

Breathing was heavy here. The sky above, the narrow strip we could see, seemed under a cloud, not the bright, friendly, open desert sky we knew. At Cairns and all along the coastal Alps, we had observed how the heavy, moist clouds hang over the beautiful, forested peaks.

As we ate our simple meal we laughed and talked in low tones. But soon we "quietened down," as the Aussies say, and went inside the bug net stretched from the side of the car to the tree. Ann was most fussy that night about parking. She seemed to have some feeling about "not blocking the road." She fussed about and inched the car into one side, leaving a partially clear track, just as though traffic had to pass! I joked with her about it at the time, but she had her way.

The moment blackness descended, that forest around us came alive. First there were the sounds of hops and jumps and rustlings, familiar to any nature lover, and the dry skitterings of lizards on tree trunks. We lay peacefully listening to them. Then came snorts, hisses and crashes of big branches of the kind that send one sitting bolt upright in the darkness.

A couple of the snorts were angry kangaroos or forest wallabies. The pet kangaroo at Morton had snorted like that. Other sounds were loud enough to be foraging wild pigs. "Just go to sleep," I soothed Ann. We snuggled down into our bags. It was dripping cold.

But Ann was tense. Like myself, she lay listening. A strange bird commenced to call monotonously in the near distance, and an answering call came from nearby. Boobook owls? Night hawks?

322

Parrots? Across my mind flitted movies in which savage men stalking a camp give just such calls. I didn't like the thought one bit.

Then there began, not far away, a slow, rhythmic, clinking wooden sound. Probably a beetle on a tree trunk. Yet—it sounded exactly like the wooden clack-clack sticks which Ann carried, Aboriginal souvenirs.

A hideous shiver swept over me, and was conveyed direct to Ann beside me, or her shiver to me. Under the net we each lay rigid. I thought of the words of the veteran police inspector: "We don't have any idea how many half wild men may be in the bush at any time."

"Mother, we shouldn't be here." Ann barely moved her lips next to my ear.

My mind went over all the sounds I knew in the woods. There was that big bird which could walk about the forest, the flightless black cassowary, native to New Guinea and north Queensland. I just hoped that this was a cassowary we heard, walking about the bushes, here and there. Not hopping, it took long, twig-snapping steps like a man. Tramp, tramp, the sound went purposefully and steadily first on one side of the road and then the other just below us a few yards down the slope, slipping easily through thick brush. I've never heard a cassowary walk. But there is no sound in all nature quite like that of a man walking. I heard that sound too many times in years in the bush to be mistaken.

We had no gun. Just the poor little camp shovel. We had a flashlight, but to turn it on would force a confrontation. No, no light in any case. Pretend to be asleep. Play dead. Anything but a confrontation.

And now came the sound we had been dreading—the steps of a man, bold and forthright. Steady, straight on, a man's stride, sure of himself in total darkness. He just walked right up the steep hill, coming from the direction of the highway, and registering no surprise, passed on by our "sleeping" bodies beside the car. The steps never faltered, but went on past us on top of the rise and down the other side, following the old dim track into the deeps of the forest, like a midnight ghost on a familiar round.

It was no ghost. It was a man, barefoot. Steps of a man who has been here before, who has a pattern of walking about after midnight, without carrying a light. A man who sees in the dark.

Past us I heard him cough and clear his throat.

By now Ann and I were shaking so that the net practically rattled. "If he comes back," I whispered in Ann's ear, "whatever you do, don't scream or raise your voice. He's got to think we're powerful white men sleeping inside the net. He won't dare bother us."

"How about a spear?" Ann whispered. "A spear could go right through this little net, Mother, do you realize that?"

"Well, you're right, Ann. Of course, there is that possibility."

"I think we should make a rush for it and get out of here."

"I'm too scared," I said.

"We should be gone out of here when he comes back this way. Look, Mom, we have a lot of attractive equipment here. Nobody would even know where to begin to look if we should just disappear between Cairns and Mount Isa, along a five-hundred-mile run."

"Yes, yes." A search would probably not get started for some weeks, if we disappeared.

At last Ann's sensible arguments carried. At a signal we made a concerted rush out of the net. Ann dove into the Toyota, got to the headlights, and switched them on. Their glare harshly lit up the horrid forest alley.

Making each move count, we threw our junk aboard. Never was any camp broken with such dispatch, born of urgent fear. Start the engine. Thank God it worked. All doors and tail gate clang into lock. Turning around meant many back-ups into crackling brush. We made it. Roughly the Toyota walked down to the lonely highway, driven by wild-eyed ladies in nightgowns.

Ann did not stop until the Atherton Tablelands faded out into wide open desert and a friendly dry creekbed off the road offered a place for the sleeping bags under the starry sky. Safe, we slept.

On into desert where the kite-hawks sailed like buzzards and the country turned red, and I said to Ann next day: "I think I may have an explanation for Nightmare Alley. All the birds we heard. . . ."

"The birds? What would a man want with birds?"

"Stealing rare tropical birds out of their native forests is a big business now. Probably four hundred thousand birds are being shipped out of here illegally each year to supply U.S. and European pet shops. The business has never been bigger.

324

Exotic pets are in demand, and there are more people wanting them every year.

"Well, you get a public demand like that, and there are always sneak thieves and criminal types who will supply the demand. Wholesale dealers in birds will claim the birds are raised in captivity, but lots of times they're stolen. And the forests are robbed and left empty places. Well, this may have been what we ran into, you see.

"The worst of it is, from the humane standpoint, that only about one bird in four lives through the shipment in tiny boxes. That means that maybe a million birds have been stolen from Australia in the past year. Last year there were something like forty convictions of bird thieves, I read, but it looks like the punishment they get under present different state laws is just a little fine and wrist-slapping."

"So you think the midnight walker was visiting his secret bird traps?"

"Yes. He could even be some farm worker in the area, or even the farmer himself."

"Or maybe," Ann reflected, "it was just blackfella business. And nobody knows what blackfella business is, but to them perhaps it is not strange to go walk-about at night."

We were pulling up to a large, bleak, yellow-with-gingerbread hotel at Croydon, which sat starkly all by itself in the harsh sun. Croydon on the Beef Road to Normanton, is a defunct gold town. Entering the frilled iron structure, whose interior would have a colder winter and hotter summer than any city man knows, we took seats at a table in the dim, ancient dining room, where the owner-manager, grizzled Bill Blaise, said that a sandwich might be obtained. Pulling out just then was a large Ansett tourist bus with golden-agers aboard. Bill Blaise was still smiling.

"My daughter and I had a fright when we were camping last night." He sat down in interested concern.

Yes, he had in fact lumbered years ago in the area I described. He asked detailed questions, and we got down to fine points.

"You were in what we call the Forty Mile Scrub," he concluded. "I know the area. It's rain forest, but a peculiar type of rain forest. Nothing exactly like it any place else, I guess. No farmhouses there for forty or fifty miles."

"All the time I thought there were a couple of farmhouses and a cleared valley probably right over the hill!"

"Oh, no. Not there. It's a lonely place. The Forty Mile Scrub is fairly isolated. It's a depressing sort of place, I'll agree to that. There is a strange thing about it, we always said. There's a lot of birds in there, but nobody has ever found any surface water. They can't figure how all those birds get water, though it stands to reason they must be getting it. Cockatoos and pigeons, now you know they're never found more than six miles flight from a waterhole. Well, I wouldn't blame you women for getting scared there because the place gives anyone a peculiar feeling. Even in the daytime. But, don't you think, well, you imagined things out of the natural bush noises?"

"No, it was a man all right. Maybe more."

"You ever see 'im?"

"Nope. The darkness was so black. We heard him walk within three feet of where we lay, and he thought we were white men asleep there."

"Do you think it could have been a cassowary?"

"No bird-brain cassowary," I reiterated. "It was a man, bare-footed."

"Well, if he was barefoot and carried no torch, it must 'ave been a blackfella, that's all it could have been. Could be a crazy white man expert in the bush, sometimes you find a crazy white man. But it must have been an Aborigine or two, I'm betting. You were up against a real bushman there, whoever he was. A real bushman."

Bill Blaise would see that the news got around, and probably later some mean-tempered Aussie—and may we all be glad for mean-tempered Aussies in this world, Aussies who are not afraid of the devil himself in the spookiest of forests—would go out there in the night on a stake-out, and check the matter out.

Onward, south of the Gulf of Carpentaria, with small flies sticking like demons, we camped fifty miles out of Mount Isa. Two horses brought their friends around our camp, nickering all night long. They smelled our water cans. It was pitiful. This country was dying of drought. These horses would be dead before the Wet came again.

Altogether, we stayed at Mount Isa Mines, an American-owned

company but now completely Aussie-operated, for about ten days, taking our meals at the cafeteria, and enjoying the usual Single Girls' Quarters. This mine operates on fifteen levels to a depth of twenty-four hundred feet to get at the silver-lead-zinc ore bodies (later copper) and is said to be one of the most mechanized mines operating in the world, complete with a computer housed in an air-conditioned room. The company operates two generating stations providing power for mining activities and the town of Mount Isa. A seventy-two-mile transmission line also carries power for the town of Cloncurry. Coal is railed eight hundred miles for this power station on Mica Creek. Lake Moondarra, fourteen miles north of the station, a rockfill dam formed on the Leichhardt River, furnishes water for the little isolated island of civilization here in this vast northwest Queensland. The town of Mount Isa beside the mines numbers eighteen thousand.

This modern installation is the outgrowth of seventy-five years of pioneer mining in the region known as the Cloncurry field. The original quest in this region, using camel trains and mule trains, was for gold and silver. Back in 1907 the mines operating on this field were already floated on the Melbourne Stock Exchange, before the railways crossed the Nullarbor Plain to tie together the East and the West. In those days only the brave and the foolhardy were prepared to face the heat, the dust and the apparent scarcity of water out here—but they did so, nonetheless. The first prospectors died from thirst, fever, bad rum, and the spears of blacks; the first mines were worked with machinery dragged across vast plains by teams.

Mount Isa Mines then came into the hands of American Smelting and Refining Company (ASARCO), an empire which straddled the American continent from Chile and Peru to Alaska in 1930.

Except for motor lorries the settlement for several years was cut off from the world, without a telephone or telegraph. The town had no bank although the wages were nearly five thousand pounds a month. The majority of the "gougers" here were drawn from ghost copper towns of the Cloncurry field. This extreme isolation was broken by plane by the missionary John Flynn and his Flying Doctor Service coming on trips from Alice Springs. (A beautiful Flynn church here commemorates this service, as a part of the two million square miles of Outback served by Flynn and the Australian Inland Mission.) The railway came through, and the population rose from three hundred to three thousand. When the whistle sounded on payday hundreds of dusty men ran, rode bikes, or crowded on trucks to file along the track to two hotels, and when the hotels closed they adjourned to the bush to drink and sing, or fight in a circle of swaying spectators. Each year a quarter of the population was charged in court with drunkenness. But out of it all, a community grew, and it was upon this scene that our friend of a friend, Julius Kruittschnitt, who was to win a name among the greats of world mining, arrived.

Years of struggles with recalcitrant blast furnaces followed. The designers of the smelter had blundered. Radical and expensive remedies were necessary. The milling and floatation section of the treatment plant were inefficient. It was found that the grains of silver and lead in the hard rock were so exceptionally fine and intergrown that man here must deal with an ore of rare complexity which deceived the metallurgical advisors of the company, deceived their microscopes, lab tests, and pilot plants. Now ASARCO itself was in so deep financially that it could not get out. The great gamblers in the mercurial world of mining held on. Mount Isa was saved by the world upcurve price in metals. After about twenty years, the long-suffering shareholders of the world were at last to receive their dividends for the first time, and profits rolled in.

Copper development, coming of age late in Mount Isa's struggles, helped to save Australia during World War II. The soaring consumption of lead in assembly line and defense stockpiles in the U.S. brought sudden prosperity. High profits from lead eased the task of financing a new copper mill and smelter. ASARCO, which for eighteen years had financed and guided the mine indirectly through the Mining Trust (British company), acquired more direct control. Today the American company owns 53 percent of the shares.

The town became a boom town when the prosperity bonus, conceived in 1924 by Broken Hill managers and miners, came into effect to award employees a higher reward when the price of lead was high. Although popularly conceived as a bonus to compensate for the hazards of lead poisoning, it was really a venture in profit-sharing by companies which made huge profits for forty years. Now men lined up to get the most prized jobs in the land, with wages three times as high as they earned in Melbourne and Brisbane. Shop-

328

keepers of the town raised their wages to keep employees, and raised their prices.

In the Korean War America demanded more lead, while the company went ahead building houses and community facilities, and as chimney of the new copper smelter rising over three hundred feet above the plain, man's most prominent landmark in north Australia today. Here now was the largest mining company in Australia. Its annual income, even allowing for inflation, surpassed the richest Australian mining corporations of the past.

Post-war prospecting by big companies has continued through north Queensland and the Northern Territory, stimulated by the story of Mount Isa. The government opened uranium prospecting to everyone in 1953, permitting a lifeblood of speculative capital to accelerate this country.

Massive pitchblend was found forty miles from Adelaide, the most uranium-conscious of Australian cities. Radioactive mineral was found on Western Australia goldfields and New South Wales tin fields. Uranium was found 20 miles north of Mount Isa on the Calton Hills cattle station, and the value of Mount Isa Mines shares jumped a million in a day. Uranium fever captured Mount Isa.

Prospectors rushed to buy geiger counters from every shop. The hills were said to radiate a faint luminous light at night, a mystic sign that whole ranges were radioactive. Newspapers reported that a pig had produced high readings, infallible proof that he came from radioactive country. A new, modern phase for "pegging" (staking claims) dispersed all manner of camps of corrugated iron, while the aircraft of the more affluent flew fifty to a hundred feet above the prospectors and sought uranium with scintillometers. Through aerial prospecting Mount Isa Mines added thirteen leases to its terrain of radioactive outcrops.

Large checks were paid for untested uranium leases, and shafts were sunk on the outcrops: Flat Tyre, Mighty Glare, Pickwick, Pelican, Six Kangaroos, Glowing Hills, Anderson's Lode. An Aussie named Walton, who was a frugal taxi driver, sold an untested outcrop to Australasian Oil Exploration Ltd. for 250,000 pounds in cash and a royalty on all uranium mined. It was the largest sale of any untested mine ever to take place. A year later a winding road led off through the pink hills to the new Mary Kathleen Mine of the Northern Territory. The controling interest was purchased by Rio Tinto, a strong

329

British company which had worked the famous Spanish mine by
that name. The uranium ore proved constant. Settlement grew with
certainty and swiftness, and now Mary Kathleen is known all over
the world: but the overseas market for uranium flagged, and by the
end of 1963 only the caretakers remained.

The old traditional metals—lead, zinc, copper, silver—still are
going strong. Mount Isa today drills in a huge strip of rugged country stretching from the old Great Australia, the first mine on Con-
curry, to a new lead ore body near Borroloola, five hundred miles
northwest. The new searches spring from optimism and wealth,
with Mount Isa the pulse of mineral expansion, the pivot of that
vast terrain from the bauxite of Cape York in the East to the uranium of Rum Jungle and the copper of Tennant Creek. Nearly
thirty years after the discovery of Mount Isa the company's leases
have been far from explored; yet the richest unfound lodes seem to
lie beneath the streets and houses and gardens of Mount Isa itself.

But there are problems. If the company's industry were located
at Melbourne or Sydney, the problem of supplying water, power,
transport and amenities for thousands of people would be no concern
to the company directors. If the company produced steel or cars or
goods that fluctuate less in price, it would be easy to predict the
market and the revenue. If the company but knew the dimensions
and wealth of the ore bodies it would be able to decide on an optimum rate of production. But a mine is always capricious, with a
heart of its own. On what scale should a mine be worked? On what
scale financed? The imponderable problems hang in the balance
from year to year. On what scale will a new administration decide
to tax it?

Soon we were making friends, and the North West *Star* reporter,
"Tony," from England, brought around old Tom Biddolf, a miner
who was an honorary game warden and curator of rock paintings,
for me to talk with. Four of us drove out to a gorge with a small
pool of water and pictographs. Tony said that pictographs are most
often associated with water. He was soon going off on his holiday
to visit the bird and crocodile regions beside the Gulf, along the
Arthur River.

We drove out to see Lake Moondarra, that lake created in the
Leichhardt River bed, of which we had seen posters of people water-
skiing and swimming. But in ten years this lake had filled just three

330

times. Today in the Dry, aquatic growth choked its shores, preventing access for anything but waterfowl. A typical instance of the damming of rivers in a desert, the reservoir lost enough water by evaporation daily to perhaps serve a city of one hundred thousand.

Such water loss seems almost criminal. This is a part of the world which can least afford any water loss whatsoever. This lake was losing five feet of water a week now in the Dry.

"Who built this lake?" I asked.

"Utah Construction was aked to come from America," was the reply in the company cafeteria. "But they gave up. They were too slow building the dam before the floods took 'er away. They couldn't get along with our unions. So, we said, 'good on you, go home then; and they went and the Theiss Company of Australia has finished the work nicely, as you can see."

On a desert the matter of building pumps to take water out from under the ground does not solve the long-range problems of water shortage, unfortunately. It is only a stopgap to man's needs. For, as water tables fall, the tapping of the cisterns of centuries only causes the area to become basically more improverished. In the water-rich U.S. we have already made fairly complete use of the available streamflow and dammed all available damsites. This has been done within seventy-five years. Additional opportunities for streamflow storage and diversion are very limited in the U.S.A. now.

The basic objection to dams creating stored bodies of water is twofold—loss of the precious water by evaporation, and the changing of the dry, hot, but essentially wholesome desert climate to a steamy greenhouse effect in which white man becomes completely miserable if not hard-pressed to live. Australia is like our Southwest, only more so. She will always have to depend upon stored ground water almost completely over vast areas.

Only the importation of water great distances or *reallocating the existing supplies* will enable man in arid regions to live within an annual "water budget." Water is a primary resource whose total quantity cannot be increased. Water stored underground is limited.

The conclusion, therefore, is that desert cities should court only "light industries," which discharge water that can be re-used. Man may have to get out of cattle raising and especially get out of crop raising in the desert. The closed system of horticulture, called hydroculture, and the closed system of protein raising should be used.

Trying to expand agriculture into the desert is courting eventual disaster. In crop growing, vast amounts of water are used by plants, with heavy losses occurring in irrigation and conveyance systems. In raising livestock, similarly, you have tremendously wasteful evaporation and seepage from tanks, so that within even two or three generations of cattle growers the whole land is drying up before one's eyes! In Australia the billabongs of yesterday are no more. Even the North End is drier today than it was seventy years ago. Yet both in America and in Australia businessmen and politicians are heard to cry the words we know so well: "Get more water from somewhere, for we *do* intend to build cities in the desert, and we *do* intend to push forward with our fields of sorghum and cotton and citrus, and with our livestock industry."

Researchers point out that irrigated crops, which today take 90 percent of all water used in Southern Arizona, are the most wasteful of water of any industry in economic returns to the state, with cattle raising and mining next. To figure out a desert economy you need to know the cost of water input required for each $1,000 output of each industry. Mining, while very wasteful of water, will undoubtedly continue, because man has to take the minerals where the minerals are. But other industries can be more selective. Cities of man can flourish—municipal needs for water are not the big factor in water economy—but above all, *forage crops* are the most wasteful of water of anything man could invent to try here, and the most uneconomical in dollar return.

After Mount Isa Ann and I hit the road to Camoolweal (sounds like Camelwheel).

There at the butcher's chill domain a white-bearded, regal old patriarch went striding past, and we hastened to overtake him. He was Harry Skinner, who was paid a fee as "water diviner" for Camoolweal. Water divining has not passed from the earth; in fact, it has never had more advocates than now, and the art flourishes.

Harry Skinner could find water by walking about carrying a stick or even a piece of wire in his hand; he was pulled irresistably toward where water lay under the ground. His travels as a water diviner had taken him through much of Australia in his day.

The track that day was a rough and noisy ride, on through Doomagee, a remote Gulf mission. We could barely see each other inside the car, in choking dust mixed with our pepper, which had got loose.

332

At Doomagee the hospitable missionaries had us into the mission for tea: an hour of vacuous, heat-numbed small talk as the afternoon quickly wanted.

With this we proceeded through more bulldust, carrying two gift slices of beef liver, hoping to make camp alongside one of the billabongs of the Nickelson River bed. We stopped in the road when a red truck intercepted us carrying two grimy, red, but alert-looking young men covered with bulldust.

It turned out that they were part of an aerial survey team mapping this country, working with a helicopter and served by ground crew and trucks. They had been camping here for three weeks.

Having stumbled upon this interesting windfall of companionship, Ann and I made camp near the men and shared evening tea around their campfire. Outback residents have a legend for vast friendliness to travelers, but Ann and I did not usually find this so. It is not easy to communicate with the Potato Famine Irish who are still mad at everybody, nor is it easy to communicate with all longtime resident missionaries.

Along the Gregory River another day, a tiny, deep, still stream fifteen feet wide and perhaps ten feet deep, we drove down below the level of the dry savannah and made our camp among hidden pandanus palms. Strange fishes shimmered in the green, translucent depths of the Gregory, decked in a miniature forest of its own. Silently I walked from pool to pool, as the day's sweat dried on me, and the approaching dusk laid on its witchery spell. How tempting to take a swim along that deep, serene channel. But one would not dare with those overhung banks, holding their secret caves. One would only dare to dip a bucket to pour over the head for the evening bath ashore.

When I climbed up the embankment a mob of bullocks started toward me ominously. They came forward as one, horns lowered.

"Oh, you don't have the respect for a sheila afoot that you have for a sheila riding along in a car," I told them out loud. Suddenly they turned as one and ran back and bunched up. Then suddenly together the several tons of bullocks charged right at me.

I had not reckoned fully how little respect wild cattle may have toward their betters and elders. Luckily for me the Gregory River was there. I ducked for it down below the prairie level, and once out of their sight, they forgot me.

Morning in the wilderness again. Slam the tailgate on the Toyota. In the car follow Ann's streamers of violet toilet paper strung through the open savannah on little bushes. Pick them all up as we go, so as not to litter. The road, that thin lifeline, is so easy to lose. I had drawn an arrow in the sand there with a stick.

At an eighty-year-old rock-walled homestead, windowless because it was built during the Aboriginal wars, we stopped, and said hello to Mrs. Tom Burton whom people four hundred miles back said was the "only woman in these parts." We found her working in her vegetable garden beneath a battered straw hat, and followed her into an open-air shed. Childless, in her late forties, slim and tough as rawhide, the Outback woman usually helped her husband Tom and the blackfellas at mustering, and she loved to sleep out on the ground, exploring far parts of their bushland, far better than she loved confinement in the ancient fortlike house.

Women grow old fast in the cruel, lonely Outback. The classic features of a fair English beauty could still be seen beneath the weathering, as well as the exuberant personality for which, during early years, she was renowned. But she was psychologically weary. There had been too little to break the monotony of endless toil and heat, and fifteen men to feed each day, mostly on beef and damper, from a wood-burning stove.

Kangaroo Downs, twelve hundred square miles. Its Brisbane-born mistress had not been to Darwin in nearly a quarter of a century, and only once visited the neighbors at the next station beyond. A few times a year people happened by. That was all.

As we rested briefly in the shed a half dozen of the great Australian pelicans could be seen floating on the pond near the house where the river widened out, an enchanting sight.

Pelecanus conspicillatus is the hugest, most conspicuous pelican you ever saw in your life, with white plumage, black wings and tail, a pink bill the size of a barrel, yellowish pouch, and the wing spread of perhaps *ten feet*. One of the largest birds in the world that flies, it builds a three-foot, very smelly nest on the hot ground, often on islands of the ocean but upon inland waters as well, and is classed as a "bird of the Australian bush." Two eggs are laid, characterized by thin, red, longitudinal stripes. Repulsively funny young are

334

hatched, "shiny like a gelatin bag, and full of gawky bones." They babble and screech. They are born naked, blind, and helpless, and are long dependent. But there remains much yet to discover about the lives of the dignified, regal adults.

"Oh dear me. Look at those nasty pelicans on our pond," cried the ranch mistress. "When Tom comes in I'll have to git him to git the gun and git after them."

I was astounded. "But why?"

For a moment she was nonplussed. The why hadn't really occurred to her. "They eat fish fer one thing."

"Do you and your husband eat the fish?"

"Oh, no"—impatiently—"nobody bothers with them."

"What's wrong with the pelicans, then?"

She brushed her hand across her overheated brow. "Well, they stir up the bottom. We get our water from there. Nasty things. Tom always shoots them when he can."

"We have an international treaty which protects all our pelicans now," I mentioned guardedly. "We think highly of all the migratory wildfowl, and three countries, the U.S., Canada, and Mexico, cooperate in laws to protect them."

"Well, I never heard of that," she said, weary and mystified. We followed her to the meat house then, and she generously gave us some prime beef for our traveling.

The Helmericks Expedition was now doing the best eating done in a year of batting around. These ranchers knew beef and they ate the best of their herds. Grateful, Ann and I grabbed a big hunk of beef thick with tallow, and took off.

Afternoon found us bumping through a dry bottom and there we met three Commonwealth mapmakers out of Canberra, and as it was a good stop for tea and talk, we sat there in the shade with them for a bit. These three young beards went out for seven months at a time on their expeditions. They used two International trucks having four-wheel drive and carrying a gross four tons each of supplies, under lace-on canvas. Their fuel range was a thousand miles.

Exchanging views with them about the "locals" was a help in getting a balanced view. The fellows explained the usual indifference of station people to travelers as disenchantment with the increasing numbers of outsiders who, driving through their properties, leave the gates open, leave careless campfires burning, leave

335

trash at waterholes, fire guns indiscriminately, and in general expect
a hospitality which they have done nothing to deserve.

The traveler seeing a dwelling along his way expects dinner or
tea, said the men, but has no concept of the primitive conditions
under which the Outback dwellers live out their days. It is necessary for someone to chop wood to supply each cup of tea. Dirt is
everywhere in the old homestead, which consists mainly of poles
supporting the tin roof kept in place by rocks on top. There may or
may not be running water. Snakes and mice crawl in. It is just as
biting cold for the homesteader to face each dawn inside his spacious
stone-iron castle as it is for the camper outside on the ground, if not
more so. Residents may feel, resentfully, that outsiders are far more
affluent in style of living than themselves.

Why should these workworn graziers and wives invite in the
casual wayfarer? Yet I can say that from the stranger's standpoint
he looks forward to seeing a dwelling along his way, and he looks to
it as a shelter in the wilderness, or a break in the monotony of his
solitude at the least.

When Ann and I reached Woolargarang, an enormous property
straddling northwest Queensland and the Northern Territory, late
in the day, it was to find none of the Americans of whom we had
been advised for a full year in residence. Driving up to the house,
it was difficult to imagine Americans living there. The old man, a
stern and weathered Mormon of considerable years, had, as a matter
of fact, become discouraged, broken his partnership, and returned to
America by the time we got there. Our information was out of date.

We found an Australian there who had taken over as manager.
He was a man bumped over with what could have been arthritis in
the spine. Wrinkled like a pomegranate, burned, horny-handed,
with several missing teeth, he and his group there suffered also
from sandy blight and barcoo rot.

Reluctantly he introduced his brown-skinned cook, whom he
called his wife. The widow and mother of eleven had no means to
live other than to move in with a man who himself was in such shape
from toil and beer that perhaps none but an ignorant brown woman
would have had him. Here the dear souls huddled, worked to death,
never clean, with her small sons with sore eyes playing in the dirt.
Shut off to themselves. Heat, flies, loneliness. Leprosy country.
Embarrassed, they sent Ann and me right on. We learned they

336

always did that if people came. Such was our year-long anticipation of an invitation to visit a real American-Australian cattle empire. Oh, well. Bless 'em.

A few yards down the road we found a police officer, to our vast surprise, stationed on the state border housed in a new, modern unit. The house was self-sustained with its own electric generator, water tank, and complete plumbing. He had a pretty, young wife and two rosy, immaculate babies. They too, lived in isolation. The cleancut young officer told us at tea that it had cost the Commonwealth government $78,000 to place an officer here in a livable home by modern standards. From this quotation, if accurate, we could understand why station homesteads were so poor in comforts and amenities.

The duty of the officer was to apprehend persons running from the law toward the territory. His domain of jurisdiction embraced seventeen thousand square miles, almost altogether roadless. He was about twenty-five.

Next day in the Northern Territory we arrived at Ringer Hill Station homestead. Its home paddocks and fences were in excellent condition and the congenial family took us trucking about a small part of their 1,800-square-mile domain, where we learned to correctly identify such things as Mitchell grass, spear grass, and kerosene grass, and the red-backed spider, a relative of the black widow of North America, and a desert tree in delicate purple bloom. We viewed three deluxe bulls which had been purchased for five thousand dollars for the lot. We were taken to view from a "jumpup" an expanse of open forest where fires had ranged last year for three months, coming close to destroying the house.

Ringer Hill employed twenty-nine hands of whom all but one were blackfellas. Wages over here in the territory are less by ten dollars, being just thirty-five dollars a week for stock hands, white or black. Working temporarily at the ranch and not counted were two European lads. They were handicapped by lack of English. The Australians found them "useless" in these far tropics, and did not consider them to be worth their pay.

Animals shot on sight at this property by the professional manager were dingoes (also methodically poisoned with strychnine baits), cockatoos (occasionally, when in the mood), kangaroos and walleroos, the odd wild buffalo bull (he breaks down fences), the brumby

337

or wild horse (a dozen were due for liquidation this week), along with all snakes including the gentle python, and as many goanna lizards as the blackfellas could catch to eat. Quail and wild pigeons and noble bustard were shot for occasional food and sport.

Ann and our host climbed up a rock cleft to explore a cave opening one hundred feet up a rock canyon, Ann being an expert rock climber by training, and he an Aussie who dared anything. He tore some dripping moist ferns off the cliff to take home to plant. An Aborigine was asked, in return for sweets, to go get some different types of desert lizards so that the visitors would be able to see the species. Within the hour our hands held the limp and broken little jewels which had not survived the kind of catching they got.

We were invited to stay the night and we slept in real beds, and had a tub bath, too. Eight turns of the faucet made the sun-heated water run. Eight turns back shut the faucet off. We were shown every hospitality which these good-humored, kindly people afforded.

This Gulf property, "owned" by a city doctor who seldom had the time to fly in, represented an investment of twenty thousand dollars five years ago, and today the manager said it was valued at half a million dollars. The lease ran for ninety-nine years.

Once a year a government agent comes around to check on how many improvements have been made on the station according to lease terms. If these terms have not been met the individual loses his "spread." Reverting to Crown land, these properties nowadays are being grabbed up by well-to-do individuals, or more often, corporations, who are waiting in line to begin the rebuilding of the land with Townsville lucerne and sorghum fields and deluxe bulls for breeding stock. Still others continue to abuse the land as long as they can with trampling hooves beat into the raw earth for a quick profit.

Chapter 21

TIP OVER, THE COUNTRY RACES, AND GOOD-BYE DARWIN

Borroloola is a famous old place at the end of nowhere. We knew it was right near the Gulf. It would have a store, some missionaries and four policemen, and we were told you have to drive across the tide-water MacArthur River to reach the town. If the tide is in, you wait until it goes out.

Nobody was expecting us. The newspaper at Mount Isa, the North West *Star*, had sent out radio messages into the land where we were going, but after four hundred miles we had got out of range anyway, even if anyone picked it up at the remote stations. I asked the police officer on the border to send out a message, but his radio bands only operated backwards into Queensland.

Well, Ann was driving us along about fifteen or twenty miles an hour which I felt was entirely too fast for the circumstances, but Ann was always like that. She brought us around a bend with no visibility, and the road was eroded and kind of washed out at that spot, and that time she couldn't make it. We hit red clay, the Toyota slammed into a soft bank on the right, and over she went onto her side, right in the road, just like a big, square box.

For a moment we lay inside the thing, hung upsidedown by our tightly-drawn shoulder straps. Ann, on the upper side of me, hung

339

on to the steering wheel so her weight would not crash down onto me. I pushed the button to unlock my seat belt. "Turn off the ignition," was all I said, disgusted.

Ann turned it off. We had no broken bones. We were okay. Desert heat poured suffocatingly into our metal box, as we gingerly climbed out the high, upper side, and from there stepped easily over onto the grass of the embankment. How silent the wilderness was! Even before the dust settled I heard that silence.

Reaching my hand up to the back of my head, I felt something messy, trickling. My hand came away covered with blood.

"Look, Ann. Blood!"

"Oh, Mother, Mother!" she gasped. Then quickly, concealing her fear, "I'll take charge here, Mother," she said firmly. "You could have a fractured skull and you must lie down at once. Remember, I studied first aid! I'm going to make you a bed under the net on the grass, in the shade of this tree. You mustn't move a finger. Just do as I say, and I'll take care of everything. . . ."

"Get the water cans first. See they don't leak. . . . " I was mumbling a bit dizzily. "Get the food and gas out. Get everything out. I'd better give you a hand. . . ."

"Oh, no, Mother, *please* stop wandering around, and lie down here. . . ."

I lay back and let her work. It seemed to me that it was good for her. As Ann remarked later, "It is a terrible feeling when you realize that you have nearly killed your own mother with the car."

Within minutes Ann had excavated the essential things, starting with the bug net, which she hung on the limb of a little tree. Stillness.

"What time is it?"

"About four-thirty," said Ann. "Now, just relax, dear. I'm going to bathe your scalp wound and dust it with this antibiotic powder. . . ."

"Don't bathe it," I said. "The blood has clotted. Just powder it. Have you assessed our water supply?"

"Don't think about anything, Mother, just relax."

"I think we're going to have to do some careful thinking," I said from my bed under the net.

"Trouble is," said Ann, "we don't really know where we are, do we? The road isn't on the maps, and we can't tell how far we drove along it because we don't have a watch, and the speedometer went out, you recall, a few weeks ago."

"Makes a problem in arithmetic, doesn't it?"

"Well, not knowing the constant factors, all we can do is make a calculated guess as to where we are," said Ann capably. "But I always keep a pretty good eye out as we travel and I keep track in my mind. I'm quite sure that we're not more than forty miles from Borroloola, and I could walk it if I had to, so don't worry."

"That's just the point," I said. "I certainly dread to have you start out walking that road alone. But you're going to have to, aren't you? Nobody is ever going to come by here."

"Maybe I should start out right away?" she suggested.

"No," I decided thoughtfully. "Eat and sleep now. Tomorrow start just before dawn."

Our water cans held seven gallons—only a couple of days' supply. We had enough food for a while.

It is not wise to walk through wild country known to possess poisonous snakes which might be about at night. Also, by night everything else may be on the move: truculent wild buffalo, herds of equally pugnacious wild cattle, and wild pigs could take a mind to follow and molest a person afoot, not to mention the possibility of running into Aborigines of unknown characteristics.

Ann would start early and try to complete the entire walk in one day. If she didn't make it, she would halt at sundown and lie down near the road in the bush, and just stay put—not wander about after dark. That way she probably wouldn't run into trouble. If daytime trouble came along, at least she had a good chance of seeing the trouble before it saw her.

Darn it, in any part of our eight hundred miles beyond the bitumen there would be some traffic—but oh, no, not here of all places. The question Ann and I pondered for a bit was which way she should walk. Back towards the fencing crew we had passed earlier, or farther towards Borroloola? That fencing crew might not stay put. What if they were gone when she finally reached their billabong? We couldn't risk it. Borroloola had to be the goal, crossing the river and all.

The time element was pressing. Each person uses a gallon of water a day, conservatively, in such heat, not counting washing or any such nonsense. One gallon to drink. Ann could carry only one quart in the canteen on her belt. Creeks she might cross could be salty, being in the tidal influence in these lowlands. All she could take was the knife on her belt, her matches, a hunk of fat brisket. A person can live and travel at length on fat brisket, so long as water is available.

As dawn reddened the sky Ann took off, a slim and capable young explorer.

I got to thinking about the Richardson Station people whose side road we had passed. Would they possibly decide to make a trip to town? Or had they already gone for the week? *Who* might possibly come by here?

Early in the day I thought I heard the sound of a very distant vehicle coming along our yesterday's track, but it was only the rising wind through the forest. I could see Ann in my mind's eye, nimbly striding off the miles. What would she do if that unknown road forked, and forked yet again, and there were of course no road signs? She could walk forever in the Never-Never. I well knew that. We could see her passing by anthills twenty feet high and thirty feet in circumference. Striding through open forest, an eye out on every side and behind, she must see all dangers before they are encountered.

I am happy to report that this young explorer's rescue walk through this very wild country lasted but three hours. Had not a pickup truck actually come along to my camp, hers would have indeed been a full 45-mile journey. And, aside from a pond of water right near us—unknown to us, originally, of course—the rest of the way was bone dry.

It was the fencing contractors, Pat O'Brien and his wife Mavis, who came along. I had managed to hang spare clothing on sticks along the road, so that a second crash would not occur at the bad turn. You can believe that when I heard that truck coming, I rushed out like a glad gazelle.

The capable O'Briens just set right to work. With an adroit fastening of his winch chain to get the full angle of leverage needed for a difficult uphill pull, and wasting not a single motion about it, Pat O'Brien jerked the battered Toyota onto its feet.

While it lay on its side all the clutch fluid had drained out of the Toyota. Pat then climbed behind the Toyota wheel, and with

342

my camp luggage hastily thrown aboard, now did the truly impossible: he drove it with no clutch down that track to where we picked
up our gallantly-trudging Ann, and Wife Mavis carrying me beside
her in the pickup, we followed right along that track to the Mac-
Arthur River crossing and into Borroloola.

At the trading post it was my treat: canned cold drinks and
candy bars, following which our party took ourselves to the riverbed
and set up a picnic with sandwiches under the trees, and with a can
of asparagus, a perennial favorite about which all Australians are
utterly mad, no matter how inflated its price.

Ann and I reached Darwin and stayed two nights. With a rush
we completed our business: laundry done by coin machines belonging to our astute landlady, and the usual refill of the jerry cans and
tucker box, and the scrubbing down of the vehicle interior.

The Toyota was crumpled on one side. "Gee, I hate to give
back our Toyota in this condition," I said.

"Oh, well, at least they'll know that the sheilas really went bush,
and that is what a Toyota is supposed to do," Ann surmised. "How
do you feel, Mom?"

"Let's make just one more quick bush trip," I said. "Then I'll
have to wind it up, I guess."

Ann and I had hoped very much to be able to enter that most
wild of native reserves known as Arnhem Land, but at Darwin our request was turned down. The government was in the position of having
to turn down requests like ours constantly, to preserve the privacy of
the last remote Aborigines, in order to keep these people from being
trampled to death by all of the writers, explorers, investigators, and
news media who desired to pursue them.

"If we had only come here ten years ago. . . ."

"Except," Ann reminded me, "that ten years ago I was only
seven."

"Yes, unfortunately—too young for exploration's demands."

A great number of letters went out now to pull together the
end of the expedition and its scattered members, and wires were sent.
Ann would stay in Darwin a few days after I left. She would use the
Toyota as long as she needed it there, and then turn it in to the local
dealer. Then she would fly from Darwin to Perth to meet Jean's ship
when it came into port. Together the girls would collect our baggage

343

scattered all over Australia, and catch their flights—separately, as it turned out—across the Pacific to American shores some weeks after I left Australia.

In all our time in Australia we had never had the opportunity to attend the annual "country races" (pronounced *rices*) which are held at various times in different parts of the land. Now came our chance. We had learned from travelers that *rice dies* (race days) were coming at Brunette Downs here in the Northern Territory. So off we set in the crumpled Toyota with the old jerry cans and tucker box and tools and the familiar cooking pots, and in keeping with that grand old Australia custom, we drove six hundred miles through bush to go to a party.

The bush race meeting developed from the old stockroute days. It is an event at which the cattle people of a whole region converge upon one station which plays the host for neighbors who manage and work vast Outback properties.

When the locals go to the rices they go for a week. They take with them a couple of sides of beef for their food, perhaps a dozen tents, a converted water tank for use as showerroom, and beds, pillows, blankets, mirrors, vanities, folding chairs, bedrolls, horses, trucks, tools. The old and the young go, and babies in their cribs. All of the station blackfellas go in their own trucks and make their own camp in a separate spot nearby. The same camping places stay on reserve year after year as belonging to this station or that, and the Blacks in their camps "know their place" and look forward to the festivities as much as anyone, as the most important single event in the social calendar of an Outback year.

Blackfellas have gone out weeks ahead of the great event in many cases, to work and prepare the camps for the whites. Brush is chopped; a big windbreak is made; firewood is collected in piles the size of a house; swags, frocks, and truckloads of beer are stashed ahead.

The diet of the party-goers consists basically of meat, damper, and beer. It's much the same diet as they live on at home, except for mountains of beer and except for the chance to see other people: and that's what makes a party, naturally.

Routinely enough, Ann and I drove south on the Stuart Highway, stopping only for tea and gasoline. Once I got out of the car and weightily dragged off from the road the carcass of a mangled

344

and very odorous kangaroo, so that the wedge-tail eagle which was feeding upon it would not be in danger from the occasional traffic.

At dark, sixteen miles south of Elliott and over four hundred miles out of Darwin by bitumen, we turned east onto an unmarked dirt beef road, a good clear one. Quite worn out from days of rushing about town and from our continuous life on wheels, we were ready to call it a day as we took the Toyota bush along the Beef Road, hastening by flashlight and a small twig fire to lay out our swag and have a tea comprised of only that—tea and bacon fry.

Desert spinifex scarred our shins for the last few times now. The sky above was glorious, bursting with light as its enormous Milky Way stretched across the zenith, and within the Milky Way, very deep, a connected series of gigantic black nebulae serpentined like a Chinese dragon, like an Australian monitor lizard, across the entire heavens. No, the black inky dragon was not just empty space. The inky mass was *something* there in the heaven, as you can see from deep within Australia, for you can see the outlines of black density because light from the bright Milky Way outlines the mystery beautifully here.

The morning was too breezy for a fire. We took our bacon and instant coffee on the burner. Now driving on across level grass plains, treeless except for the occasional mirage-like distant shadow of a tree, we found ourselves upon the famous Barkly Tablelands.

Burned yellow Mitchell grass stretched endlessly on these great grass plains, reminiscent of pictures of Africa. Just grass and horizon, with streams of well-fed shorthorn beef cattle, and everything else shimmering into distance. Many a rider crossing these Barkly Tablelands perished in the old days.

Time hung suspended, broken only by the dutiful opening and closing of paddock gates along the narrow but excellent dirt track. Plains turkeys (noble bustard), white corellas (somewhat smaller than our white cockatoos), in a mob of a thousand, galahs with their rosy breasts, a big healthy dingo with cocked ears, all stood for our camera. A number of windmills pumped water into tanks from bores.

With a seasonal rainfall varying from eight to twenty inches and unreliable, the plains have retained much of their presettlement characteristics as tree and shrub savannah grasslands famous in the world. The risk remains great for destruction of the native grasses and erosion.

345

At last the homestead dwelling loomed up. We were on the Eva Downs property, often called an exemplary one. It is completely fenced around its outside boundaries, enclosing a 1,080-square mile property on lease by Australian Estates Pty. Ltd, which has eighteen stations in Queensland also, and "other properties," an English investment, Australian-managed. It is one of three fine properties in this region, the others being Cresswell Downs and Walhollow, all of which run Australian shorthorns only.

Eva was the first station in the Territory to take up the use of road trains! They had built all their own roads before the government. This was fairly easy to do on the plains. But until quite recently the cattle were driven along the old stock trails, of which we saw bits and snatches here and there today, even in 1969.

The managers at Eva had come from New South Wales, and like many, they admitted to little previous experience in pastural development, a fast-growing and very new concept here. The management family had been in residence here for six years, and had done very well indeed.

I went to the door and asked directions about getting to the rices. I asked to buy meat, too. I had learned the language.

So of course the people said they wouldn't *sell* meat, but they would give it away to us. I was taken by the wife to meet the husband in his rough lumber office, and I sat down there with both, chatting, nonchalantly holding a six-pound piece of beef loin in my left hand.

After a while, having looked me over and heard my yarn, they said, "Look, why don't you invite your daughter to come in from the car?"

"Well, I reckon I could."

Meanwhile I was carrying the six-pound piece of beef, and finally the wife said, "Look, why don't you and Ann stay over with us, and we'll take you to the rices when we go, in just another *die*.

Eighty miles easy drive next day found us at Brunette Downs Rice Camp. The camp was laid out in such a way as to provide literally miles of elbow room for each visiting company to have its own privacy in this land of great wealth of space. We were miles away from the Brunette Homestead itself, and were never to see it. At intervals private aircraft flew overhead taking visiting VIP Brunette visitors, presumably Texans, on tours over the range. The Duke and Duchess of Gloucester were among that party, we heard, but we bushies did not meet any of these.

The Eva Downs Camp was a couple of miles from the racetrack and its little, shaded open grandstand where we would commute each day for the events and to purchase some of our meals in the Clubhouse where a contract crew of women were busily cooking.

Here converged every man, woman, and child drained from tens of thousands of square miles. In the feed line waiting for our free steaks that first evening I met "Stan the Firestone Man," from Mount Isa, whose sales beat covered half a million square miles, he believed. He was a good talker, fit and tanned in the usual tropical wear of shorts and knee socks.

That night Ann and I went to the dance in the old Clubhouse which was decorated with streamers and posters of each station's jockey colors, and by assorted balloons. The building was of the expected corrugated iron walls and sheet iron roof. Cooking in back was by wood-burning stove. The worn old wooden dance floor and the decorations combined to convert it into a potential tinder box, yet somehow it lasted.

Many of the women who had worked with such feverish activity for days to prepare for the great holiday of the year, did not attend this first-nighter dance. After all the hair put up into curlers, after all the ironing, pressing, bathing, and powdering and meal-preparing for families, after all the sharp cockney words and shrewish remarks to errant husbands, wives stayed in tent camps very often with little ones, unhappily shut out from the social doings which their husbands attended, for there is no servant class in Outback society.

Scene at the dance: young women seated on straight chairs all around the walls have been brought in by busload somehow, most of their expenses paid, from Alice Springs—the single nursing sisters. Their presence at the dance did little to make the wives feel any better, but was touted as a boost for Outback morale. Of far superior education and higher wage-earning ability than most of the jackeroos whose evenings they graced, the female townies seemed to enjoy the chance to visit the Outback for adventure.

Soon every available woman was dancing. Ann of course

had brought her turquoise eyelids and had woven pearls into her long, blonde hair. She had her retinue of oddly-assorted followers.

One fellow I watched kept dancing all by himself. He made extravagant gestures and contortions around the dance floor, very drunk. He would fall hard upon the floor, pick himself up, and start over again, reaching his hands supplicatingly to heaven. Everyone thought he was funny. He was in a complete world of his own, not able to ask a real live girl to dance or to communicate with him. His weathered face reflected long, lonely, endless Outback years. To me he was not funny, but sad.

After the first night there were black eyes and split lips. Men appeared with large white bandages wound about their heads like mummies.

At the dance two older men near my own age came up and said I was to dance with them, regardless of my excuses. These were not Outback men. They had pale, greedy-looking faces, and were Sydney-siders in business suits, and had a patronizing air toward us bushies.

"What are you, anyway?" I finally asked them rudely, since they acted patronizing. "Are you two crooks some kind of low-down bookies?" The bookies were here in numbers, arranging the betting as they followed Australia's country rice shows around the calendar. Keen professionals out of the cities, they despised the very land they fed upon.

"No, we're in the oil business," gruffly replied one.

"I don't trust you for one minute," I said. "You've got on white shirts and black ties, and I think you are a no-good pair of sidewinder rattlesnakes and death adders."

Their eyes popped at that. One hastened to present his oily card.

"What kind of monkey business is this oil, anyway?"

"Good God, Hibbert," mumbled the one to his mite. "This woman's crazy."

"Common, luv, you're a pretty country girl. Don't you rally want to dance? What's the trouble with your foot, luv?"

"Barcoo rot," I said. (It was, too.)

Luckily my friend Stan the Firestone Man came up, and he took me away for tea at the long tables in the furnace-hot kitchens,

348

or I would have been into my last fight in Australia, perhaps just because it was fun to turn into a mean Outback Aussie meself.

The living environment of the six hundred or more people who camped at Brunette in cars, trucks, and tents was not one which would pass strict health laws.

Now thousands upon thousands of brown empties covered the grandstand grounds for miles about. Empty cartons, papers, and rubbish piled up. Big barrels were supplied by our hosts, but few used them.

A large number of rats had proliferated over these traditional campgrounds through the years, due to the garbage. At night my light caught rats rustling among the dry leaves of our *wurlie*, our bough shed, where we cut our bread and hung our beef. Fighting, snapping, hissing squeaking, their red eyes glaring in the night, the rats swarmed. One was advised to sleep up off the ground on a cot and to keep all articles of apparel off the ground. The rodents could carry a disease which may cause yellow jaundice.

In the distance we could see the blackfellow camp. They laid down along a small creek and used its water. Not only they but some whites were getting water from this creek, oblivious to the possibility of typhoid contagion or hepititis or intestinal interitus.

Open tin wall privies had no lid, and no chemical disinfectant made its debut here. Flies crawled, buzzed, and swarmed happily.

As an Outback lady picked her way from dance hall to distant ladies toilet she teetered, full of beer, through a bog of mud and stones—for typically, there was no drinking water available at the club or rice stand, water not playing a big part in the Australian intake, hundreds of gallons of the precious stuff was at the same time pouring out of the side of a large silver tank and flowing over the ground.

Each day's rices ended with the Aboriginal rice. By this late time of day nobody had much interest in this event. The hat was passed to take up a collection for a stingy little Aboriginal prize. I put a two dollar bill into the hat. These riders had no jockey suits, but were the most skilled riders and horsemen of the lot.

Evenings around the Eva campfire at our tent camp under the moon found a colorful collection of ringers from Alexander, Brunette, Cresswell, and Anthony's Lagoon. Young ringers had caked blood on their faces. Others limped painfully. One older man, genteel with the gentleness of the real oldtime man of the bush, when I asked his name, at first only would say: "They keep me to gather the firewood and boil the billy for tea." He was a Brunette man, very loyal to Brunette and to the manager, whom all liked much.

Outback games are simple. A bottle was placed on top of our tin can stove to explode—a joke. Two jackeroos on hands and knees were playing "bull." This game consists of butting heads together until somebody's skull is nearly fractured. Whoever can least "take it" usually gives up and quits, often lying down in the dirt. There is no campfire singing or playing of the guitar. No one here knew how to play a musical instrument, or had one.

What we did find was several writers and photographers gathered at the rices from long distances, attracted by all the "material." Among them Ann's English friend from Mount Isa had flown out, doing some free-lancing, from which Ann's picture appeared enlarged, wearing a broad-brimmed hat donated by a jackeroo suitor, upon that full page in the daily *Australian*, which is devoted to Australian beauties.

Another journalist, twenty-three, tall and very good-looking, came from Norway with his mite, a photographer. The Norwegians, speaking almost no English, were on an assignment for one of Norway's most prominent magazines.

Although the Norwegians had been around Australia and New Guinea for five months, we found they had seen far less of Outback life, particularly the more remote parts, than we. It was our pleasure to introduce the intelligent young Norwegian travelers to Cresswell Station's local Norwegian and to permit the latter to speak his native tongue for the first time in some years. Into our campfire mob with its primitive diet of beef and bread and beer we brought the journalists who privately considered the Outback people and their land to be wild in every respect. Many bottles rolled underfoot. Outback women told me how the blacks go off walk-about each season, and despite local efforts to save them, lose many of their babies and small children by malnutrition and exposure on the three-month walks.

Ann shot pictures at the rices, replete with black eyes, blood stains, and bandages. The Aborigines provided material for Ann's camera, too. They were not allowed inside the clubhouse or to the dancing or food and drink therein. The reason given was that station owners who were "neighbors" paid annual dues, and this was a private club.

It was pointed out to us by sincere club members that the blacks were always potentially "dangerous." If they were allowed to mix socially with whites violence invariably broke out among the white young men toward the blacks, as it did, anyway, toward each other. It was pointed out that "Blacks cannot handle their liquor." Most white Aussies here believed that the Aborigines were a primitive people, "primitiveness" being a fixed and static quality one is born with, and which is at best unlikely to change much for many generations. Nobody of course would care to admit that there was some curious sociological force at work in their white structure of society which would logically continue by every means at its disposal to make sure that the primitive people so classified would remain exactly that way.

It was a fascinating piece of sociological evidence to observe that the basic laws of human behavior relate here in Australia, in microcosm, and are not peculiar just to America, by any means. "The Aborigines are roight, so long as they remain in their place."

This same Aussie also says, "Women are roight, so long as they remain in their place," with the same complacency, though his trumpeting on this subject may be more muted in the interests of keeping peace at home.

The last day at Brunette Rices is devoted to the rodeo. With their love of rough sports, it is not surprising that the Aussies would take to that American sport of making frightened horses and cattle buck in an arena so that they can be mastered by the superior species. Originally the Aussie cowboy "gentled" the wild horse by a series of training maneuvers which were calculated to get quick results, as did the original American on the old ranch.

The rodeo we watched showed many skills but was set back in time some hours because some joker the night before had turned loose all the livestock which was to provide the entertainment. Mustering the beasts was the real exhibition of skill of the day.

The party was over. Our Outback year was over.

Ann and I said our farewells and went off in the Toyota, leaving our multiple hosts folding up cots and tents and dismantling the electric generator, and piling high the babies' cribs atop big trucks.

We helped ourselves to gas at Eva Downs homestead and left a note and cash on the kitchen table, got a drink of water, on our hands and knees, from the spigot which came out just ten inches above the kitchen floor and went on off through that endless mirage of an empty world, camping at sundown, where I heard my last dingo howl. He was far, far away.

By dodging the car just in time, we saved a last Taipan snake in the road, a race horse goanna, covered with lovely pink and white beads, and a nice seven-foot black-headed python.

On the bitumen to Darwin we passed a man slumped asleep over his suitcase along the roadside, and others out like a light on the grass under the trees. Drugs, possibly: hippies now on their way to Darwin among the green grass budgerigars and bush pheasants and kangaroos.

Poor wretches, they weren't wanted anywhere. Excess population. Australian youth cultists, they hoped to find the Promised Land somewhere across the water in Southeast Asia. But several Asian nations already were no longer letting them in, or if they did, simply jailed the disillusioned youth.

We picked up one for a ride who was from New Zealand, finally. Just under twenty-one, obviously a reader of books, son of a professor, he was a drop-out from electrical engineering.

The boy's tresses hung shoulder-length. He had that thinness and peculiar yellow pallor that comes from malnutrition often combined with drugs, or at least a kind of mental illness which has become so familiar to us with over-populated America's soul-sick youth. He threw trash from our moving car, and littered the land.

He was very cynical. Rejecting emphatically the capitalistic system of Australia, he was quite fearful of arrest by the police, whom he had heard among his "set" were prejudiced against long hair and brutal in what he considered to be a barbaric country, this Australia.

Yet this boy, in order to be able to go outside of his own highly socialized little country, was forced literally, to take to the road with a pack on his back. For his country permitted such a small amount of money to be taken out that it would last him only a week or ten days away, were not the hospitality of the "working holiday" extended indiscriminately to all Commonwealth travelers by a generous and prospering Australia.

When we dropped off the boy at that special hamburger stand in Darwin which has become known as a contact place for dropout youth who wear beads and beards and who are helping each other on their way to Asia, we turned toward our rooming house wordlessly.

On another day soon I was packed and dressed to catch my plane, bound for Sydney's chill winter clime. Then, Ann lost the car keys. I almost thought I wouldn't ever get back to America, hopping on my one good foot, but fortunately an English technician picked me up and got me to the airport on time. Ann hotwired the half-smashed Toyota at the last minute and arrived for goodbyes just at plane take-off.

I would long hear that Aussie accent in memory, the colorful blunt words, see tables sodden with beer dripping onto tanned hairy knees, think of a country with a million things needing to be done, a country of tomorrow. Petty meanness must be rooted out. It is like a gray thread running through a culture which aspires to a brighter fabric. I returned to America exploding hearty "good-oh's" and "fair dinkums" for quite a time afterwards.

Each of us who has ever been there would always want to go back. We would get this funny feeling whenever we would see a Jeep or Toyota going along some road some place, with its young sweaty occupants covered with dust and that 500-mile stare in their eyes. It was then that Australia would always beam its siren call. Just knowing it is out there gives a person this feeling of a good world. It was then that my heart beat young again when the thought of Australia loomed in my mind, of our mites there, the people we met, and the times we had.

References and Bibliography

The Australian Aborigines. Government bulletin published by the Department of Territories, with the Ministers responsible for Aboriginal Welfare in the Australian States, 1967.

Australian Council of National Trust. *Historic Homesteads of Australia,* vol. 1. Melbourne: Cassell Australia, Ltd., 1969.

Baker, Sidney J. *The Australian Language.* Sydney: Currawang Pub. Co., 1945, 1964.

Bates, Daisy. *The Passing of the Aborigines.* Melbourne: Wm. Heinemann, Ltd., 1938, 1966.

Beatty, Bill. *Tasmania, Isle of Splendor.* Melbourne: Cassell Australia, Ltd., 1963, 1967.

Bergman, Dr. G. F. J. *Gustav Weindorfer of Cradle Mountain* (booklet). Hobart: Mercury Press, 1959.

Blainey, Geoffrey. *Mines in the Spinifex.* Sydney: Angus & Robertson, Ltd., 1962, 1965.

Carson, Rachel. *Silent Spring.* Boston: Houghton-Mifflin, 1962.

Carter, Jeff. *Outback in Focus.* Adelaide: Rigby, Ltd., 1968.

Clarke, Arthur C. *The Coast of Coral.* New York: Harper & Bros., 1955.

Cotlow, Lewis. *In Search of the Primitive.* Boston: Little, Brown & Co., 1966.

Desrosier, Norman W., Ph.D. *Attack on Starvation.* West Point, Connecticut: Avi Pub. Co., 1961.

Dexter, Lewis Anthony. *The Tyranny of School.* New York: Basic Books, Inc., 1964.

355

Durak, Mary. *Keep Him, My Country.* Sydney: Angus & Robertson, Ltd., 1966.
Gunn, Aeneas. *We of the Never-Never.* London: Hutchinson, 1908, 1966.
Hill, Ernestine. *The Great Australian Loneliness.* Melbourne: Robertson & Mullens Pty. Ltd., 1949.
Hill, Ernestine. *The Territory.* Sydney: Angus & Robertson, Ltd., 1951, 1968.
Horne, Donald. *The Lucky Country: Australia Today.* Baltimore: Penguin Books, 1964.
Idriess, Ian L. *In Crocodile Land.* Sydney: Angus & Robertson, Ltd., 1946, 1966.
Idriess, Ian L. *One Wet Season.* Sydney: Angus & Robertson, Ltd., 1949.
Idriess, Ian L. *The Wild North.* Sydney: Angus & Robertson, Ltd., 1960.
Kaberry, Phyllis M. *Aboriginal Women.* Sydney: University of Sydney, 1939.
Lindsay, Harold A. *The Bushman's Handbook,* 3rd ed. Brisbane: Jacaranda Press, 1963.
Lockwood, Douglas. *Crocodiles and Other People.* Adelaide: Rigby, Ltd., 1963, 1966.
Lockwood, Douglas. *I, the Aboriginal.* Adelaide: Rigby, Ltd., 1962, 1968.
Lockwood, Douglas. *We, the Aborigines.* Melbourne: Cassell Australia, Ltd., 1963.
McGinnies, William G., ed. *Deserts of the World.* Tucson: University of Arizona Press, 1968.
Marshall, A. J. *The Great Extermination.* Melbourne: Wm. Heinemann, Ltd., 1966.
Martin, William E., and Bower, Leonard G. "Patterns of Water Use in the Arizona Economy." A paper financed by Rockefeller grant, under the series *Water in Relation to Social and Economic Growth in an Arid Environment.* Tucson: University of Arizona, 1968.
Meerloo, Joost A. M., M.D. *The Rape of the Mind.* New York: Grosset & Dunlap, 1956.
Menninger, Karl, M.D. *The Human Mind.* New York: Alfred A. Knopf, Inc., 1945.
Monkman, Noel. *From Queensland to the Great Barrier Reef.* New York: Doubleday and Co., Inc., 1966.
Moorehead, Alan. *Coopers Creek.* New York: Harper & Row, 1963.
Moorehead, Alan. *The Fatal Impact.* New York: Harper & Row, 1966.
The Modern Encyclopedia of Australia and New Zealand. Sydney: Horwitz-Grahame, 1964.
Morcombe, M. K. *Australian Western Wildflowers.* Perth: Landfall Press.
O'Reilly, Bernard. *Green Mountain.* Fortitude Valley, Brisbane: W. R. Smith & Paterson Pty., Ltd., 1942.
"Origin of the Australian Aborigines." Bulletin of the Dept. of Aboriginal Welfare (Federal), 1969.
Reader's Digest Complete Atlas of Australia, Including Papua-New Guinea. Sydney: The Reader's Digest Assn. Pty. Ltd., 1968.
Rosenberg, Jerry M. *The Invasion of Privacy.* New York: Random House, 1969.

356

Serventy, Vincent. *A Continent in Danger*. London: Reynal & Co., Trinity Press, 1966.

Smith, Adam. *The Money Game*. New York: Random House, 1967.

Smith, Patsy Adam. *Moonbird People*. Adelaide: Rigby, Ltd., 1965.

Spicer, Edward, ed. *Human Problems in Technological Change: A Case Book*. Russell Sage Foundation, 1952.

Te Chow, Ven. *The Handbook of Applied Hydrology*. New York: McGraw Hill, 1964.

Turnbull, Clive. *Black War: The Extermination of the Tasmanian Aborigines*. Melbourne: Cheshire Pty., Ltd., 1948.

Wilson, A. R. W., Pender, E. B., and Carter, E. K. *Peaceful Uses of Nuclear Explosives—An Evaluation, for Australian Purposes, of Proposed Civil Engineering and Mining Applications*. Tech. Mission to the U.S.A., September-October 1963.